The Question of Linguistic Idealism

The Question of Linguistic Idealism

Edited by
RICHARD GASKIN

OXFORD
UNIVERSITY PRESS

OXFORD
UNIVERSITY PRESS

Great Clarendon Street, Oxford, OX2 6DP,
United Kingdom

Oxford University Press is a department of the University of Oxford.
It furthers the University's objective of excellence in research, scholarship,
and education by publishing worldwide. Oxford is a registered trade mark of
Oxford University Press in the UK and in certain other countries

© Oxford University Press 2025

The moral rights of the authors have been asserted.

All rights reserved. No part of this publication may be reproduced, stored in a retrieval system,
transmitted, used for text and data mining, or used for training artificial intelligence, in any form or
by any means, without the prior permission in writing of Oxford University Press, or as expressly
permitted by law, by licence or under terms agreed with the appropriate reprographics rights
organization. Enquiries concerning reproduction outside the scope of the above should be sent
to the Rights Department, Oxford University Press, at the address above.

You must not circulate this work in any other form
and you must impose this same condition on any acquirer.

Published in the United States of America by Oxford University Press
198 Madison Avenue, New York, NY 10016, United States of America

British Library Cataloguing in Publication Data

Data available

Library of Congress Control Number: 2024952587

ISBN 9780192872654

DOI: 10.1093/9780191968617.001.0001

Printed and bound by
CPI Group (UK) Ltd, Croydon, CR0 4YY

Links to third party websites are provided by Oxford in good faith and
for information only. Oxford disclaims any responsibility for the materials
contained in any third party website referenced in this work.

The manufacturer's authorised representative in the EU for product safety is
Oxford University Press España S.A. of El Parque Empresarial San Fernando de Henares, Avenida
de Castilla, 2 – 28830 Madrid (www.oup.es/en or
product.safety@oup.com). OUP España S.A. also acts as importer into Spain
of products made by the manufacturer.

Contents

The Contributors   vii

1. Introduction: The Question of Linguistic Idealism   1
   Richard Gaskin

2. Conditions, Necessity, and Transcendental Linguistic Idealism in Wittgenstein's *Tractatus*   31
   Chon Tejedor

3. 'Simplex Sigillum Veri' and the Question of the Limits of Language   58
   Hanne Appelqvist

4. Transcendental and Linguistic Idealism   82
   Bernhard Weiss

5. World and Truth in Conflict   111
   John Collins

6. Metaphysics First or Language First: The Notion of a Single Object   138
   Friederike Moltmann

7. Linguistic Instrumentalism   160
   John A. Keller and Lorraine Juliano Keller

8. Abstract Objects and the Philosophy of Language   194
   William Stirton

9. Mathematics and the Limits of Language   219
   Silvia Jonas

10. Isomorphism and Idealism   237
    Michael Morris

11. Representation, Alien Languages, and Linguistic
    Idealism   260
    Matti Eklund

12. Linguistic Idealism and the Genealogy of Negation   283
    Richard Gaskin

Index   310

The Contributors

Hanne Appelqvist (PhD, Columbia 2007) is the Director of the Helsinki Collegium for Advanced Studies at the University of Helsinki. Her research has focused on the affinities between Kant and Wittgenstein. She is the author of *Wittgenstein and Aesthetics* (CUP, 2023), editor of *Wittgenstein and the Limits of Language* (Routledge, 2020), and has published a number of articles in Wittgenstein's philosophy of logic, the philosophy of religion, aesthetics, and ethics. She has been the Editor-in-Chief of *Estetika: The European Journal of Aesthetics* since 2018, and the President of the *Nordic Wittgenstein Society* since 2021.

John Collins is Research Professor at the University of the Basque Country (UPV/EHU) and Ikerbasque, in the Department of Linguistics and Basque Studies. His research is focused on the philosophy of language, the foundations of generative grammar, polysemy, and the syntax/semantics interface. He has published widely in these areas and is the author of three monographs: *Chomsky: A Guide for the Perplexed* (Bloomsbury, 2008), *The Unity of Linguistic Meaning* (OUP, 2011), and *Linguistic Pragmatism and Weather Reporting* (OUP, 2020).

Matti Eklund is Chair and Professor of Theoretical Philosophy at Uppsala University. He works mainly on topics in metaphysics, the philosophy of language, the philosophy of logic, and metaethics. He is the author of *Choosing Normative Concepts* (OUP, 2017), and *Alien Structure: Language and Reality* (OUP, 2024).

Richard Gaskin is Professor of Philosophy at the University of Liverpool. He has taught and researched at the universities of Bonn, Mainz, Oxford, and Sussex. He specializes and has published widely in the philosophy of language, metaphysics, the history of philosophy, literary theory and criticism, and the European literary tradition. His most recent book publications are *Language and World: A Defence of Linguistic Idealism* (Routledge, 2021), and *Othello and the Problem of Knowledge: Reading Shakespeare through Wittgenstein* (Routledge, 2023).

Silvia Jonas is Professor of Philosophy at the University of Bamberg. Her primary areas of research are in the philosophy of mathematics and science, epistemology, and metaphysics. She graduated from Oxford University and holds a PhD from the Humboldt University in Berlin. Central questions of her research are how mathematics shapes the philosophical conceptualization of reality, whether reality exceeds the physical realm, and if there can be knowledge beyond the limits of language. She is author of *Ineffability and its Metaphysics: The Unspeakable in Art, Religion, and Philosophy* (Palgrave, 2016).

John A. Keller (PhD, Notre Dame 2010) is Associate Professor of Philosophy and the Rev. Joseph S. Hogan Chair at Saint Joseph's University in Philadelphia. He works in the areas of metaphysics, epistemology, philosophy of language, and philosophy of religion, and is the editor of *Being, Freedom, and Method: Themes from the Philosophy of Peter van Inwagen* (OUP, 2017).

Lorraine Juliano Keller (PhD, Notre Dame 2012) is Associate Professor of Philosophy at Saint Joseph's University in Philadelphia. She works on philosophy of language, metaphysics, and the philosophy of religion, and has published articles on the metaphysics of propositions, logical form, divine ineffability, and real and notional assent.

Friederike Moltmann (PhD, MIT 1992) is Research Professor at the French Centre Nationale de la Recherche Scientifique (CNRS) in Nice, France. She has held visiting positions at the Universities of Padua, New York, and Düsseldorf. Her research focuses on the interface between natural language semantics and philosophy (metaphysics, but also philosophy of mind, philosophy of language and philosophy of mathematics), often in relation to generative syntax. She is author of *Parts and Wholes in Semantics* (OUP, 1996), *Abstract Objects and Semantics of Natural Language* (OUP, 2013), and *Objects and Attitudes* (OUP, 2024).

Michael Morris is Emeritus Professor of Philosophy at the University of Sussex. He is the author of *The Good and the True* (OUP, 1992), *An Introduction to the Philosophy of Language* (CUP, 2007), *Routledge GuideBook to Wittgenstein and the Tractatus* (Routledge, 2008), *Real Likenesses: Representation in Paintings, Photographs, and Novels* (OUP, 2020), and a number of articles in the philosophy of language, metaphysics, the philosophy of art, and ancient philosophy.

William Stirton lives in Edinburgh. He has published articles in mathematical logic, the philosophy of mathematics and the philosophy of language. He has spoken at conferences on mathematical logic and the neo-Fregean philosophy of mathematics. On the historical-scholarship side, he served in the team who created the one and only complete English translation of Frege's *Grundgesetze der Arithmetik*.

Chon Tejedor After lecturing at the Universities of Oxford and Hertfordshire, Chon Tejedor joined the Philosophy Department of Universitat de València in 2017. She works mainly on Wittgenstein, the epistemology of responsibility, and intercultural understanding. She is co-Principal Investigator of 'The Epistemology of Responsibility in Agency-Stultifying Situations' and was Principal Investigator of 'Intercultural Understanding, Belonging and Value: Wittgensteinian Approaches', both projects funded by the Spanish Ministry for Innovation and Universities. She is Fellow of the RSA and was for several years Editor and Executive Committee member of the British Wittgenstein Society. Her publications include *The Early Wittgenstein on Metaphysics, Natural Science, Language and Value* (Routledge, 2015) and *Starting with Wittgenstein* (Bloomsbury, 2011).

Bernhard Weiss is Professor of Philosophy at the University of Cape Town. He is interested in the philosophies of language and of logic. A strong focus of his work has been use-based theories of meaning, taking inspiration from the writings of Wittgenstein, Michael Dummett, and, more recently, Robert Brandom. In addition to publishing a number of papers in the area he has published two books: *Michael Dummett* (Princeton, 2002) and *How to Understand Language* (Routledge, 2010).

1
Introduction

The Question of Linguistic Idealism

Richard Gaskin

1.1

This collection of essays derives its title, *The Question of Linguistic Idealism*, from Elizabeth Anscombe's famous paper of the same name. Anscombe is primarily concerned to investigate whether Wittgenstein was, in his later writings, a linguistic idealist, but in the course of addressing that exegetical problem she has interesting things of a systematic nature to say about the relation between language and the world. Contributors to this collection were invited to write on any aspect of the topic of linguistic idealism that interested them, and the result is a rich variety of approaches and perspectives, both historical and systematic. In this first section of the Introduction I shall present a thumbnail sketch of the various strategies adopted by the contributors. Then, in the rest of the Introduction I shall offer, by way of providing some orientation, a polemical defence of one version of linguistic idealism, so that readers have at least an initial, and positive, conception of the doctrine before they work their way through the contributions, several of which adopt, to a greater or lesser extent, a negative attitude to it.

The collection begins with three papers looking at various aspects of the Kantian and Wittgensteinian background. There has been much dispute concerning the question whether, and if so to what extent, and in what way, Wittgenstein endorses any form of transcendental idealism in the *Tractatus*. In her contribution, **Chon Tejedor** maintains that Wittgenstein in that work considers two forms of transcendental linguistic idealism, according to the first of which the world is what is given to the transcendental willing subject in representation, and according to the second of which possible representation determines the possibilities of the world; she argues that he aims to dissolve the doctrine in both these forms. If Wittgenstein rejects transcendental idealism, it follows that he must reject the idea of the synthetic a priori, and one interpretation of the *Tractatus* indeed aligns the a priori with analyticity. By contrast, **Hanne Appelqvist** contends in her contribution that Wittgenstein appeals in the *Tractatus* to a species of fundamental insight that, by Kantian lights, would count as synthetic a priori. First, she suggests that spatio-temporality is, for Wittgenstein, part of the necessary, transcendentally grounded structure of reality; secondly, she notes the role that 'a priori insights about the form in which the propositions of natural science can be cast' (*Tractatus* 6.34) plays in Wittgenstein's thinking. In his contribution, **Bernhard Weiss** distinguishes between an idealism that rejects the view that reality is independent of our representations, on the one hand, and, on the other, an idealism that rejects the view that our representations are responsible to reality. He argues that, while the first, Kantian strategy is beset by well-known difficulties, the second strategy, in a specifically linguistic version, is supported by the later Wittgenstein's reflections on the autonomy of grammar.

Linguistic idealism comes in various versions, but a theme that one could expect to find near the core of the doctrine in any form is the thesis that, to put it telegraphically, semantics drives ontology, that what there is, in some sense, drops out—is a precipitate—of meaningful language. The collection continues with several papers discussing this thesis from various perspectives. **John Collins** holds, against the linguistic idealist, that semantics is no reliable guide to ontology. He focuses on the phenomenon of copredication, which allows a single non-ambiguous noun phrase to take predicates of quite different sorts, as when we say 'The book is dog-eared and interesting' or 'Sam slammed the glass on the bar and promptly downed three more'. Collins argues, on the basis of examples like these, that rather than saying, as semantics might lead us to think, that in these cases there is a single object with a highly variegated collection of properties, we should take the noun phrase to divide its reference. Although not drafted in direct response to Collins, **Friederike Moltmann**'s contribution offers some countervailing considerations, maintaining that our conception of *a single object* is language-driven. The range of entities and combinations of entities which we are prepared to count, depending on context, as single objects is so diverse, and so apparently lacking in any kind of restriction from the side of the world, that unity in these cases emerges almost as a *façon de parler*—at any rate as something imposed by language. We then return to a more critical approach to the thesis that language drives ontology in the contribution by **John A. Keller** and **Lorraine Juliano Keller**, which defends a form of anti-realism about linguistics that the authors call 'linguistic instrumentalism'. According to this idea, a principle that many commentators (including linguistic idealists) accept, namely that for something to be the meaning of a linguistic expression that thing must exist, is false. Against this, these authors argue that linguistic principles can be correct without being true. What matters is that these principles should be useful, or empirically adequate, and these latter statuses do not, at least as far as linguistics goes, import a truth requirement.

The linguist idealist's idea of ontology driven by semantics has clear connections with recent initiatives by neo-Fregean philosophers to ground a case for platonism concerning numbers in considerations drawn purely from the philosophy of language. Frege abandoned his initial attempt to achieve this grounding in the light of the notorious 'Julius Caesar' objection that he raised against himself. In his contribution, **William Stirton** argues that the Julius Caesar problem has not been solved by neo-Fregeans and linguistic idealists and continues to offer stubborn resistance to any effort to found the existence of abstract objects, such as numbers, on the linguistic use of abstract terms, such as numerals. The mathematical context of Stirton's discussion is broadened in **Silvia Jonas**'s contribution, which contends that our understanding of mathematics goes beyond linguistic formulation. On the basis of several case studies (the rule of *modus ponens*, consistency of formalisms, statistical models of the prime numbers), Jonas argues that we have a language-independent access to the mathematical domain, which accordingly turns out to be metaphysically prior to linguistic description of it.

The collection concludes with three chapters on specific, but important, aspects of the linguistic idealist's case: two of these chapters are sceptical of the doctrine's prospects; one is supportive of it. **Michael Morris** examines the idea of a structural isomorphism between language and reality. The linguistic idealist of course accepts the existence of such an isomorphism (and in addition puts an idealistic spin on that acceptance). Morris argues that belief in the relevant structural isomorphism imports a commitment to what he calls the idea of the Linguistic Given, according to which the world can justify particular uses of language (language use in general) only if it is itself linguistically organized. He then maintains that it is possible to conceive the world as standing in the required justificatory relation to language *without* signing up either to the notion of a structural isomorphism between language and reality in general or to linguistic idealism in particular.

If linguistic idealism is not to be trivial, there must be some substantial constraints on what is to count as a language, and as the 'linguistic organization of reality'. I note this point below in this Introduction, suggesting that the language to which the linguistic idealist appeals in maintaining that the world is in some sense the precipitate of language must stand in some reasonably close relation of accessibility to specifically *human* language. That then gives the doctrine of linguistic idealism its distinctive, and controversial, anthropocentric underpinning. Part of this idea is the claim that there cannot be radically alien languages: that something sufficiently alien to our way of conducting ourselves linguistically would no longer be a language. Only so can the doctrine of linguistic idealism have some bite. In his contribution, **Matti Eklund** subjects this point to scrutiny: he argues, contrariwise, that we can in some sense accommodate the idea of radically alien languages, with the consequence that the linguistic idealist cannot justifiably read off worldly structures from (for example) the subject–predicate structure of familiar natural languages. Finally, **Richard Gaskin** investigates the genealogy of negation and contends that careful consideration of the way in which negation entered the language according to one popular and quite plausible story—which suggests that negation embodies the idea of exclusion/incompatibility—actually supports the case for linguistic idealism. The essential thought here is that the idea of incompatibility imports the subsidiary idea of a collection of non-identical *incompatibility ranges*, and that that non-identity is linguistic in origin, since these ranges are categories, and categories are, *au fond*, subject matters, topics of discourse.

So much by way of summary of the chapters in this collection. In the rest of this Introduction I aim, as I have indicated, to provide the reader with some initial orientation on the topic of linguistic idealism. And since, in philosophy, the best way of getting into a topic is to consider the polemics of it, I offer that orientation in the form of an unashamedly non-neutral defence of a particular version of linguistic idealism. I shall begin with Anscombe's discussion of Wittgenstein, but soon broaden the scope of the discussion with the aim of delivering a general and systematic defence of the position. I hope, if not to persuade readers of the truth of linguistic idealism, at least to start up some lines of thought in their minds. Readers who consider my points and perhaps formulate arguments of their own, whether for or against the position I defend, will thereby be in the thick of the debate. And that is the best way of coming to understand a philosophical question.

1.2

What exactly is linguistic idealism? Near the beginning of her paper (1981, ch. 13) Anscombe quotes, from *Philosophical Investigations*, I, §371,

Wittgenstein's aphorism that '*Essence* is expressed (*ausgesprochen*) by grammar'.[1] This looks like a nice compendious statement of the doctrine, or at least of a central feature of it, and at least as Wittgenstein himself might be taken to propound it—insofar as he does, a question which will be of subsidiary interest in the sequel, alongside my main systematic purpose. It would have been useful if Anscombe had added to her quotation of §371 the two sections that follow it (she does supply us with the first of these later on in her discussion): 'Consider: "The only correlate in language to an intrinsic necessity is an arbitrary rule. It is the only thing which one can milk out of this intrinsic necessity into a proposition (*Satz*)"' (§372). And: 'Grammar tells us what kind of object anything is. (Theology as grammar)' (§373).

Instead of reminding us of these latter two passages at this point, Anscombe quotes—and indeed begins her article with—an equally famous, but also more difficult and obscure passage from near the end of the *Investigations*, where Wittgenstein writes:

> If anyone believes that certain concepts are absolutely the right ones, and that having different concepts would mean not realizing something that we realize—then let him imagine certain very general facts of nature to be different from what we are used to, and the formation of concepts different from the usual ones will become intelligible to him. (1977, II, §xii)

Again, it would have been good if Anscombe had continued the citation to the end of the section. Wittgenstein adds:

> Compare a concept with a style of painting. For is even our style of painting arbitrary? Can we choose one at pleasure? (The Egyptian, for instance.) Is it a mere question of pleasing and ugly?

Note the double appearance, in the Wittgensteinian texts quoted so far, of the word 'arbitrary'. We appear to be headed in opposite directions in the two places where this word is used, the first quoted passage (*Investigations*, I, §372) seeming to suggest that our rules, conventions, and ways of carrying on are arbitrary, the second (II, §xii) that they are not. We can reconcile the apparent tension by adducing further texts. At *Zettel* (1981), §§357-8, Wittgenstein writes:

---

[1] All translations from the *Investigations* are Anscombe's (in her 1968 edition); ditto for *Zettel* (in the 1981 edition).

> We have a colour system as we have a number system.
> Do the systems reside in *our* nature or in the nature of things?
> How are we to put it?
> —*Not* in the nature of numbers or colours.
> Then is there something arbitrary about this system? Yes and no. It is akin both to what is arbitrary and to what is non-arbitrary.

Elsewhere we are told that grammar is arbitrary in the sense that it has no justification, and that we could frame its rules differently; it is non-arbitrary in the sense that its rules might, from a psychological point of view, come naturally to us (the sense hinted at in the passage from the end of *Investigations* II, §xii, quoted above).[2]

The fact that Anscombe starts her article in the way I have indicated, not with 'Essence is expressed by grammar' but with 'If anyone believes...', is puzzling, and the mystery is only compounded when she goes to on to remark that 'If anyone believes...' is one of the passages that arouses in her mind the question whether Wittgenstein was a linguistic idealist in his late phase. As David Bloor remarks (2018, 340), it is hard to see why this particular passage should arouse that particular thought. The difficulty is this, I think (I shall come to Bloor's diagnosis in Section 1.6): whether 'If anyone believes...' ought to prompt thoughts about a Wittgensteinian linguistic idealism depends on exactly how we are supposed to construe the phrase 'very general facts of nature'. In particular: is Wittgenstein alluding to facts about *our mindedness*—facts concerning what we find natural—or is he talking utterly generally about *empirical reality*, physical as well as psychological, inanimate as well as animate? If the *latter*, then the passage surely points towards not any form of idealism, but rather to an opposing realism: the idea that general empirical facts drive our concepts is a distinctively *realist* one. It emerges in the rest of Anscombe's article that she does indeed, at least sometimes, conceive of Wittgenstein's 'very general facts of nature' in this second way. Two examples she gives of such facts (as she supposes Wittgenstein takes them to be) are that 'colour and shape are independent' and that 'the sequence of phenomena' comprising my judgement 'I can't be making a mistake' together with my later coming to believe (rightly or wrongly) that I was then not competent to judge 'is rare'.[3] So it remains puzzling precisely why *Anscombe* finds herself entertaining *idealist* thoughts when she reads the passage in question.

---

[2] Wittgenstein 1980, 49, 57; 1973, p. 126. For discussion see Gaskin 2001, 201–8.
[3] Anscombe 1981, 113, 133, with reference to Wittgenstein 1979a, §§643–5. Cf. Moore 1997, 128.

Nevertheless, I think she is right that the passage *ought to* prompt such thoughts in the reader. For the continuation of 'If anyone believes . . .', quoted above, together with *Zettel*, §§357–8, also quoted above, suggest that by 'very general facts of nature' Wittgenstein in *Investigations* II, §xii, means the *first* of the two aforementioned options, namely facts about what we find natural. And if that way of construing Wittgenstein's phrase is factored into one's understanding of 'If anyone believes . . .', the passage now *does* look as though it implies some kind of idealism. Further, when this passage, understood as I have recommended, is put together with '*Essence* is expressed by grammar', assuming, as is plausible, that the concepts Wittgenstein is concerned with in 'If anyone believes . . .' *are* essences, it further looks as though a distinctively *linguistic* form of idealism is in question.

But, though the slogan 'Essence is expressed by grammar' would certainly convey a *linguistic* form of idealism, assuming that it *is* idealistic in purport, Anscombe's view is that it falls short of being fully idealistic. A properly idealistic slogan, she supposes, would need to say that essence is *created* by grammar (1981, 112). However, I suggest that the contrast that is here being invoked is, at least in this context, spurious. For when we put 'Essence is expressed by grammar' together with the two sections that immediately follow it, as I did above, it surely transpires that Wittgenstein's version and Anscombe's rewrite come to the same. Given the arbitrariness of grammar, if grammar tells us what kind of object anything is, it follows that grammar *is* creating essence; an 'essence' that was merely *expressed* by an arbitrary grammatical rule in any sense of 'express' that fell short of *create* would not *be* an essence, but a mere accident. After all, in claiming that essence is expressed by grammar Wittgenstein must intend to assert a necessary truth, not a mere contingency. The rules of grammar are, as we have seen, said by Wittgenstein to be arbitrary, which means that they could have been framed differently, and it must be assumed that Wittgenstein holds that, in the counterfactual scenario in which they *were* framed differently, essence would *still* be expressed by grammar—by the grammar of the language of that counterfactual situation. So, necessarily, grammar expresses essence: here the modal operator has wide scope; the claim is that in any possible world, the grammar of *that* world expresses the essences of *that* world. But now necessity is, for Wittgenstein, *itself* a grammatical matter. Not only do we have it that, however different an object's nature might be in other, counterfactual circumstances, grammar always, in those circumstances, expresses that nature; it is also Wittgenstein's view that this fact is itself a *grammatical* one, and this in turn is tantamount to the doctrine that grammar not merely expresses but indeed creates essence. That such really is

Wittgenstein's view emerges clearly, as I have said, from the immediate sequel to his assertion that essence is expressed by grammar.

1.3

Anscombe's discussion is unfortunately infused with versions of the muddle I have just diagnosed; correspondingly, as one reads through her article the doctrine of linguistic idealism moves in and out of focus. Sometimes she has it clearly in view. For example, in commenting on Wittgenstein's 'You learned the *concept* "pain" when you learned language' (1977, I, §384), Anscombe writes (1981, 114):

> That is, it is not experiencing pain that gives you the meaning of the word 'pain'. How could experience dictate the grammar of a word? You may say: doesn't it make certain demands on the grammar, if the word is to be the word of *that* experience? But the word is not just a response to that experience at that time: what *else* is the word to apply to? The experience can't dictate what is to be put together with it.

The individual experience cannot tell you, as Anscombe goes on to remark, what other things are to count as relevantly *similar* to it (i.e., relevantly similar either to the experience itself as a mental event or to its object). And the similarity that is expressed by a word—the similarity that collects its instances—does not come *before* the use of that word. So far, so pellucid.

But Anscombe then almost at once forgets what she has just said. Having noted, correctly, that 'if there had never been humans around talking about horses, that is not the slightest reason to say there wouldn't have been horses', she continues 'These essences, then, which are expressed by grammar, are not created by grammar' (1981, 114). This is a *non sequitur*: the point Anscombe had made about 'pain' and pains applies equally to 'horse' and horses. What *collects* horses into a natural kind—the essence of *horse*—is not something supplied by individual horses or by any other chunk of reality considered independently of linguistic practices. It is a matter of how we find it natural to group things together, and that constraint applies every bit as much to the counterfactual world in which there are horses but no humans as to the actual world in which there are both. After all, that counterfactual world is being contemplated by *us* here and now from *our* perspective, and we are of course equipped with *our* concept horse and *our* feelings of similarity: the existence or otherwise of language users in the counterfactual scenario under consideration is neither here nor there. The linguistic idealist says that essence *is* created by grammar, while insisting that it by no means follows that if there had been no humans or indeed if there had been no empirical languages there would then have been no essence of equinity, and so no horses either. Horses and their essence, equinity, could certainly have existed in a world without languages and language users, notwithstanding the fact that essence is a creature of grammar.

There are two places in Anscombe's discussion of linguistic idealism where the confusion we have identified comes into the open in a particularly instructive way. Here is one. She writes:

> I understand or mean or think of a kind of animal when I hear, read, or say 'horse'. But those terms don't signify a mental act such as forming an image or having a representation before me. No image or representation could determine future or past application of the word, i.e. what I and others have called and will call a 'horse'. *This* is determined by the grammar's expressing an essence. (1981, 115)

But there is an obvious antinomy between 'determined' and 'expressing' in this last sentence: for if grammar merely *expresses* essence in Anscombe's sense— that is, if grammar expresses essence in a manner that falls short of *creating* it— then grammar is not in a position to *determine* anything, any more than, say, the imprint of a signet ring in soft wax, an imprint which expresses the form of the ring, is in a position to determine that form. To bring this passage into line with Anscombe's good observations about 'pain', quoted above, we need either to change 'expressing' in its last sentence to 'creating', or read the former word as being, in context, tantamount in meaning to the latter.

The tension I have diagnosed also emerges in a later passage where Anscombe writes that the existence of 'horses and giraffes, colours and shapes' is not 'the product of human linguistic practices', either for Wittgenstein or in fact; 'but', she continues, 'the metaphysical necessities belonging to the nature of such things—these *seem* to be regarded by [Wittgenstein] as "grammatical rules"' (1981, 121), and at this point she brings in *Investigations* I, §372, quoted above. The emphasis that Anscombe puts on the word 'seem' in the passage I have excerpted is slightly misleading, since it could be taken to imply that the appearance is non-veridical: in fact Anscombe thinks that we should embrace, both as our interpretation of Wittgenstein and as our preferred systematic position, what she calls a 'partial idealism', according to which, on the one hand, 'the existence of human concepts can be somewhat generally equated with the existence of a great variety of human linguistic practices', while, on the other, this 'by no means implies any dependence on human thought and language, on the part of the things that fall under the concepts' (1981, 118).

The problem is that you cannot have both of these positions. In the first place, individual horses cannot exist unless the essence of equinity exists. In general, concrete spatiotemporal individuals have essences: Anscombe indeed herself makes this point (1981, 114). But then there is an obvious transition to metaphysical necessities—essences just *are* such necessities—and if the latter are being fixed by arbitrary grammatical rules it follows that the former must, in some sense, be a 'product of human linguistic practices'. Moreover, if the essence of equinity is a product of linguistic practices, then the individual horse, which could not exist without that essence, must somehow be a product of them too. This only sounds worrying if we suppose that production by linguistic practices is in competition with (in the case of horses) biological reproduction; but of course there is no such competition. We can put the requisite point by saying that horses are produced empirically by their parents, but transcendentally they are products of language. What *that* means is that the existence of individual horses and of the essence of equinity depends on the *possibility* of their being talked about in language. (Any language? Or specifically human language? For the moment I assume with Anscombe that the latter is in question, but we shall return to this point in Section 1.6.) Linguistic idealism, as I understand it, is a transcendentalist doctrine.[4]

In the second half of her paper Anscombe turns to examine rules, rights, and promises, three things 'whose existence *does* depend on human linguistic practice' (1981, my emphasis). But if these things depend on human linguistic practice, and given that *any* use of language is rule-governed (and indeed right- and promise-governed), it follows, as she had recognized in the case of 'pain' but then appeared to forget, that the meanings—in the first instance the senses, but then a fortiori the referents, too—of *all* words depend, in *some* manner, on human linguistic practice, which makes individual horses just as much as their common essence so dependent. Individual horses do not determine the correct application of the word 'horse' any more than individual pains dictate the grammar of the word 'pain'. Whether anything counts as a *horse* depends on the use of the word: it is a matter of the application

---

[4] Dilman construes it empirically, with the result that a linguistic idealist would hold that, had there been no empirical language, there would have been no horses, either (2002, 4–5): but that would be a very flat-footed version of the doctrine. He also, oddly, builds into his version of linguistic idealism the thesis that grammar 'exist[s] in isolation ... from our life and its activities' (2002, 80).

of a grammatical rule; and rules embody our feelings of similarity. What Anscombe said about pains applies exactly, mutatis mutandis, to horses, and to everything else that we talk about. Her attempt to combine 'partial' linguistic idealism, supposed to apply to spatiotemporal objects like horses, with 'full' linguistic idealism, supposed to apply only to rules, rights, and promises, therefore collapses.[5] In the context of adopting a 'full' linguistic idealism for rules, *any* attempt to commit oneself no further than to a 'partial' idealism in respect of horses will fail, since both the essence of horse and what counts as an individual horse depend on the rule-governed activity of our use of words.

1.4

I have argued that Wittgenstein's insistence on the arbitrariness of grammar entails that his slogan 'essence is expressed by grammar' must in context be read—as one would anyway, given the sequel, be disposed to read it—so that it amounts to nothing less than the claim that essence is created by grammar. But how can grammar create essence? In his middle and later period Wittgenstein often wrestles with this difficulty, which can be cast as a tension between the senses, noted in Section 1.2, in which grammar is and is not arbitrary: grammar is said to be arbitrary in the sense that it has no justification, and that we could frame its rules differently, but non-arbitrary in the sense that its rules might, from a psychological point of view, come naturally to us. Do these theses about grammar, taken together, not imply that even if we cannot actively think ourselves into or imagine occupying alternative grammatical conventions we can at least conceive the possibility of such alternative conventions, and therewith make sense of the idea of alternative metaphysical necessities? But if we admit so much, are we not reneging on the *necessity* of the metaphysical 'necessities' we started with?[6] And surely Wittgenstein does not wish to 'bargain any of its rigour out of logic'? (cf. 1977, I, §108). Yet time and time again he gives the impression of flirting with transcendental idealism in a substantial, Kantian sense, according to which, though we cannot see past our own forms of thought, we are not allowed to conclude from the existence of that limit on our capacities that reality necessarily accords with those forms;

---

[5] 'Partial idealism' is Anscombe's own term; 'full idealism' is helpfully supplied by Bloor (2018, 335).
[6] If we start with a necessary proposition, a background logic of S4 will suffice to exclude the possibility that it might not be necessary; if, on the other hand, we start with a non-necessary proposition, we will need the S5 axiom to enable us to rule out the possibility that it is necessary.

rather, it is implied that the fundamental nature of reality is an open question, and is possibly quite alien to the way we think and talk.

One place where this style of thinking emerges in Wittgenstein's post-Tractarian writings comes in his 1929 paper, 'Some Remarks on Logical Form'. It is worth quoting the relevant section at length:

> Now we can only substitute a clear symbolism for the unprecise one by inspecting the phenomena which we want to describe, thus trying to understand their logical multiplicity. That is to say, we can only arrive at a correct analysis by, what might be called, the logical investigation of the phenomena themselves, i.e., in a certain sense *a posteriori*, and not by conjecturing about *a priori* possibilities. One is often tempted to ask from an *a priori* standpoint: What, after all, can be the only forms of atomic propositions, and to answer, e.g., subject–predicate and relational propositions with two or more terms; further, perhaps, propositions relating predicates and relations to one another, and so on. But this, I believe, is mere playing with words. An atomic form cannot be foreseen. And it would be surprising if the actual phenomena had nothing more to teach us about their structure. To such conjectures about the structure of atomic propositions, we are led by our ordinary language, which uses the subject–predicate and the relational form. But in this our language is misleading: I will try to explain this by a simile. Let us imagine two parallel planes, I and II. On plane I figures are drawn, say, ellipses and rectangles of different sizes and shapes, and it is our task to produce images of these figures on plane II. Then we can imagine two ways, amongst others, of doing this. We can, first, lay down a law of projection—say that of orthogonal projection or any other—and then proceed to project all figures from I into II, according to this law. Or, secondly, we could proceed thus: We lay down the rule that every ellipse on plane I is to appear as a circle in plane II, and every rectangle as a square in II. Such a way of representation may be convenient for us if for some reason we prefer to draw only circles and squares on plane II. Of course, from these images the exact shapes of the original figures on plane I cannot be immediately inferred. We can only gather from them that the original was an ellipse or a rectangle. In order to get in a single instance at the determinate shape of the original we would have to know the individual method by which, e.g., a particular ellipse is projected into the circle before me. The case of ordinary language is quite analogous. If the facts of reality are the ellipses and rectangles on plane I the subject–predicate and relational forms correspond to the circles and squares in plane II. These forms are the norms of our particular language into which we project in

ever so many different ways ever so many different logical forms. And for this very reason we can draw no conclusions—except very vague ones—from the use of these norms as to the actual logical form of the phenomena described.⁷

'And it would be surprising if the actual phenomena had nothing more to teach us about their structure': this is as far away as can be imagined from the assertion that 'Grammar tells us what kind of object anything is', not to mention the well-known remark in *Zettel* that 'Like everything metaphysical the harmony between thought and reality is to be found in the grammar of the language' (§55, tr. Anscombe).

What about the *Tractatus*? Peter Hacker, commenting on the above passage from 'Some Remarks', avers that the 'programme' set out therein 'coheres perfectly with the *Tractatus*' (2000, 375). He is not alone in so thinking. In fact, the realist idea that the world exists independently of language, and that it is then the business of language structurally to reflect that already constituted world, has been quite commonly read into the *Tractatus*. David Pears, for example, tells us that, according to this work, 'logic reveals the structure imposed on all factual discourse by the ultimate structure of reality. That is its connection with the world.'⁸ But, as a number of commentators have pointed out, any such realism is quite antithetical to the spirit of the *Tractatus*.⁹ We *do* find hints of realism in the *Notebooks*,¹⁰ but by the time of the *Tractatus* it has disappeared, to be replaced by a form of linguistic idealism. In particular the transcendental deduction of the existence of objects that is offered in 2.02–2.0212 and 3.23 exemplifies that idealism: 3.23 states that 'the requirement of the possibility of simple signs is the requirement of the determinacy of sense'; indeed, in the *Notebooks* draft of 3.23 Wittgenstein had even written 'simple things' instead of 'simple signs' ('The demand for simple things *is* the demand for definiteness of sense': 1979c, 63). And, however exactly the difficult sections 2.02–2.0212 are to be understood, it seems clear that their burden, taken together with 3.23, is that the existence of objects does not come first, metaphysically speaking, in the order of creation, but is rather transcendentally deduced as a necessary condition of the meaningfulness of language. Intelligible language is the

---

⁷ Wittgenstein 1929, 163–5 (= 1993, 30–1). Cf. 1974, 204–5; 1975, 118–19; 1979b, 41–2; Hacker 2021, 163–4, 175.
⁸ Pears 1987, 27. Cf. 1987, 8; 1988, 206. See also Harrison 1973, 40, 48, 84–5; Malcolm 1986, 14; Schroeder 2006, 96.
⁹ See Ishiguro 1969, 20–1; Sullivan 1996, esp. 204–9; McGuinness 2002, 82–94. Cf. McGinn 2013, 200–1.
¹⁰ See Pears 1996, 203–5; McGinn 2006, 6 n. 5.

given—'By means of sentences we make ourselves understood' (4.026)—and then (that is a logical 'then') the substance of the world, the objects, are its transcendental precipitate; facts are composed of objects, which means that for Wittgenstein the world, the totality of facts, depends for its constitution on language.[11]

In the light of this, we can see that a move that Wittgenstein makes in his middle period, which both he and many of his commentators take to be a fundamental shift *away from* the metaphysics of the *Tractatus*, is in reality no such thing: I mean the move 'from simples to samples'.[12] In *Philosophical Remarks* Wittgenstein states:

> What I formerly called 'objects', the simple, is simply what I can refer to without having to worry that it perhaps does not exist, that is to say, it is that for which there is neither existence nor non-existence, and that means: what we can speak about *whatever may be the case*.... If I want to communicate to someone what colour a material is to have, I send him a sample (*Muster*), and clearly this sample belongs to the language. (1975, 72–3)

The 'new' position is then clearly articulated in *Philosophical Investigations*:

> We can put it like this: This sample is an instrument of the language used in ascriptions of colour. In this language-game it is not something that is represented, but is a means of representation.... And to say 'If it did not *exist*, it could have no name' is to say as much and as little as: if this thing did not exist, we could not use it in our language-game.—What looks as if it *had* to exist, is part of the language. It is a paradigm in our language-game; something with which comparison is made. (1977, I, §50)[13]

But if my summary of the linguistic idealism of the *Tractatus* was on the right lines, then it would seem that in the first of these passages Wittgenstein gives a rather misleading description of his erstwhile position. In the *Tractatus*, as we have said, meaningful language is the given, and objects drop out of that language as a condition of its meaningfulness; the existence of objects is transcendentally deduced from the existence of meaningful language. So for the Tractarian Wittgenstein there is no question of our 'having to worry', in general, that an object 'perhaps does not exist': if my language is meaningful—and the criteria for that are internal to the language-game itself, a matter of whether

---

[11] Here I shall have to leave the claims made about the *Tractatus* in this paragraph at the level of sheer assertion, deferring their detailed defence, as well as a presentation of my favoured reconstruction of the argument at 2.02–2.0212, to another occasion.

[12] See, for example, Hacker 2021, 76–8, 113–15, 128–9; Beaney in Wittgenstein 2023, lix–lxi.

[13] See also Wittgenstein 1974, 40–1, 97; 1980, 101–3; 1993, 56.

the signs I purport to employ do indeed have a use—then whatever objects my words can be interpreted as referring to *eo ipso* exist. For to say that my words refer to objects is just another way of saying that these words are indeed meaningful: ontology is merely a reflex of meaningful language.[14] In the passage from *Philosophical Remarks* quoted above, Wittgenstein writes as though his Tractarian position had been a realist one, as if objects had to exist first, independently of language, as an external pre-condition and determinant of language's being meaningful; but in fact his position was the idealist one of insisting that objects are a transcendental product of meaningful language.

Of course, I can refer to an object *only if* it exists: alternatively put, an object's existence is a *necessary condition* of my ability to refer to it. But what are the metaphysical dependencies underlying these equivalent formulations? Is it that I can refer to an object *because it exists* (realism), or does the object exist *because I can refer to it* (idealism)? From an empirical perspective, realism holds. But, as I shall explore in §§5–7, when we think about the matter transcendentally, idealism is seen to be right. The later Wittgenstein appears to have forgotten just how idealistic the *Tractatus* was. The *Tractatus* in effect *already* thinks that 'What looks as if it *had* to exist, is part of the language.' The early sections of *Philosophical Investigations* repeat the misunderstanding of the *Tractatus* that we find in the *Remarks*. Again, the earlier work is attacked as having been more realistic than it was. Indeed, in the *Investigations* Wittgenstein persistently treats the 'object and designation' model of meaning as being more substantial than it needs to be or was in the *Tractatus*.[15] The later Wittgenstein would have said of the Tractarian statement 'Objects form the substance of the world' (2.021) that 'That is a grammatical remark.'[16] But this is what the *Tractatus* thinks too. To say 'What I used to call simple objects are really samples and belong to the language' is just to put new clothing on an old form. Tractarian simple objects in effect *were* samples and *were* part of the language.[17]

1.5

According to the linguistic idealism of the *Tractatus*, the world necessarily echoes the subject–predicate form of sentences (4.24, 4.5, 5.471, 5.4711). We are told at 4.22 that elementary sentences are combinations of names, but 4.24 makes clear that they can be represented as evincing subject–predicate

---

[14] Cf. Wittgenstein 1977, I, §13.
[15] See Gaskin 1996, 94–104.
[16] Cf. Dilman 2002, 11.
[17] Cf. Wittgenstein 1979b, 43.

form (using this label to include relational form) at a higher level of description. If, for the sake of illustration, '*abc*' is an elementary sentence, we could employ any of '*f*(*a*)', '*g*(*a*, *b*)', and '*h*(*a*, *b*, *c*)' to represent it (and there are further such representational possibilities, of course). Representational sentences like the ones just mentioned have, in general, function–argument form (4.24, 5.47), and the linguistic idealism of the *Tractatus* then sees to it that the world mirrors that form. The long passage quoted above from 'Some Remarks' is a reaction against that Tractarian idealism; equally, it gives us an excellent picture of exactly what the linguistic idealist is reacting against. For a good way of conveying the linguist idealist's starting point is to say that the idea that Wittgenstein advances in this passage—the idea that the form of language might not be an adequate guide to the form of reality; in particular, the idea that the 'phenomena' might not be accurately capturable in language's subject–predicate-shaped (in general: argument–function-shaped) net—does not add up: when pressed it collapses into contradiction. (As an aside, one might ask why Wittgenstein thinks, at the end of the quoted passage from 'Some Remarks', that, compatibly with all he has said, we might get even so far as drawing 'very vague' conclusions about the nature of reality from our linguistic forms? If the realist perspective that the passage adopts is right, then from our linguistic forms we can draw *no conclusions at all* about the shape of reality. If our linguistic forms warrant even 'very vague' conclusions about the nature of reality, those forms must be very roughly accurate; and what underpins that accuracy? It would appear that Wittgenstein cannot keep his new-found realism in focus.)

The contradiction arises because the world is necessarily structured in argument–function form, simply by virtue of being complex. In his Introduction to the *Tractatus*, Russell suggests that commonality of form between language and reality is 'perhaps the most fundamental thesis' of the work.[18] At the most general level of abstraction, what world and language have in common is that they are both complex—they both involve structurings of objects—and complexity imports function–argument structure (5.47). Of course, the sheer fact of commonality of form between language and world does not in itself settle the question whether the realist or linguistic idealist (if either) gives the right account of which side of the mirroring relation determines which; but

---

[18] Russell at Wittgenstein 1922, 8. Russell's assertion is contested by Ramsey in his 'Critical Notice' of the *Tractatus*. Ramsey is right to reject Russell's additional suggestion that Wittgenstein is concerned with 'the conditions that would have to be fulfilled by a logically perfect language' (1931, 270–1, quoting Russell at Wittgenstein 1922, 7); but the fact that Wittgenstein's 'doctrines apply to ordinary language' (Ramsey 1931, 270) does not, as Ramsey supposes, diminish the cogency of Russell's gloss on the fundamental purport of the *Tractatus* (though, as I will note in the text, the gloss is incomplete).

we have seen that the Tractarian Wittgenstein answers in favour of linguist idealism, and below in this section I shall argue that this is the right answer.

Wittgenstein follows the 'Some Remarks' passage that I excerpted in Section 1.4 with a geometrical case intended to illustrate its main claim. Ironically, however, so far from supporting that claim the example actually works against it. Wittgenstein first suggests that the 'logical analysis of phenomena' requires that 'for their representation numbers (rational and irrational) must enter into the structure of atomic propositions' (1929, 165). He then specifies an example in which the exact location of a rectangular red patch in the visual field is given by the Cartesian co-ordinates [6–9, 3–8]: this means that the base of the rectangle is a continuous interval from point 6 to point 9 on the x-axis, and its height a continuous interval from point 3 to point 8 on the y-axis. The sample atomic proposition specifying the position and colour of the patch may then, he tells us, take the form '[6–9, 3–8] R', where 'R' symbolizes the colour red. But here the linguistic idealist will object that '[6–9, 3–8] R' exhibits argument–function structure, indeed is a subject–predicate sentence.[19] After all, this piece of notation merely abbreviates the ordinary English sentences that I used to expand it, and those sentences have that form. In general: descriptions of reality that employ some kind of mathematical symbolism *cannot* obviate the subject–predicate structure of ordinary language, since mathematical symbolism simply *abbreviates* natural language. So how can the example illustrate the alleged possibility that ordinary language, with its subject–predicate structure, might fail to represent reality accurately?

His example is a simplified one, Wittgenstein assures us; but that assurance does nothing to help us see how atomic forms might be unforeseeable, or how they might take a non-subject–predicate shape. How could 'the actual phenomena' have 'more to teach us about their structure' than is foreseen by grammar? Is the idea that, in order for reality to teach me about its real structure, I should take off the linguistic spectacles that I wear, with their subject–predicate tint, and look directly at the 'actual phenomena'?[20] But, to pursue this analogy, it is not a mere pair of removable spectacles that supply the tint: it is my whole visual system; it is the entire physical arrangement of matter, at least as that bears on perception; it is everything in the nature of things that empowers me to look at anything at all. In order to 'look directly at

---

[19] The same objection applies against Wittgenstein 1979b, 41–2 (cf. n. 7 above), as well as to an attempt by Hintikka and Hintikka (1986, 123) to represent elementary states of affairs without calling in aid subject–predicate structure.

[20] One might think of comparing 1977, I, §103, but here the polemic is surely directed, not against linguistic idealism as such, but against a wrong-headed platonistic version of that doctrine, one involving the idea of supermechanism. Cf. Gaskin 2006, 188–93; Moore 2013, 243 n. 10.

the actual phenomena' I would have to circumvent all of that; but then I would no longer be seeing anything.

A different analogy which Wittgenstein at one point uses in this connection is telling. In a context where Frege's theory of number is in question he writes:

> You can of course treat the subject–predicate form (or, what comes to the same thing, the argument–function form) as a norm of representation, and then it is admittedly important and characteristic that whenever we use numbers, the number may be represented as the property of a predicate. Only we must be clear about the fact that now we are not dealing with objects and concepts as the results of analysis, but with moulds into which we have squeezed the sentence (*Satz*). And of course it is significant that it can be fitted into this mould. But squeezing something into a mould is the opposite of analysis. (If you want to study the natural growth of an apple tree, you don't look at an espaliered tree—except to see how *this* tree reacts to *this* pressure.) (1975, 136–7, tr. adapted)

Actually, an espaliered tree gives you information not merely about how *this tree* responds to the restrictions that have been imposed on it, but how, in general, *plants of a certain kind* do so. But the key objection to this passage is that Wittgenstein's analogy fails in a crucial respect: we *can* study apple trees in their 'natural' state, but we *cannot* get behind language to look at reality 'in itself'. For the analogy to hold, it would have to be the case either that we could examine reality 'neat', before the imposition of our subject–predicate structures, or that apple trees were only ever encountered in espaliered form, and indeed that we could not conceive how they might exist in any other condition. The first option is evidently incoherent, but the second is hardly less so. If the state of things envisaged therein obtained, 'being espaliered' would amount to 'having the particular plant biology of apple trees'. And then the idea that apple trees had been *forced* into possessing that biology—that in their 'natural' state they would take a *different* (perhaps non-biological) form—would plainly make no sense. Just so, says the linguistic idealist, with the idea that reality might 'in itself' exist beyond or apart from subject–predicate (argument–function) form.

If we adopt the view that there is a fundamental mirroring relation between language and reality—that, to put it generally, they share argument–function structure—the linguistic idealist, I have claimed, gives the right answer to the question which side drives which: according to this idealist, following the Tractarian Wittgenstein, (i) it is *because* language has argument–function structure that reality does, too; correlatively, it is not the case *either* (ii) that reality's form drives that of language, *or* (iii) that neither side determines the shape of the other. This latter option, (iii), actually divides into two sub-options: if neither side determined the other that might be either (a) because there was no determination in the picture anywhere; or (b) because both sides of our dichotomy were simultaneously determined to be the way they were, and to match one another, by some third thing.

A very general reason why (i) must be right is based on modal considerations: it is only if the mirroring relation between language and reality is driven from the side of language that this relation will evince the requisite *necessity*. (In addition, (iii)(b) is ruled out by the point that there is in any case nothing deeper than language and reality to do any determining of these two things.) If either (ii) or (iii) obtained (in either version (a) or (b)), language's mirroring of reality's fundamental structure would be a mere accident of fate; nothing would logically guarantee that the mirroring relation held. We could conceive of the two coming apart, which would in turn generate a sceptical puzzle: how do we know that there *is* a match between the structure of the language we use and reality? That sceptical doubt *would* be licit: for both in the case of (ii) and (iii)(b)—supposing, in the case of (ii), that the structure of language were driven causally from the side of the world, and in the case of (iii)(b) that the matching structures of language and reality were driven causally by something else—and even more evidently in the case of (iii)(a), the structure of language would be merely contingently related to the structure of reality. But it is *not* coherent—either in fact, or in the context of Tractarian metaphysics—to suppose that the structures of language and reality might be related in that merely contingent way. To ensure the necessity of the mirroring relation between them, we need language to be in control; we need it to be the case, as I shall explore further in the next section, that alternatives to the fundamental structure of reality that we have *do not make linguistic sense*. (Peter Sullivan notes that, on the so-called 'resolute' interpretation of the *Tractatus*, according to which most of the work's sentences—those not belonging to the 'frame'—are pure nonsense, no such explanatory asymmetry is available: 'If both "*p*" and "*q*" are empty, then "*q* because *p*" and "*p* because *q*" are equally empty.'[21] For me that constitutes an important consideration telling *against* the resolute reading of the *Tractatus*; but I shall not pause here to pursue this exegetical matter.)

Once we have got straight on that point, we can give due weight to Wittgenstein's concession, in the last quoted passage, that the world *can* be expressed in

---

[21] Sullivan 2002, 48.

language. Wittgenstein even describes this fact as 'significant', though he does not say what he thinks the significance of it is, and the immediate sequel seems to cancel the concession. I suggest that the significance is this: that the world *can* be expressed in language is *itself* a necessary truth, and so is itself driven by language. And when we have said so much, it comes to seem pointless to try to reserve a sense in which language falls short of the world, a sense in which it does not fully embrace the world's essence. For if it is essential to the world that it *can* be described in language, what more or what less—in short, what *else*—can there be to the world at the fundamental level? If a state of affairs is such that it *can* be truly—or even falsely—described by the sentence 'the cat is sitting on the mat', in what sense might language be supposed to be *inadequate* to reality? How can that sentence fail more badly than simply by being *false*?[22]

1.6

The reasoning I have just given closely imitates Kant's argument that the limits of reality are determined by the limits of thought, and not vice versa. (He also rules out the possibility that both sets of limits have a distinct common cause.)[23] Adrian Moore suggests that this argument is bound up with transcendental idealism in Kant's sense, that is, with an idealism which conceives the *limits* of thought to be *limitations* (2013, 249–50). To construe the limits of thought as limitations amounts, in turn, to supposing that there is (or could be) *something beyond* those limits. The question to what extent the *Tractatus* exemplifies a transcendental idealism in that Kantian sense has been the subject of a rich series of exchanges between Moore and Sullivan.[24] Moore—if I may attempt a crude summary—has argued that Wittgenstein, in the *Tractatus*, is alive to the incoherence of transcendental idealism, but that he also shows some sympathy with it (Sullivan agrees so far), and that the doctrine is indeed in *some* sense still standing at the end of the work (here Sullivan demurs). And, in connection with the Kantian (and so indirectly with my) argument that, in the mirroring relation between thought or language, on the one hand, and reality, on the other, one side (thought/language) determines and explains the fundamental constitution of the other (reality), Moore writes that,

---

[22] Cf. Wittgenstein 1977, I, §402; Gaskin 2018, 343–7; 2019, 1339.
[23] Kant 1998, A92–3/B124–6, B166–8. Kant often uses this pattern of argument: see also, e.g., B41 (space); A31/B47 (time); A111–14 (categories); A195–6/B240–1 (causation).
[24] See entries for both authors in the Bibliography, esp. under 2003, 2011, 2013; also Moore 1997, *passim*, esp. chs 7 and 9. See further Morris 2008, *passim*, esp. ch. 6.

as Wittgenstein helps us to appreciate, if these limits [i.e., the limits of thought/language, on the one hand, and the limits of reality, on the other] really were *limits, simpliciter*, and not limitations, there would be no question of any such determination and no need for any such explanation. The limits would be as they are because, in the most austere sense of the word 'could', they *could* not be otherwise. And their coincidence would still be knowable *a priori*. (2013, 250)

But against this: it does not follow, from the hypothesis that the structure of thought or language drives reality, that we must construe their limits as limitations. It is not, as Moore implies, simply a brute fact that these limits could not be otherwise: there is a reason why they could not *be* otherwise, namely that we could not *make sense* of their being otherwise. When we try to do so, we find that the attempt breaks down, and this is precisely because—here supplementing Wittgenstein with Davidson (see below)—we could not *translate* 'speakers' who were radically other-minded. We could not recognize the purported 'other-mindedness' of such 'speakers' *as a way of being minded* at all. But that means that the relevant beings would not *be* minded.[25] And this is a *linguistic* matter: it is a matter of what makes sense in our language.

Is the argument I have just given verificationist and, if so, is that a strike against it? Jonathan Lear suggests, in connection with the claim that recognizing the basic laws of logic is a condition of being minded at all, that

This is not verificationism, for no claim is being made that we (humans) must in principle be able to recognize every form of life. Perhaps there are Martians who speak a language which because of some kinks in our hardwiring we will never be able to recognize as such. The point is that if they are speaking a language, living a form of life, they too will be generally obeying the law of non-contradiction. (1998, 279–80)

We should agree with the implication of this passage that one would be committed to an objectionable form of verificationism if one insisted that we humans be able *in practice* to recognize every form of life. But what if we substitute 'in principle' for the emphasized phrase of the last sentence? After all, it is surely also implied in the quoted passage that the kinks in our wiring, to pick

---

[25] See further B. Williams 1981, ch. 12; Lear 1982, 386, 389; 1998, chs. 11 and 12; Gaskin 2001, 208–14; 2019, 1334–8; 2021, 243–5, this latter passage correcting some aspects of my 2019 account, in particular clarifying the point that the position both includes an element of verificationism and is right to do so (see next paragraph).

up on Lear's example, are just *contingent* limitations, and that they therefore *could* be ironed out. To insist that it must be *in principle* possible for us to recognize Lear's Martians as having a form of life is to say that, if the kinks in our wiring *were* ironed out, we *would be* in a position to arrive at that recognition. The linguist idealist, I think, must insist on some such condition of *in-principle* recognizability. Aliens, if they are to count as genuinely possessing a form of life, must in some such sense be *accessible* to us. If we wish to call that a form of verificationism, then we should add that so much verificationism is acceptable and indeed mandatory.

What is it to say that a form of life, in order to count as such, must be accessible to us humans? This is not an easy matter to spell out in detail, but minimally it must mean, putting it abstractly, that there is a finite series of intelligible steps taking us from here to there. If the form of life in question is not immediately intelligible to us it must be mediately so; it must stand to us in a relation which is some suitable ancestral of 'is intelligible to'. And, one should add, the number of steps in any suitable chain of intelligibility relations must be not just finite but quite small. But the key point is that there should indeed *be* such a chain. This condition is what gives bite to the doctrine of linguistic idealism: for clearly, if no restrictions were placed on what it was for something to count as a language, it would carry no weight to assert that reality must be expressible in language. (At the limit, such a liberal dispensation might even permit reality to count as its own linguistic expression.) So the idea of intelligibility must be grounded in that of intelligibility-to-us-humans.

But the other side of that coin is that, so long as they are accessible to us in the mediate sense just explored, forms of life that are possessed and languages that are spoken by non-human beings are entirely conceivable. This suggests that when we talk about 'our mindedness' or 'our language' the first-person plural should be keyed not merely to members of the species *homo sapiens*. As Bernard Williams pointed out in his seminal essay 'Wittgenstein and Idealism' (reprinted in his 1981), to which Anscombe in her essay on linguistic idealism was probably in part responding, 'thinkers and speakers' cannot simply be identified with a particular empirical group: in fact no empirical limits can be placed on who (or what) might belong to the community of thinkers and speakers.[26] Temporal and other constraints may affect the extent to which mutual intelligibility between different members of this wider community is practically *achievable*, but mutual intelligibility must in principle, in

---

[26] B. Williams 1981, 160: in the writings of the later Wittgenstein, 'one finds oneself with a *we* which is not one group rather than another in the world at all, but rather the plural descendant of that idealist *I* [sc. of the *Tractatus*] who also was not one item rather than another in the world'.

the mediated sense, *be* achievable. To put Williams's point in terms that Saul Kripke (1982, 37) has made familiar, the extension of 'thinkers and speakers' must be fixed normatively, not (merely) descriptively, since the idea of intelligibility is essentially a normative one. (That has the consequence that this extension cannot at any point in time be definitively *fixed*: it is always the case that more can join the group.) But—to reiterate the point that I made above, in agreement with the linguistic idealist—while membership of the group of mutually intelligible interpreters living a form of life does not *stop* with human beings, it does *start* with them.

According to linguistic idealism, then, in the version of that doctrine which I favour, the world is constituted by language in the following sense: worldly structures mirror linguistic structures at the deepest level and as a matter of their essence; and because of the non-contingent and non-accidental nature of this mirroring relation between worldly and linguistic structures it follows that worldly structures are driven by linguistic structures, rather than the determining relation's running in the opposite direction, or in neither. (And there is nothing deeper to fix both sets of structures simultaneously.) It is because *language*—and that, as I have just been reflecting, means ultimately if not immediately *human* language—is the way it is that the world is, in broad terms, the way *it* is. And since linguistic structures, as a matter of their constitution, make sense to language users, these users' understanding of their language enables them, in consequence, to 'make sense' of the world. This asymmetrical dependence of world on language puts language users in a certain position of power and privilege: it does not of itself enable them, in general, to settle what is true and what is false; to do *that* usually requires investigation of one sort or another.[27] But the dependence does warrant our adopting as our metaphysic a form—a linguistic form—of anthropocentricism or idealism.

As I have, I hope, made clear, for the linguistic idealist the dependence of world on language is a transcendental not an empirical one, so that there is no fear lest the doctrine force us to suppose that the world sprang into existence with the historical evolution of empirical language. Rather, for the world to exist it must be expressible—its nature must be describable—in language. Whether or not any empirical languages happen to be around to express it and describe its nature is of no consequence as far as the sheer existence of the world goes; it only matters to the world's existence that it and its nature should be capturable in language. But the fact, if it turns out to be a fact, that over the course of the universe's entire history there will have been no empirical

---

[27] Gaskin 2021, §36.

language existing in most places and at most times does not unsettle the linguistic idealist, who agrees with common sense on the independence of the world from empirical language. Even so, linguistic idealism ought to sound like quite a startling view. That is because, as I have hinted, it is not vacuous to say that the world must be expressible in language, given that the expressing language must either be a human language, which is an empirical, contingent, evolved phenomenon, or at least be a form of language that is accessible to humans, perhaps an adaptation or extension of human language. Something—language—which is capable of accidental empirical evolution, and which has in fact evolved as a matter of sheer empirical accident, is controlling the very nature of the world, is driving its fundamental describability and intelligibility. Human beings are only a tiny and insignificant bit of reality, and yet it is a condition on there being such a thing as reality in the first place—a reality for humans to have evolved in—that it be linguistically intelligible to them. There is a sense in which, notwithstanding Copernicus, planet Earth is the centre of the universe after all. (Kant's 'Copernican Turn'[28] is, in another sense, anti-Copernican!)

Earlier (Section 1.2) I noted Bloor's puzzlement, which I shared, that Anscombe should start her article on linguistic idealism with the particular passage of Wittgenstein that she chose, namely 'If anyone believes . . .' (1977, I, §xii). Bloor's own suggestion for resolving the puzzle is that 'linguistic idealism is an account of the ontology of social institutions' (2018, 341). Now, this might initially seem like an unpromising manoeuvre. After all, one is tempted to object, linguistic idealism surely has much grander ambitions than merely advancing the claim that social institutions generate their own objects, which is, one would have thought, a rather anodyne thesis: even the most hardened realist will grant that *a maximum break, a shot to nothing,* and *a plant* are objects generated by, and internal to, the game of snooker, while seeking to hold the realist line when it comes to the sticks, balls, and tables. But I think this dismissal would be premature. Bloor goes on to propose that socially generated objects such as promises and other performative acts are 'linguistic idealism in action' (2018, 345): a particularly telling example he gives is that of a bank's soundness or unsoundness. These objects are bootstrapped into existence by the beliefs of economic agents: if enough of the relevant people *believe* that a bank is unsound, for example, then it *is* unsound; in this context, that is exactly what unsoundness amounts to. Of course, objects that are brought into existence by social institutions are *empirically* so created; by contrast, I have been

---

[28] Kant 1998, BXVI–XVII, XXII n. 1.

insisting that the linguistic idealist propounds a *transcendentalist* thesis about the language-dependence of objects in general. In a world without human or similar beings there would be no banks in existence to be either sound or unsound, but there might well be physical objects of various kinds, whose existence would, according to the linguistic idealist, be transcendentally constituted by human (or similar) language. But we can improve the prospects for Bloor's model if we adduce the Wittgenstein–Davidson point about the veridical tendency of beliefs.[29] For an object to exist most actual (if there are any actual) and counterfactual beliefs about its existence have to be true; otherwise those (actual and counterfactual) beliefs would not *be* beliefs about that object. Mistakes, error, falsity in general, depend for their existence on their having an exceptional status. So there is a sense in which the (un)soundness of a bank does serve as quite a good model of the linguistic idealist's treatment of objects in general. (And, going back to my snooker example, observe that not merely are the rules of the game and the objects they generate cultural artefacts; the sticks, balls, and tables are such artefacts too.)

1.7

I said above (Section 1.5) that argument–function form generalized subject–predicate form, and the reader will have noticed that in the apple-tree passage Wittgenstein observes that (for his occurrent purposes) these two forms 'come to the same'.[30] But surely, one might object, they are *not* the same thing: subject–predicate form is grammatical, argument–function form logical. In one way this objection is right. The phrase 'the grammatical subject–predicate distinction' is usually used to mean a low-level distinction that applies to natural languages in a fixed way: for example, in the English sentence 'Socrates sits', we are taught that 'Socrates' is the subject and 'sits' the predicate, not the other way round. By contrast, if we construe that sentence or the proposition to which it refers in argument–function terms, we have a choice of representations: we could take 'Socrates'—or, at the level of reference, Socrates—to be an argument to the function '[sit]'—at the level of reference, the concept *sitting*—or alternatively vice versa. And these two options are not the only ones: there are infinitely many others, in fact, for we could take both

---

[29] Wittgenstein 1977, I, §§240–2; 1979a, §§155–6; 1982, §§252–71; 1992, 20; Davidson 1982, 220–3, 236–7; 1984, 137, 152–3, 159, 168–9, 192, 196–201; 2001, esp. essays 10–14. See McGinn 2004, 245–7; M. Williams 2004, 252–3; Coliva 2010, 114–15; Trächtler 2021, ch. 5.

[30] Cf. *Tractatus* 4.126(d), where it is implied that proper (as opposed to formal) concepts (*Begriffe*) can be represented by functions.

'Socrates'/Socrates and '[sit]'/sitting as arguments to a copulative/ instantiation relation, and so on into Bradley's regress.[31] The logical distinction is a grid or schema that can be placed on the natural language sentence (and the proposition that it refers to) in various, equally good, ways, corresponding to different analyses of the sentence (proposition). Grammar allows us no such leeway: on the ordinary understanding of the grammatical subject–predicate distinction, the sentence 'Socrates sits' has just one analysis.

Of course, one can construct more etiolated senses for 'the subject–predicate distinction', and I have done this elsewhere.[32] At the limit, one might use the phrase to mean the same as 'the argument–function distinction':[33] in that case one might more perspicuously speak of a distinction between 'logical subject' and 'logical predicate'; and one could then treat '[sit]' as the logical subject of 'Socrates sits', and 'Socrates' as that sentence's logical predicate (and correspondingly for the relevant proposition). This move simply mimics the phenomenon of type-raising as that occurs in, for example, Frege's syntactic and semantic hierarchies: instead of analysing the sentence 'Socrates sits' as composed of a zeroth-level name and first-level predicate, these being argument and function respectively, we may treat the first-level predicate as argument (logical subject) and the zeroth-level name as function (logical predicate), thereby raising it for these purposes to the second level of the hierarchy. (Correspondingly, *mutatis mutandis*, for the hierarchy comprising entities at the level of reference.) If we wanted a natural-language translation of the sentence so analysed, we might try 'Sitting Socratizes' (i.e., 'Sitting is instantiated by Socrates').

As I have said (Section 1.5), following *Tractatus* 5.47, argument–function structure is a reflex of complexity, and that means that in its analytical application to complexity it can be wielded in every which way. Suppose that some verbal or non-verbal entity is an argument: that is, suppose that, on some occasion in which we are engaging in analysis, this entity *serves as* an argument. Well, so far that implies nothing about any status that the relevant entity might have, or acquire, *independently* of its role on this occasion as an argument. And there will be alternative analytic strategies that accord the same entity a functional status. No sense attaches to the idea that an entity might have a status, in the relevant sense, independently of the status which it acquires pursuant to a particular analysis: independently of any particular analysis, neither 'Socrates',

---

[31] See Gaskin 2008, esp. ch. 6. It is the very fact that there *are* all the options supplied by Bradley's regress that unifies the sentence/proposition, in my view.
[32] Gaskin 2008, 215–21, 292–314.
[33] This is how Ramsey, in discussing the Picture Theory in his 'Critical Notice', uses 'subject' and 'predicate': 1931, 273.

nor 'sits' has a status in the relevant sense—ditto for the referents of these expressions, and indeed for any (names of) relations of instantiation that we might wish to adduce in our analysis of the proposition *that Socrates sits* (the sentence 'Socrates sits'). Hence 'argument' and 'function' do not correlate with interesting ontological categories. As far as anything we have said here goes, independently of any particular application of the argument–function dichotomy, everything has the same ontological status, in which case we may as well aver that everything counts as an object.[34]

Philosophers have often tried to deploy the grammatical subject–predicate distinction in such a way as to yield ontological dividends: they have wanted to say, for example, that Socrates is an object whereas sitting (that concept or property) is not. But the fact that the grammatical subject–predicate distinction is, as I put it above, *low-level*, and that it can be *generalized* to a logical distinction which is just the distinction between argument and function, shows that, fundamentally, grammatical distinctions have no metaphysical depth. In particular, as far as the question of the unity of the sentence is concerned, we must say that *all subsentential expressions*, not just conjunctions and similar, are, to speak with the medievals, syncategorematic; correspondingly, as far as the question of the unity of the proposition is concerned, we must say that *all referents of subsentential expressions*, not just concepts (functions), are, to speak with Frege, unsaturated.[35] The obligation to say both these things is imposed on us by the context principle. Words are made for sentences, and they are fitted up to combine with other words in forming those sentences: no special importance attaches to any particular kind of subsentential expression (or corresponding referent) in effecting the moment of sentential (propositional) unity. As Ramsey saw, there is no justification for the Frege–Russell view that the grammatical predicate (concept) has a privileged role in effecting unity; all the semantically significant parts of a sentence (and all the corresponding parts of the proposition referred to) stand in equal need of each other. In the case of the distinction between *logical* subject and *logical* predicate (and their referents)—equivalently, in the case of the distinction between argument and function—there *is* an asymmetry: the logical predicate (function) constitutively carries an argument place for a logical subject. But that is just a trivial consequence of the way that distinction has been drawn up (and of the definitions of 'argument' and 'function'): as we have said, the distinction *in se* carries no implications for its *application* to particular sentences and their referents.

[34] Cf. Gaskin 2008, 196.
[35] See Gaskin 2008, ch. 3, esp. §§40–2.

Sullivan (2020, 195) notes the Ramseyan point that there is a symmetry between grammatical subject and predicate, in the sense that the former needs the latter just as much as vice versa: for the purposes of explaining sentential (propositional) unity, no grammatical category (no sort of referent) is privileged; the dependence of one grammatical category on another is mutual. This contrasts, he thinks, with a logical asymmetry. 'In the role of explaining quantificational validity the dependence is that of a function on its values. This dependence is essentially asymmetric: it is the ground of the hierarchy of types. In a word, logic is well founded; grammar (apparently) is not' (2020, 195). But the asymmetric dependence that Sullivan has in mind, namely the dependence on the sentence of the elements that compose the Fregean hierarchy of subsentential expressions, is just an echo of the grammatical asymmetry between incomplete subsentential expressions and the complete sentence, which in turn is a reflection of the context principle. The sentence is metaphysically prior to its semantically significant subsentential components, its words (in general, morphemes): these are *made for* sentences. The Fregean hierarchy is itself asymmetric, of course, in the sense that it has a lowest but not a highest level. That mirrors the asymmetry of the argument–function structure, but in both cases the asymmetry is purely formal.[36] There are alternative, equally good ways of assigning subsentential expressions to the levels of a syntactic hierarchy,[37] just as there are alternative, equally good ways of discerning argument–function structure in the sentence (proposition), or indeed in any complex. Low-level grammar—the syntax of empirical languages—has no metaphysical significance: for when one generalizes grammatical subject–predicate form to arrive at logical subject–predicate form (= argument–function structure) nothing constrains the generalizing from the side of the world. Who thus generalizes does not risk omitting, or distorting, any feature of reality. Once again language is in the driving seat, and reality tags along behind.[38]

References

Anscombe, E. 1981. *From Parmenides to Wittgenstein* (Cambridge: CUP).
Davidson, D. 1982. *Essays on Actions and Events* (Oxford: Clarendon Press).
Davidson, D. 1984. *Inquiries into Truth and Interpretation* (Oxford: Clarendon Press).
Davidson, D. 2001. *Subjective, Intersubjective, Objective* (Oxford: Clarendon Press).

[36] Cf. Ramsey 1931, 133–4; Sullivan 2022, 61–2.
[37] See Gaskin 2008, ch. 4.
[38] For their comments on a previous version of this Introduction I would like to thank Barry Dainton, Matti Eklund, Adrian Moore, and William Stirton.

Bloor, D. 2018. 'The Question of Linguistic Idealism Revisited', in H. Sluga and D. Stern (eds), *The Cambridge Companion to Wittgenstein*, 2nd edn. (Cambridge: CUP), 332–60.
Coliva, A. 2010. *Moore and Wittgenstein: Scepticism, Certainty, and Common Sense* (Basingstoke: Palgrave).
Dilman, I. 2002. *Wittgenstein's Copernican Revolution: The Question of Linguistic Idealism* (London/New York: Palgrave Macmillan).
Gaskin, R. 1996. '"Kein Etwas, aber auch nicht ein Nichts!": kann die Grammatik tatsächlich täuschen?', *Grazer Philosophische Studien* 51, 85–104.
Gaskin, R. 2001. 'Nonsense and Necessity in Wittgenstein's Mature Philosophy', in R. Gaskin (ed.), *Grammar in Early Twentieth-Century Philosophy* (London: Routledge), 199–217.
Gaskin, R. 2006. *Experience and the World's Own Language: A Critique of John McDowell's Empiricism* (Oxford: Clarendon Press).
Gaskin, R. 2008. *The Unity of the Proposition* (Oxford: OUP).
Gaskin, R. 2018. *Tragedy and Redress in Western Literature: A Philosophical Perspective* (London: Routledge).
Gaskin, R. 2019. 'From the unity of the proposition to linguistic idealism', *Synthese* 196, 1325–42.
Gaskin, R. 2021. *Language and World: A Defence of Linguistic Idealism* (London: Routledge).
Hacker, P. 2000. 'Was he trying to whistle it?', in A. Crary and R. Read (eds), *The New Wittgenstein* (London: Routledge), 353–88.
Hacker, P. 2021: *Insight and Illusion: Themes in the Philosophy of Wittgenstein*, 3rd edn. (London: Anthem).
Harrison, B. 1973. *Form and Content* (Oxford: Blackwell).
Hintikka, M. and Hintikka, J. 1986. *Investigating Wittgenstein* (Oxford: Blackwell).
Ishiguro, H. 1969. 'Use and reference of names', in P. Winch (ed.), *Studies in the Philosophy of Wittgenstein* (London: Routledge), 20–50.
Kant, I. 1998. *Kritik der reinen Vernunft*, ed. J. Timmermann (Hamburg: Felix Meiner).
Kripke, S. 1982. *Wittgenstein on Rules and Private Language: An Elementary Exposition* (Oxford: Blackwell).
Lear, J. 1982. 'Leaving the world alone', *Journal of Philosophy* 79, 382–403.
Lear, J. 1998. *Open Minded: Working out the Logic of the Soul* (Cambridge, Mass.: Harvard University Press).
Malcolm, N. 1986. *Nothing Is Hidden: Wittgenstein's Criticisms of his Early Thought* (Oxford: Blackwell).
McGinn, M. 2004. 'Living with the Problem of the Other: Wittgenstein, Cavell and Other-Minds Scepticism', in D. McManus (ed.), *Wittgenstein and Scepticism* (London: Routledge), 240–59.
McGinn, M. 2006. *Elucidating the Tractatus: Wittgenstein's Early Philosophy of Logic and Language* (Oxford: Clarendon Press).
McGinn, M. 2013. 'Simples and the Idea of Analysis in the *Tractatus*', in G. Kahane et al. (ed.), *Wittgenstein and His Interpreters: Essays in Memory of Gordon Baker* (Oxford: Blackwell), 200–20.
McGuinness, B. 2002. *Approaches to Wittgenstein: Collected Papers* (London: Routledge).
Moore, A. 1997. *Points of View* (Oxford: OUP).
Moore, A. 2003. 'Ineffability and nonsense', *Proceedings of the Aristotelian Society*, supp. Vol. 77, 169–93.
Moore, A. 2011. 'Response to Sullivan', in R. Read and M. Lavery (eds), *Beyond the Tractatus Wars: The New Wittgenstein Debate* (London: Routledge), 190–5.
Moore, A. 2013. 'Was the author of the *Tractatus* a transcendental idealist?', in P. Sullivan and M. Potter (eds), *Wittgenstein's Tractatus: History and Interpretation* (Oxford: OUP), 239–55.
Morris, M. 2008. *Wittgenstein and the Tractatus Logico-Philosophicus* (London: Routledge).
Pears, D. 1987. *The False Prison*, vol. 1 (Oxford: Clarendon Press).
Pears, D. 1988. *The False Prison*, vol. 2 (Oxford: Clarendon Press).
Pears, D. 1996. 'The Relation between Wittgenstein's Picture Theory of Propositions and Russell's Theories of Judgment', in C. Luckhardt (ed.), *Wittgenstein: Sources and Perspectives* (Bristol: Thoemmes), 190–212.

Ramsey, F. 1931. *The Foundations of Mathematics and Other Logical Essays* (London: Routledge).
Schroeder, S. 2006. *Wittgenstein: The Way out of the Fly-Bottle* (Cambridge: Polity).
Sullivan, P. 1996. 'The "Truth" in Solipsism, and Wittgenstein's Rejection of the A Priori', *European Journal of Philosophy* 4, 195–219.
Sullivan, P. 2002. 'On Trying to be Resolute: A Response to Kremer on the *Tractatus*', *European Journal of Philosophy* 10, 43–78.
Sullivan, P. 2003. 'Ineffability and Nonsense', *Proceedings of the Aristotelian Society*, supp. vol. 77, 195–223.
Sullivan, P. 2011. 'Synthesizing without Concepts', in R. Read and M. Lavery (eds), *Beyond the Tractatus Wars: The New Wittgenstein Debate* (London: Routledge), 170–89.
Sullivan, P. 2013. 'Idealism in Wittgenstein: A Further Reply to Moore', in P. Sullivan and M. Potter (eds), *Wittgenstein's Tractatus: History and Interpretation* (Oxford: OUP), 256–70.
Sullivan, P. 2020. 'Varieties of Alien Thought', in S. Miguens (ed.), *The Logical Alien: Conant and His Critics* (Cambridge, Mass.: Harvard University Press), 183–201.
Sullivan, P. 2022. 'Anscombe, Stenius, and Ramsey on the *Tractatus*', in A. Haddock and R. Wiseman (eds), *The Anscombean Mind* (London: Routledge), 59–99.
Trächtler, J. 2021. *Wittgensteins Grammatik des Fremdseelischen* (Berlin: Metzler).
Williams, B. 1981. *Moral Luck: Philosophical Papers 1973–1980* (Cambridge: CUP).
Williams, M. 2004. 'Wittgenstein, Truth, and Certainty', in M. Kölbel and B. Weiss (eds), *Wittgenstein's Lasting Significance* (London: Routledge), 247–81.
Wittgenstein, L. 1922. *Tractatus Logico-Philosophicus*, tr. C. Ogden (London: Routledge).
Wittgenstein, L. 1929. 'Some Remarks on Logical Form', *Proceedings of the Aristotelian Society* supp. vol. 9, 162–71.
Wittgenstein, L. 1974. *Philosophical Grammar*, ed. R. Rhees (Oxford: Blackwell).
Wittgenstein, L. 1975. *Philosophical Remarks*, ed. R. Rhees (Oxford: Blackwell).
Wittgenstein, L. 1977. *Philosophische Untersuchungen* (Frankfurt/Main: Suhrkamp), tr. E. Anscombe, *Philosophical Investigations* (Oxford: Blackwell, 1968).
Wittgenstein, L. 1979a. *On Certainty*, ed. G. von Wright and E. Anscombe (Oxford: Blackwell).
Wittgenstein, L. 1979b. *Ludwig Wittgenstein and the Vienna Circle*, ed. B. McGuinness (Oxford: Blackwell).
Wittgenstein, L. 1979c. *Notebooks 1914–1916*, 2nd edn., ed. G. von Wright and E. Anscombe (Oxford: Blackwell).
Wittgenstein, L. 1980. *Wittgenstein's Lectures: Cambridge 1930–1932*, ed. D. Lee (London: Rowman and Littlefield).
Wittgenstein, L. 1981. *Zettel*, 2nd edn., ed. G. von Wright and E. Anscombe (Oxford: Blackwell).
Wittgenstein, L. 1982. *Last Writings on the Philosophy of Psychology*, vol. 1, ed. E. Anscombe et al. (Oxford: Blackwell).
Wittgenstein, L. 1992. *Last Writings on the Philosophy of Psychology*, vol. 2, ed. G. von Wright et al. (Oxford: Blackwell).
Wittgenstein, L. 1993. *Philosophical Occasions: 1912–1951*, ed. J. Klagge and A. Nordmann (Indianapolis: Hackett).
Wittgenstein, L. 2023. *Tractatus Logico-Philosophicus*, tr. introduction and notes by M. Beaney (Oxford: OUP).

2
Conditions, Necessity, and Transcendental Linguistic Idealism in Wittgenstein's *Tractatus*

Chon Tejedor

2.1 Introduction

In this chapter, I argue that Wittgenstein aims to dissolve, rather than uphold, transcendental linguistic idealism in the *Tractatus*.[1] I take idealism generally to advance the view that there is (in some respect to be specified) a definite direction of determination from language, thought, and/or the self to the world: language, thought, and/or the self determine the world and do so in a manner that is asymmetrical, since the world necessarily depends on them for its determination, but not vice-versa. Linguistic realism, in turn, posits the opposite, equally asymmetric, direction of determination: from world to language, thought, and/or the self. I will use the expression 'linguistic idealism' to refer to any idealist position that treats language as a central aspect of that which determines the world.

There is broad consensus among commentators to the effect that the early Wittgenstein considers empirical idealism to be nonsensical: the *Tractatus* aims to dissolve any version of idealism centred around the notion of empirical 'thinking subject' or self.[2] The question whether the *Tractatus* upholds a transcendental form of idealism remains outstanding, however, and is a highly complex one. This is so, not just because the textual evidence is notoriously ambiguous and lends itself to differing interpretations, but also because the

---

[1] This chapter was written as part of the research project PID2022-139226NB-I00, funded by the Spanish Ministry of Science and Innovation.
[2] See Levine 2013, 170–238; Tejedor 2015, 46–73; Hacker 2021, 81–90.

versions of transcendental idealism most relevant to discussing Wittgenstein's work are intricate and, therefore, potentially elusive and difficult to pinpoint.[3]

In his early texts, Wittgenstein considers a variety of idealist proposals (some empirical, others not). Two of these encompass key aspects of transcendental linguistic idealism.[4] According to the first, *the world is the world as given to the transcendental willing subject (i.e., to me) in representation*; according to the second, *possible representation determines the possibilities of the world*. In both cases, representation includes language, as well as other types of representation (for instance, mental representation in thought and experience). The former kind of idealism is articulated around the notion of transcendental subject (or transcendental first-person: *me*): on this view, the transcendental subject, through its willing, renders representation—and, thereby, the world as given in representation—possible. The latter idealism includes no such commitment to the transcendental subject but turns instead on the view that possible representation (notably, in language and thought) imposes, in itself (i.e., independently of any first-personal subject), a restrictive limit on world possibilities. Let us call these positions, respectively, the Subject-based and the Representation-based versions of transcendental linguistic idealism.[5] One of the most striking characteristics of both versions of idealism is their scope. It is telling that, in *TLP* 5.6ff, the terms 'world' and 'language' come to acquire the broadest of extensions, since they are used to encompass, respectively, all possibilities (including, but not restricted to, those possibilities that obtain as facts in empirical reality: *TLP* 5.61; cf. 1, 1.1), and all language endowed with sense (including, but not restricted to natural languages currently in use).[6] As we will see below, this is a deliberate decision on Wittgenstein's part: focusing on the broadest versions of idealism will enable him also to dismantle, in one clean sweep, the narrower versions of the doctrine implicit in the broader ones.

In the first two sections of this chapter, I examine the textual evidence with a view to showing that the *Tractatus* aims to dissolve, respectively,

---

[3] See Williams 1981; Moore 2003, 2007, 2013; Sullivan 2003, 2013; Appelqvist and Pöykkö 2019; Gaskin 2021; Appelqvist 2023.

[4] Tejedor 2015, 53–73.

[5] These two versions of transcendental idealism are partly linguistic since both maintain that language is a central aspect of that which determines the world.

[6] Wittgenstein's use of these expressions is multivocal in the *Tractatus*. Note, for instance, that his use of 'the world' aims to capture the totality of facts in *TLP* 1 and 1.1 and the totality of possibilities in 5.61. As we will see below, his use of the term 'limit' is also multivocal and sometimes aims to capture this notion of totality as well. On the difficulties surrounding the *Tractatus*'s understanding of totality see Sullivan 2000, 175–92. It is unclear that Wittgenstein was fully aware of these difficulties when he wrote the *Tractatus*, however: see Ramsey 1923, 478.

the Subject-based and the Representation-based versions of transcendental idealism. In the third section, I examine in more depth Wittgenstein's philosophical reasons for abandoning these two forms of transcendental idealism. I argue that idealism requires, in order to get off the ground, a non-analytic understanding of necessity that Wittgenstein rejects as self-subvertingly nonsensical. For Wittgenstein, the prevalence of this notion of necessity is part of a more general, self-defeating tendency in traditional metaphysics that seeks to fuse together the methods of the natural sciences with a priori philosophical considerations. In the fourth and final section of the chapter, I consider an aspect of the *Tractatus*'s position in which the shadow of transcendental idealism could be said to linger: the notion of purpose at the heart of Wittgenstein's distinction between sense and nonsense. As we will see, however, the *Tractatus* ultimately empties itself of any remnants of idealism with respect to this.

2.2 Transcendental Idealism and the Subject

Let us begin by considering the Subject-based version of transcendental idealism, one that Wittgenstein is most likely to have drawn from Schopenhauer's *The World as Will and Representation*, but which he explores in a modified, broader-scoped version in the *Tractatus*.[7] The version of transcendental idealism he targets proposes that the world (understood as the totality of possibilities) is *the world as given to the transcendental willing subject in representation* (where representation includes all—i.e., any—language, thought, and experience). In this version of idealism, the subject is transcendental in that it is not *in* the world but yields the unifying perspective that renders representation—and, thereby, the world as given in representation—possible. The willing subject therefore acts as a condition for the world: it imposes a restrictive limit on the world understood as the totality of possibilities. There is, in this respect, a definite relation of determination from the willing subject through representation (including language) to the world, a relation that is necessary (i.e., non-contingent) and asymmetrical, since the world depends on the willing subject's representation for its determination, but not vice-versa.

As we will now see, plotting the evolution of Wittgenstein's thinking in the *Notebooks* and the *Prototractatus* suggests that, by the time he comes to

---

[7] There is no doubt that Wittgenstein read Schopenhauer's work: see Monk 1990, 30–1, 151–64. Schopenhauer is indeed included in the list drawn up by Wittgenstein of the thinkers who have exerted the greatest influence on his work (*CV*, 16).

write the *Tractatus*, he has discarded the two central planks of this version of transcendental idealism: the view that representation is unified through being perspectival and the view that the perspective in question is that of the transcendental willing subject.

2.2.1 A Unifying Perspective?

There are important reasons to suggest that Wittgenstein has abandoned the view that representation is perspectival by the time he comes to write the *Tractatus*. Consider his discussion of the eye metaphor in *TLP* 5.633 and 5.6331:

> Where *in* the world is a metaphysical subject to be found?
> You will say that this is exactly like the case of the eye and the visual field. But really you do *not* see the eye.
> And nothing *in the visual field* allows you to infer that it is seen by an eye. (*TLP* 5.633)
> For the form of the visual field is surely not like this:[8]

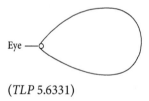

(*TLP* 5.6331)

The *Tractatus*'s discussion of the eye metaphor is often interpreted as advancing, first and foremost, the thesis that the subject (i.e., the eye) cannot be located in the representational (i.e., visual) field.[9] Understood in this way, the aim of the metaphor would be to reject any empirical version of idealism centred around the thinking subject (i.e., a subject that could be located inside representation and the world).[10] This rejection would, of course, be compatible with endorsing the Subject-based version of idealism, according to which the subject is not located in the world and representation, but provides the unifying perspective that renders possible the world as given in representation. Wittgenstein's use of the eye metaphor in the texts prior to the *Tractatus* casts

---

[8] See also Pears 1987, 153–90.
[9] See, for instance, Pears 1987, 179–80; Hacker 1993, 38–50.
[10] Pears 1987, 153–90. This understanding of the eye metaphor is partly motivated by the fact that *TLP* 5.633 follows immediately after 'The subject does not belong to the world; rather, it is a limit of the world' (5.632). However, Wittgenstein's numbering system indicates that 5.633 is a comment on 5.63 not on 5.632, 5.633, and 5.6331 are therefore best read as commenting on and seeking to counter the claim that 'I am my world. (The microcosm)' (5.63).

serious doubt on this interpretation, however. Consider the precursors of *TLP* 5.6331 in the *Notebooks* and the *Prototractatus*:

> The eye makes its appearance in philosophy through the world's being *my* world. The visual field has not e.g. a form like this:
>
>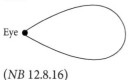
>
> (*NB* 12.8.16)
>
> For the form of the visual field is surely not like this:
>
>
>
> (*PTLP* 5.335431)

Note that the drawings in the *Notebooks* and the *Prototractatus* do *not* locate the eye (i.e., the subject) *inside* the visual (i.e., representational) field. When Wittgenstein writes in these earlier texts that the form of the visual field is *not* as presented in the drawing, the target of his criticism is not therefore the idea of a thinking subject locatable *inside* such a field. The use he makes of the eye metaphor in these earlier texts shows that his aim is not merely to discard the empirical notion of a thinking subject and, with it, empirical idealism. Instead, the eye metaphor seems consistently and primarily concerned with conveying that the *shape* of the representational (i.e., visual) field is *not perspectival*: that the field is not 'constituted differently in length from breadth' (*NB* 20.10.16). This, however, runs counter not just to empirical idealism, but also to the Subject-based version of transcendental idealism.

Although *NB* 20.10.16 seems to endorse the view that representation is perspectival, Wittgenstein's decision not to reiterate this view in the *Prototractatus* and the *Tractatus*, together with his decision to retain in these texts the claim that 'the form of the visual field is surely *not* like this' (*TLP* 5.6331, *PTLP* 5.335431; my italics) shows that, by the time he writes the *Tractatus*, he has discarded the view that representation is perspectival. He has, in other words, abandoned the first plank of the Subject-based version of transcendental idealism.[11]

---

[11] Wittgenstein does not deny that representation by human beings may, *as a matter of fact*, be perspectival: this would be an empirical question for the natural sciences. What he seeks to dissolve is the view that, from the point of view of what is *essential* (i.e., from the point of view that matters to *philosophy*), it is a metaphysical condition that representation should necessarily be perspectival.

2.2.2 Representation without a Willing Subject

The view that Wittgenstein has abandoned this version of transcendental idealism by the time he comes to write the *Tractatus* is further reinforced when one considers his discussion of the willing subject in the *Notebooks*. As noted earlier, his position during this period is in flux. Although some of the *Notebooks* entries appear to endorse the notion of willing subject (notably *NB* 5.8.16), the discussion concludes with two remarks that disavow this:

> Is belief a kind of experience?
> Is thought a kind of experience?
> All experience is world and does not need the subject.
> The act of the will is not an experience. (*NB* 9.11.16)
> What kind of reason is there for the assumption of a willing subject?
> Is not *my world* adequate for individuation? (*NB* 19.11.16)

NB 9.11.16 states that experience (and more generally thought, i.e., mental representation) does not require the willing subject.[12] In the next entry (*NB* 19.11.16), the questions Wittgenstein asks suggest that he is reaching an even stronger conclusion: that there is, in fact, no reason whatsoever to posit a transcendental willing subject; that such a subject is not, after all, a condition of representation of any sort, be it mental or linguistic.

After these entries from November 1916, Wittgenstein never uses again the expression 'willing subject' in the *Notebooks*, the *Prototractatus*, or the *Tractatus*.[13] Some commentators have attempted to minimize the significance of this by suggesting that Wittgenstein continues perhaps to endorse this notion of the subject albeit under a different label: that of 'metaphysical subject'.[14] This suggestion could, on the face of it, seem convincing. After all, the expression 'metaphysical subject' does continue to appear in the *Prototractatus* (*PTLP* 5.33552) and the *Tractatus* (*TLP* 5.641). What is more,

---

[12] It is widely acknowledged that Wittgenstein uses the expression 'willing subject' to indicate the transcendental, Schopenhauerian subject and the expression 'thinking subject' to indicate the empirical subject locatable within introspective experience that is discussed by Descartes and Russell. For a defence of this, see Tejedor 2015, 46–72 and Hacker 2021, 81–108. That by 'subject' in *NB* 9.11.16 Wittgenstein means the transcendental willing subject (rather than the empirical thinking subject) is clear since both the entry that immediately precedes this (*NB* 4.11.16) and the one that immediately follows it (*NB* 19.11.16) explicitly mention the willing subject. In *NB* 4.11.16, for instance, Wittgenstein writes: 'the subject is the willing subject'.

[13] Wittgenstein does mention the 'will' in the latter two works, i.e., in *PTLP* 6.44, 6.441 and *TLP* 6.43. But the numbering and organization of *PTLP* 6.44, 6.441 and *TLP* 6.43 (as indeed those of *NB* 6.7.16, 7.7.16, and 8.7.16) show that the will, in these entries, is the *empirical* will of embodied human beings, not the will of a transcendental subject.

[14] See Pears 1987, 179–80; Hacker 1993, 38–50.

in the *Tractatus*, the expression 'metaphysical subject' acquires paramount importance, since it is explicitly associated with the notion of philosophical self that Wittgenstein actively endorses in the concluding entry of the *TLP* 5.6s, namely *TLP* 5.641:

> Thus there really is a sense in which philosophy can talk about the self in a non-psychological way.
> What brings the self into philosophy is [...] that 'the world is my world'.
> The philosophical self is not the human being, not the human body, or the human soul, with which psychology deals, but rather the metaphysical subject, the limit of the world—not a part of it. (*TLP* 5.641)

In fact, however, there is no good reason to suppose that Wittgenstein uses the expressions 'willing subject' and 'metaphysical subject' interchangeably in any of these texts, or that these two expressions are intended to capture the same notion. Note indeed that, although both expressions ('willing subject' and 'metaphysical subject') appear in the *Notebooks*, they are never used alongside each other in the same entries; and there is nothing in those *Notebooks* entries in which they do appear (i.e., separately from each other) to suggest that Wittgenstein regards them as interchangeable (*NB* 4.8.16, *NB* 2.9.16, *NB* 2.8.16, *NB* 5.8.16, etc.). Furthermore, there is a serious difficulty with arguing that the metaphysical subject of *TLP* 5.641 *is* the transcendental willing subject of the *Notebooks*. For *TLP* 5.641 proposes, in a surprisingly unambiguous manner, that 'there really is sense in which philosophy can ['must' in *NB* 11.8.16] talk about' the metaphysical subject. If the metaphysical subject were the willing subject of the *Notebooks*, *TLP* 5.641 would be suggesting that it is possible to *talk about* the transcendental willing subject that acts as a condition of the world. Such a claim would of course be highly surprising, since any attempt to *talk* about such a subject would be nonsensical, in Wittgenstein's view.[15] Those interpretations of the *Tractatus* that endorse the notion of illuminating or substantive nonsense might well suggest that it is possible to *talk*—i.e., convey substantive information or insights that could be new to the listener—*about* the transcendental willing subject by means of nonsensical propositions.[16] As I have argued elsewhere, however, this interpretation is problematic.[17] Note that there is indeed nothing in the sections of the *Tractatus* in which Wittgenstein discusses the role of philosophy (especially *TLP* 4.112,

---

[15] Both Williams (1981, 146) and Pears (1987, 184–5) acknowledge that this poses a serious difficulty for their readings.
[16] See notably Hacker 2021.
[17] See Tejedor 2015, 2–7, 46–90, 156–8. On this, see also, notably, Sullivan 2003 and McGinn 2006, 1–27.

4.114, 4.115, 4.116, and the Preface) to suggest that the task of philosophy is to *talk*—i.e., convey substantive, potentially new information or insights—*about* representation, the world or the subject, by means of nonsensical propositions. Instead, in the *Tractatus*, Wittgenstein seems to use nonsensical propositions as examples or case studies, in order to illustrate the way in which these seemingly substantive insights ultimately 'fall apart' in our hands.[18] In Section 2.5, I propose an understanding of Tractarian nonsense that obviates these difficulties.

All of this should, at the very least, give us pause. Since there is no textual evidence in the *Notebooks* to indicate that Wittgenstein uses the expressions 'willing subject' and 'metaphysical subject' interchangeably and since understanding them as interchangeable poses a serious difficulty when it comes to interpreting *TLP* 5.641, we ought to seek an alternative way of understanding of Wittgenstein's use of 'metaphysical subject'. This will be the task of Section 2.3.

2.2.3 'Transcendental Twaddle'

The textual evidence from Wittgenstein's early writings makes a strong cumulative case for the view that Wittgenstein has abandoned the Subject-based version of transcendental idealism by the time he writes the *Tractatus*. Although he may have seriously considered embracing aspects of this doctrine at several junctures in the *Notebooks*, he has given it up by the time he is writing the *Tractatus*. This change of heart regarding transcendental idealism is reflected in Wittgenstein's wartime exchanges with Paul Engelmann. In the autumn of 1916, following a series of acts of valour in battle, Wittgenstein is promoted to officer and sent to the town of Olmütz to train in this capacity. This is where he first meets Engelmann, with whom he strikes up a life-long friendship.[19] Wittgenstein's thoughts on the Schopenhauerian position crescendo during the weeks he spends with Engelmann, whom he meets in October 1916.[20] The strongly Schopenhauerian remarks end abruptly in the *Notebooks* in late November 1916, with the two entries quoted above (*NB* 9.11.16 and *NB* 19.11.16). Shortly thereafter, Wittgenstein leaves Olmütz to spend Christmas in Vienna and then returns to the Front. By the time Engelmann and Wittgenstein meet again in December 1917, it is clear to Engelmann that Wittgenstein has had an important change of heart. The following month, in

---

[18] See Goldfarb 1997, 71.
[19] Monk 1990, 148–9.
[20] See notably *NB* 12.10.16, 15.10.16, 17.10.16, 20.10.16, 4.11.16, 9.11.16, and 19.11.16.

January 1918, Engelmann writes a letter to Wittgenstein in which he mentions this change. In his reply, Wittgenstein writes:

> *I am clear about one thing*: I am far too bad to be able to ruminate randomly[21] about myself [...] *Only let's cut out the transcendental twaddle* when the whole thing is as plain as a sock on the jaw. [My italics in the last instance] (Engelmann 1967, 11)

In my view, this reply is further confirmation that, by the winter of 1917–18, when Wittgenstein is writing the remarks that would come to form the *Prototractatus*, he has altogether given up on the Schopenhauerian outlook and, with it, on the Subject-based version of transcendental idealism: he has come to regard the entire thing as 'twaddle'. Having seriously entertained this form of transcendental idealism in the *Notebooks*, he seems to have abandoned it by the time he writes the *Tractatus*, following his discussions with Engelmann in Olmütz.

2.3 Transcendental Idealism and Possible Thought

Let us now consider the second variety of transcendental idealism of relevance to the *Tractatus*'s discussion: the Representation-based view, according to which *possible thought, expressible in language, determines the world* (understood as the totality of possibilities) (cf. *TLP* 5.61). The Representation-based version of transcendental idealism is more minimal than the Subject-based version, insofar as it does not posit a first-personal subject as a condition of the world or help itself to the view that representation is perspectival. The view nevertheless qualifies as a form of idealism in that it posits an asymmetrical direction of determination from thought (expressible in language) to the world. And it qualifies as transcendental, rather than empirical, insofar as it turns on the notions of all possible thought (here: all mental representation with a sense, including experience, beliefs, memories, etc.),[22] all language endowed with sense and the world understood as the totality of possibilities. In order to shed light on Wittgenstein's treatment of this variety of transcendental idealism, it is important to revisit his use of the expression 'metaphysical subject'.

---

[21] I am grateful to the editor for this suggested translation of the German term 'spintisieren'.
[22] For a defence of this understanding of thought in the *Tractatus*, see for instance Hacker 2021, 65–81.

2.3.1 The Metaphysical Subject

It is clear that the notion of metaphysical subject is of great importance to Wittgenstein. He mentions it on repeated occasions, in the *Notebooks*, the *Prototractatus*, and the *Tractatus* (NB 4.8.16, 2.9.16; PTLP 5.33552; TLP 5.641). In Section 2.2, we saw that there were serious difficulties with interpreting this notion as equivalent to that of transcendental willing subject. Let us therefore consider an alternative way of understanding it. I propose that, for Wittgenstein, any investigation into the metaphysical subject is an investigation into the question whether there is a *distinctively philosophical* approach to the self: is there a viable notion of the self that is *specifically philosophical*? It is because Wittgenstein has this question in mind that he associates 'philosophical I' with 'metaphysical subject' in TLP 5.641 (quoted above).

In his search for a distinctively philosophical notion of the self, Wittgenstein considers three candidates: the empirical notion of thinking subject located in the world, the transcendental notion of willing subject, and that of metaphysical subject. By the end of his discussion of the thinking and willing subjects, Wittgenstein has come to the conclusion that neither of these two notions of the subject (where the subject is understood as imposing a condition on the world, a 'limit' in the sense of *restriction*) is viable.

Having discarded these two restrictive, philosophical notions of the self, Wittgenstein endorses a different philosophical understanding of the self: the 'metaphysical subject' of *PTLP* 5.33552 and *TLP* 5.641, which is different from both the Schopenhauerian 'willing subject' of the *Notebooks* and the empirical 'thinking subject'. Wittgenstein tells us that the metaphysical subject is 'the limit of the world—not a part of the world' (*TLP* 5.641). I suggest, with Marie McGinn, Adrian Moore, and Peter Sullivan, that his use of the term 'limit' here does not seek to capture the notion of a restrictive *condition*.[23] Instead, Wittgenstein is using the term 'limit' to capture the notion of *totality*. After all, this notion of *limit as totality* repeatedly emerges elsewhere in the *Tractatus*, notably in *TLP* 4.51, where Wittgenstein writes:

> Suppose that I am given *all* elementary propositions: then I can simply ask what propositions I can construct out of them. And there I have *all* propositions, and *that* fixes their limits. (*TLP* 4.51)

---

[23] That 'limit' need not be understood as capturing such a notion is persuasively argued by McGinn, Moore, and Sullivan, although their understandings of this notion ultimately differ from mine. See McGinn 2003, 491–513, 2006; Moore 2003, 169–93; Sullivan 2003, 195–223.

Wittgenstein uses the term 'limit' in connection with the notion of *totality* at several junctures in the *Tractatus*, notably at *TLP* 5.556.[24] In line with this, I suggest that the expression 'metaphysical subject' of *TLP* 5.641 is intended to encompass *all possible thought*. One cannot go beyond all possible thought: *that* is the limit. The philosophical notion of the self—i.e., the metaphysical subject—endorsed by Wittgenstein in *TLP* 5.641, is thus the totality of possible thoughts.

This may seem a surprising candidate for the role of philosophical self. Note, however, that it is in line with a notion of the self proposed by Ernst Mach, one that is highly influential during this period and of which Wittgenstein is certainly aware. We know that, in the middle of the war, Wittgenstein becomes acquainted with Weininger's writings and, through them, with the following view held by Mach:[25]

> If I now call the sum of my mental aspect, sensations included, my ego in the widest sense (in contrast with the restricted ego) then in this sense I could say that my ego contains the world (as sensation and idea).[26]

Mach's view turns essentially on the idea that my mental life ('my ego in the widest sense') coincides with the world: the sum total of the contents of my mind (my thoughts, experiences, sensations, etc.) coincides with the world, *and does so perfectly*. Mach's view is not concerned with the question whether the subject (either the thinking or willing subject) imposes a metaphysical *restriction* on the world. It simply notes that the contents of one's mind and the contents of the world are perfect reflections of each other: that they are, in an important respect, identical to each other. If Mach's notion of the mental life of a human being can be regarded as an approximation to the notion of self, so can, by extrapolation, Wittgenstein's notion of metaphysical subject, understood as the totality of thoughts or of mental representations. I suggest that the metaphysical subject of *TLP* 5.641 is an elaboration of Mach's notion: it is the Machian ego, maximally generalized so as to encompass not just the mental life of a human being but all possible mental life, all possible thoughts, all mental representations endowed with sense.

Interpreting the expression 'metaphysical subject' in this way enables us to account in a satisfactory manner for Wittgenstein's claim, in *TLP* 5.641, that

---

[24] I am grateful to John Preston for a critical remark that enabled me to clarify this point.
[25] See Monk 1990, 19; McGuinness 2002, 134.
[26] Mach 1976, 6–7. This passage is also cited in McGuinness 2002, 131.

philosophy can *talk* about the metaphysical subject. Philosophy can talk about the metaphysical subject in the sense that, given the understanding of thought at work in the *Tractatus*, all possible thoughts *can* be expressed in language.[27] In the light of this, Wittgenstein's suggestion, at the end of *TLP* 5.641, that the metaphysical subject is not 'a part of the world', should not be taken to imply that the metaphysical subject cannot be described or talked about in language. Instead, we should simply draw from this that the metaphysical subject is not *restricted* to *particular* mental facts or thoughts, for example, to a particular human self, namely *mine* (as in Mach's original view). The metaphysical subject endorsed in *TLP* 5.641 encompasses all *possible* thinking, not just the thoughts associated with some particular human being. It is in *this* respect that the metaphysical subject is not 'a part'—that is, a *section*—of the world ('ein Teil der Welt' in the original) for Wittgenstein.

2.3.2 The World Is My World

One of the strengths of interpreting Wittgenstein's notion of metaphysical subject in this way is that it enables us to make sense of the respect in which 'the world is my world' is 'quite correct' for Wittgenstein (*TLP* 5.62).[28] Given the context, the expression 'The world is my world' can be paraphrased as: 'the totality of possibilities ("the world") is the totality of possible thoughts'. The crux here is to note that both the original sentence and its paraphrase can be read in a number of ways.[29] When it is used to express the modified version of the Machian view—that is, when 'my world' is used exclusively to capture *all possible thoughts* (i.e., the modified Machian subject)—the inclusion of 'my' no longer purports to impose any metaphysical restrictions: there is simply no first-personal subject acting as a *restrictive metaphysical condition* on the world or on thought.[30] 'My world' thereby becomes interchangeable with 'all possible thought'; and 'the world is my world' with 'the totality of possibilities is the totality of possible thoughts'.

For Wittgenstein, when 'the world is my world' is understood in this way, it 'cannot be said' because it is senseless. But it is also 'quite correct' because it

---

[27] But, as observed in n. 6, there are serious difficulties with Wittgenstein's notion of totality in the *Tractatus*.

[28] I am grateful to Adrian Moore for a critical discussion that greatly helped in developing this section.

[29] On this, see Floyd 1998, 85.

[30] There is here no first-personal subject in the singular (no *I*) imposing such a restriction; and indeed no first-personal subject in the plural either (no *we*). There is no first-personal subject of any sort playing the role of imposing such a restriction.

is tautologously true—hence the decision to begin *TLP* 5.62 by signalling that we are now dealing with the question 'to what extent solipsism is a *truth*' (my italics).

As a tautology, 'the totality of possibilities is the totality of possible thoughts' does not constitute an attempt to express a substantive necessary truth. For we know that tautologies express nothing of substance for Wittgenstein: they convey *no information about the state of reality* (*TLP* 4.461); and they convey *no logical information* either, as emerges in his discussion of the propositions of logic (*TLP* 6.1ff). Tautologies simply reflect a practical ability that language users already demonstrate in their everyday linguistic practices: the ability to construct tautologous zero-sum games out of propositions that are bivalent and bipolar (cf. *TLP* 6.121). Tautologies, like contradictions, are a by-product of the way in which signs are used to express propositions with a sense. It is precisely for this reason that they are incapable of conveying any *new* information, that is: any information we don't already possess by virtue of our mastery of language and thought. Those who already possess the ability to construct propositions with a sense will extract no insights that are not already implicit in their linguistic practice: at most, they will be reminded of their already existing know-how. And those lacking the ability in question will be unable to make anything out of tautologies and contradictions.

For Wittgenstein, tautologies are senseless in that that they convey no new information about reality (*TLP* 4.461, *TLP* 4.462) or about logic (cf. *TLP* 6.1251, *TLP* 6.1261). Tautologies are therefore wholly unsubstantive. I suggest that, for Wittgenstein, 'the world is my world' is senselessly tautologous in precisely this respect. This may seem puzzling. After all, far from appearing unsubstantive, 'the totality of possibilities is the totality of possible thoughts' (the modified Machian paraphrase of 'the world is my world') appears to convey a substantive insight into the nature of possibility and the nature of thought, one that could come as a *surprise* to the reader, that could be regarded as providing new information of a sort.

'The totality of possibilities is the totality of possible thoughts' can indeed, especially in the hands of philosophers, come across as an attempt to impose a substantive metaphysical restriction on the world of the possible. This is precisely the way it is used in the Representation-based version of transcendental idealism, according to which all possible thought, expressible in language, imposes in itself (independently of a first-personal subject) a restrictive condition on the world understood as the totality of possibilities. As we saw above, this version of transcendental idealism posits a definite, necessary, and asymmetrical direction of determination from the totality of possible thoughts to the totality of possibilities. Wittgenstein, however, warns us against falling for this version of transcendental idealism in *TLP* 5.61:

> Logic pervades the world: the limits of the world are also its limits.
> So we cannot say in logic, 'The world has this in it, and this, but not that'.
> For that would appear to presuppose that we were excluding certain possibilities, and this cannot be the case, since it would require that logic should go beyond the limits of the world; for only in that way could it view those limits from the other side as well.
> We cannot think what we cannot think; so what we cannot think we cannot *say* either. (*TLP* 5.61)

Placing a metaphysically restrictive spin on 'The totality of possibilities is the totality of possible thoughts' can mislead us into committing the kind of mistake described in *TLP* 5.61: that of thinking that one can demarcate what is impossible (i.e., what cannot possibly exist) by mapping out what cannot possibly be thought; the mistake of trying to say 'in logic, "The world [of the possible] has this [i.e. possibility] in it, and this, but not that"' (*TLP* 5.61). However, demarcating or mapping out *A* by means of *B* presupposes specifying and therefore thinking of *B*. Trying to demarcate what cannot possibly exist by appealing to what cannot possibly be thought involves trying to *think* what cannot be thought. This, however, is clearly self-subverting: 'what we cannot think, [...] we cannot think' (*TLP* 5.61); we cannot 'think what cannot be thought' (*TLP*, Preface).

Unlike other tautologies, 'the totality of possibilities is the totality of possible thoughts' does not, on the face of it, show that it says nothing. Wittgenstein is well aware of this. Indeed, he suggests that its senselessness only becomes manifest when one considers that 'the limits of the language (the only language which I understand) mean the limits of *my* world' (*TLP* 5.62).[31] In line with our previous discussion, I propose that we interpret 'the limits of language' in *TLP* 5.62 as standing for the *totality* of propositions (see *TLP* 4.51, quoted above). 'The limits of language' in (*TLP* 5.62) are the same as 'the limits of my language' in *TLP* 5.6: for whether it is me using language or anyone else, the limit remains *everything that can be said*. The totality of propositions (everything that can be said with a sense) includes not just all ordinary-language propositions, but

---

[31] Cf. *TLP* [PM] 5.62. It is clear from the positioning of 'allein' in the German original ('der Sprache, die allein ich verstehe') that Wittgenstein means here the only language I understand, rather than the language that only I understand: Pears 1987, 173.

also all elementary propositions. That 'the limits of the language mean the limits of *my* world' only comes into view, therefore, when one considers what would emerge if we carried out a complete logical analysis all the way to the level of elementary propositions. If we carried out the complete analyses of, on the one hand, all propositions with a sense and, on the other, of all possible thoughts, these two processes would ultimately yield, when analysed, *the same elementary propositions*.

For Wittgenstein, coming to see this enables us to recognize that 'the world is my world' is 'quite correct' but 'cannot be said'. In other words, it enables us to recognize that 'the totality of possibilities is the totality of thoughts' is both tautologously true and senseless: that it is necessarily true but also, by the same token, altogether unsubstantive, that is, that it is incapable of informing us of anything not already implicit in our ordinary linguistic and thinking practices.

2.4 Self-subverting Metaphysics

2.4.1 Non-analytic Necessity

For Wittgenstein, the Subject- and the Representation-based versions of transcendental idealism, like, indeed, empirical versions of idealism, are part of a self-subverting attempt to impose in an a priori manner a restrictive condition on the world. At the heart of such attempts is the notion of non-analytic necessity: a form of necessity that is not analytic insofar as it is not derived from the internal relations between propositions, and which is intended to be substantive and informative. This form of necessity is at work in the transcendental idealist views that the willing subject or, alternatively, possible thought *necessarily determine* the world. For this relation of *determination* is not intended to be a merely contingent relation. At the same time, it is not intended to be conceptual or analytic either. On the contrary, this notion of determination is intended to capture substantive aspects of the world, of which we might be unaware. The notion, in other words, is intended to be *informative*. This treatment of necessity as non-analytic, substantive and informative emerges in a surprisingly varied number of contexts in the history of metaphysics, from the Kantian notion of the synthetic a priori through to the notion, criticized by Hume, of causation understood as involving a necessary connection.

Wittgenstein regards this non-analytic notion of necessity as nonsensical. This is not mere dogged (or dogmatic) insistence on his part that necessity *must be* logical and analytic; nor is it a matter of this notion running counter to a theory of meaning he defends in the *Tractatus*. Wittgenstein discards non-analytic necessity in the *Tractatus* because he comes to the conclusion that it is self-subverting, that it defeats itself. In order to shed light on this point, let us briefly revisit his treatment of language and thought.[32]

In my view, the *Tractatus* does not set out to defend a particular theory of language. Its aim is rather to shed light on ('elucidate', as McGinn puts it) our ordinary language use, that is, aspects that are already part of our everyday use of signs.[33] Wittgenstein suggests that, in ordinary language, one can tell whether a proposition (or, indeed, a thought) is contingent or necessary, simply by attending to its internal characteristics, without having to check anything external to it. He takes this to be an aspect of our use of signs that will be obvious to anyone with a mastery of everyday language and thought. This idea emerges in Wittgenstein's discussion of propositions (*TLP* 4.021, 4.024, 4.026) and in his discussion of internal relations (*TLP* 5.2, 5.23, 5.231).[34] That one should be able to tell, simply by attending to its internal characteristics, whether a proposition is contingent (and thus in principle verifiable), is, in Wittgenstein's view, a key aspect of ordinary linguistic communication: if someone says 'it is raining', I need to be able to tell, simply by attending to the proposition, that it stands in need of verification, that its truth can and needs to be ascertained before I decide to take an umbrella (for instance). This is a central aspect of propositions and thoughts of all types, including those featuring relations of entailment (*TLP* 5.133–5.1363).[35] Compare for instance the following two propositions: 'If Alex is a bachelor, Alex is a man' and 'If it is raining, there is a traffic jam.' Both of these propositions feature an entailment relation. The first is necessarily true and I can tell this simply by attending to its internal characteristics: the proposition is true under all circumstances, irrespective of the facts, simply by virtue of the internal or analytic relation between the concept of bachelor and that of man. Similarly, I can tell that the proposition 'If it is raining, there is a traffic jam' is contingent simply by attending to its internal characteristics, without having to check any facts external to it.

In contrast, the relation of determination at the heart of the idealism–realism debate is a relation of *necessary entailment* that involves a *non-analytic understanding of necessity* (cf. *TLP* 5.1363). According to this understanding, some propositions are necessary, not by virtue of their internal characteristics,

---

[32] Tejedor 2019.
[33] See McGinn 2006.
[34] McGinn 2006, 75–133, 210–29; Tejedor 2015, 15–45.
[35] McGinn 2006, 210–29; Tejedor 2015, 15–45, 91–118.

but by virtue of certain necessary yet substantive (i.e., informative, non-analytic) laws—for instance, in linguistic idealism, laws concerning the necessary direction of determination from language to the world.

This may not strike us as problematic. We might tell ourselves that the cases in which non-analytic necessity applies are such a tiny minority that our linguistic and thinking practices can, for the most part, remain unaffected by them: so long as the exceptional cases are indeed rare enough, accommodating them need not be disruptive. For Wittgenstein, however, the problem runs deeper than this. For accepting non-analytic necessity means accepting that *we can no longer be confident as to the logical status of a proposition* (whether it is contingent or necessary) *merely by attending to its internal characteristics.* For, in the non-analytic view, necessity can be substantive: it can be informative and therefore capable of surprising us. Consider the proposition: 'It is raining in Paris.' Ordinarily, proper attention to the internal characteristics of this proposition would entitle me confidently to conclude that it is contingent: 'It is raining in Paris' can be either true or false and is in principle verifiable. If non-analytic necessity were ruled in, however, I would no longer be entitled to this confidence in my conclusion. For there could *always* be some as yet undiscovered law (i.e., undiscovered by metaphysicians) to the effect that it is *necessarily* raining in Paris.

The moment we allow for non-analytic necessity, we are surrendering the *normative authority* we ordinarily possess, *by virtue of our mastery of language and thought,* to determine the logical status of propositions (and, more broadly, of pictures, including thoughts) by attending to their internal structures alone. The non-analytic view of necessity thereby inadvertently undermines our entire linguistic and thinking practices, the very practices on which it relies in order to get off the ground. This, of course, destabilizes the view. For, if we no longer enjoy normative authority over our linguistic and thinking practices, any attempts to defend or justify non-analytic necessity in language or thought must collapse with them.

The non-analytic notion of necessity draws its apparent credibility from the resemblance of non-analytic to analytic necessity, which *is* familiar to us insofar as it is part of our ordinary linguistic and thinking practices. As we saw above, necessity, in its analytic form, is utterly familiar to us, since the ability to construct necessary tautologies and contradictions is part of our ordinary linguistic and thinking practices. Non-analytic necessity subverts these practices—the very practices that lend it its credibility. It is, in this respect, self-subvertingly nonsensical. I suggest that it is with this in mind, and not out of dogmatic stubbornness, that Wittgenstein writes:

> There is no compulsion making one thing happen because another has happened. The only necessity that exists is *logical* necessity. (*TLP* 6.37)
> Just as the only necessity that exists is *logical* necessity, so too the only impossibility that exists is *logical* impossibility. (*TLP* 6.375)

2.4.2 The Self-subverting Mechanics of the Idealism–Realism Debate

For Wittgenstein, the non-analytic view of necessity lies at the heart of the determination debate between idealists and realists. The view results from a powerful but misguided urge to view philosophy as a special type of natural science.

> Philosophy is not one of the natural sciences.
> (The word 'philosophy' must mean something whose place is above or below the natural sciences, not beside them.) (*TLP* 4.111)

Part of the aim of the natural sciences is to produce a body of true propositions capable of describing the possibilities that obtain as facts in reality (*TLP* 4.11), as well as the contingent mechanisms that connect such facts. Idealism, like realism, involves attempting to identify what are in effect a priori mechanisms: mechanisms that are intended to operate in a non-analytic necessary manner. For Wittgenstein, however, this attempt ends up nullifying itself.

> This is the way I have travelled: Idealism singles men from the world as unique, solipsism singles me alone out, and at last I see that I too belong with the rest of the world, and so on the one side nothing is left over, and on the other side, as unique, the world. (*NB* 15.10.16)

If idealism and solipsism advance the view that the world is dependent on the self, then this view, together with its denial (i.e., realism), dissolves when the notion of non-analytic necessary determination disintegrates: 'and so on the one side *nothing* is left over, and on the other side, as unique, the world' (my italics, *NB* 15.10.16). The understanding of 'the world' that emerges 'as unique' at this point is metaphysically neutral in that it presents all of the world's contents as being on the same level: no *section* of the world is any longer of special metaphysical importance (*TLP* 5.641, discussed above). Empirical selves, human beings, propositions, thoughts, physical bodies, etc. are all factual: they are all metaphysically on a par, there is nothing metaphysically salient about any of them. This idea emerges in the *Notebooks*, where the view that they are on a par is linked to a remark concerning the subject as boundary of the world that is clearly the precursor of *TLP* 5.641:

> The philosophical self is not the human being, not the human body or the human soul with the psychological properties, but the metaphysical subject, the boundary (not a part) of the world. The human body, however, my body in particular, is a part of the world among others, among beasts, plants, stones etc., etc. [cf. *TLP* 5.641]
> Whoever realizes this will not want to procure a pre-eminent place for his own body or for the human body.
> He will regard humans and beasts quite naïvely as objects which are similar and which belong together. (*NB* 2.9.16)

Idealism and realism begin by drawing up a priori divisions between domains, some of which are then treated as philosophically salient or more significant than the others: the self *versus* the world; possible thought *versus* the world; the world *versus* representation; etc. With these a priori divisions in place, idealism and realism proceed to ask what relations of determination hold (in a non-analytic necessary manner) between them. For Wittgenstein, however, this a priori division into (purportedly) philosophically significant domains is misconceived.

> This is connected with the fact that no part of our experience is at the same time *a priori*. Whatever we see could be other than it is. Whatever we can describe at all could be other than it is. There is no *a priori* order of things. (*TLP* 5.634)

Wittgenstein's rejection of such an 'a priori order of things' is implicit from the start in his understanding of propositions and thoughts (*TLP* 2.1–3.34; 4). Thought is not metaphysically or representationally privileged, as would be the case, for instance, if thoughts were inherently representational and propositions were representationally inert. This is made evident in Wittgenstein's reply to Russell's question about 'Gedanke' in his letter from Monte Cassino of 19.8.19, which indicates that the psychical or mental signs that are the constituents of thoughts play the *same role* as that played by word-signs of linguistic propositions:

> 'Does a Gedanke consist of words?' No! But of psychical constituents that have the same sort of relation to reality as words. (*NB*, 131)

That the mental and the linguistic are on a par in this way, that neither is more fundamental than the other with respect to representation, is further corroborated by the fact that thoughts and propositions are defined in terms of each other in the *Tractatus*: a proposition is a thought propositional sign; a thought is a proposition with a sense. Neither thoughts nor propositions are presented as ontologically prior to or as more fundamental than the other.

> We use the perceptible sign of a proposition (spoken or written, etc.) as a projection of a possible situation.
> The method of projection is to think of the sense of the proposition. (*TLP* 3.11)
> I call the sign with which we express a thought a propositional sign.—And a proposition is a propositional sign in its projective relation to the world. (*TLP* 3.12)

Conversely:

> A thought is a proposition with a sense ['der sinnvolle Satz']. (*TLP* 4)

2.5 Purpose, Nonsense, and the Ladder Metaphor

2.5.1 One Logical Space

Instead of imposing a priori metaphysical divisions, Wittgenstein repeatedly and very deliberately emphasizes *oneness*. The *Tractatus* starts off with the notion of one reality: the world as the totality of facts (*TLP* 1, 1.1). Since reality contains all of the possible states that obtain as facts (*TLP* 1.11) and since pictures and propositional signs are themselves facts (cf. *TLP* 2.141, 3.14, 3.142), reality must be regarded as encompassing both *representing and represented* facts. Representing and represented facts are both subsumed under this one—unique (*NB* 15.10.16)—reality. This is not a mere quirk. It is not a mere terminological or classificatory matter either. On the contrary, I suggest that this emphasis on *one* world of facts (one reality that includes both represented and representing facts) is intended to convey that there is no philosophically or metaphysically significant, a priori distinction to be drawn *between* representing and represented facts: neither are metaphysically more salient—more fundamental, more substantive, more *real*—than the other. Indeed, from the point of view of philosophy (i.e., from the point of view of clarifying what is essential), what makes the difference between a representing fact and a represented one is not the *stuff* that these facts happen to be made of, for example, whether they are made of linguistic signs, of mental signs, of physical stuff, etc. The difference between representing and represented facts lies, instead, in their *use*. A chalk mark on a classroom blackboard, when it is used as a picture representing a possible state, is analysable into elementary propositions; when it is itself represented by a picture (e.g., by a painting of the classroom that includes a representation of the blackboard with its chalk mark), it is part of a possible state, analysable into states of affairs.

The determination debate between idealists and realists begins by imposing an a priori division between a domain encompassing the depicted world and a domain of representations or pictures. For the determination question to get a grip, one of these two domains needs to count as ontologically prior to the other: the idealist view that representation (in language or thought) determines the world, for instance, turns on the thought that representation is prior in this way. Wittgenstein's approach, already in the *Tractatus*, consists in noting that, far from constituting two independent domains demarcated by sharp boundaries, pictures and depicted possible states are *correlative* or conceptually co-dependent: a picture represents a possible state; a possible state is that which is represented by a picture.[36] Representations (i.e., pictures) and represented states *emerge simultaneously with use*: the depicting and the depicted cannot be specified independently of each other, since neither of the two is ontologically prior to the other. Instead, both representations and represented states belong to the *one* common domain: logical space (*TLP* 2.202), which includes all arrangements of elements that can be logically decomposed all the way to the fully analysed level. This sheds light on Wittgenstein's remark:

> A gramophone record, the musical idea, the written notes, and the soundwaves, all stand to one another in the same internal relation of depicting that holds between language and the world.
> They are all constructed according to a common logical pattern.
> (Like the two youths in the fairy-tale, their two horses, and their lilies. *They are all in a certain sense one.*) (*TLP* 4.014, my italics).

2.5.2 Purpose and Nonsense

For Wittgenstein, our ability to judge how and to what purpose signs are used is not dependent on our being presented with a theory of language, thought or

---

[36] McGinn 2006, 75–133; Tejedor 2015, 15–45.

representation.[37] On the contrary, insofar as we already have mastery of ordinary language and thought, we already have the *ability* (whether we exercise it correctly or not) to make such judgements.

> Man possesses the ability to construct languages capable of expressing every sense, without having any idea how each word has meaning or what its meaning is—just as people speak without knowing how the individual sounds are produced. (*TLP* 4.002)
> The essential in a proposition is therefore that which is common to all propositions which can express the same sense.
> And in the same way in general the essential in a symbol is that which all symbols which can fulfil the same purpose have in common. (*TLP* 3.341)
> Signs which serve *one* purpose are logically equivalent, signs which serve *no* purpose are logically meaningless. (*TLP* 5.47321)
> In fact, all the propositions of our everyday language, just as they stand, are in perfect logical order. [...]
> (Our problems are not abstract, but perhaps the most concrete that there are.) (*TLP* 5.5563)

'Our problems are not abstract' in that they are not problems to be resolved by getting to grips with an abstract theory of language. For they do not stem from the lack of such a theory (*TLP* 4.002). Instead, they result from the fact that, although we already have the know-how to use signs with a purpose and to recognize the purposeful use of signs (inasmuch as we already have mastery of language and thought), our disposition to act on this know-how is at times eroded by our self-subverting philosophical tendencies—tendencies such as those manifested in the idealism–realism debate. Our failure, on those occasions, is not the kind of failure that results from the lack of an abstract theory of language: it is a failure in our *practical understanding*, a failure in our disposition to use signs with a purpose. Since it is our disposition (our *tendency*) to *act* (i.e., to use signs) that needs to be corrected, only an *activity* can genuinely be of help. Philosophy, properly understood, is precisely such an *activity*, for Wittgenstein (*TLP* 4.112).[38] The aim of philosophy—i.e., the aim of this activity—is to enable us to fine-tune our thinking and linguistic abilities, to orient our disposition to use signs away from the production of self-subverting nonsense.[39]

---

[37] Tejedor 2015, 16–22.
[38] Tejedor 2015, 119–68; 2019.
[39] Tejedor 2015, 119–68; 2017.

In order to effect this transformation in us—that is, with this *purpose* in mind—Wittgenstein presents us with a careful arrangement of sentences in the form of the *Tractatus*.[40] Some of the sentences included in his text are presented in an intentionally ambiguous manner so as to invite us to consider different possible readings of them whilst exercising our thinking and linguistic abilities.[41] An instance of this would be the expression 'the world is my world': as we saw in Section 2.3.2 'the world is my world' can be read as a self-subverting attempt at expressing a substantive, non-analytic form of metaphysical necessity ('the world is *my* world', *TLP* 5.62); or it can be read as a senseless, empty, unproblematic tautology ('the totality of possibilities is the totality of thoughts') that can be had by me or anyone else without a restrictive emphasis on the first-personal subject (*TLP* 5.641). Interestingly, both Ramsey and Engelmann, who were among the first to read the *Tractatus* and to discuss it with Wittgenstein, mention that he deliberately includes ambiguous sentences in his book, as part of his philosophical method. In a letter to his mother dated 20 September 1923, Ramsey writes:

> His [Wittgenstein's] idea of his book is not that anyone by reading it will understand his ideas, but that some day someone will think them out again for himself, and will derive great pleasure from finding in this book their exact expressions. [...] Some of [Wittgenstein's] sentences are intentionally ambiguous having an ordinary meaning and a more difficult meaning which he also believes.[42]

In the light of this, the following remarks by Engelmann strike a particularly strong chord:

> Yet we do not understand Wittgenstein unless we realize that it was philosophy that mattered to him and not logic, which merely happened to be the only suitable tool for elaborating his world picture.
> This the *Tractatus* accomplishes in sovereign fashion, ending up with implacable consistency by nullifying the result, so that the communication of its basic thoughts, or rather of its basic *tendency* [my italics]—which, according to its own findings, cannot on principle be effected by direct methods—is yet achieved indirectly. He nullifies his own world picture, together with the 'houses of cards' of philosophy (which at that time at least he thought he

---

[40] Tejedor 2015, 119–68. See also Floyd 1998, 85.
[41] See also the discussion of riddles in Diamond 1991, 267–89.
[42] Quoted in McGuinness 2008, 139, and in Schulte 2013, 16.

had made collapse), so as to show '*how little is achieved when these problems are solved*'. What he wants to demonstrate is that such endeavours of human thought to 'utter the unutterable' are a hopeless attempt to satisfy man's eternal metaphysical *urge* [my italics].[43]

2.5.3 The Ladder Metaphor

The sentences that make up the *Tractatus* are intended to serve a purpose. This purpose is the clarification of language and thought (*TLP* 4.0031, 4.112), that is, the re-orientation of our disposition to use signs away from self-subverting nonsense. This notion of *purpose* is one of the keys to unlocking the *Tractatus* (*TLP* 3.341, 5.47321).[44] For, according to Wittgenstein, nonsense amounts precisely to *lack of purpose*. Philosophical nonsense in particular (such as that arising in metaphysically substantive views such as restrictive idealism and realism) involves the disintegration of purpose through self-subversion: it involves using signs for a putative purpose, in a manner that in fact subverts that very purpose.

According to Wittgenstein, so long as sentences are used for a purpose, the propositions that they express avoid collapsing into nonsense. The *Tractatus* therefore recognizes a far wider variety of propositions than is often acknowledged in the literature: among the propositions that avoid nonsense are included not only propositions with a sense (i.e., sentences used with the purpose of representing possible states) and senseless tautologies and contradictions (the by-product of our ability to construct propositions with a sense), but also, for instance, *principles*. Principles are sentences that are used with the purpose of giving instructions for the construction of propositions with a sense within particular systems—for instance, within the optional systems of the natural sciences (TLP 6.32–6.3611).[45]

All of this applies to the propositions that make up the *Tractatus* as well. For Wittgenstein, so long as we continue to be tempted by substantive (i.e., restrictive) metaphysics, the propositions that make up the *Tractatus* have a purpose to serve and are therefore *not* nonsensical. However, once this 'tendency' or 'urge' (as Engelmann puts it in the above-quoted letter) is overcome, the propositions that make up the *Tractatus* become redundant, that is,

---

[43] Engelmann 1967, 96.
[44] I discuss this in Tejedor 2015, 91–137, 156–68, 2017, 2019, 275–89. See also Kremer 2001, 39–73.
[45] I discuss this in more detail in Tejedor 2019.

purposeless. It is at *this* point that they become nonsensical.[46] Thus, the point at which the *Tractatus* fully achieves its own purpose of clarification is precisely the point at which we come to recognize that it is time to let go of the sentences of the book, just as we might let go of a ladder once we have used it for the purpose of climbing to the top:

> My propositions serve as elucidations in the following way: anyone who understands me, eventually [*am Ende*; literally, 'at the end'] recognizes them as nonsensical, when he has used them—as steps—to climb up beyond them. (He must, so to speak, throw away the ladder after he has climbed up it.) He must overcome [*überwinden*] these propositions and then he will see the world aright. (*TLP* 6.54)

Having reached this stage in the discussion, we may find ourselves in a quandary as to the status of this very notion of purpose. We may, for instance, feel the *urge* to ask questions such as: is Tractarian purpose essentially *human* purpose? Is it essentially part of representation (as opposed to, e.g., of reality)? If Tractarian purpose were essentially *human* or if it were essentially part of the domain of representation, the shadow of idealism would continue to linger over the Tractarian position. I suggest that this is not the case. For Wittgenstein's position has emptied itself of two ingredients that are essential to the distillation of idealism: non-analytic necessity; and the a priori division of logical space into stable, sharply demarcated domains, some of which can be specified independently of and enjoy ontological priority over others. With the vanishing of these two ingredients, substantive metaphysical questions can no longer get a grip and Tractarian purpose can no longer be assigned a metaphysical status: it no more (essentially) belongs to the domain of the *representational* than to that of the *represented*, to the mind than to physical reality, to the human than to the non-human. Purpose, pictures, and possible states of the world are correlative: they emerge simultaneously out of the one, unique, metaphysically neutral logical space.

The *Tractatus* engages us in a process of clarification that culminates in the end (*am Ende*: *TLP* 6.54) in coming to recognize that questions such as those posed by restrictive metaphysics, like the very propositions of the *Tractatus*

---

[46] Metaphysical and resolute readings coincide in interpreting this as indicating that, for Wittgenstein, (most of) the *Tractatus*'s propositions just *are* from beginning to end nonsensical (illuminatingly or plainly so) and that this is central to the method at work in his book: cf. Conant 1991; Hacker 2021. In this respect, my view does not align itself with either of these two readings. On this, see also Tejedor 2015, 1–7, 156–68.

itself, have become idle, that is: nonsensical. A recognition that ultimately reveals itself in our disposition to remain silent with respect to them.

What we cannot speak about we must pass over in silence (*TLP* 7).

References

Appelqvist, H. 2023. *Wittgenstein and Aesthetics* (Cambridge: CUP).
Appelqvist, H., and Pöykkö, P. 2019. 'Wittgenstein and Levinas on the Transcendentality of Ethics', in H. Appelqvist (ed.), *Wittgenstein and the Limits of Language* (New York: Routledge), 65–89.
Conant, J. 1991. 'Throwing Away the Top of the Ladder', *Yale Review* 79, 328–64.
Diamond, C. 1991. *The Realistic Spirit: Wittgenstein, Philosophy and the Mind* (Cambridge, Mass.: MIT).
Engelmann, P. 1967. *Letters from Ludwig Wittgenstein. With a Memoir from Paul Engelmann* (Oxford: Blackwell).
Floyd, J. 1998. 'The Uncaptive Eye: Solipsism in the *Tractatus*', in L. Rouner (ed.), *Loneliness* (Notre Dame: Boston Studies in the Philosophy of Religion), 79–108.
Gaskin, R. 2021. *Language and World: A Defence of Linguistic Idealism* (London: Routledge).
Goldfarb, W. 1997. 'Metaphysics as Nonsense: On Cora Diamond's *The Realistic Spirit*', *Journal of Philosophical Research* 22, 57–73.
Hacker, P. M. S. 1993. 'The Agreement between Thought and Reality', in J. V. Canfield and S. Shanker (eds), *Wittgenstein's Intentions* (New York: Garland), 38–50.
Hacker, P. M. S. 2021. *Insight and Illusion: Themes in the Philosophy of Wittgenstein* (London and New York: Anthem Press).
Kremer, M. 2001. 'The Purpose of Tractarian Nonsense', *Noûs* 35, 39–73.
Levine, J. 2013. 'Logic and Solipsism', in M. Potter and P. Sullivan (eds), *Wittgenstein's Tractatus: History and Interpretation* (Oxford: OUP), 170–238.
Mach, E. 1976. *Knowledge and Error—Sketches on the Psychology of Enquiry*, trans. T. J. McCormack and P. Foulkes (Dordrecht: Reidel).
McGinn, M. 2003. 'Between Metaphysics and Nonsense: Elucidation in Wittgenstein's *Tractatus*', *Philosophical Quarterly* 99, 491–513.
McGinn, M. 2006. *Elucidating the Tractatus: Wittgenstein's Early Philosophy of Logic and Language* (Oxford: OUP).
McGuinness, B. F. 2002. *Approaches to Wittgenstein: Collected Papers* (London: Routledge).
McGuinness, B. F. 2008. *Wittgenstein in Cambridge* (Oxford: Blackwell).
Monk, R. 1990. *Ludwig Wittgenstein: The Duty of Genius* (London: Vintage).
Moore, A. W. 2003. 'Ineffability and Nonsense', *Proceedings of the Aristotelian Society, Supplementary Volume* 77, 169–93.
Moore, A. W. 2007. 'Wittgenstein and Transcendental Idealism', in G. Kahane, E. Kanterian, and O. Kuusela (eds), *Wittgenstein and His Interpreters: Essays in Memory of Gordon Baker* (Oxford: Blackwell), 174–99.
Moore, A. W. 2013. 'Was the Author of the *Tractatus* a Transcendental Idealist?', in P. Sullivan and M. Potter (eds), *Wittgenstein's Tractatus: History and Interpretation* (Oxford: OUP), 239–55.
Pears, D. 1987. *The False Prison*, vol. I (Oxford: Clarendon Press).
Ramsey, F. 1923. 'Critical Notice of L. Wittgenstein's *Tractatus*', *Mind* 32, 465–78.
Schulte, J. 2013. 'Ethics and Aesthetics in Wittgenstein', in L. Perissinotto (ed.), *The Darkness of this Time: Ethics, Politics and Religion in Wittgenstein* (Milan: Mimesis International), 1–17.
Sullivan, P. M. 2000. 'The Totality of Facts', *Proceedings of the Aristotelian Society* 100, 175–92.
Sullivan, P. M. 2003. 'Ineffability and Nonsense', *Proceedings of the Aristotelian Society, Supplementary Volume* 77, 195–223.

Sullivan, P. M. 2013. 'Idealism in Wittgenstein: A Further Reply to Moore', in P. Sullivan and M. Potter (eds), *Wittgenstein's Tractatus: History and Interpretation* (Oxford: OUP), 256–70.
Tejedor, C. 2015. *The Early Wittgenstein on Metaphysics, Natural Science, Language and Value* (London: Routledge).
Tejedor, C. 2017. 'Scientism as a Threat to Science: Value and Principles in the *Tractatus*', in J. Beale and I. J. Kidd (eds), *Wittgenstein on Scientism* (London: Routledge), 7–28.
Tejedor, C. 2019. 'Wittgenstein on Physics', in S. Wuppuluri and N. da Costa (eds), *Wittgensteinian (adj.): Looking at Things from the Viewpoint of Wittgenstein's Philosophy* (New York: Springer), 275–89.
Williams, B. 1981. 'Wittgenstein and Idealism', in *his Moral Luck* (Cambridge: CUP), 144–63.
Wittgenstein, L. 1961a. *Notebooks 1914–1916*, ed. G. H. von Wright and G. E. M. Anscombe, trans. G. E. M. Anscombe (Oxford: Blackwell). [*NB*]
Wittgenstein, L. 1961b. *Tractatus Logico-Philosophicus*, trans. D. Pears and B. F. McGuinness (London: Routledge). [*TLP*]
Wittgenstein, L. 1971. *Prototractatus*, ed. B. F. McGuinness, T. Nyberg, and G. H. von Wright, trans. B. F. McGuinness and D. Pears (London: Routledge). [*PTLP*]
Wittgenstein, L. 1998. *Culture and Value*, eds G. H. von Wright and H. Nyman, rev. A. Pichler, trans. P. Winch (Oxford: Blackwell). [*CV*]

3
'Simplex Sigillum Veri' and the Question of the Limits of Language

Hanne Appelqvist

3.1 Introduction

In his 1960 commentary on the *Tractatus*, Erik Stenius proposed that 'Wittgenstein's philosophical system could be called "Critical Lingualism" or "Transcendental Lingualism" or even "Linguistic Idealism"' (Stenius 1960, 220). As the labels reveal, the proposal was made in explicit reference to Kant's critical or transcendental idealism. Like Kant, who takes the form, if not the material content, of reality to depend on the forms of our judgments, Wittgenstein takes the form of reality to depend on the form of language. Here, reality means the domain of possibilities with which logic is concerned (*TLP* 2.0121). And as Wittgenstein writes, 'A thought contains the possibility of the situation of which it is the thought. What is thinkable is possible too' (*TLP* 3.02).

Wittgenstein draws no essential difference between language and discursive thought. Meaningful propositions and thoughts alike are pictures of possible facts, and thus are judgments about empirical reality (*TLP* 3, 3.5, 4). But logical form, which thought and reality must share in order for picturing to be possible, is not itself among the expressible facts of the world (*TLP* 2.18, 4.12). Nor is the formal isomorphism between thought and reality grounded in the empirical subject, which is a complex fact inhabiting the empirical world. Instead, logical form as the limiting condition of possible thoughts emerges together with the metaphysical subject to which the thoughts belong. Hence, Stenius argues, '[t]he limits of the world of the metaphysical subject, or rather, the limits of the metaphysical subject's "logical space" of possible worlds, is determined by the limits of his language' (Stenius 1960, 221; see *TLP* 5.6–5.62). That the limits are determined by something outside the scope of what is limited, that is, outside the totality of empirical facts, including propositions, is what makes the idealism of the *Tractatus* transcendental.¹

Adrian Moore and Peter Sullivan have since engaged in a long and sophisticated debate on the role of transcendental idealism in the *Tractatus*. On Moore's reading, the early Wittgenstein is a transcendental idealist, whereas Sullivan argues that, though considering the position, Wittgenstein rejects it. Both agree that, for the *Tractatus* to be a work of transcendental idealism, the limit of language it espouses must be a limitation. It is not enough for the limit to signify the essential, formal features of language and the world. To count as evidence of Wittgenstein's commitment to idealism, the limit should exclude something, just as for Kant the limits of theoretical reason exclude what he, in the Preface of the *First Critique*, labels 'faith' (*CPR* Bxxx). When formulated thus, the position certainly seems to resemble the *Tractatus*'s project. After all, Wittgenstein characterizes the limit of language as excluding things that language cannot express. 'The aim of the book', he writes, 'is to draw a limit to thought, or rather—not to thought, but to the expression of thoughts' (*TLP*, p. 3). Moreover, as he explains to Ludwig von Ficker, the point of doing so is to protect ethics from 'babbling': 'my book consists of two parts: one of which is here, and of everything which I have *not* written. And precisely this second part is the important one' (Luckhardt 1979, 94–5).

Stenius mentions a wide range of things that fall outside the expressive resources of language. These include logical form, mathematics, the form of general laws of nature, the metaphysical subject, ethics, the will as the subject of ethical attributes, God, and the world as a limited whole.² These notions cannot be expressed by propositions, because they do not have empirical content, which is required for sense. For Stenius, this is enough to indicate that Wittgenstein's limit of language does exclude something, namely, the very items that for Kant fall outside the bounds of knowledge. Moore zeroes in on the same parallel. Like Kant, who draws a contrast between thoughts with and without empirical content, Wittgenstein draws a contrast between propositions with sense and nonsensical pseudo-propositions. Adding to Stenius's list of Tractarian ineffabilia knowledge of objects, understanding of propositions, understanding of Wittgenstein, and the practice of philosophy, Moore argues that Wittgenstein 'recognizes modes of rational engagement with things other than thought'.³

---

¹ Stenius 1960, 220–1; on Kant's transcendental idealism, see Moore 1997, 116–26; on the relation between Kant's transcendental idealism and the *Tractatus*, see Moore 2011 and 2013.
² See Stenius 1960, 219–22; *TLP* 4.121, 6.21, 6.32–6.361, 5.632, 6.421, 6.423, 6.432, 6.45.
³ Moore 2013, 253; see also Moore 2020, 38–40; *TLP* 2.0123–2.0124, 4.022, 4.024, 4.1212, 4.11–4.115, 6.54.

Given that Stenius and Moore see Wittgenstein's early position as 'shaped and motivated in ways like Kant's', they take the early Wittgenstein to endorse transcendental idealism (Sullivan 2013, 257). However, unlike Stenius who, in Sullivan's words, 'swallows the suggestion whole', Moore's position on the role of transcendental idealism in the *Tractatus* is more reserved (Sullivan 2013, 261). This is because, on his view, transcendental idealism is ultimately incoherent and Wittgenstein himself was aware of its incoherence. Such awareness is manifest in Wittgenstein's route to the view as understood by Moore. According to him, we find in the *Tractatus* 'a kind of nonsense born of the urge to combat nonsense of that very kind; a disease for which it itself purports to be the cure' (Moore 2013, 247).

Sullivan grants that Wittgenstein's statements that 'logic is transcendental' and that 'ethics is transcendental' are echoes of Kant (*TLP* 6.13, 6.421). However, on Sullivan's reading, the two echoes are not connected as they are connected for Kant. It is imperative for Kant's purposes to draw a 'substantive restriction on knowledge and hence on the reality to which fully contentful thought is answerable' (Sullivan 2013, 264). For Kant, knowledge and faith are 'claimants of the same territory. [...] what faith stipulates, and knowledge attains, are truths' (2013, 265). But it is difficult to see what, for Wittgenstein, could be such a shared territory that the limit of language divides. The viable candidates—truth, thought, and meaning—all belong exclusively to the domain of language. Accordingly, Sullivan argues, the transcendentality of logic cannot be at all like the transcendentality of ethics, albeit that Wittgenstein's 'clumsy first expression of the thought' seems to suggest otherwise (2013, 259).[4] According to Sullivan, 'the notions of language and world [...] are the interdependent notions of formal totalities', the interdependence of which requires no philosophical explanation of the kind that transcendental idealism purports to offer (Sullivan 1996, 209).

The decisive move in Sullivan's argument is his claim that to render the limit a limitation, the restriction on language must be substantive. To count as evidence of transcendental idealism in the *Tractatus*, the a priori limits of language should be synthetic. And according to Sullivan, the Tractarian limits are strictly analytic: 'the requirement for something to be thinkable is not the tightening up of any broader conceptual space. In thought, the requirement

---

[4] The expression in question reads: 'Ethics does not treat of the world. Ethics must be a condition of the world, like logic. Ethics and aesthetics are one' (*NB* 77). Given that, for Sullivan, Tractarian logic boils down to the intrinsic truth-directedness of propositions, it is understandable that he denies the plausibility of reading Wittgenstein's early ethics as consistent with his 'theoretical philosophy' (Sullivan 1996, 197, 209). This would entail a quasi-realist conception of ethics, which obviously goes against the letter and spirit of the *Tractatus*.

excludes nothing, and in language nothing is excluded but straightforward, ordinary nonsense' (Sullivan 1996, 200). Hence, while a priori, logic has, on Sullivan's view, nothing either substantial or synthetic about it, as, he thinks, Wittgenstein's remark according to which '[t]here is no a priori order of things' clearly shows.[5] That the limits of language are not limitations seems to be similarly indicated by Wittgenstein's remark:

> We cannot say in logic, 'The world has this in it, and this, but not that.'
> For that would appear to presuppose that we were excluding certain possibilities, and this cannot be the case, since it would require that logic should go beyond the limits of the world; for only that way could it view those limits from the other side as well. (*TLP* 5.61)

If the limit of language excludes no possibilities, then the contrast needed for reading the exclusion of the Tractarian ineffabilia from the domain of language as an indication of transcendental idealism dissolves. Otherwise put, given that Wittgenstein denies the key assumption on which Kant's position is built, namely, the idea of synthetic a priori, he cannot be committed to transcendental idealism.

Moore agrees that there is no synthetic a priori in the *Tractatus* (Moore 2013, 250). He also grants that in 5.61 Wittgenstein seems to deny that the limits of language could be construed as limitations (2013, 245). Nevertheless, on Moore's reading, Wittgenstein speaks *in propria persona* when he mentions ways of encountering reality that escape the expressive resources of meaningful language (2013, 248). For an example from Wittgenstein's theoretical philosophy, Moore mentions Wittgenstein's concession that logic is 'prior to the question "How?", not prior to the question "What?"', which he reads as a reference to ineffable knowledge of objects and as such counteracting the claim that there is no stepping outside the limits of language (*TLP* 5.552; see Moore 2013, 245). While not warranting the proposition 'The world has this in it', the remark testifies to Wittgenstein's acknowledgement of a kind of a limitation in our discursive mode of thought.

Another example of a non-discursive way of engaging with the world, evoked by Moore, is evaluation. Like logical form, value is not an expressible fact. Given that propositions can only picture accidental states of affairs, what is 'higher' remains inevitably out of their scope (*TLP* 6.42). Wittgenstein mentions ethics, aesthetics, and the feeling of the world as a limited whole as things

---

[5] *TLP* 5.634. See Sullivan 1996, 198; 2013, 264.

that 'lie outside the world' of facts, thus testifying to his transcendental idealism (*TLP* 6.41; see Moore 2013, 252-3). Sullivan, too, considers the possibility that, in the *Tractatus*, thought might be limited by *feeling* (see Sullivan 2013, 267). After all, Wittgenstein refers to feeling in contexts that do not allow expression by means of propositions—most notably in his remark on 'feeling the world as a limited whole', which resonates with Kant's treatment of the notion of a world-whole in the *Third Critique* (*TLP* 6.45).[6] However, as Sullivan sees no viable connection between Wittgenstein's remarks on ethics and his theoretical philosophy, he concludes that Wittgenstein's denial of knowledge to make room for faith cannot be relevantly similar to that of Kant.

3.2 Wittgenstein's A Priori: The Received View

It is a more or less universally accepted view that there is no synthetic a priori in the *Tractatus*. According to Stenius, 'Wittgenstein rejected the possibility of any synthetic propositions a priori' (Stenius 1960, 214). Hans-Johann Glock, who also reads Wittgenstein against the backdrop of Kant's transcendental philosophy, takes it as a given that Wittgenstein discards 'the idea of synthetic a priori truths' (Glock 1996, 199). And as noted, Moore concedes that, for Wittgenstein, 'there is no a priori knowledge of limitations' and hence no synthetic a priori (Moore 2013, 250). According to Moore, 'Wittgenstein can at most countenance that which finds *apparent* or *attempted* expression' of things that remain outside the limits of discursive thought (2013, 252).

The difference between Wittgenstein and Kant stems from the fact that Wittgenstein, in Stenius's words, 'moves the limits of theoretical reason to the limits of language', thereby rendering the idealism of the *Tractatus* 'linguistic' (Stenius 1960, 218). Since there is no principled difference between meaningful propositions and thoughts, the limits of language coincide with the limits of the thinkable. Accordingly, what for Kant can still be thoughts—albeit *empty* thoughts without sensible, empirical content—becomes mere nonsense in Wittgenstein's hands.[7] Moore explains the contrast as follows:

---

[6] In the *First Critique*, Kant famously denies *knowledge* of the world as a whole (*CPR* A426-33/B454-61). However, the *Third Critique* sets out to argue that, while the *discursive* perspective cannot furnish us with knowledge of a world-whole, the *reflective* perspective, which relies on feeling rather than concepts, allows us to *see* the world as a limited, purposive whole, albeit that this seeing does not amount to knowledge (*CPJ* 20:247-51; *CPJ* 5:379).

[7] See *TLP* 5.1362, 6.421-6.43, 6.431-6.4312, 6.432.

Thoughts without content, for Kant, are nonetheless thoughts. They involve a genuine exercise of concepts (B146). And they are true or false (A820–831/B848–859). By contrast, nonsense, for Wittgenstein, is just nonsense. It comprises words to which no meanings have been assigned (5.4733 and 6.53). (Moore 2013, 252).

Wittgenstein's identification of language and thought thus entails that the limits do not exclude anything of a sort that we could think, express, or hold as truth-apt.

It is indisputable that no meaningful proposition, and hence no thought in Wittgenstein's strict sense of the term, can be true a priori (*TLP* 2.225, 3). This is because the *sense* of propositions just means their capability of being true and of being false about empirical facts (*TLP* 4.023). Propositions picture reality by having their *form* in common with the pictured state of affairs but also by their constituents (names) being correlated with objects as constituents of states of affairs (*TLP* 2.151, 2.1513–2.1515, 3.2). Objects, in turn, are content as well as form (*TLP* 2.025). It follows that every meaningful proposition has material, empirical content: 'it is only by means of propositions that material properties are represented—only by the configuration of objects that they are produced' (*TLP* 2.0231). Accordingly, to determine whether a proposition is true, 'we must compare it with reality' (*TLP* 2.223; also 4.05). This entails that the truth value of every meaningful proposition is a posteriori. By contrast, 'A priori knowledge that a thought was true would be possible only if its truth were recognizable from the thought itself (without anything to compare it with)' (*TLP* 3.05).

At first sight, Wittgenstein seems to offer an even more comprehensive denial of the possibility of syntheticity a priori. Immediately after his famous drawing in 5.6331 of the way in which the eye and its visual field are not related, Wittgenstein writes:

This is connected with the fact that no part of our experience is at the same time a priori.

> Whatever we see could be other than it is.
> Whatever we can describe at all could be other than it is.
> There is no a priori order of things. (*TLP* 5.634.)

This denial of an a priori order of things is often treated as conclusive evidence of Wittgenstein's denial of a synthetic a priori (see Sullivan 1996, 198;

Moore 2013, 250). However, rather than being an outright denial of any a priori order whatsoever, the remark can be read as yet another affirmation of the inexpressibility of the a priori. Wittgenstein explains the notion of an order in question by reference to description and hence by reference to meaningful propositions with empirical content. Similarly, his mention of parts of experience implies that what is at stake pertains to *actual* facts with determinate material properties. Heikki Kannisto has argued that 'the order of things' [*die Ordnung der Dinge*] is 'meant to refer [...] to the contingency of any particular configuration of objects' (Kannisto 1986, 152). However, as Kannisto continues, '[l]ogical form [...] is not meant to be part of the world in that sense. It is the *order of possibilities*, and as such prior to any experience of facts' (1986, 152, emphasis added; cf. *PI* §97).[8] Also 5.61, which forbids the 'saying' of what there is, may be read as placing the emphasis on the inexpressibility of the question 'What?'.

Kannisto takes the transcendental idealist reading of the *Tractatus* further than most by arguing that Wittgenstein's answer to his 'great problem round which everything that I write turns is: Is there an order in the world a priori?' is in fact affirmative (*NB* 53; see Kannisto 1986, 115). According to Kannisto, logical form 'is not merely a question of analytical principles governing a few privileged relations between objects and states of affairs. It is with the forms of objects themselves, as well as their configurations, that logic is concerned' (1986, 125). This is to say that the possibilities with which logic deals are *real* possibilities in Kant's sense: they are not merely possibilities of thought, revealed by applying the principle of contradiction, but presuppose the subsistence[9] of (forms of) objects (1986, 121–4).[10] In spite of arguing that Tractarian possibilities concern things and not just concepts, Kannisto sides with other commentators in treating expressibility as an indispensable feature of syntheticity, claiming that 5.634 'is indeed a denial of synthetic *a priori*: no describable part of my experience is a priori' (1986, 152).

---

[8] Incidentally, the same could be said about the metaphysical subject, which clearly is not a *part* of my experience (of seeing the Necker cube, say). Yet, the possibility of my experiences belonging to 'me' depends on there being a unique point of view from which the facts of the world are seen (*TLP* 5.631–5.633, 5.641).

[9] Objects do not exist in the sense in which states of affairs (i.e., actual, contingent constellations of objects) exist. The objects subsist as simple and unalterable phenomenal types, similar in kind to, for example, redness (see *TLP* 2, 2.023; *PI* §57; Kannisto 1986, 140).

[10] Kant writes: 'I can think whatever I like, as long as I do not contradict myself, i.e., as long as my concept is a possible thought, even if I cannot give any assurance whether or not there is a corresponding object somewhere within the sum total of all possibilities. But in order to ascribe objective validity to such a concept (real possibility, for the first sort of possibility was merely logical) something more is required.' (*CPR* A10/B14.) Wittgenstein, in turn, states: 'Nothing in the province of logic can be *merely* possible. Logic deals with every possibility and all possibilities are its facts' (*TLP* 2.0121, emphasis added).

If expressibility is taken to be a necessary condition of syntheticity, then there cannot be syntheticity a priori in the *Tractatus*, given that meaningful propositions always have contingent material content. This is how Glock reads Wittgenstein. Contrasting Wittgenstein's view (albeit from a later period) with Kant's claim that mathematical propositions are synthetic a priori as they seem to anticipate reality, he notes that Wittgenstein 'insists that necessary propositions are not *about* anything and hence not synthetic'.[11] In the same vein, Moore suggests that synthetic truths are 'used to make substantial claims about the world' (Moore 1997, 127).

But is this too quick? Recall that, according to Sullivan, the requirement of thinkability 'excludes nothing, and in language nothing is excluded but straightforward, ordinary nonsense' (Sullivan 1996, 200). Since truth, thought, and meaning all reside within the limits of language and each notion already presupposes determinate content, the limits do not look like limitations. There is no *conceptual* space to be 'tightened up' if by conceptuality we already mean propositions' ability to '*touch*' empirical reality (1996, 200; *TLP* 2.15121). However, Wittgenstein is as committed to the distinction between form and content as Kant is, applies the distinction to empirical facts and judgments about those facts, and concedes that whatever is a priori can pertain to form only (*TLP* 2.025, 3.31, 5.4731). Articulating syntheticity in terms of expressibility, that is, by reference to meaningful propositions, conceals this distinction. Without the distinction, the notion of aboutness remains ambivalent: it is one thing for an insight to be about the structural features of reality, grounded in logical form, another to be about specific (structured) facts with contingent content (see *TLP* 2.033).

Besides, if by 'language' we mean *contentful* language, then its expressive resources exclude things mentioned in the *Tractatus* that do *not* amount to 'straightforward, ordinary nonsense'. The primary example is logical form, which cannot be expressed by meaningful propositions, because it is mere form without empirical content (see *TLP* 3.13, 3.31–3.311). Yet Wittgenstein insists that, while not expressible in meaningful language, the form of reality 'expresses *itself*' (*TLP* 4.121). It does this most overtly in propositions of logic that are not nonsensical in spite of lacking sense (i.e., direction that points to a specific empirical fact) (*TLP* 4.4611). Rather than being bipolar, they are unconditionally true (*TLP* 4.461). Granted, Wittgenstein states that propositions of logic are tautologies and as such analytic (*TLP* 6.11). But do the

---

[11] Glock 1996, 132; see also Glock 1992, 19–20.

analytic propositions of logic encompass all that is necessary and known a priori? In the following, I argue that they do not.

3.3 Synthetic A Priori Revisited (I): Space and Time

If the early Wittgenstein was a transcendental idealist, then the relevant model of syntheticity a priori should reflect Kant's understanding of the notion. And it is not clear that, for Kant, expressibility, conceptuality, or even aboutness is required for an insight to be synthetic a priori.

Kant defines syntheticity a priori in contrast to analyticity. Analytic judgments are a priori in virtue of the principle of contradiction: they express nothing in the predicate that has not already been included in the concept of the subject. By contrast, synthetic a priori judgments amplify this concept and require another, additional principle. (*CPR* A6/B10; *P* 4:266–7.) However, the ways in which Kant employs the notion of syntheticity in the investigation of different kinds of a priori judgments reveal a more multifaceted picture. Pure concepts of understanding, typically held up as the primary model of synthetic a priori, have a necessary relation to empirical objects and yield synthetic a priori knowledge about nature (*CPR* A85/B117). The a priori principle of practical reason is a synthetic a priori proposition, but one that governs the supersensible domain of freedom and is thinkable only as something that ought to be the case (*G* 4:420). The first instance involves a priori concepts, the second a conceptual a priori principle. Both are applied to a given domain, nature and freedom respectively, and can be understood in terms of aboutness or expressibility in a sense that Wittgenstein's early account cannot accommodate.[12]

However, for Kant, pure judgments of taste, too, as well as mathematics and geometry are synthetic a priori. In all these cases, syntheticity is grounded in space and time as pure forms of intuition and does not presuppose 'genuine exercise of concepts' (cf. Moore 2013, 252). Instead of proceeding from concepts, these synthetic insights rely on direct *seeing* (in the case of mathematics) or *feeling* (in the case of pure judgments of taste) of a spatio-temporal form. For this reason, it is also unclear whether the resulting insights count as 'thoughts'

---

[12] According to Kant, we cannot know whether an action is grounded in the Categorical Imperative, but we can know whether the action is in conformity with it. Wittgenstein, of course, denies the availability of any absolutely commanding ethical laws and the possibility of any empirical action being either good or bad (see *TLP* 6.41, 6.422).

in the strict discursive sense of the term. In *Prolegomena*, a work arguably known to Wittgenstein at the time of the *Tractatus*'s composition, Kant argues that our knowledge of mathematics is 'always *intuitive*; in the place of which philosophy can content itself with *discursive* judgments *from mere concepts*' (*P* 4:281; see *CPR* A711/B739; Proops 2004, 109). The contrast between intuitive and discursive judgments reflects the subject's modes of relating to reality. Cognitive judgments, as a paradigm case of conceptually determined discursive judgments, subsume empirical intuitions under concepts of understanding, where an essential feature of concepts is their object-directedness or aboutness (*CPJ* 5:179–80; *CPR* A320/B377). In this respect, they resemble Wittgenstein's meaningful propositions that have empirical content in virtue of a propositional form's being projected onto reality, thus being 'intrinsically truth-directed' (see Sullivan 1996, 197; *TLP* 3.11, 3.13). By contrast, the intuitive mode is one of direct seeing or—in the absence of a concrete object—imagining (see *CPR* B151).

Transcendental aesthetic, which investigates pure forms of intuition, abstracts away from the concepts of understanding and eliminates all material content from the intuitions (*CPR* A22/B36). Yet, even without concepts, it yields synthetic a priori knowledge. For example, Kant argues that our knowledge that $7 + 5 = 12$ is not analytic, because we cannot derive the meaning of 12 from the combination of 7 and 5: 'we could never find the sum through the mere analysis of our concepts, without making use of intuition' (*P* 4:269). Similarly, that space is three-dimensional can 'by no means be proven from concepts, but rests immediately upon intuition, and indeed on pure *a priori* intuition, because it is apodictically certain' (*P* 4:284–5). We need not compare geometrical theorems with reality to know that they are true, because our grasp of geometry relies on space and time as the necessary forms of intuition independently of any actual empirical facts. Accordingly, as Stenius puts it, 'an investigation of what is imaginable to us shows what is *a priori* true with regard to perception' (Stenius 1960, 217; see *P* 4:287). In this respect, then, mathematics and geometry precede the conceptual apparatus of the understanding.

Wittgenstein's statement that thinkability discloses the realm of possibilities accords with Kant's view of imaginability as the source of a priori knowledge of the formal features of the sensible domain (*TLP* 3.02). Since possibilities are grounded in the form of thought, any 'imagined world [...] must have *something*—a form—in common' with the real world (*TLP* 2.022). This form, Wittgenstein claims, is perceivable not just in tautologies of logic but also in mathematical equations. We *see* the a priori truth of logical propositions as well as the correctness of mathematical equations directly from the propositions themselves without comparing them with actual facts.[13] At the same time, while not *descriptions* of the world, mathematical equations are applicable to empirical reality. Indeed, for Wittgenstein, the possibility of using mathematics in inferences from non-mathematical propositions to other non-mathematical propositions is an essential aspect of mathematics.[14]

As I have said, propositions of logic are analytic (*TLP* 6.11). However, for the early Wittgenstein, mathematics is not reducible to logic, and mathematical equations are not tautologies but 'pseudo-propositions'.[15] According to Pasquale Frascolla, this means that, unlike propositions of logic that are tautologically equivalent since the two sides of a biconditional have the same sense, mathematical equations 'attempt to express a metalinguistic relation—in particular—a semantic relation' (Frascolla 1994, 28). This relation can be seen either from the original equation or from the calculation that proves the correctness of the equation, calculations being symbolic processes of transforming one mathematical expression into another. Accordingly, Frascolla argues, mathematical equations have 'informative content', albeit of a kind that cannot be expressed in meaningful language (1994, 29; see *TLP* 6.23). But if this is the case, then Wittgenstein's stance on the 'old objection against identity in mathematics', which he mentions in an early *Notebook* entry, must be that 2×2 is *not* 'really the *same* as 4' (*NB* 4). That it is not is, of course, Kant's point in claiming that pure mathematics is synthetic a priori. Later, in 1929, Wittgenstein concurs with Kant's conclusion explicitly: 'What I said earlier about the nature of arithmetic equations and about an equation's not being replaceable by a tautology explains—I believe—what Kant means when he insists that $7 + 5 = 12$ is not an analytic proposition, but synthetic *a priori*' (*PR* §108).[16]

---

[13] *TLP* 4.461, 6.113–6.1222, 6.2321.
[14] *TLP* 6.211; cf. *CPR* A39–40/B56–7. On Kant's explanation of the apriority and applicability of mathematics, see Shabel 2005.
[15] *TLP* 6.2; see Floyd 2021, 10; Rodych 2018; Potter 2000, 181.
[16] In 1929, Wittgenstein alludes to Kant's example of imagined fingers or points that are needed for getting 12 out of 5 and 7 and claims that what 'tells us that the 5 strokes and the 7 combine *precisely to make* 12 is always only insight into the internal relations of the structures—not some logical consideration' (*PR* §104; see *P* 4:268–9). Moreover, he insists that no investigation of concepts, but only 'direct insight' reveals the truth of the mathematical equation (*PR* §107). While most commentators assume that these remarks indicate Wittgenstein's change of heart on the issue, I am not convinced (see, e.g., Stern 1995, 112–13). For me, the role assigned to direct insight into structural relations, figuring centrally already in the *Tractatus*, suggests a continuity with his early view. For Wittgenstein on the synthetic a priori, see also *RFM* 245–6, 338.

It is clear that Wittgenstein himself saw a connection between Kant's treatment of mathematics and his own project. In the *Notebooks*, he suggested that his 'theory of tautologies' could cast '[l]ight on Kant's question "How is pure mathematics possible?"' (*NB* 15; *P* 4:280). In the *Tractatus*, Wittgenstein returns to Kant's answer. He writes:

> The question whether intuition [*Anschauung*] is needed for the solution of mathematical problems must be given the answer that in this case language itself provides the necessary intuition. The process of *calculating* serves to bring out that intuition. Calculation is not an experiment. (*TLP* 6.233)

The remark is characteristically enigmatic and has been interpreted in contradictory ways. Juliet Floyd takes it to express a 'logicist-inspired criticism of Kant' (Floyd 2012, 231). David Stern, while noticing that Kant's transcendental aesthetic makes an appearance in the *Tractatus*, claims that Wittgenstein 'unequivocally dismissed the role of intuition [*Anschauung*] in mathematics'.[17] Stenius argues, in diametrical opposition, that Wittgenstein actually endorses Kant's view. According to him, Wittgenstein assumes that intuition in the Kantian sense of '*concrete visual observation*' of spatio-temporal structures is needed as a source of evidence in formal proofs even when the intuition is directed to linguistic expressions used in those proofs (Stenius 1989, 57). Hence, while not backing off from his claim that Wittgenstein denies the availability of synthetic a priori *propositions*, Stenius leaves room for what Kant would count as synthetic a priori knowledge (cf. Stenius 1960, 214). Frascolla does not connect Wittgenstein's remark to Kant, but explains its role in a way that is roughly in harmony with Stenius's interpretation. According to Frascolla, calculation, used to prove mathematical equations, is 'construction of a sign figure that shows the mutual reducibility of the two forms' on the two sides of the equation (Frascolla 1994, 32). The role of calculation is to make directly visible the transformability of one to the other and hence allow one to *see* the correctness of the equation from the formal structures of the signs. These formal structures serve as the '"object" of intuition' 1994, 33).[18]

The peculiar status of mathematics in the *Tractatus* is most evident in Wittgenstein's remarks on geometry. He contrasts geometry with physics by

---

[17] Stern 1995, 113; see Stern 1995, 51–2, 110 n. 64; *TLP* 2.0121–2.0131.
[18] In a later article, Frascolla writes that 'intuition, if it is directed to the way the world is, is banished from the processes of solving mathematical problems', connecting the point to Wittgenstein's claim that calculations are not empirical experiments (Frascolla 2017, 310; see *TLP* 6.2331). This is true if 'the way the world is' means specific empirical facts. However, pure intuition is not directed to empirical reality even if its forms apply to it (see *CPR* A40/B57).

noting that while it is possible to represent a state of affairs that violates the laws of physics, it is impossible to represent one that violates the a priori laws of geometry (*TLP* 3.0321). He also points out that geometry abstracts away from any specific spatial constellations in spite of being applicable to them. Geometry is a 'network', presupposed for the possibility of saying something about actual spatial structures. This network 'is *purely* geometrical; all its properties can be given a priori' (*TLP* 6.35). So, in geometry, just as in logic, 'form is the possibility of structure' (*TLP* 2.033; see also *TLP* 3.411). But although logic and geometry are alike in being formal and hence excluded from meaningful language, Wittgenstein does not run the two together. Instead, he puts logic and geometry on a par as distinct sources of a priori insights: 'It is as impossible to represent in language anything that "contradicts logic" as it is in geometry to represent by its co-ordinates a figure that contradicts the laws of space, or to give the co-ordinates of a point that does not exist' (*TLP* 3.032).

Sullivan takes notice of Wittgenstein's alignment of logic and geometry but treats geometry as nothing more than Wittgenstein's preferred model or analogy for the aprioricity of logic. Besides, according to him, the analogy between the two 'breaks down all over the place' (Sullivan 1996, 199). While the requirement to construct the concept of a triangle in intuition does impose a constraint tighter than the concept of a triangle provides, in language no such tighter constraint is in sight (1996, 200; see Sullivan 2011, 172). What I am suggesting is that Wittgenstein's appeal to geometry is not an appeal as to a mere model. Instead, spatio-temporality belongs to the 'form of reality' as part of the transcendentally grounded phenomenal architecture of the 'world as I found it' (*TLP* 2.18, 5.631).

Indeed, some remarks of the *Tractatus* imply that Wittgenstein's early account incorporates the very transcendental ground that, for Kant, serves to establish the syntheticity of a priori knowledge of mathematics and geometry, namely, space and time. According to Wittgenstein, objects 'constitute the unalterable form' of reality, and 'space, time and colour (colouration) are forms of objects' (*TLP* 2.023, 2.0251; translation modified[19]). Moreover, he repeatedly evokes necessities that are grounded in these forms. For instance, he writes that 'we are quite unable to imagine spatial objects outside space or temporal objects outside time'—a point that, for Kant, serves to establish

---

[19] The original reads 'Raum, Zeit und Farbe (Färbigkeit) sind Formen der Gegenstände' (*TLP* 2.0251; see Frascolla 2004, 377).

the a priori character of space and time.[20] And he claims that the impossibility of the simultaneous presence of two colours at the same place in the visual field springs from the 'logical structure of colour'.[21] Addressing time, Wittgenstein denies the possibility of comparing temporal processes with time itself: 'We cannot compare a process with "the passage of time"—there is no such thing—but only with another process (such as the working of a chronometer)', adding that the same applies to space (*TLP* 6.3611). This remark, too, could be read as an indication of the transcendental ideality of time and space: both are conditions for the possibility of representing spatio-temporally structured facts, but do not belong to the totality of expressible facts.

Finally, while the aforementioned necessities cannot be captured by meaningful propositions, which always picture contingencies, Wittgenstein suggests that the subject knows or is acquainted with them. In the very beginning of the book, he talks about knowledge of objects and claims that to know an object means that 'I know [*kenne*] all its possible occurrences in states of affairs' (*TLP* 2.0123). I know the object's internal properties, which are determined by the object's form, such as colouration. I need not know what the colour of a given speck in the visual field is, as this can only be established by empirical investigation. But I can know that the speck must have *some* colour without comparing this insight with reality.[22] It is difficult to understand such claims as analytic statements springing from the principle of contradiction. The necessities in question are rather established by the impossibility of imagining their opposite regarding experience. For Kant, such necessities would be synthetic on account of their reliance on pure forms of sensibility.

---

[20] *TLP* 2.0121; see *CPR* A24/B38; *TLP* 2.013–2.0131. P. M. S. Hacker notes that 2.0121 looks like a synthetic a priori proposition but argues that Wittgenstein 'did not think that to know one of these (non-analytic) a priori propositions was correctly characterized as *knowing the truth of a description of how things necessarily are in nature*' (Hacker 2013, 35). On his view, rather than being a priori descriptions of the scaffolding of nature, such propositions are norms of description. I agree that there is no room for '*true descriptions*', that is, meaningful propositions about such necessities. However, on my reading, the necessities pertaining to space, time, and degrees of colour are not *just* norms of description but pertain to the form of *reality* itself (see *NB* 118; *TLP* 2.18, 4.121; *RLF*; Appelqvist 2024). If thinkability gives the norm, if what is thinkable is possible, and if the necessities are determined by an investigation into the domain of the possible, then how can we distinguish between the scaffolding of reality and the norms of description?

[21] *TLP* 6.3751; see *TLP* 4.123. For Kant, colours do not belong to *pure* forms of sensibility and hence sensations of colours are given only a posteriori. However, he grants that 'their property of having a degree can be cognized *a priori*' (*CPR* A176/B218; see *TLP* 2.0131).

[22] *TLP* 2.0123–2.0131; 3.05; *CPR* A176/B218.

3.4 Synthetic A Priori Revisited (II): Application of Logic

The second example of synthetic a priori judgments from Kant's transcendental aesthetic makes an even more radical break with conceptuality and aboutness. Recall Moore's parallel between Wittgenstein's nonsensical pseudo-propositions and Kant's thoughts without content. According to Moore, the latter 'are nonetheless thoughts', 'involve a genuine exercise of concepts', and 'are true or false' (Moore 2013, 252). The characterization matches Kant's view of conceptual thoughts about, for example, God, and the noumenal subject, which do not correspond to intuitions (*CPR* A2–3/B6–7; see Moore 2020, 39). However, in addition to such empty thoughts, Kant's account accommodates blind judgments that do not involve any concepts (*CPR* A51/B76). The paradigm example of a judgment that makes a legitimate claim to necessity independently of concepts is the judgment of beauty. Moreover, rather than being confined to matters of taste, Kant takes his analysis of the judgment of beauty to have direct relevance for the application of concepts to nature as well as for the possibility of natural science.

Pure mathematical cognition does not proceed from concepts, but it does involve 'construction of concepts' by exhibiting a priori intuitions corresponding to concepts (*P* 4:272; *CPR* A713/B741). And while geometrical intuitions are not conceptually grounded, they lead to conceptually expressible theorems that are applicable to spatiotemporally organized nature. By contrast, the judgment of beauty neither relies on nor leads to concepts (*CPJ* 5:209). It is not *about* anything either, because without concepts it cannot attribute properties to objects (*CPJ* 5:184, 5:211). Instead, the judgment of beauty makes a claim about a necessary connection between a sensuously given form and the subject's *feeling* of pleasure (*CPJ* 5:203). What justifies the claim to necessity is that the power of judgment, which is the faculty engaged in the non-conceptual contemplation of the form, has its own a priori principle, which warrants transcendental investigation.[23] Hence, Kant concludes, 'this problem of the critique of the power of judgment belongs under the general problem of transcendental philosophy: How are synthetic *a priori* judgments possible?' (*CPJ* 5:289).[24]

---

[23] At the time of writing the *First Critique*, Kant thought that pure judgments of taste do not warrant a transcendental investigation (*CPR* A21/B35). However, by the time of the *Third Critique*, he had changed his mind about this.

[24] Kant's explanation reads as follows: 'That judgments of taste are synthetic is readily seen, because they do go beyond the concept and even the intuition of the object, and add to that as a predicate something that is not even cognition at all, namely the feeling of pleasure (or displeasure). However,

The a priori principle governing the power of judgment is the principle of formal purposiveness, also known as 'lawfulness of the contingent as such' (CPJ 20:217, 5:404). Unlike the principles of understanding and of practical reason, which legislate a domain, the principle of the power of judgment lacks a domain of its own. It does not ground claims *about* nature as cognitive judgments do by determining particulars under concepts; nor does it determine what one should will as practical judgments do by reference to the concept of freedom (*CPJ* 5:174–6). The principle simply governs the *reflective use* of the power of judgment, namely, the kind of use that does not begin from concepts but from the sensuously given particular (*CPJ* 5:185–6). As a result, and in contrast with other a priori principles that are capable of grounding a *doctrine*, the principle of formal purposiveness is merely a principle for *critique* (*CPJ* 5:194; cf. *TLP* 4.0031, 4.112). And yet, Kant argues, the principle of formal purposiveness, uncovered by analysing the judgment of beauty, is required for 'cognition in general' (*CPJ* 5:218; see *CPJ* 5:287).

When introducing the a priori principle of the power of judgment, Kant calls it the principle of 'purposiveness of nature (in the multiplicity of its empirical laws)' (*CPJ* 5:181). He notes that, at first sight, the principle 'seems rather to be tautological and to belong to mere logic' (*CPJ* 20:211). However, as logic is incapable of explaining why different *particular* objects of nature should fall under a given concept without launching a regress of conceptual justifications on the application of concepts, the principle must be transcendental and synthetic (see *CPR* A133; *CPJ* 20:211). To avoid the regress, we must be able to *see* the particulars as unified and as such fitting for concepts by relying on a judgment that is based on a feeling rather than a concept (*CPJ* 5:218).[25] Hence, Kant claims, the principle of formal purposiveness is a 'condition of the possibility of the application of logic to nature' (*CPJ* 20:212).

In the *Tractatus*, Wittgenstein famously argues that unless the world had objects, then the sense of one elementary proposition would depend on the truth of one another—a conclusion he is not willing to consider on pain of the

---

that such judgments, even though the predicate (of *one's own* pleasure that is combined with the representation) is empirical, are nevertheless, as far as the requisite assent *of everyone* is concerned, a priori judgments, or would be taken as such, is already implicit in the expressions of their claim.' (*CPJ* 5:288–9).

[25] The problem of how to apply concepts to particulars (manifolds of intuitions) is first presented in the *First Critique* (*CPR* A131–6/B169–75). In the Preface of the *Third Critique*, Kant returns to the problem and suggests that his analysis of pure judgments of taste as non-conceptual judgments contains the key to its solution (*CPJ* 5:169). According to Moore, the 'feeling of unity', which Kant evokes as the core of his solution, is a 'type of inexpressible knowledge' (see Moore 2007).

regress lurking therein (*TLP* 2.021–2.0211).[26] He also suggests that the subject knows the objects as regards their forms (*TLP* 2.01231). This knowledge, which cannot be expressed, amounts to knowledge of the limits of empirical reality, which is 'limited by the totality of objects' (*TLP* 5.5561). Now consider Wittgenstein's remark:

> The 'experience' that we need in order to understand logic is not that something or other is the state of things, but that something *is*: that, however, is *not* an experience.
> Logic is *prior* to every experience—that something *is so*.
> It is prior to the question 'How?', not prior to the question 'What?' (*TLP* 5.552)

It is hard not to read the 'What' as referring to objects, which give the world its unalterable form (*TLP* 2.023). For Moore, the remark is evidence of an urge to 'say what grounds the very essence of reality, conceived as something to which not even logic is prior', suggesting that the limits of language could be construed as limitations (Moore 2013, 245). Sullivan criticizes what he calls 'object-centred' interpretations of the *Tractatus*, because he takes them to render the Tractarian account 'quasi-extensional' (Sullivan 1996, 197). On his view, Wittgenstein's reference to knowledge of objects amounts to nothing but one's having the formal notion of an object (see 1996, 207). However, if the objects are considered only in respect of their forms, including their spatio-temporal form, independently of their material content, then the extensionality in question acquires a more formal character.[27] While there are a priori relations between thought and reality more substantial than analytic propositions can accommodate, these relations are still independent of any actual, expressible matters of fact. We need no experience about what states of affairs actually obtain to understand logic; that is, we need not know how objects are actually combined. But we do need the 'non-experience' of there being something. Insofar as this amounts to knowing, for example, that visual spots must have *some* colour, notes *some* pitch, etc., then that something is already seen as lawful.

---

[26] Wittgenstein's later treatment of the problem of 'rule-following' (*PI* §201) is better known, and has been discussed in relation to Kant's treatment of the problem (most notably in Bell 1987; Moore makes the connection in Moore 2007, Sullivan in Sullivan 2011; see also Appelqvist 2023, 48–58). However, as acknowledged by Sullivan, the problem is essentially the very same as the problem of the limits of language which the *Tractatus* addresses (see Sullivan 2011, 173).

[27] See *TLP* 2.0231; Kannisto 1986, 138–43; Appelqvist 2024.

Wittgenstein's own explanation of why logic is not prior to 'What' reads as follows:

> And if this were not so, how could we apply logic? We might put it this way: if there would be a logic even if there were no world, how then could there be a logic given that there is the world? (*TLP* 5.5521)

If read in the light of Kant's discussion of the a priori principle of the power of judgment as a condition of the possibility of applying logic to nature, Wittgenstein's enigmatic remark becomes understandable. Logic cannot be prior to the question 'What?', because that to which logic is applied must already be *seen as* malleable to the conceptual structure of the general propositional form (see *TLP* 4.5). And this can only be if there is an a priori connection between our way of judging the world and the world 'as I found it' (*TLP* 5.631).

For Kant, the connection manifest in reflective judgment is not limited to the applicability of concepts to empirical particulars. According to him, the systematicity of empirical laws of nature similarly relies on the principle of the power of judgment. This is to say that the very enterprise of natural science rests on the a priori assumption that particular laws of nature can be subsumed under more general ones. For Kant, this assumption manifests itself in such heuristic maxims as the law of parsimony, the law of continuity, and that principles should not be multiplied beyond necessity. While traditionally presented as 'pronouncements of metaphysical wisdom', such maxims are neither derived from nature nor demonstrable from concepts (*CPJ* 5:182). Instead, they are but expressions of the a priori principle of the power of judgment that for all things in nature we 'can always presuppose a form that is possible for general laws cognizable by us' (*CPJ* 20:212).[28]

Now, in the *Tractatus*, we read:

> Men have always had the presentiment that there must be a realm in which the answers to questions are symmetrically combined—a priori—to form a self-contained system.
> A realm subject to law: Simplex sigillum veri. (*TLP* 5.4541; see *NB* 83.)

Later, immediately after his remarks on mathematics, Wittgenstein addresses the status of laws of nature. He begins by claiming that the 'exploration of logic means the exploration of *all lawfulness [aller Gesetzmäßigkeit]*' (*TLP* 6.3, tr.

---

[28] Kant addresses this point in *CPJ* 20:210–18; 5:181–6; cf. *CPR* A652/B680.

altered). He denies that the law of induction could be a 'law of logic' and a priori, because it is a proposition with sense and accordingly with material content (*TLP* 6.31). However, the same does not hold for the law of causality. According to Wittgenstein, 'the law of causality is not a law but a form of a law' (*TLP* 6.32). While not analytic in any obvious way, it is a priori. On Stenius's reading, Wittgenstein's point boils down to the ineffable idea that 'we can give our hypotheses of "connections" in nature the form of general laws—and Kantianism is right in so far as this logical form is the only form under which *connections* in nature are thinkable'.[29]

Echoing Kant's argument, Wittgenstein claims further that people have assumed that there must be '*a* "law of least action" before they knew exactly how it went' (*TLP* 6.3211). The conclusion he draws is that this a priori insight is formal and hence belongs to logic. In the same vein, he denies a priori *belief* in the law of conservation, but states that we have 'a priori *knowledge* of the possibility of a logical form' (*TLP* 6.33). According to Wittgenstein,

> All such propositions, including the principle of sufficient reason, the laws of continuity in nature and of least effort in nature, etc. etc.—all these are a priori insights about the forms in which the propositions of science can be cast (*TLP* 6.34).

The examples Wittgenstein adduces here correspond to the heuristic principles that Kant mentions as expressions of the principle of purposiveness of nature. Moreover, as far as I can see, Wittgenstein's reasoning accords with Kant's explanation of the role of the a priori principle of the power of judgment. Wittgenstein denies that laws of nature are (meaningful) explanations of natural phenomena (see *TLP* 6.371). Instead, in order for the 'corpus of the natural sciences', which consists of meaningful propositions, to have structure—i.e., to be hierarchically organized—we must rely on a formal principle that makes that structure possible (*TLP* 4.11).

Sullivan acknowledges that Wittgenstein's remarks on natural science, along with his discussion of mathematics and the subsequent remarks on value, are reflections of Kant's philosophy (Sullivan 1996, 198 n. 9). But given that he takes the a priori in the *Tractatus* to be strictly analytic, he reads Wittgenstein as attacking rather than agreeing with Kant. Contrasting Wittgenstein's

---

[29] Stenius 1960, 219–20; see *TLP* 6.361.

view with Kant, he writes that '[t]o be a law-giver to Nature would be a grand thing: to be a dispenser of tautologies less so' (Sullivan 2013, 261). The contrast is fair enough if the model of a priori legislation of nature is Kant's pure concepts of understanding, treated in the *First Critique*. The *Tractatus* cannot accommodate a priori true propositions or beliefs about nature, given that whatever is a priori pertains to form and never to content, and given that for him, unlike for Kant, sense requires both. However, if we take our lead from the *Third Critique*, then the a priori insights cast in 'minimum-principles' such as the law of least action need not make meaningful, truth-apt statements about facts (*TLP* 6.321). They need not attribute anything to nature if they are taken as expressions of the a priori principle governing our way of *seeing* nature as lawful.

3.5 Conclusion: The Challenge from Sullivan

According to Sullivan, the transcendentality of logic cannot be like the transcendentality of ethics, because the Kantian contrast required for construing the limits of language as limitations just is not there in the *Tractatus*. Thought and language do not exclude any possibilities because, for the early Wittgenstein, there is no synthetic a priori. There is no shared territory that the limit of language would divide into two. So while it may look as though Wittgenstein contrasts thinking with feeling, thereby introducing a genuine limitation to thought, such Kantian integration between Wittgenstein's theoretical and practical philosophy is 'too much integration to hope for' (Sullivan 2013, 265).

I have argued that, although the *Tractatus* cannot accommodate synthetic a priori *propositions*, the text suggests that not 'all lawfulness' is reducible to the analytic propositions of logic (*TLP* 6.3).[30] The examples I have given—mathematics, geometry, and, for short, 'Simplex sigillum veri' as the heuristic principle guiding natural science—accord, not with Kant's transcendental logic, but with his transcendental aesthetic. If the proposal is plausible, then logic and ethics are connected by a bridge not unlike the bridge Kant himself envisions between the two in the *Third Critique*.

---

[30] This proposal entails that, in the *Tractatus*, Wittgenstein must be using the notion of logic in a narrow and broad sense, the narrow sense corresponding to propositions of logic (cf. *TLP* 6.1–6.11) and the broad sense to '*everything that is subject to law*' (*TLP* 6.3; see also *TLP* 6.361).

What is divided into two by the limit of language is the world. It is not divided as a garden is divided by a fence, but the division is effected by the subject's way of judging that world (cf. Sullivan 2013, 266). The world understood as the totality of possible facts can be pictured by meaningful propositions, relevantly similar to Kant's determining judgments. The world understood as the totality of actual facts is pictured by true propositions, that is, by the propositions of natural science. But the same world may also be judged, not by *saying* something true or false about it, but by *seeing* its necessary form. This contrast in modes of judging, which Wittgenstein takes to be strictly exclusive, reveals that neither discursive thought considered on its own nor intuitive seeing considered on its own provides us with a complete conception of the world (see *TLP* 4.1212).

According to Kant, that our cognition itself is divided between the discursive and the intuitive modes shows that our human understanding is but one possible way of grasping the world (*CPJ* 5: 406). The division is particularly pronounced in our relation to nature, which can be approached either discursively or by means of reflection. The first approach, investigated by theoretical philosophy, presents nature as an aggregate of contingent facts to which the mechanical laws drawn from conceptual understanding apply. The latter approach, spelled out in the *Third Critique*, presents the same nature as a purposive whole, where that which for discursive judgment is contingent is *seen as* lawfully organized (*CPJ* 5: 385–8.) The judgment does not warrant knowledge of a world-whole, because it relies on the judging subject's feeling rather than concepts. Yet, it allows us to see nature as hospitable to the will's moral exercise.

I have argued that Wittgenstein's remarks on natural science echo Kant's discussion of the principle of the power of judgment. After claiming that the hypotheses of natural science rely on a priori insights into forms of language, Wittgenstein turns to ethics. He denies the expressibility of each of the notions that form the foundation of Kant's moral philosophy, namely, the good or bad exercise of the will, happiness, eternity, immortality, and God (*TLP* 6.42–6.432). Moreover, Wittgenstein reinterprets each notion in such a way that no connection to a transcendent domain, still relevant for Kant's purposes, is available.[31] However, in this string of otherwise negative pronouncements there is one exception. Wittgenstein writes:

> The intuition of the world sub specie aeterni is the intuition of it as a whole—a limited whole.

---

[31] See Appelqvist and Pöykkö 2020.

The feeling of the world as a limited whole is what is the mystical. (*TLP* 6.45, translation altered[32])

The remark accords with the culmination of Kant's argument in the *Third Critique*. As an *intuition*, the intuition of the world as a limited whole is not discursive. The world is not pictured by a complete list of true propositions, which is what the natural sciences provide, but it is *felt* in the subject's contemplation of the existence of the world (see *TLP* 6.44). The difference with Kant's other notions of practical philosophy is the character of the a priori principle grounding the judgment. The principle has no domain of application and does not allow one to *say* anything about the world. Accordingly, it fits into an account that denies the possibility of synthetic a priori propositions while taking the relation between the world and thought to be governed by a priori insights beyond mere tautologies.[33]

References

Works Cited by Abbreviation

CPJ   Kant, I. 2000. *Critique of the Power of Judgment*, P. Guyer (ed.), P. Guyer and E. Matthews (tr.) (Cambridge: CUP).
CPR Kant, I. 1998. *Critique of Pure Reason*, P. Guyer (ed.), P. Guyer and A. W. Wood (tr.) (Cambridge: CUP).
G   Kant, I. 1997. *Groundwork for the Metaphysics of Morals*, M. Gregor (tr. & ed.) (Cambridge: CUP).
NB   Wittgenstein, L. 1961. *Notebooks 1914–1916*, G. H. von Wright and G. E. M. Anscombe (ed.), G. E. M. Anscombe (tr.) (Oxford: Blackwell).
P   Kant, I. 2004. *Prolegomena to Any Future Metaphysics* (Cambridge: CUP).
PI   Wittgenstein, L. 2009. *Philosophical Investigations*, G. E. M. Anscombe, P. M. S. Hacker, and J. Schulte (tr.). Revised fourth edition by P. M. S. Hacker and J. Schulte (Oxford: Blackwell).
PR   Wittgenstein, L. 1975. *Philosophical Remarks*, R. Rhees (ed.), R. Hargreaves, and R. White (tr.) (Oxford: Blackwell).

---

[32] The original German reads: 'Die Anschauung der Welt sub specie aeterni ist ihre Anschauung als—begrenztes—Ganzes. Das Gefühl der Welt als begrenztes Ganzes ist das mystische'.

[33] I want to express my gratitude to Anssi Korhonen, Gabriel Sandu, Richard Gaskin, Panu Raatikainen, and Andre Maury for their comments on an earlier version of this chapter as well as to Frode Kjosavik for a stimulating conversation on syntheticity a priori in Kant's philosophy at the Norwegian Academy of Science and Letters on 9 November 2022. Thanks also to Amanda Häkkinen and Anna Konijn for their help in the final stages of preparing the manuscript.

RFM Wittgenstein, L. 1983. *Remarks on the Foundations of Mathematics*, G. H. von Wright, R. Rhees, and G. E. M. Anscombe (eds.), G. E. M. Anscombe (tr.) (Cambridge Mass: MIT Press).

RLF Wittgenstein, L. 1993. 'Some Remarks on Logical Form', in J. Klagge and A. Nordman (eds), *Philosophical Occasions 1912–1951* (Indianapolis: Hackett), 28–35.

TLP Wittgenstein, L. 1961. *Tractatus Logico-Philosophicus*, D. F. Pears and B. F. McGuinness (tr.) (London: Routledge).

Other Sources

Appelqvist, H. 2023. *Wittgenstein and Aesthetics* (Cambridge: CUP).

Appelqvist, H. 2024. 'The Fish Tale: The unity of language and the world in light of *TLP* 4.014', in J. Zalabardo (ed.), *Wittgenstein's Tractatus Logico-Philosophicus: a Critical Guide* (Cambridge: CUP), 69–89.

Appelqvist, H. and Pöykkö, P. M. 2020. 'Wittgenstein and Levinas on the transcendentality of ethics', in H. Appelqvist (ed.), *Wittgenstein and the Limits of Language* (New York: Routledge), 65–89.

Bell, D. 1987. 'The art of judgment', *Mind* 96, 221–44.

Floyd, J. 2012. 'Das Überraschende: Wittgenstein on the surprising in mathematics', in J. Ellis and D. Guevara (eds), *Wittgenstein and the Philosophy of Mind* (Oxford: OUP), 225–58.

Floyd, J. 2021. *Wittgenstein's Philosophy of Mathematics* (Cambridge: CUP).

Frascolla, P. 1994. *Wittgenstein's Philosophy of Mathematics* (London: Routledge).

Frascolla, P. 2004. 'On the nature of Tractatus objects', *Dialectica* 58, 369–82.

Frascolla, P. 2017. 'Wittgenstein's early philosophy of mathematics', in H. J. Glock and J. Hyman (eds), *A Companion to Wittgenstein* (West Sussex: Wiley Blackwell), 305–18.

Glock, H. 1992. 'Cambridge, Jena or Vienna: The roots of the *Tractatus*', *Ratio* 5, 1–23.

Glock, H. 1996. *Wittgenstein Dictionary* (Oxford: Blackwell).

Hacker, P. M. S. 2013. *Wittgenstein: Comparisons and Context* (Oxford: OUP).

Kannisto, H. 1986. *Thoughts and Their Subject: A Study of Wittgenstein's Tractatus*. Acta Philosophica Fennica Vol. 40 (Helsinki: Societas Philosophica Fennica).

Luckhardt, C. G. 1979. *Wittgenstein: Sources and Perspectives* (Ithaca, NY: Cornell University Press).

Moore, A. W. 1997. *Points of View* (Oxford: OUP).

Moore, A. W. 2007. 'Is the feeling of unity that Kant identifies in his *Third Critique* a type of inexpressible knowledge?', *Philosophy* 82, 475–85.

Moore, A. W. 2011. 'A response to Sullivan', in R. Read and M. A. Lavery (eds), *Beyond the Tractatus Wars: The New Wittgenstein Debate* (New York: Routledge), 190–95.

Moore, A. W. 2013. 'Was the author of the *Tractatus* a transcendental idealist?', in P. Sullivan and M. Potter (eds), *Wittgenstein's Tractatus: History and interpretation* (Oxford: OUP), 239–55.

Moore, A. W. 2020. 'The bounds of nonsense', in H. Appelqvist (ed.), *Wittgenstein and the Limits of Language* (New York: Routledge), 27–45.

Potter, M. 2000. *Reason's Nearest Kin: Philosophies of Arithmetic from Kant to Carnap* (Oxford: OUP).

Proops, I. 2004. 'Wittgenstein on the substance of the world', *The European Journal of Philosophy* 12, 106–26.

Rodych, V. 2018. 'Wittgenstein's philosophy of mathematics', in E. N. Zalta and U. Nodelman (eds), *Stanford Encyclopedia of Philosophy*.

Shabel, L. 2005. 'Apriority and application: Philosophy of mathematics in the modern period', in S. Shapiro (ed.), *The Oxford Handbook of Philosophy of Mathematics and Logic* (Oxford: OUP), 29–50.

Stenius, E. 1960. *Wittgenstein's Tractatus: A Critical Exposition of Its Main Lines of Thought* (Oxford: Blackwell).
Stenius, E. 1989. '*Anschauung* and formal proof: A comment on *Tractatus* 6.223', in I. Pörn (ed.), *Erik Stenius: Critical Essays II. Acta Philosophica Fennica* Vol 45 (Helsinki: Societas Philosophica Fennica), 56–69.
Stern, D. 1995. *Wittgenstein on Mind and Language* (Oxford: OUP).
Sullivan, P. 1996. 'The "truth" in solipsism, and Wittgenstein's rejection of the a priori', *The European Journal of Philosophy* 4, 195–219.
Sullivan, P. 2011. 'Synthesizing without concepts', in R. Read and M. A. Lavery (eds), *Beyond the Tractatus Wars: The New Wittgenstein Debate* (New York: Routledge), 171–89.
Sullivan, P. 2013. 'Idealism in Wittgenstein: A further reply to Moore', in P. Sullivan and M. Potter (eds), *Wittgenstein's* Tractatus: *History and Interpretation* (Oxford: OUP), 256–70.

4
Transcendental and Linguistic Idealism

Bernhard Weiss

I am interested in contrasting two idealist positions: Kantian Transcendental Idealism and—what I'll label—Linguistic Idealism. I also aim to provide some, though limited, support for the latter. Both idealisms should be distinguished from empirical idealism, what Kant called dogmatic and problematic idealism. Each of dogmatic and problematic idealism depends on a scepticism or agnosticism about the external world; that is, each bases itself on an epistemic thesis which privileges the internal. Transcendental and Linguistic Idealism (at least, as I construe the latter) each question realism, on the grounds that it conflicts with the necessary conditions for the possibility of representation.

4.1 The Kantian Background

Let me begin with Transcendental Idealism and some broad features of Kant's monumental vision. His route to the idealist destination starts by taking the Copernican Turn (Kant 1929, Bxvii). Having problematized the possibility of metaphysical knowledge, he suggests a potential resolution of the conflict of reason with itself. Rather than persisting in thinking that empirical knowledge should conform to pre-given objects, we should instead 'experiment' with the idea that the object of knowledge should conform to our modes of knowing. From this point the investigation takes on a reflective cast; we turn from a metaphysics of the world independent of thought and knowledge to an attempt to make explicit our ways of thinking and knowing about the world. However, importantly, the investigation *is* tentative; it *is* a trial. Why so? I think we do well to notice the following two features of the project.

First, the account has to secure the claim that the objects of our representations warrant the accolade of *objects*. As Strawson (1966, 24) says, Kant needs to show that what we represent is distinct from our representations. Strawson terms this the thesis of objectivity. In the implementation of the programme this entails (at least, very often) that the focus is on objectivity rather than on objecthood. Our employment of the categories, for instance, is justified by their role in drawing a principled distinction between the subjective and the objective, between *mere* appearance and reality. A nice example of this is provided by the Second Analogy's attempt to justify our employment of the category of causation (Kant 1929, 218–32). Epistemological scepticism is also transformed rather than dissipated in the new momentum of the Copernican Turn. No longer does it pose the question whether our modes of knowing succeed in making available an independent reality; instead, it poses the question whether the standards we employ in putative knowledge claims are standards which yield objectivity.

That's one large and important feature of the journey. The second feature I want to notice is this. The Copernican Turn is supposed to make possible metaphysical knowledge; in other words, it is supposed to make possible substantive a priori knowledge of objects. Though independent of the trial brought on by the Copernican Turn, Transcendental Idealism is integral to its *success*. The reason for this is simple enough. Thinking of the object *as* the object of representation achieves a significant reconception of our metaphysical ambition only if the form of our cognition imposes substantial requirements on the nature of objects, that is, only if the Turn takes us to a point where we are able to see the object of representation as distinct from the object as it is in itself. (As Kant says, 'we can know a priori of things only what we ourselves put into them' (Kant 1929, xvii).) If it does so, then the reflective investigation of our ways of knowing can hope to reveal substantive, yet a priori knowable, features of objects. Metaphysical knowledge becomes possible. If it does not, then the Turn does not effectively change the nature of our investigation; the reflective investigation of our ways of knowing reveals nothing substantive about objects, and metaphysical knowledge remains as vexed as ever. So, though distinct, the Copernican Turn and Transcendental Idealism are indissolubly linked: the success of the former depends on the truth of the latter.

Though this is the merest sketch of these Kantian themes, I want now to dwell for a moment on some of the difficulties with Kant's project. The Copernican Turn shifts the focus of attention from the objects to our ways of knowing about the objects; and the success of the Copernican Turn—the validation of Transcendental Idealism—depends on manifesting our contribution to the nature of objects, objects as they are *for us*. Making out this contribution is, for Kant, making out the a priori elements in our cognition, and this, in turn, involves accepting and detailing realms of synthetic a priori knowledge.

The more detailed incarnation of this programme in the first *Critique* depends on establishing the a priori spatio-temporal form of intuition, and the objective validity of the pure schematized concepts of the understanding, the categories.

4.2 Tensions in the Framework of Transcendental Idealism

This discovery (if that is what it is) that the character of the objects we know about is, in part, a contribution *we* make, is one that is hard to recognize. We appreciate the contribution by finding synthetic a priori elements in our cognition. Because these are a priori, and so universally applicable, they enjoy a kind of necessity. But, because they are features of our contingent natures, they admit of alternatives, though to be sure, alternatives whose detail we cannot contemplate. So objects *for us*, are necessarily subject to the laws of arithmetic and geometry, yet objects *as such* cannot be claimed to be so subject. The result is an awkward attempt to cover two, quite widely separated stools: accepting the necessity of arithmetic and geometry, while conceding their contingency; taking the object to be an object *for us*, when we conceive of it as being dependent on a contribution of our contingent nature, but as simply an *object*, when we take arithmetic and geometry to be universally applicable.

Another source of tension in Transcendental Idealism is that it entails limits to what it makes sense to say or to claim to know; yet its own metaphysics forces us to transgress these limits. As Wittgenstein remarks in the preface to the *Tractatus*, drawing a limit to thought seems to require us, absurdly, to think both sides of the boundary; but setting up limits in language appears equally problematic, unless we can ensure, as Wittgenstein did not, that the language used to state the limits of sense is itself meaningful.

It can also seem that, rather than making the philosophical endeavour (the search for a priori insight) easier to envisage, it becomes harder, in the reconceived landscape, to carve out a territory for it. For, if the objects we know about are merely objects for a contingent set of subjects, with one among many possible forms of cognition, then doesn't the reflective investigation of those forms of cognition become an empirical investigation of one set of knowers among others? Ought not empirical psychology to replace transcendental logic? Moreover, if we fail to mark the parochiality of the objects of our knowledge, how do we recognize our distinctive contribution to the construction of knowledge?[1]

---

[1] See Lear, 'The Disappearing We' (1998a), at pp. 238–40. In 'Transcendental Anthropology' (1998b) Lear explores the tension between transcendental investigations and empirical anthropology, attempting to supplement Kant with Wittgenstein to found a transcendental anthropology.

The problem lies in the felt need to recognize alternatives. Our contribution emerges by detecting synthetic a priori elements of knowledge. But recognizing them as *our* contributions forces an admission of alternatives, alternatives which pass beyond the bounds of sense, alternatives which place us in the invidious position of seeing the synthetic a priori as both necessary and contingent.

A worry about this kind of idealism exercises Anscombe, though her focus is on Wittgenstein.[2] The worry is that once we make objects constitutionally dependent on the forms of our cognition then their existence seems somehow dependent on us. It is tempting to say that had we not existed then the objects would not have existed. And this stands in tension with what we also want to say, namely, that the existence of the objects in no way depends on us. Of course, there are ways of dealing with the tension. On the one hand, one might say that the empirical claim is perfectly fine as an observation about the empirical self, a dated self of finite duration. Empirical objects, we learn, generally exist independently of this empirical self. But the Idealist thesis is about the transcendental self. Empirical reality is not independent of the transcendental self, which forms a condition for the possibility of empirical reality. In the particular case of Kant's transcendental Idealism the framework of space and time are features of objects only as they are for us; so the question of dependence of objects on the temporal existence of the transcendental self is simply confused and meaningless. But this feels very much like a merely technical victory, and one which doesn't dissipate the underlying strain. What the Transcendental Idealist wants to say is that the objects—the only objects of which we can conceivably have experience—are objects shaped by our cognition; but—and this distinguishes her from the Empirical Idealist—that, despite this, those objects are independent of being experienced. It is, however, as Kant urges, very hard not to think of those objects—the objects of experience, which are shaped by the form of our cognition—as appearances, as the product of some kind of encounter between the transcendental self and a transcendental reality. And once we do that the problem seems to resurface. It can be pushed down, but only by refusing to think about the sense in which the objects of experience are mere appearances. Only at the cost, that is, of making the metaphysics of Transcendental Idealism impossible to express.

The source of these tensions in the structure of transcendental idealism is, I want to suggest, its strategy of attempting to deny realism by discerning our contribution to the construction of reality. For, with this as our goal, we

---

[2] See her 1981.

embark on a mission of: (i) searching for the synthetic a priori; (ii) attempting to see our contribution as both necessary and contingent; (iii) seeing the contingency of our contribution in terms of the possibility of alternatives whose details cannot be conceived; (iv) explaining reality in terms of a metaphysics whose contours surpass our powers of description because it requires description of the world independently of our contribution; and (v) making sense of a kind of 'double think' in which empirical reality is both objective, and so independent of us, yet dependent on us. My claim here isn't that the framework of transcendental idealism cannot be braced against these strains. That would be an argument for another occasion, and is one I am not able (nor, as it happens, keen) to make. Rather, I simply want to notice the tensions in order to motivate the search for a contrasting way of pushing the (or an) idealist agenda.

4.3 Realism and Two Idealist Strategies

For the purposes of this discussion, the following captures my understanding of Realism:

> Representation is responsible (that is, in some appropriate sense, answerable) to a world independent of representation.

This is, of course, a vague and therefore inadequate definition. Here's one illustration of its inadequacy. As Strawson points out, the burden of Kant's necessary validation of a notion of objectivity is to secure a sense in which what we represent is distinct from our representation of it. So there must be a sense in which what we represent is independent of our representations. But despite this, there is also a sense in which what we represent is not independent of representation, because it is conditioned by the forms of our cognition. So, the notion of *independence* clearly awaits determination. The observation doesn't however discourage me. The point is that the definition of Realism suffices to direct attention to a set of possible concerns that the idealist might raise; making the debate precise will be a task that falls to the idealist. It'll be her obligation to make clear, for instance, in exactly what sense she denies the independence of the world from its representation. The definition of realism need not anticipate the various forms of idealist rejections of it. Another reason why I am not discouraged by the vagueness in the definition is that it suffices for what I am interested in right now. It enables me to point to two broad strategies of idealist denials of Realism.

The first strategy is to focus on the notion of independence. Pursuing this strategy will require making good some claim to the effect that the world is in some way dependent on representation. And, even if it's not the only way of doing so, a very obvious way of arguing this is to find our contribution to the form of reality. This takes us back to some version of Kantian Transcendental Idealism.[3]

The second strategy is to focus on the notion of responsibility: the idealist might argue that representation is not (in some appropriate sense) responsible to the world. Let me immediately qualify this suggestion, a qualification that is both an attempt to avoid absurdity and a move towards clarification. We form representations which are truth-evaluable; and, since truth-value depends on content *and* on how it is with the world, representation is responsible to the world. An idealist position which denies this is not worth taking seriously. So, I shall take the notion of responsibility to engage not with the truth-evaluation of contents, but with the formation of truth-evaluable contents. Specifically, the idealist will claim that the formation of such contents is not grounded in reality. Once again, I cannot pretend that this claim is clear. I hope to make some progress in clarifying it below, both through ostensible failures to avoid such 'grounding' and through a potential success. However, let's begin by noting an egregious failure. Referential theories of meaning or of mental content precisely ground the formation of truth-evaluable representations in worldly relations of reference (perhaps themselves reduced to, say, causal relations). So, such theories count as realist.[4] To be sure, I don't think that the idealist needs to *reject* theories of reference; rather she rejects theories of content *based on* theories of reference.

I have deliberately framed the discussion in terms of the notion of representation, taking it that this is neutral between psychological and linguistic representations. It'll now become important to me to distinguish psychological from linguistic representation. For what I want to suggest is that the second idealist strategy—denial of worldly grounding—appears hard to pursue when the focus is purely psychological (as it is in Kant); but more plausible when the shift to a linguistic focus is made.

---

[3] I think Dummett's anti-realism can be read as a different way of denying the independence claim. But rather than making out our contribution to the character of the world, Dummett argues that the only sense we can make of representation being responsible to the world requires that the world be conceived as knowable, and in that way, not independent of the knower.

[4] Unless the world itself is seen to be dependent on representation. But this takes us back to the first idealist strategy.

4.4 The Psychological Setting

A natural place to look for accounts of the formation of truth-evaluable mental content which eschews a worldly grounding is to those versions of Conceptual Role Semantics which focus on mental content rather than on linguistic meaning. Conceptual Role Semantics encompasses an extremely broad range of views; but among the variety on offer are some which give an account of a concept by focusing on its role in a thinker's cognitive economy, and so, seemingly, set worldly involvement to the side. To take an example, Field (1977) gives such an account by focusing on a thinker's subjective probability function as it applies to beliefs (or judgements) involving the concept. And to take another example, Peacocke (1992) individuates concepts in terms of their possession conditions, namely, a condition a thinker must fulfil in order to grasp the concept and which is explicated in terms of forms of transitions between judgements which a speaker finds primitively compelling (and whose status as such is causally explained by the thinker's sensitivity to such forms).[5]

The first problem I want to raise about such accounts depends on assuming that the psychological is what is shared by oneself and one's Twin Earth twin. It's a problem Field himself acknowledges and uses to motivate inclusion of a theory of reference as an additional component in the theory of content. I quote at some length:

> To know whether the German sentence 'Beethoven wohnte in Deutschland' is true, it is natural to say that we need to know only two things: first, whether Beethoven lived in Germany; and second, what the German sentence means. This condition is met by an account of meaning that includes referential meaning as one component. But it does not appear to be met by any pure conceptual-role account of meaning: given only (i) the conceptual role that the string of symbols 'Beethoven wohnte in Deutschland' has for a given speaker and (ii) the fact that Beethoven lived in Germany, it is not at all clear how to determine whether or not the German sentence is true. In fact, it seems evident that such a determination is in principle impossible: for whether the sentence is true depends on what the terms in it refer to, and what the terms refer to depends on factors outside the speaker's head. (For example, if Evans is right, it depends on the causal role that external objects and external properties have on the formation and retention of our beliefs involving

---

[5] Let me be clear: I'm mooting Field's and Peacocke's theories as accounts that an Idealist might find congenial; I am not suggesting either of these philosophers has any such interest—in fact, quite the reverse is true.

these terms.) Meaning is a matter not of conceptual role (i.e., role in individual psychology) but of sociological role: one aspect of the sociological role of a term is the role that term has in the psychologies of different members of a linguistic community; another aspect, irreducible to the first, is what physical object or physical property the term stands for. (Field 1977, 397–8)

Though Field speaks here of language, it is clear that the point would apply to any purely psychological account of the bearers of content: any account of concepts which focuses purely on their role in individual psychology will fail to include those factors external to the thinker which determine referential relations and, in so doing, render thoughts and beliefs truth-evaluable.

It would be possible to reject this train of thought by rejecting its narrow-minded assumption. So, I might insist that my twin and I differ in our psychologies precisely because, while I have water thoughts, he has twater thoughts. Adequately to deal with the scenarios which are thrown up by semantic externalist arguments, one would also have to allow that Putnam and the botanist expert to whom he defers in his use of 'beech' each have beech thoughts, despite the difference that these play in their individual psychologies.[6] It's hard to see that these differences in psychological contents can be accounted for on the basis of the kinds of mechanisms implicated in Conceptual Role Semantics, such things as primitively compelling transitions between contents and subjective probabilities. It is one thing to admit these differences (samenesses) in psychological content, quite another to explain them in terms acceptable to a requisite form of Conceptual Role Semantics.

Moreover the guide to mental content now seems to depend on competency in a public language, either in terms of a thinker's use of such a language (in making assertions and avowals) or in terms of the public attribution of mental states (or both). So this takes us from the psychological mode of framing the debate toward the linguistic mode.

I want to raise issues of normativity, in part because these will figure in our discussion of language and help make a contrast between the psychological and linguistic modes of framing the debate. A thinker, if she is indeed a *thinker*, must have her employment of concepts normatively constrained. Whence do these constraints arise? There is no judging (or thinking) nonsense: there are merely certain kinds of failures to judge (or, more broadly, to think). So there is no employment of a concept in ways which fail to make sense. Thus, there is no

---

[6] See Putnam 1975, 215–71.

normative constraint on this level of our use of concepts: where we seek impermissibility we merely find impossibility. On the other hand, uses of the concept in a range of inferences or judgements are not constrained by the individuation of the concept itself, because, unless more is said about conceptual role, these are simply held to determine the concept. So, the relevant constraint can only emerge via some requirement of fidelity to the content of the concept *as determined by those content-determining uses*. Peacocke argues that this requires a determination theory, namely a theory which maps the concept as individuated by its possession conditions onto a semantic value. If he's right, then normativity in concept use is grounded in worldly relations. Let's consider the point in slightly more detail.

Possession conditions are, for Peacocke, transitions which a thinker finds primitively compelling and whose being so is (causally) explicable in terms of their forms. These forms are not themselves normative. Let's consider his example of the possession conditions for the concept of addition. A thinker possesses the concept *plus* iff she finds transitions of the form:

$$\frac{(m\,C\,k) \text{ is } n}{(m\,C\,s(k)) \text{ is } s(n)}$$

primitively compelling and finds them so because of their form; and likewise for transitions of the form '$(m\,C\,0)$' is 'm' (cf. Peacocke 1992, 138; I've made minor alterations in the wording).[7] The first component of the possession condition corresponds to the recursive clause in the definition of addition—call it R—and the second component to its base—call it B.

To this Peacocke now adds a clause of a determination theory which assigns a semantic value to the concept thus individuated. So, the semantic value of the concept *plus* is that function for which instances of R are always truth-preserving and instances of B are true. It then turns out, unsurprisingly, that instances of R are always correct (in the sense of being valid) and instances of B correct (in the sense of being true). Normativity emerges via the determination theory; or, put differently, fidelity to the concept, as determined by its possession conditions, is managed by the determination theory.

Though Peacocke has his own particular take on the components of the story, I think the broad form is convincing. Possession of a concept is rightly linked to a certain capacity; then we need normativity to constrain uses of the concept. If the capacity is itself viewed in normative terms, we need to explain whence the normativity arises. No plausible answer presents itself

---

[7] 'm', 'k', and 'n' are numerals and 's' is the successor function.

on Peacocke's account; so we need to look elsewhere. Since Peacocke views correctness, as is appropriate for representational success, in semantic terms, the obvious and presumably the only place to consider is semantic theory or, as he calls it, the theory of determination. Crudely, when viewed in the individualistic mode forced on us by the psychological setting, there is no alternative but to ground the normativity of concepts in their semantic valuation. The second idealist strategy thus seems unfeasible on this approach.

I want to conclude that the second idealist strategy—denying worldly grounding—is a difficult, perhaps impossible, path to tread when the debate is framed psychologically. Let me turn then to the linguistic mode of prosecution.

4.5 The Linguistic Setting

I begin this attempt to explicate and to motivate a Linguistic Idealism[8] by turning to Anscombe's classic discussion of the issue as she sees it in Wittgenstein's philosophy. I too shall want to make use of Wittgenstein's writings but will do so in a way that is more influenced by Hacker than by Anscombe.

The question before us is whether and how we can motivate a denial of the claim that meanings are grounded in the nature of things. As we are often reminded, it is a question Wittgenstein puts to himself in *Zettel*:

We have a colour system as we have a number system.
Do the systems reside in *our* nature or in the nature of things?
How are we to put it?—*Not* in the nature of numbers or colours. (1967, §357)

We seem to have Wittgenstein considering the second idealistic strategy and, somehow, favouring it. But how might we follow him in this?[9]

---

[8] One might wonder about relocating the *Transcendental* Idealist claim to the linguistic setting. There is, perhaps, a strategy here—one we find in Sellars and Brandom—which sees meaning as the product of inferential relations, which, since meaning-determining, are given a priori, but are substantive too. I don't think that this delivers anything worth calling idealism, though, since, as Brandom argues, the role of logical vocabulary (and certainly *a* role) is to make these inferential commitments explicit as claims and thus brought into the business of asking for and giving reasons. So here the alternatives to these substantive but a priori inferential commitments are easily contemplated, discussed and, perhaps, adopted. The point is that, on this conception, the substantive a priori features of language are seen as, in effect, making claims about the nature of the world, which we can come to see as plainly false.

[9] Let me be clear that, although I'll be drawing on Wittgenstein's writings, and those of his commentators, I shall not be defending a reading of Wittgenstein.

Anscombe's 'test question' is 'Does this existence, or this truth, depend upon human linguistic practice?' (Anscombe 1981, 116). She argues that Wittgenstein has different views about different existences or truths: ordinary objects such as shoes and ships and sealing wax do not so depend; essences and metaphysical necessities, she says, '*seem* to be regarded as grammatical rules' (1981, 121); promises, rules, and rights are also dependent on conventions incorporated into language. I'm not now concerned with the merits of these particular arguments (though I'll return to borrow from them later); my concern is rather with Anscombe's 'test question'.

I don't think that the Linguistic Idealist is making a claim about the ontological status of a range of objects. If she were, and if she were not to 'make herself look ridiculous'[10] in the eyes of science, then, since science contemplates a vast array of phenomena independent of human observers, her idealism would have to be extremely limited, as it is. The more ambitious alternative would be to reconstruct a Kantian distinction between the empirical and the transcendental, so that viewed empirically objects are independent of observers, but viewed transcendentally they are not. But this choice—either restriction of one's idealism or the metaphysics of transcendental idealism—is not forced. Rather the limitation that the idealist should accept is in her claim. Her claim is just about the grounding of linguistic practice in a prior ontology; not about the ontological status of inclusions in that ontology. Put differently, the question is about whether that ontology provides a substantive constraint on the adequacy of a linguistic practice. Denying that it does so need not entail denying the existence of objects in that ontology independent of the practice. In short, to accept that fallacious entailment is just to assimilate the second idealist strategy to the first. It is a conflation we ought not to tolerate.

Anscombe's discussion goes on to consider the kinds of irresoluble disagreements in world views that Wittgenstein describes in *On Certainty*. The kinds of case at issue are cases where interlocutors differ in what counts as bedrock. So, for the one it is a real possibility that someone has been to the moon; for the other not. Wittgenstein's claim is that if one were to encounter this kind of disagreement one could not respond by providing reasons which buttress one's putative knowledge. Rather the difference is deeper, concerning as it does what holds firm for each disputant. This is not simply a matter of knowledge and reason-giving, but the frame of the whole business of providing reasons; what counts as a reason depends upon the frame and so elements of the frame are not themselves supported by reasons. The disagreement is thus not amenable

---

[10] See Winch 1958, 2.

to being settled by rational exchange; rather, it becomes a matter of persuasion, of changing a person's way of seeing the world, perhaps by making apparent the pragmatic advantages of the shift. I am not sure why Anscombe places this discussion in the wider context of her investigation of Linguistic Idealism. Wittgenstein's concern is clearly not meaning—since disputants genuinely disagree; they agree on meanings—but on the mechanics of knowledge claims. So let me draw back from this particular discussion and think instead about the general role of contemplating alternatives.

It is tempting to think that if a linguistic practice is not grounded in the nature of things then it is not forced on us by something external and so admits of alternatives. And, indeed, Wittgenstein is wont to describe alternative linguistic communities which have, for example, very different ways of measuring. Wittgenstein's aims here are the subject of much debate; but it seems to me that he is attempting to shake a presumption that the practice is constrained by a requirement to reflect extra-linguistic reality. Rather it is constrained by one's 'form of life', which includes one's natural inclinations, interests, needs, and saliencies. So, it seems to be a way of pursuing my favoured linguistic-idealist approach. Perhaps so. But let me note the following. First, if the approach is successful, it is sufficient for making a linguistic-idealist claim. But it is not necessary. So, it is only one way among others of pursuing that idealist strategy. Second, it has its dangers. The danger is that it threatens, if we add flesh to the notion of a form of life, to develop into one or another version of relativism. And, if we do not spell out the alternatives, then it is not the mere abstract possibility of such alternatives that substantiates Linguistic Idealism, but the rejection of a linguistic grounding in the nature of things and a replacement of it with observations about how a practice is moulded by natural and social history. I think we do better to concentrate simply on that argument, without the titillation provided by piquant examples of outlandish alternatives.

The version of Linguistic Idealism I want to investigate claims that it is mistaken to invoke, in our account of the formation of truth-evaluable contents, semantic relations to the world. Earlier, I noted that, on the psychological construal of this position, this (namely, not invoking semantic relations to the world) is a hard trick to pull off, since focusing on individualistic psychology fails to deliver genuinely truth-evaluable representations; and, in addition, fails to generate adequate normative constraints on a thinker's employment of her concepts. These are not obviously problems for the linguistic construal of the idealist position. Indeed, I submit that we have promising models for how to fill out the position. The combination of Brandom's (1998) semantic deflationism with his normative pragmatic account of content will, it would seem, fit the bill nicely. The point is that once we migrate out of the individualistic psychological setting, we have a means of normatively constraining practice and of locating practice in a worldly setting, and so allowing for the development of the usual gamut of truth-evaluable representation. Here I won't defend Brandom's broad approach, nor any of its details. Instead, I want to offer an argument for Linguistic Idealism and then experiment with some ideas about how its insights might be realized.

4.6 Model-Theoretic Indeterminacy

The argument for Linguistic Idealism I find in model-theoretic indeterminacy results. Here my inspiration is, of course, Putnam, though I shan't be defending either his account or my account as a reading of his. Let me present the framework of the core of my argument. I'll then fill in its detail and finally urge my linguistic-idealist conclusion.

> Premise 1: Reference is a notion used to think systematically about our pre-theoretic notion of aboutness.
> Premise 2: Aboutness is not indeterminate.
> Sub-conclusion 1: Reference is not indeterminate. (From 1 and 2)
> Premise 3: Model theory is a formal theory about a technical notion which we'll call semantic value. (Stipulative choice of terminology)
> Sub-conclusion 2: Model-theoretic indeterminacy reveals that semantic value is indeterminate. (From 3, given Putnam's use of the indeterminacy results)
> Conclusion: Reference is not semantic-value.

I'll speak now to each premise in turn. First, let's think about reference and aboutness. Many, including Davidson (1984, essay 16) and Gaskin (2021, 57–65), argue that reference is a purely theoretical notion, the latter arguing strongly against attempts to connect it with aboutness. Rejecting the pre-theoretic notion of reference and aboutness as multifarious and indefinite, Gaskin recommends employment of 'reference' or 'semantic value' as theoretical terms in linguistic theory constrained by success in interpretation. Davidson doesn't make the point in quite these terms, but there's every reason to think the two would march in step here. The issue is too large to address fully here; so, let me register a difference of view. I think one might either see one's task in the philosophy of language as driven by an attempt to gain this kind of external perspective on our practice, or one might see it as a reflective exercise, as an attempt to make the workings of our practice clear to ourselves. When seen in the latter way the enterprise is distinctively Kantian, and Dummett is surely its most eloquent proponent.[11] And, as he recommends, the basis of philosophical explanation of meaning is mundane explanations of meaning supplied within the practice, which are then pressed with a rigour and systematicity that *is* theoretical in aim, the aim being to understand not just an element of practice but the practice as a whole. So unclarity in the pre-theoretic notion of aboutness is not crippling to the project, but, in part, motivates it, since it reveals why we need a systematic approach. I'll return in a moment to the attempt to sugar the pill of referential indeterminacy. But let's move on to Premise 2: aboutness is not indeterminate. To suppose that, in general, aboutness is indeterminate would be to concede that we do not know what we're talking about. Meaning determines what we are talking about; so, if aboutness were indeterminate, then so too would be meaning. This is a brand of meaning scepticism which we ought strenuously to avoid. Premise 3 is stipulative and merely creates a space between the formal treatment of semantic value, and the notion of reference built on the pre-theoretic notion of aboutness. The second conclusion all but follows from the indeterminacy results, such as the premutation argument recruited by Putnam; but not quite. Here I think that the way Putnam uses the argument is important. For he shows its relevance to reflection on natural language. So let me very briefly outline Putnam's point.

Putnam argues that if we take a description of a natural language, which is as non-miraculously rich as you like, short of detailing semantic relations, then the model-theoretic results show that semantic relations for the language are radically indeterminate.[12] What model theory shows is that given the syntax of a formal language, indefinitely many assignments of semantic value can be reconciled with stipulations of truth-values for sentences, even with stipulations of their truth-values across all possible worlds. This might seem to have no direct relevance to natural language, because one supposes that constraints on our use of natural language in context suffice to determine semantic values, that is, suffice to determine the intended interpretation. However, Putnam

---

[11] See, for example, his 'Can Analytical Philosophy be Systematic, and Ought It to Be?', essay 25 in his 1978.
[12] See 'Models and Reality' (1983, 1–25) and chapter 2 of *Reason, Truth and History* (1981, 22–47).

shows that, short of helping oneself to miraculous non-naturalistic intentionality, nothing, neither idealized operational nor theoretical constraints, can do this work. Such constraints merely limit the form of the theory expressed in language and, given the Context Principle, fix truth-value assignments to sentences; and these are grist to the mill of the indeterminacy results.

The conclusion thus follows: reference is not semantic value. As I've made clear, the conclusion only follows under the premise that reference ought to mesh with aboutness and therefore that referential indeterminacy would be repugnant. At this point I can say a few words about why, even when construed as a theoretical notion, referential indeterminacy is not a palatable option. I focus on Gaskin. Gaskin (2021, 68) employs a distinction between an object language and metalanguage, and notes that from the object-language perspective there is no indeterminacy about what we mean, while from the metalinguistic perspective there is indeterminacy of reference. The indeterminacy is acceptable since from the metalinguistic perspective we are aiming at an adequate theory of interpretation, which isn't jeopardized by referential indeterminacy. The distinction between object- and metalanguage is, however, hard to impose on an unregimented natural language. So, if the aim is to understand our own practice, it is not an easy distinction to which to help oneself. Additionally, it is hard to see how the two perspectives cohere. Admittedly they are being adopted from different linguistic points of view; but they are contemplated by a single mind. How does such a mind accept both that 'cat' and 'cherry' differ in meaning but that 'cat' might equally be taken to refer to cats or to cherries? And what linguistic point of view enables Gaskin to talk about the relation between all object-language and metalinguistic points of view? So, even if it is a purely theoretical notion, I am not at all sure that referential indeterminacy is acceptable. Nonetheless, I reject it here not primarily for these reasons but because I am insisting on basing reference on aboutness.

How then do we resist the assimilation of reference to semantic value? I think we do this by rejecting the pretence of model theory.[13] That pretence is that we can, as Putnam suggests, describe fully the use of language in context and then ask for its referential grounding. Once we do that, we think of language as one structure and the world as another and then ask how they fit together. The indeterminacy results show that there can be no answer (or, better, that there are too many answers) to this question. The Realist precisely endorses the model theoretician's pretence; it is denied by

---

[13] I do not deny that it is often a useful and revealing pretence.

Linguistic Idealism, according to which we cannot make sense of holding language, in this way, responsible to the world.

I don't claim that this is a conclusive argument; rather, I hope, it maps out a not implausible route to Linguistic Idealism. Let us suppose that we agree with this suggestion. Accepting that language and the world are indissolubly linked is not to provide an account of how they are so. For this aspect of my argument I want to move from model theory to Wittgensteinian ideas about the autonomy of grammar, ideas which precisely deny that language is responsible to the nature of things.

4.7 The Autonomy of Grammar

Wittgenstein rather delightfully notes that 'Language must speak for itself' (*PG*, §2), drawing this as a conclusion from the observation that

> What is spoken can only be explained in language, and so in this sense language itself cannot be explained. (*PG*, §2)[14]

He is a trifle more expansive in the *Philosophical Remarks*:

> [A]ny kind of explanation of a language presupposes a language already. And, in a certain sense, the use of language is something that cannot be taught, i.e. I cannot use language to teach it in the way in which language could be used to teach someone to play the piano.—And that of course is just another way of saying: I cannot use language to get outside language. (*PR*, §6)

And he goes on,

> I do not call a rule of representation a convention if it can be justified in propositions: propositions describing what is represented and showing that the representation is adequate. Grammatical conventions cannot be justified by describing what is represented. Any such description already presupposes the grammatical rules. That is to say, if anything is to count as nonsense in the grammar which is to be justified, then it cannot at the same time pass for sense in the grammar of the propositions that justify it (etc.). (*PR*, §7)

---

[14] Also at §3: 'One can say that meaning drops out of language; because what a proposition means is told by yet another proposition.' (Thanks to the editor for pointing this out.)

It's worth moving quite slowly through this collection of ideas, despite their seemingly obvious appeal to a kind of circularity. The first quote from *PR* (and that from *PG*) focuses on explanation and on what we might call first-order, practitioners' use of language. The focus here is on explanation and on the limits placed on linguistic attempts to employ language to explain language, and is reminiscent of *TLP* 3.263: 'The meanings of primitive signs can be explained by means of elucidations. Elucidations are propositions that contain the primitive signs. So they can only be understood if the meanings of those signs are already known.' But the second quote hints at something quite different; it gestures towards the possibility of reflective attempts to justify—rather than explain—a practice. And it speaks directly to my concern here about grounding language in the nature of things. But the distinction between explanation and justification isn't patent and doesn't align with that between practitioners' and reflective perspectives. For what serves as an explanation of use can be used in a justification of one's use. In *PI*, Wittgenstein makes the point about practitioners' use in terms of justification:

'How am I able to obey a rule?'—if this is not a question about causes, then it is a question about the justification for my following the rule in the way that I do.
If I have exhausted the justification I have reached bedrock, and my spade is turned. Then I am inclined to say: 'This is simply what I do'. (*PI*, §217)

Nonetheless I think it is important to think through the somewhat distinct range of considerations that apply *in* the practice and when reflecting *on* the practice.

As far as practitioners are concerned, one might suppose that ostensive definitions would be the most important technique for fixing a relation between words and world and thereby conferring a meaning on the former. In this connection, there are two main lines of thought in Wittgenstein's later writings: the first concerns the role of ostensive teaching, runs through much of the opening sections of *PI*, and is present in *PG* (e.g., pp. 60–3); the other, about ostension and samples, is more prominently present in *PG* (but see also *PI*, §50). I'll be brief about the first because this is well-worn territory and less pertinent to my issue of grounding language in the nature of things.

Wittgenstein rejects the foundational role attributed to ostensive definition in Augustinian pictures of language because successful ostension requires considerable linguistic stage setting: in particular, it needs to be clear for the learner and so made clear by the teacher what kind of object is being ostended. The Augustinian picture seems to concede as much, conceiving of the learner as having to arrive at the appropriate determination by means of conjectures. But this distorts language learning, by portraying learning one's first language as akin to learning a second language (see *PI*, §32). So, though ostensive teaching has a role in learning and teaching language, it isn't a linguistically naïve procedure which forges the connections between words and worldly items. In other words, it isn't a procedure which can, independently of language, link words to worldly items, themselves given independently of language.

Perhaps more intriguingly Wittgenstein writes that '[t]he ostensive definition may be regarded as a rule for translation of a gesture language into a word language' (*PG*, §45). Hacker (1986, 186–7), plausibly, unpacks this as the claim that ostensive definition fails to forge the link between word and object, but instead forges links *within* the ambit of representation; it is a 'rule of *translation*'. And this he presents as a primary illustration of the autonomy of grammar. Let me illustrate briefly my understanding of the claim before I attempt to discuss and to link it with other concerns. The idea seems to be that when, for instance, in teaching the meaning of 'blue' I point to an appropriate object and say 'This is blue', I am not making an assertion about the object—though, I think importantly, in other circumstances I might be doing so with the very same words (see *PR*, §6). Rather the object is being taken into one's system of representation; it is an object of comparison. The blue object, in being used as a sample, applies to other objects—so can be used as an instrument of predication—and, given that one knows this use of a sample, provides a means of introducing the word 'blue'—which then can itself be used as an instrument of predication.

I want now to consider an objection to this reading of Wittgenstein's example. In some ways, the phenomenon he describes is reminiscent (again) of a view in the *Tractatus*. There we are given examples of spatial pictures which represent spatial states of affairs. The spatial form of the picture mirrors that of the state of affairs, and once the elements of the picture are put in correspondence with the objects of the latter the former is enabled to represent the latter. So too it seems here. The sample inhabits a certain 'space'—in this case the space of colours. And because of its location in that space it is enabled to represent a range of items. So, in our example, the sample is blue and, because of its nature *as such*, it is able to represent (or perhaps better, apply to) a range of items, viz., the blue things. The problem is that this seems a beautiful illustration of just what I earlier aimed to deny, namely, a grounding of meaning in the nature of things.

There are a few things to say here. First, the position I wanted to deny was one which claimed that meanings can be grounded in the nature of the things represented. That isn't so here; meaning is grounded in the nature of the thing which represents. Perhaps, but in Tractarian terminology it's the *shared* form that is essential to representation; and so realist readings of the *Tractatus* can argue that representation is grounded in the form of the represented things. More pertinently, in the *PG* Wittgenstein goes on to argue that samples are not essential to connecting language and reality. Instead, he seems to think that they have, at most, a causal/psychological function but are not essential to language. And, perhaps more importantly, he argues that systems of samples do not determine their own use; rather, any number of uses are possible: a sample of blue can be used to represent yellow etc. We determine a use, despite the undoubted fact that using a blue sample to represent blue is overwhelmingly natural. As Wittgenstein notes in the *Tractatus*, 'every picture is *at the same time* a logical one' (2.182); so, though the logic of representation might exploit shared spatial form, it is the abstract isomorphism that matters. And so here too we might say all representation is conventional, even if the convention exploits natural facts.

Wittgenstein draws out this equipollence between the word and the sample by drawing attention to the similarity in role between, say, a sample of red and the word 'rouge', when each is used to explain the meaning of 'red' to a suitably qualified learner; given an understanding of 'rouge' one can exploit this in explaining 'red' as synonymous with 'rouge', and, given a capacity to use samples appropriately, the sample can be used to explain the meaning of 'red'. Neither is essential.

> Can one perhaps say, ['primary' signs, samples] don't really any longer need to be *understood*?—If that means that they no longer need to be *interpreted*, that goes for words too; if it means, they *cannot* be further interpreted, then it's false.[15] (*PG*, §48)

So, ostensive teaching of the meaning of words is not in tension with the autonomy of grammar; rather when seen aright it illustrates its autonomy. It makes vivid too my lesson from model theoretic indeterminacy, namely, that model theory distorts things by setting up the world and language as separate structures. For here the very same thing—the sample of blue—can both

---

[15] Wittgenstein begins the section by talking about the interpretation of written and spoken signs by ostensive definition and then about ostensive definition as a rule for translation from gesture to word language. So, it's likely that he is working with a notion of interpretation which he uses later, namely, that an interpretation is 'the substitution of one expression of the rule for another' (*PI*, §201; to which I return below).

appear on the linguistic side of things, as a means of representation, and as an object referred to.[16] So the world cannot be set over against a separate linguistic structure. Wittgenstein makes my point:

> One is inclined to make a distinction between rules of grammar that set up 'a connection between language and reality' and those that do not. A rule of the first kind is 'this colour is called "red"',—a rule of the second kind is '~~p = p'. With regard to this distinction there is a common error: *language is not something that is first given and then fitted onto reality.* (PG, §46, my emphasis)

So I think it would be a mistake to read the autonomy of grammar as a claim which separates language from the world, as a claim which replaces responsibility to the world with some kind of linguistic freedom from the world. No; the point surely is that language is based in normative practice which itself is world-involving. Linguistic rules cannot be adequately described except in world-involving terms. But this doesn't mean the world grounds or justifies the rules; rather the world is constitutively integrated into the rules.

Let me leave there matters relating to practitioners' justifications and explanations and turn to reflective justifications of language. There are three points to be made: (i) the justification of language by describing what it represents exploits the very same features of language we aim to justify and so is circular; (ii) the kinds of proposition developed in justification are not statements of fact but what Wittgenstein calls grammatical propositions; and (iii) language has no function in terms of which its adequacy can be gauged.

The first point is mentioned in the quotation above from PR. Here is Wittgenstein returning to the point in PG:

> The rules of grammar cannot be justified by shewing that their application makes a representation agree with reality. For this justification would itself have to describe what it represented. And if something can be said in the justification and is permitted by its grammar—why shouldn't it also be permitted in the grammar I am trying to justify? Why shouldn't both forms of expression have the same freedom? And how could what the one says restrict what the other can say? (PG, §124)

It's worth noting a difference between this quote and the one in PR. In the latter he seems to assume that the very same grammatical rules will be invoked in

---

[16] This is not the same as being able to refer to words. The point here, as I mention in the text, is that the very same form of words can employ the sample as a representation and as an object referred to.

the justification. Here he separates the grammar to be justified from that in which the justification is given. The point is easier to make where there is no distinction between grammars. For Wittgenstein very plausibly seems to be observing that there can be no mismatch between what we might call object languages and metalanguages. If the metalanguage succeeds in representing then so too does the object language, independently of what *else* is said in the metalanguage. If the object language fails to represent then so too does the metalanguage.

Here—in *PG*—the quote ends with three questions. The first two drive a similar point. Wittgenstein seems to be saying that if such a justification could be given then it wouldn't be needed. For if it could be given, it would have to make sense. And if it made sense—succeeded in representing a portion of reality—then there'd be no reason for questioning the representative success of the original grammar. One might counter thus: suppose the first-order grammar purports to represent Xs; the second-order grammar, by representing Xs, explains *how* the first-order grammar represents Xs. And, in explaining how it does so, it justifies its doing so. So, this explanation is not nugatory. I think Wittgenstein's third question now becomes pertinent; because, if such justifications can succeed, then they can also fail. But his question is: how could this be? How can what we say in the one grammar—which represents Xs—restrict the other grammar's representational success?

Well, a justification for a grammar might be aimed at addressing a number of different concerns. One might be troubled by the sceptical thought that reference to Xs is illusory; in which case the justification seems to fail for the reasons Wittgenstein describes. But one might have no real concern *that* the grammar refers to Xs but want an explanation of *how* it does so. In that case it is far from obvious that it fails. The distinction bears resemblance to Dummett's distinction between explanatory and suasive justifications (Dummett 1978, 296). So, the best way of reading Wittgenstein here is to say that he is discussing justification as focused on a kind of sceptical worry about representational success. We can't pretend to move outside language and question whether a certain kind of representational success occurs nor satisfy ourselves that it does. For we cannot ask whether we can talk about Xs nor affirm that we do, without talking about Xs. And so, both the question and the affirmation are valueless. However, we *can* talk about how reference to Xs is an important and useful part of our lives, and about how, for instance, such talk meshes with our natural history. That kind of explanatory endeavour is not—nor should it be—a casualty of Wittgenstein's remarks.

Surely there is a non-circular way of pursuing questions about representational success by adopting a metalinguistic perspective. If one took a certain ontology to be privileged then one might ask of a grammar which purportedly refers to Xs, whether reference to Xs can be justified in terms of this privileged ontology; whether, say, reference to moral properties or numbers can be justified in terms of reference to a naturalistically acceptable ontology. I think that this version of the question needs to be ruled out by a reinterpreted Copernican Turn which rejects a privileged ontology, taking ontology instead to be determined solely by the theory of meaning—not by a prior commitment to, for example, naturalism; rather the object is the object of representation. Error theories would thus be rejected, because they raise scepticism about reference to an ontology by privileging a certain other ontology. So interpreted, the Copernican Turn becomes of a piece with the Linguistic Turn.

The final riposte Wittgenstein considers is that one might justify language by pointing to reality. He dismisses pointing as delivering justification, for its lack of 'multiplicity' (*PG*, §134), admitting only that it might reveal the cause of our speaking one way rather than another but as failing to provide a reason. It would be hard to argue that Wittgenstein's point here is obvious, but presumably he is worried about how pointing, independently of a good deal of referential, and thus question-begging, stage setting, has the specificity of a justification; and how mere confrontation with the world can deliver justification. I think again he is noticing that successful ostension is not more basic than, but relies on the same mechanisms as, linguistic reference.

Wittgenstein also questions the kinds of justification we are apt to give. We cannot justify, for example, the first-third personal asymmetry of talk about sensations by appeal to the nature of sensations, nor of colour talk by appeal to the nature of colours, because the propositions which we thereby construct, though sharing a form with fact-stating (empirical) propositions, are merely grammatical. So, these are not justifications for our way of speaking by appeal to the world, but mere encapsulations of our ways of speaking. For example, to insist that only I know that I am in pain is not to have an insight into the (metaphysical) nature of pain, but to state a feature about the grammar of 'pain', viz., that first-personal avowals of pain have a certain authority and are not subject to the same kinds of error as are third-personal attributions of pain. Similarly, to say that white is lighter than black is not to have an insight into the nature of colours, but to state a fact about our use of colour vocabulary. Essence for Wittgenstein is not embedded in the world but is a product of grammar.

The point about colour links with the earlier discussion of samples. It is worth dwelling on it for a moment.[17] Consider two circular patches, a white one, A, and a black one, B:

Here we might say patch A is lighter than patch B, explaining a perfectly mundane empirical fact about two uniformly coloured patches. But each patch might be used as a sample and, when they are used as such, we cannot say that the colour of patch A is lighter than the colour of patch B, nor therefore that white is lighter than black. At least, we could not say this and be taken to be saying something about the world; we would be stating a grammatical proposition. Likewise, we could use the fact that patch A is lighter than patch B as a sample of being *lighter than* and use this in explaining that a particular white patch is lighter than a red patch.[18]

Let's consider the enterprise of trying to justify pain talk by appeal to the essential nature of pains. Doing so would involve talking about pains and discussing their essential properties. But, in doing this, we would be imposing the very same framework as is employed in mundane talk about pains. So, it would justify, for example, the first-third personal asymmetry of pain-talk by detailing the first-third personal asymmetry of pains, which was already present in the grammar used in that detailing enterprise. The project would be circular.

We might also recommend Wittgenstein's conception of essences as expressed by grammar by raising concerns about Realist construals of essences. What would it be to be confronted with an essence in being confronted with an object? And, if indeed confrontation with an object brings in its train confrontation with essences, which essence, on a given occasion, is relevant to the meaning of a word? Is the donkey over there presenting the essence of being a donkey, being an equine or being a mammal? There is no answer till we decide what kind of object it is being taken to be; but, since the object's kind is co-ordinate with which rule we take to be in operation, there

---

[17] See Wittgenstein *RFM*, I, §105.

[18] I think this phenomenon, viz. cases in which an assertion can be taken as an assertion of ordinary empirical fact and again as fixing a meaning, is important too in Wittgenstein's philosophy of mathematics. There he seems to observe that reporting that there are two walnuts and three pecan nuts, and five nuts in all, can be taken to be a statement of empirical fact (the upshot of an experiment) and can be taken to be the result of calculation, as fixing that 2 + 3 = 5 (see, inter alia, *RFM*, I, §§ 95–100; III, §§22–4, 69–76; IV, §§51–3; VI, §§5, 23, 36; VII §§1–4, 17).

is no non-question-begging answer to this question. As Anscombe remarks, since we now need to appeal to the meaning of the word to decide this question, meaning is not grounded in essence; quite the reverse.

Earlier I applauded Field's reminder of the lessons of semantic externalism. But, as is well known, these seem to justify a realism about some essences: the essence of water is a matter of its chemical constitution, irrespective of anything to do with language. So, is there a tension between my endorsements of semantic externalism and of Wittgenstein's linguistic construal of essences?

I don't know of anywhere Wittgenstein specifically addresses the issue. So, a response needs to find its way speculatively and indirectly. A first thing to note is that Kripkean statements of essence, for example, 'Water is H_2O', differ in important ways from typical cases of grammatical propositions, statements such as 'Nothing is simultaneously red and green all over', 'You can be mistaken about my being in pain; I cannot.' The latter but not the former are knowable a priori, and knowability a priori might well be a plausible requirement to place on something's being a grammatical proposition. Certainly, there seems to be a difference in discussing whether or not something can be red and green all over, at the same time, and whether or not water is H_2O. In the former case the mistaken view is senseless; in the latter case it is denial of a necessary truth but is surely not senseless. So, a swift response might be just to put statements of Kripkean essence in a separate category from Wittgensteinian grammatical propositions, and thus both accept the lessons of semantic externalism and learn too the Wittgensteinian lesson of the autonomy of grammar. Moreover, the upshot of combining these two sets of lessons would not be anodyne, since Witttgensteinian grammatical propositions still form an interesting enough bag to focus a substantive claim that grammar is not justified by the nature of things.

I think, though, that we can do a little more to bring Kripkean statements of essence closer to Wittgenstein's conception of grammatical propositions. Let's focus on the term 'water' and treat it as typical of natural-kind terms. Plausibly, 'water' is introduced by demonstration of a sample, exploiting a criterion of identity: 'Water is the same stuff as this'. And here, by 'same stuff' we mean: *stuff with the same chemical composition.*[19] So, in the Wittgensteinian way of looking at this, the sample becomes an instrument of representation, and determines an extension for 'water' by means of a criterion of identity, which renders our use responsible to the sample's underlying composition, whether or not this is known. So, the statement 'Water is H_2O' emerges in this way:

---

[19] Note that I assume that the community must contain speakers with a grasp of the relevant criterion of identity. So, a community lacking a science of chemistry would not be able to have this concept of *water*.

1. This [the sample] is H_2O.
2. Water is the same stuff as this [the sample].
3. So water is H_2O.

Here the second premise is given by a conferral of meaning; and the first is not a statement about the world but a statement about the sample, an instrument of representation and, importantly, about that feature of it employed in representation. The conclusion of the argument—the Kripkean statement of essence—is thus, in a certain sense, purely the product of our use of language: (i) our choice of an instrument of representation (a sample), (ii) our choice about how to use that instrument in representation, and (iii) its nature. Given that our choice in (ii) may hold our use responsible to an unknown nature there is no surprise that the conclusion is knowable only a posteriori; but given that it emerges purely from our representational activity, there's also a sense in which it counts as grammatical. So, in this extended sense, the Kripkean lesson can be accepted and we can also see statements of Kripkean essence as grammatical.

Let me explore the curious status of (1) a little further. The colour of a colour sample, the shape of a sample of shape, and the length of a unit of measurement (for length) are for Kripke contingent features of the object which it is known to have a priori; 'The metre rule is one metre long' is known a priori, yet it states a contingent fact. But Wittgenstein says that

> There is *one* thing of which one can say neither that it is one metre long, nor that it is not one metre long, and that is the standard metre in Paris.—But this is, of course, not to ascribe any extraordinary property to it, but only to mark its peculiar role in the language-game of measuring with a metre rule.—Let us imagine samples of colour being preserved in Paris like the standard metre. We define: 'sepia' means the colour of the standard sepia which is there kept hermetically sealed. Then it will make no sense to say of this sample either that it is of this colour or that it is not.
> We can put it like this: This sample is an instrument of the language used in ascriptions of colour. In this language-game it is not something that is represented, but is a means of representation. (*PI*, §50)

Here I don't think that Wittgenstein is saying that we cannot say 'This [the metre rule] is one metre long' but that, when we do so, we are stating a grammatical proposition which fixes the meaning of 'metre'. Nor is the conclusion that the metre rule is something whose length—even when length is conceived in metres—is something which somehow evades the language-game; quite the reverse. To say that the metre rule is longer/shorter/neither longer nor shorter than *X*, is to say *X* is less than/more than/exactly a metre in length. Precisely analogous remarks apply to the use of colour samples; and indeed apply, I think, in the case of natural-kind samples too. The difference is this: in each case we incorporate into the functioning of the language-game a mode of comparison, or, equivalently, a criterion of identity. In the cases of colour and length the mode of comparison is incorporated into the language-game and is, in a certain sense, final. We simply inspect an object to see whether it is the same colour as another; likewise to determine relative lengths. Though we might make mistakes, there is no further court of appeal, and so no analogue of (1). In the case of natural-kind terms there is. Though we *may* use (Putnamian) stereotypes to compare two bits of stuff, the underlying criterion of identity appeals to chemical composition. So, whilst in the cases of length and colour there is nothing to be said about the feature of the sample which is employed by the language-game as a mode of comparison, in the case of natural kinds there is. That is the role of (1). So, though (1) is knowable only a posteriori its assertion is not like asserting, 'This [the sample] is in Paris', because (1) shapes the language-game, but the latter does not. So, in a broad sense, (1) is grammatical. Put differently, it isn't just that (1) exposes a feature of the sample but that it exposes that feature we fix on in making comparisons, that feature we are using to determine sameness.[20]

Another way of attempting to ground grammar in the world is by testing whether or not it fulfils its purpose. Wittgenstein, however, denies that language has a purpose,

> Language is not defined for us as an arrangement fulfilling a definite purpose.... Language is of interest to me as a phenomenon and not as a means to a particular end. (*PG*, §137)

He suggests a number of things wrong with the alternative, for instance, with claims such as that the purpose of language is the communication of thoughts. Such a conception imposes a false uniformity on the ways in which language functions (see *PI*, §491). It also pretends to have latched onto a definite purpose but only by failing to take note of the variety of things that might fall under the description 'communicating a thought'; and failing too to notice that 'the concept of language is contained in the concept of communication' (*PG*, §140). Elsewhere he ruminates on the connection between the grammar of 'invent' and that of 'language'. Conceding that we might invent a language for a particular purpose, he also talks about alternative inventions of language: extending or constructing analogies of existing linguistic systems (see *PG*,

---

[20] My thanks to the editor for pressing me on my view here.

§139). The point I think he's driving at here is one about what one might call the natural history of language. To impose a definite purpose on linguistic systems is to see them as if they were invented to serve such purposes; but their history is entirely different. In cases where he contemplates language arising in response to an attempt to achieve a purpose, Wittgenstein thinks of language as akin to a machine constructed with a certain goal in mind. Like the machine, such a language will depend on certain underlying causal processes, a psychological mechanism. The simplest such cases, he conjectures, are languages based solely on commands—so akin to the builders' language of *PI*. Here uttered words are 'designed' to bring about certain effects and the language can be appraised in terms of whether or not it enables one to bring about desired effects. But any such construal of language falls short of accommodating meaning. Wittgenstein imagines an apparently meaningless combination of words (*PG*, §§136–7). Can its being nonsense be understood in terms of language, the mechanism? Well, if it can, this is not because it might have no discernible effect, since it may well have one; the hearer may, for instance, simply stand and gape; and not because this effect may not have been desired, since it may well have been the desired effect. Despite their inexplicability in these functional terms, the bounds of sense exist in language; and the bounds may themselves be exploited in a variety of projects. How is it possible to comprehend this? Only, it would seem, by seeing language as an autonomous system of meanings that is irreducible to particular purposes, but at the service of an indefinite range of purposes, where these may exploit either meanings or their limits. Put differently, the bounds of sense—and so the concept of language—vanish on an instrumental construal of linguistic activity.

Let me mention one final point, perhaps the most profound of those rehearsed here. In his meditations on following a rule Wittgenstein concludes that our following a rule is captured solely in our policing of one another's use.

> This was our paradox: no course of action could be determined by a rule, because every course of action can be made out to accord with the rule. The answer was: if everything can be made out to accord with the rule, then it can also be made out to conflict with it. And so there would be neither accord nor conflict here.
> It can be seen that there is a misunderstanding here from the mere fact that in the course of our argument we give one interpretation after another; as if each one contented us at least for a moment, until we thought of yet another standing behind it. What this shews is that there is a way of grasping a rule

which is *not* an *interpretation*, but which is exhibited in what we call 'obeying the rule' and 'going against it' in actual cases. (*PI*, §201; emphasis in original)

So, being a rule-governed practice cannot be separated from being a practice in which practitioners appropriately police one another's use. There can be no criticism of such a practice, as a rule-governed practice per se, though there may of course be practical reforms which improve its usefulness, or its aesthetic or ethical acceptability. We cannot, for instance, imagine the appearance of rule-following being upset by a reality that it is in fact chaotic. To imagine such a situation is to imagine that what counts as *the same* can be established independently of the putative rules in operation. But Wittgenstein repeatedly reminds as that what counts as the same is co-ordinate with the nature of the rules. What we *can* imagine is an appearance of rule following, but an incapacity to follow the rules embedded in the practice. But this isn't to encounter the *mere* appearance of rule following; rather, it is to encounter limits to our own comprehension.

4.8 Conclusion

My aim in this chapter has not been to jettison Transcendental in favour of Linguistic Idealism. Rather, I have wanted to show that there is a plausible way of denying the Realist thesis which differs from that of Transcendental Idealism. It turns out, apparently anyway, that this kind of denial, the denial that representation is responsible to the world, requires a linguistic setting, that is, it privileges linguistic over psychological representation. So, it warrants the title Linguistic Idealism. The two kinds of idealism differ significantly. Transcendental Idealism has a substantial burden, namely, discerning our contribution to the nature of the world (as it is represented) and this develops a range of issues that need to be addressed: finding the synthetic a priori; explaining its equivocal modal status; distinguishing the representing subject from any empirical subject; and the postulation of incomprehensible alternative modes of representing. None of these issues needs to be addressed by the Linguistic Idealist. Her claim is primarily negative, arguing for the failure of attempts to ground truth-evaluable content in worldly semantic relations. To be sure, she needs to supplement this denial with a positive conception, but that positive conception sees representation in language as emerging via responsibility in its use to something other than worldly relations, presumably to intersubjective normative constraints. Normative practice becomes basic.

References

Anscombe, G. E. M. 1981. 'The question of linguistic idealism', in G. E. M. Anscombe, *From Parmenides to Wittgenstein* (Oxford: Blackwell), 112–33.
Brandom, R. 1998. *Making it Explicit* (Cambridge, Mass.: Harvard University Press).
Davidson, D. 1984. *Inquiries into Truth and Interpretation* (Oxford: Clarendon Press).
Dummett, M. 1978. *Truth and Other Enigmas* (London: Duckworth).
Field, H. 1977. 'Logic, meaning and conceptual role', *Journal of Philosophy* 69, 379–409.
Gaskin, R. 2021. *Language and World: A Defence of Linguistic Idealism* (London: Routledge).
Hacker, P. 1986. *Insight and Illusion*, revised edition (Oxford: OUP).
Kant, I. 1929. *Critique of Pure Reason*, tr. N. Kemp-Smith (London: Macmillan).
Lear, J. 1998a. *'The Disappearing "We"'*, in J. Lear, *Open Minded* (Cambridge, Mass.: Harvard University Press), 282–302.
Lear, J. 1998b. 'Transcendental Anthropology', in J. Lear, *Open Minded* (Cambridge, Mass.: Harvard University Press), 247–81.
Peacocke, C. 1992. *A Study of Concepts* (Cambridge, Mass.: MIT Press).
Putnam, H. 1975. *Mind, Language and Reality* (Cambridge: CUP).
Putnam, H. 1981. *Reason, Truth and History* (Cambridge: CUP).
Putnam, H. 1983. *Realism and Reason* (Cambridge: CUP).
Strawson, P. F. 1966. *The Bounds of Sense* (London: Methuen).
Williams, B. 1974. 'Wittgenstein and idealism', in G. Vesey (ed.), *Understanding Wittgenstein* (London: Macmillan), 76–95.
Winch, P. 1958. *The Idea of a Social Science and its Relation to Philosophy* (London: Routledge).
Wittgenstein, L. 1921. *Tractatus Logico-Philosophicus*, tr. D. Pears and B. McGuinness (London: Routledge) [*TLP*].
Wittgenstein, L. 1958. *Philosophical Investigations*, tr. G. E. M. Anscombe (Oxford: Blackwell) [*PI*].
Wittgenstein, L. 1967. *Zettel*, ed. G. E. M. Anscombe and G. H. von Wright, tr. G. E. M. Anscombe (Oxford: Blackwell).
Wittgenstein, L. 1974. *Philosophical Grammar*, ed. R. Rhees, tr. A. Kenny (Oxford: Blackwell) [*PG*].
Wittgenstein, L. 1975. *Philosophical Remarks*, ed. R. Rhees, tr. R. Hargreaves and R. White (Oxford: Blackwell) [*PR*].
Wittgenstein, L. 1978. *Remarks on the Foundations of Mathematics*, 3rd edn., ed. G. E. M. Anscombe, R. Rhess, and G. H. von Wright, tr. G. E. M. Anscombe (Oxford: Blackwell).

5
World and Truth in Conflict

John Collins

5.1 Introduction

Through much of philosophy of the last 150 years or so, semantics and metaphysics (/ontology) have been intimate; indeed, Dummett (1993, 5–7) characterizes analytic philosophy, at least in its origins, as the endeavour to provide semantic answers to metaphysical questions; for example, questions concerning the existence and status of number are answered by accounts of the meaning and truth of arithmetical statements. This involves what we might consider a *thin* linguistic idealism: what is to be said about ontology is exhausted by what is to be said about semantics. To be sure, analytical philosophy was born out of a rejection of idealism, whether British or Kantian, understood as a species of psychologism, which considered all claims to objectivity to be conditioned by the character of experience (cf. Hylton 1990; Coffa 1991). Yet the thin idealism I have in mind is perfectly consistent with a complete rejection of *psychological* idealism inasmuch as the mind-independence of the furniture of our world and certain abstracta are not in question, given that the governing semantic categories of truth, meaning, reference, inference, etc. are precisely not psychological; that is, thought is to be characterized in essentially objective terms as opposed to in terms of private states that are potentially unique to individual thinkers.[1] What makes for linguistic idealism of the sort I have in mind is that *what counts as real is what falls under a certain semantic specification (via truth and reference) and such a specification suffices to confer existence*. So, the idealism at issue also does not entail any kind of relativism or constructionism; the relevant sense in which ontology is a semantic matter might be a universal feature of language that enshrines a coherent notion of objectivity.

---

[1] Here I shall neglect the question whether the charge of psychologism, as made against British/Kantian idealism, was apt or not. Suffice it to say, the post-Kantian tradition sought to show how objectivity is to be established rather than taken for granted or eschewed.

One may see the latter-day resurgence of metaphysics, following Kripke's (1980) divorce of necessity from analyticity, as a move away from even a thin linguistic idealism. This is because how things are metaphysically is not constituted or underwritten by semantics; it is more that there is a natural sympathy between the semantic and the metaphysical. The present chapter will take a different tack by questioning the very concordance of semantics with metaphysics.

Thin linguistic idealism faces a severe challenge, not so much from a resurgent old-style metaphysics or a more thorough-going idealism *à la* Gaskin (2021), but internally, as it were, from the direction of semantics. The problem, in brief, is that certain semantic phenomena issue in apparently unacceptable ontology, and there is no fix to the semantics. In other words, taking semantics as our lead on matters ontological lands us with commitments we would wish to forswear. The moral will be that at least one strand of the early analytical attitude was correct: if one wants an acceptable ontology via semantics, one needs to go artificial; natural-semantic concepts of truth or quantification do not carry an ontological commitment worth the name.[2] This is because our natural idiom by itself allows us to think of anything we can talk about in a single ontological register. Thus, our natural idiom provides no serious guide to ontological commitment, a fact we only recognize once we reflect on the apparent ontology an intuitive semantics delivers as something unacceptable independent of the semantic specifications. In a sense, then, our language does make for a certain kind of idealism, but one we can eschew upon reflection via renouncing natural-language semantics as a guide to ontology.

5.2 Semantic Preliminaries

The dialectic I shall articulate is internal to a truth-conditional approach to semantics and its putative ontological commitment. I shall not dwell, therefore, on supporting the approach. Some brief remarks, however, are required to ward off misdirected objections to the sequel.

First, for formal languages, the question of a correct semantics is not a straightforward factual matter, for this kind of language is not a natural phenomenon. In this sense, 'tolerance' à la Carnap (1934) appears to reign. Yet we

---

[2] From Frege onwards, thinkers have differed over whether 'logical form' amounts to a theory of natural language or some level of content distinct from the structure of natural language.

need not be libertines, for many theoretical virtues and metaphysical considerations can be in play to sway decisions, rendering the choice of semantics more or less akin to that of other theoretical assessments where the known facts are not decisive (cf. Williamson 2013, 423–5). From here on, I shall be concerned with semantics for natural language unless otherwise made explicit.

Secondly, let a truth-conditional semantics assign compositional truth conditions to syntactically individuated sentences of a language. We may side-line further decisions on details; in particular, whether semantics is an autonomous discipline or a chapter of cognitive science will not matter to the forthcoming issues.[3] Suffice it to note that I assume full compositionality in the sense that each expression of the language will receive a value that contributes to the truth conditions of its host sentences.[4]

Thirdly, the bare idea of truth conditions does not carry substantive metaphysical presuppositions in the sense that there is no a priori proprietary vocabulary in which truth conditions are to be stated. For example, one might want to state truth conditions in a wholly phenomenal language or a wholly physical language or a wholly extensional language, and so on and so forth. Minimally, some form of disquotational truth conditions will be available, albeit expressed in a language that reflects the correct compositional structure of the sentences at issue.[5] These choices are conditioned by independent considerations, and might result in some apparent truths being rendered false. At any rate, semantics is perfectly consistent with a wide-ranging error theory; that is, it is no mark against semantics per se if it assigns truth conditions that render much of what we say false from one's favoured metaphysical perspective.

---

[3] Minimally, for semantics to be a chapter of psychology is only for it to satisfy cognitive desiderata, such as might be gleaned from considerations of acquisition and processing. A semantic theory may still happily be truth-conditional.

[4] Compositionality, it bears emphasis, is not trivial precisely because we need an independent theory of the syntax of a language that the semantics interprets; we cannot stipulate the syntax in order to support the semantics we want. For example, (ia) cannot be interpreted as (ib–c), even though the subject of the infinitive requires an understood subject bound by the quantifier phrase. Such complexities arise wherever one looks in natural language:

(i)   a.   Everyone wants to leave.
       b.   Everyone wants everyone to leave.
       c.   Everyone wants him to leave.

[5] Characteristically, truth-conditional semantics offers no conceptual analysis of lexical items and specifies their semantic contribution in terms of metalinguistic correlates. All that is made explicit is the compositional features of the items. A verb's adicity, for example, will be made explicit, as will the Boolean relation a quantifier imposes upon its restriction and scope. This results in departures from homophonic specifications (cf. Glanzberg 2014; Collins and Rey 2023).

Fourthly and correlatively, insofar as truth conditions are integral to a semantic theory, they are not equivalent to specifications of what makes a sentence true in any respect that goes beyond what a speaker understands. The truth conditions of ordinary claims about animals, say, are not constrained to include chapter and verse on genetics or cladistics. Otherwise put, truth conditions as featured in a semantic theory do not embody theories or explanations of the phenomena that our sentences are about.[6] These last two points are central to what will be argued.

Fifthly, natural language is a natural phenomenon, and so a semantic theory will be answerable to the facts in a way a theory of semantics for a formal language is not. This reveals itself in both the narrow specifics of the properties of varied linguistic constructions and in the broad design conditions of natural language.[7] A complicating factor is the question of precisely what phenomena should fall under the purview of semantics. It is widely accepted that what a speaker might literally say with a sentence such that the utterance is true or false is conditioned by both semantic and pragmatic factors; disagreement begins with how substantial a role pragmatics plays in the determination of such a content. I shall return to this matter, but for now I want to highlight a constraint from the other direction, namely syntax. Since what a semantics interprets is a syntactically individuated structure, the nature of syntax constrains interpretation. Ideally, it should provide the compositional form, although matters are not so straightforward.[8] Still, we may formulate a line of reasoning that recommends a truth-conditional semantics given the most basic fact about the nature of natural-language syntax.

---

[6] The relevant notion of 'understanding' is that which explains a speaker–hearer's competence with the language, which need not be conscious knowledge. Thus, a semantic theory records what explains a speaker–hearer's competence, not an account of the world as such.

[7] For example, it is broadly accepted within syntactic theory that all branching is binary in the sense that only two items are composed and the result is treated as an item for further composition. A semantics must thus respect this fact or else explain how it is somehow overridden in specific cases.

[8] For example, a naive syntax would render adnominal adjectival modification as

(i) [$_{NP}$ [$_{N'}$ ADJ [$_{N'}$ N]]].

A problem immediately arises with the distinctions between intersective, subsective, and non-subsective modification:

(ii) a. male nurse (male and nurse).
 b. skilful artist (skilful as an artist).
 c. fake gun (something that presents as a gun).

It doesn't follow that the semantics departs from the syntax, for there are plausible grounds to suppose that the syntax of modification is not uniformly simple (Cinque 2010). Such complications are to be expected; there is no reason to think that natural language is amenable to the most intuitive approach.

(S-S)   i. Semantics for natural language interprets natural language syntax.
  ii. Natural language syntax of the sentence/clause is intrinsic; that is, a sentence/clause has the syntax it has not due to or inclusive of any other sentences.
  iii. The interpretation the semantics provides for a sentence, therefore, cannot make appeal to the interpretation of any other sentences.
  iv. Since inference is an inter-sentential relation, semantics cannot appeal to inference in its interpretation of a sentence.

If this reasoning is correct, then inference provides semantic evidence for truth conditions, which are encoded syntactically as an intrinsic property of sentences. In other words, we explain inference via the semantics of sentences; we do not take inference to be explanatory of semantics. What a speaker does with a sentence, as it were, insofar as it means something definite, is explained (in part) by that meaning. It bears emphasis that this does not imply that inference is not crucial evidence for semantics; nor does it imply that sentences are punctate, in either semantics or syntax. The syntax of a sentence arises from its generation by a certain kind of system that generates denumerably many sentences. A semantics interprets the output of the system, and so will interpret sentences as an infinite class of structures. The crucial point is that a sentence has its syntax and so its semantics because it is generated by a certain kind of system, not because the sentence is inferentially related to any other sentence. From this perspective, classic holistic thinking from Davidson (1984) and many others is quite back to front: it takes evidence to be the very phenomena. A sentence has a certain semantic form, not because the sentence falls into a certain inferential pattern anyway, but because such a form interprets an independent syntactic structure generated by a certain kind of system, and such an interpretation explains why the inferences hold regardless of anyone's actually performing them. To be sure, when meaning is thought of in terms of inference or use, the operative notions are understood normatively, so that only 'correct' inferences or uses count as constitutive. The problem here is that there is simply no obvious way to fix which uses/inferences are to count other than by reference to some properties that are non-performative, such as structural ones. At any rate, divorcing meaning from use faces no such problem, and is perfectly consistent with systematic misuse or misunderstanding of certain constructions.

Sixthly, lexical items are assigned values, which, in an ontological register, we would describe as objects, sets of objects or properties, relations, and so on. The theory itself, however, does not enshrine any account of what such ontology might amount to or even if it is real; that is, semantic theory, as it might be, assigns names to individual-like entities without presuming that the individuals that form the class of values of names constitute any kind of natural class of thing beyond their being such values. No science, as it were, is required to group together numbers, persons, and capital cities, say. Likewise, the semantics is, without further ado, indifferent to whether a name has an actual worldly value. At first blush, it would treat *Donald Duck* and *Donald Trump* equivalently. If one desires the difference to be registered by semantics, one would have to do one of two things: either render the two names distinct in some sense, or assign different kinds of values to them. Both approaches involve a departure from semantics compositionally interpreting syntactic structure. To think of fiction as uniformly false, as do Russell (1905) and Quine (1953), because names, under analysis, encode an existential commitment (which in this case is not met) to entities that satisfy a relevant predicate, is *not* to register fiction as a semantic phenomenon; rather, it simply means that fictions happen to be false, much as *Donald Trump has a beard* happens to be false. These matters will be prominent later.

With so much said, let us consider ontological commitment.

5.3 Ontological Commitment as a Thin Linguistic Idealism

Let us suppose that no relevant party is a psychological idealist, where such an idealist thinks that to be is to meet some psychological condition. A linguistic idealist, in my terms, is happy to sanction mind-independent entities. Their claim is only that what there is is what our truths detail. If, ex hypothesi, a semantic theory is truth-conditional, then it will inform us of what there is, for it will precisely tell us what renders truths true. It will not tell us what is true, and so what in fact there is, but will do so if we independently know what is true.[9] Thus, existence is channelled via truth's status as the key evaluative notion of a semantic theory. We see this move clearly in Frege's (1884) consideration of numbers. Frege forswore any special epistemic access to numbers (by the light of rational intuition, say) and didn't enter into metaphysical speculation on how they could exist alongside the material world *à la* Aristotle in

---

[9] Gaskin (2021, 168–70) favours what he calls 'ontological generosity', under which it is not so much truth that confers existence but meaning. For present purposes, I am happy to include this broader conception.

his *Physics* or be beyond it *à la* Plato. Instead, numbers exist and form a certain class type because that is what the truth of arithmetic demands. In this light, if we assume that sentence meaning determines (or is) truth conditions, then Frege's 'context principle' may be read as saying that to be is to make a contribution to truth.

Quine can be usefully seen as generalizing Frege's basic point via his doctrine of ontological commitment:

> [A] standard whereby to decide what ontology a given theory or form of theory is committed to: a theory is committed to those and only those entities to which bound variables of the theory must be capable of referring in order that the affirmations of the theory be true. (Quine, 1953, 13)

Quine's point goes beyond explicit theoretical contexts in the sense that if a sentence is 'regimented' in a variable-involving notation, then the values of the bound variables will be whatever is required to exist in order to make the sentence true.[10] Davidson (1980, 1984) elevates the general idea to a 'method of metaphysics': what exists is what satisfies the bound variables in the semantic interpretations of our true sentences. Thus, events exist alongside objects, because the semantic interpretation of what Davidson calls 'action sentences' involves existential quantification over events. The same reasoning applies throughout much of metaphysics.[11]

It might seem invidiously misleading to describe this as any kind of idealism. One reason for thinking semantics is thoroughly non-idealist is that the operative notion of truth is not relativized in any relevant sense to human perspectives and so confers objective existence on whatever values lie in the

---

[10] Quine was not flat-footed in his application of the criterion. Quine (1960) adopts a 'double standard' according to which some quantification over dubious entities (primarily intensional ones) is accepted because no clean regimentation will export the variable outside of the relevant context. Still, the idioms are 'essentially dramatic'. More broadly, Quine ultimately tilted towards a structuralism, which took the truth of sentences to be primitive, and ontology as relative to decisions on how to incarnate structure:

> [T]here can be no evidence for one ontology as over against another, so long anyway as we can express a one-to-one correlation between them. Save the structure and you save all.... The very notion of object, or of one and many, is indeed as parochially human as the parts of speech; to ask what reality is *really* like, however, apart from human categories, is self-stultifying. (Quine, 1992, 8–9)

See Gregory 2020 for an excellent discussion of Quine's development regarding ontology.

[11] Many recent discussions in 'metaontology' have sought to discern differences of strength or commitment of quantification and associated vocabulary (*exists*, *real*, etc.). For discussion, see Chalmers 2009; Fine 2009; Schaffer 2009; Hirsch 2011; Hofweber 2016; and Sider 2016. It is unclear if such hypotheses essentially involve claims about natural-language semantics. At any rate, natural-language quantification is not polysemous (cf. Azzouni 2017; Collins 2022).

domain of the variables of the truths. Semantics, in this sense, is not intra-symbolic but a language–world relation. Indeed, this is precisely Lewis's (1970) claim against cognitive theories of semantics, which has been echoed by many others since. Still, one could go much further in a non-idealist direction. First, one might adopt an extra-linguistic criterion for existence, thinking that there is no linguistic signature of being at all. Thus, the *really* real might be that which is representation-independent, unaffected by stipulations or our conceptions of it, not essentially knowable, potentially opaque to inquiry, and so on.[12] Secondly, one might think that truth is no kind of guide at all to what is real, no matter the regimentation or semantic theory. The point here is that truth is simply orthogonal to ontological commitment. The two sometimes coincide, but generally spin free. The sequel will pursue this line, starting in the next section with some general considerations.

5.4 No Language of Being

As we saw, Quine and many following him take quantification to be a signature of ontology; other idioms, too, have often thought to play the same role. In point of fact, though, we readily employ all such idioms—quantificational and non-quantificational—to 'talk about' things we reckon not to exist according to non-semantic criteria:

(1) a. There are more Greek gods than Norse ones.
    b. Every fictional detective is smarter than Trump.
    c. Superheroes with no special powers exist—Iron Man.
    d. The peasant Anna and Vronsky dreamed of turned out to be real.
    e. It's true that Holmes used opium.

The present point is not that we are bound to take any such claims to be true, although I think they are all true (cf. Azzouni 2010; Collins 2021), but only that there is no semantic anomaly in using the supposed ontologically committing vocabulary to talk about things we reckon not to exist; at any rate, one hardly needs to be a Meinongian to find all these cases semantically acceptable. If one is minded to offer some interdiction against the cases, then it must be sought beyond the mere idioms involved, which appear to be indifferent to the ontological status of gods and ficta.

---

[12] See, for example, Devitt 2010 and Azzouni 2004, 2010 for somewhat different takes on how to employ non-semantic criteria for existence. The kind of ontology one ends up with can vary. Devitt mostly preserves our common-sense world of cats and trees, whereas Azzouni's world is far sparser. See Collins and Rey 2023 for discussion.

A natural move to make, especially for the quantification cases, is to appeal to the domain as a guarantor of true existence: the idea would be that, while we might talk as though we were quantifying over Greek gods and fictional detectives, such creatures are not genuine denizens of the domain, the domain being conceived as coincident with the extistent. This won't do, however, for reasons insightfully spelt out by Azzouni (2017; cf. Collins 2022).

An appeal to the domain of quantification is supposed to be a way of distinguishing between mere talk, as if we were quantifying over things that don't exist, and what is *really* real, for a domain is not a way of talking but the very things themselves of which we talk. The problem, however, is that while we might want some such distinction between the real and what we merely 'talk about', the idea of a domain does not establish it. The reason is simply that a domain needs specification, and it can't be specified in some brute way by pointing or kicking things into place. In general, a domain is specified as follows:

(2) $(\exists X)[(\forall y)[Fy \rightarrow y \in X]]$.

There are just two ways the values of 'y' might have an inviolate existential status. First, it might be that the *quantification* confers a really real standing upon them. Yet if quantification in the language allows us to talk of the inexistent, the quantification in (2) should do so too without further ado. What further thing can one do? One can intend for the quantification to be *really* ontologically committing, but the problem is precisely how to be clearer on what 'really' amounts to, and we have seen that bare appeal to quantification or a domain does not provide the required clarity. To be sure, we readily differentiate between Donald Duck and Donald Trump, say, but this appears not to be underwritten by any semantic knowledge, but by worldly knowledge. It is not part of the meaning of the respective names that one is fictional the other not, although to be mistaken on that score is to be seriously in error about how the world is.[13]

---

[13] Gaskin (2021, 107–9) argues that the logical form (but not 'surface syntax') of names differs with respect to whether the name is 'empty' or not. An apparent problem for this view is that names might be empty contrary to our best information ('Homer', 'Shakespeare', say); semantics, it would seem, cannot be sensitive to future discoveries about the world. Gaskin (2021, 109), however, happily acknowledges that his position denies the authority of individual speakers as regards the meaning/reference of the expressions of their language. A more general complaint, though, is that being 'empty' appears not to have a linguistic signature at all, at least, not a signature that might affect compositionality, and so 'emptiness' cannot be expressed in logical form unless we stipulate the form's character to reflect how we think the world is. The real problem, then, doesn't turn on speakers having a relevant authority; it is more that logical form, if its business is to capture compositionality, is insensitive to or invariant

The other option of making the notion of a domain enshrine the *really* real is for the *choice of comprehension predicate* '*F*' somehow to offer security of existence. But this idea is a non-starter, for '*F*' can be whatever one likes: Euclidean points, integers, cartoon characters; indeed, it is precisely the absence of an existence-conferring property that makes it at least initially attractive to seek ontological commitment in quantification.

Similar remarks hold for truth predication. We might be tempted to think that the kind of cases in (1) can't *really* be true. The basis for this thought would be the difficulty of seeing how a statement could be true unless what it is about exists. In that case, either (1)(a–e) would be false after all or they would really be about something else—intentional objects, a Meinongian realm, artefacts, or *something*. To the contrary, I think we can recognize the relevant form of sentences to have normal truth conditions, to be true, and made true by the world, which does not include Greek gods etc. Before explaining this, however, the next section will indicate that the problem posed by Greek gods et al. is far more pervasive than is often thought. There is, in short, a general mismatch between sensible conceptions of ontology (what there is) and truth conditions, along with any vocabulary supposedly revelatory of ontological commitment.

5.5 The Problem of Copredication

In the previous section we saw that vocabulary that is supposed to signal ontological commitment raises no semantic anomaly when paired with items referring to things we reckon not to exist. The issue of the truth of claims involving such vocabulary was postponed via a promissory note. A far wider phenomenon is that virtually every open-class item can occur in contexts where we would renounce the implied ontology, but competent speaker–hearers don't reflect upon the mismatch at all, and, again, the standard semantic vocabulary is insensitive to the mismatch. Here I shall restrict myself to the nominal domain.

First, let me post two definitions.

Polysemy: An item is polysemous iff it has multiple senses which are variously conceptually related and which can be selectively or simultaneously activated by context or choice of predicate.

over wordly factors, including what we might know of the world, which precisely includes 'emptiness'. Hence, modifying logical form to reflect 'emptiness' appears ad hoc at best. See Collins 2021 for further discussion.

Polysemes are not ambiguous, for the homophony between, say, *bank* (financial institution) and *bank* (side of a river) is accidental whereas the relation between the senses of a polyseme are non-accidental, conceptual. For example:

> *book*: physical volume/content;
> *London*: area/population/government/buildings;
> *school*: building/pupils/institution;
> *The Times*: physical copy/content/company
> *glass*: container/fluid;
> *window*: glass/portal;
> *Shakespeare*: products/body/mind/abstract.

What it means to say that nominals have multiple senses can be expressed in different ways, but the fundamental idea is that an item can make distinct contributions to the truth conditions of a sentence relative to a predicate. For example:

(3) a. Bill held the book.
    b. Bill memorized the book.

For (3a) to be true, some physical particular needs to be held by Bill; for (3b) to be true, no physical particular needs to be in play at all (Bill memorizes content, which could be delivered by varied means—he starts with a paperback, reads the middle online, and then is told the rest). Similarly:

(4) a. London voted Labour.
    b. London is bisected by the Thames.

For (4a) to be true, a majority of some selection of people must have acted in a certain way; for (4b) to be true, no people need to have acted in any particular way. It is useful to think of a predicate as selecting a sense of the nominal such that the nominal contributes that sense to the truth conditions of the construction.

The basic distinction between ambiguity and polysemy is reflected in the definition of copredication:

> *Copredication*: A construction C is copredicative iff C features a single nominal that is the understood argument (via any syntactic means) of two or more categorically mismatched predicates.

Let predicates be categorically mismatched if they select different senses. Here are some examples involving quantifiers where available:

(5) a. Bill memorized every book in the library, then burnt them.
   b. London voted Labour despite its increasing gentrification.
   c. Most dilapidated schools remain happy.
   d. *The Times*'s financial stability depends upon advertising and it is full of it.
   e. Sam slammed the glass on the bar and promptly downed three more.
   f. Bill painted every door in the house while the cat walked through them.
   g. Shakespeare has not been out of print in over four hundred years, although his identity remains disputed.

The prima facie problem is easily stated: in copredication, a single nominal appears simultaneously to express different senses relative to distinct predicates, but we do not take there to be *single* referent on which we confer an independent ontological status. For example, the books memorized can be counted differently from the books burnt (for (5a) to be true, Bill doesn't need to memorize each library copy of *War and Peace*, but he must burn each one); the London that votes is a population, not buildings that can be gentrified; school buildings can be dilapidated, but only the pupils can be happy; and so on. The problem has the same shape as the fiction cases. We reckon statements to be true, whether involving quantification or not, while at the same time declining to sanction any corresponding ontology. In the fiction case, this is because there is no relevant entity at all; in the case of copredication it is because there is no entity that can have all the properties the construction attributes. At any rate, no one thinks there are abstract objects with mass or buildings that can have psychological states.

It bears emphasis that neither here nor elsewhere do I intend to mount an argument against the ontological status of *ordinary objects*. From certain metaphysical perspectives, middle-sized dry goods pose various problems of both constitution and determinacy. Suppose all such problems are overcome, being susceptible to a deflation of the conditions under which we can truthfully speak of objects and confer existence upon them (cf. Thomasson 2014). Thomasson, at least, has in mind traditional concerns that quotidian objects might be open to doubt due to coincidence and vagueness worries. The current problem of copredication and the mismatch of semantics and ontology is not of this traditional form. Our problem is semantic, not metaphysical, and can be stated, as I have done, without appeal to any metaphysical presuppositions beyond truisms such as that areas can be flooded, but not happy, and persons can be happy, but not flooded. Such conundrums as to what 'London' might refer to would remain no matter how we settled the metaphysics, unless we revised the language, too.

It might be thought, however, that certain metaphysical conditions are wrapped up in the content of words. Thomasson (2014), for example, contends that expressions have 'application' and 'coapplication conditions', which are analytic rules that a competent speaker–hearer knows (not necessarily consciously) for the application and re-application of an expression. The conditions record putative conceptual truths, such as 'If x is a house, x is a building', 'If x is a baseball, x is spherical', etc. If the empirical facts indicate that the set of relevant conditions for an expression are fulfilled, then we can conclude that referents for the relevant nominals exist.[14] No further metaphysical or semantic worries are appropriate. For our purposes, there are two problems with this view.

First, it is by no means obvious how to differentiate application conditions that are mere common knowledge from ones that involve semantic competence. For sure, inferences of the kind Thomasson appeals to are by default valid, but they do not clearly hold in all cases. Is a shipping container used as a dwelling a building? Is a baseball deformed by contact with a bat still a ball? The point here is not so much that one can't cook up some plausible stories to cater for such cases one way or another, but that such stories appear not to flow from the basic competence with *house, building, container, baseball,* and *sphere.*

Secondly, even were we to suppose that the application conditions for an expression hold in a particular case, and infer that the relevant entities exist, the problem of copredication remains untouched. The problem is not whether London exists (of course it does—it is not Atlantis), but that there is no entity that can univocally satisfy the predicates of which 'London' can be an argument. To rest content with application conditions is to rest content with areas being in possession of psychological properties, which is some kind of poor pun.

Let us consider and reject various defusing moves that do at least purport to speak to the problem.

---

[14] Thomasson's principle (E) says: Ks exist iff the application conditions actually associated with 'K' are fulfilled (Thomasson 2014, 86).

a. *What's the problem?* Incredulity is never an argument, but from a certain perspective, the problem might seem chimerical. Devitt (2021, 234–5) writes:

> [W]hen I assert 'This book is real fun' I *am not* predicating a property of an 'aspect' of the book; I am predicating a property of *the book*, a property it has in virtue of having that content. It is a fact *about the world* that a certain physical object on my desk is both a book and real fun. No theory of words, a mere *semantic* theory, can gainsay that worldly fact. So when one turns to semantics, there should be no resisting the obvious view that 'This book is real fun' attributes being real fun to that particular physical object... [A]n important moral is: just because a term refers to things that have different sorts of properties, including physical properties and functional ones, does not alone show that the word has two senses.

The defusing move here is expressed in the moral: there is a problem only if we count referents on the basis of kinds of properties, but this is something we ought not to do. Thus, to say a book is heavy and fun is not to conjure up different kinds of books, one that can be heavy and one that can be fun. We should, rather, recognize that there is a single object of which we predicate different kinds of properties. After all, surely objects can have different sorts of properties.

The diagnosis offered of the problem, however, is inaccurate: the problem of copredication does not arise from an ontological incontinence that issues in many different kinds of books or cities, and so the problem is not relieved by being simple-minded about ontology.[15] The problem is that the semantics of the construction expresses distinct conditions of individuation for the value of the single nominal. Thus, books as content are individuated differently from books as material objects one can lift up. Of course it is 'obvious' that a book can have both properties, such being what books normally are. Yet that just reflects the properties of the construction. What is far from obvious is whether there is a specifiable univocal referent that can be a book—*punkt!*—from which we can understand that it might be heavy and fun. Devitt appears to assume that this is an easy task, as easy as pointing to 'a certain physical object on [his] desk'. Unfortunately, not all books are physical objects, or have contents, or pages, etc. So, if Devitt says 'Kant's

---

[15] Devitt (2021, 234) takes the putative non-univocity of polysemous nominals to mean that they have variable referents, just like ambiguities. But the very phenomenon of polysemy is that the relevant nominals, unlike ambiguities, can selectively or simultaneously express different 'senses' relative to different predicates.

first *Critique* is interesting' pointing to a physical copy, although he is referring to the physical object, what he said would be equally true if there were no physical copy on the desk, or even if all copies were destroyed (assuming that what is interesting is what Kant writes rather than the cover or binding). Not so if he said 'Kant's first *Critique* is dog-eared' in the same circumstances. The issue is not about metaphysics, but how distinct conditions of individuation can be activated with the use of a single nominal. The same issue applies across the board. This is a semantic problem, which cannot be solved by metaphysics.[16]

It is well to note here that I don't see copredication as upending any common-sense metaphysics or increasing the number of things in the world. As said, the problem is a semantic one with the consequence that ontology cannot be straightforwardly run off of the semantics. Imagine a language has two words, 'wook' and 'zook', respectively referring to books *qua* material particulars, and books *qua* contents. In time, given the coincidence of wooks with zooks, some bright spark coins 'book' to cover both cases. It would be absurd to describe such a scenario as involving the development of some new ontological scheme, for everything remains as it was save for the lexical economizing. Quite so, but we are left to say what the semantic properties of 'book' are. It can be used to refer to either wooks or zooks or both, but the world contains no such object as a thing that is both a wook and a zook. Of course, speakers of the language are not confused and use 'book' blithely. They might be confused, however, if a visiting philosopher professed there to be books, period, and offered some weird amalgam of wooks and zooks as a new ontological creature.[17]

Finally on this point, we need not deny that books (cities, etc.) have a range of diverse kinds of properties; that simply reflects how we talk of things. We only go wrong if we expect the world to be populated by entities as univocal referents for our words, without reference to any individuative conditions associated with the range of properties our predicates express.

b. *Just ambiguity*. One inviting thought is that just as ambiguity is not a problem, so polysemy isn't either. Here is King (2018, 779–80):

---

[16] Devitt is happy for some cases of 'regular polysemy' to involve distinct references, as in metonymy (Washington as legislature or city). Metonymy, however, is not happily involved in copredication:

(i) #Washington is indecisive and sits on the Potomac.

Polysemy, insofar as it gives rise to copredication, is a prima facie problem for an ontology-involving semantic theory; metonymy or metaphor does not give rise to the same kind of problem.

[17] Thanks to Richard Gaskin for the scenario.

[One might think] that count nouns like 'book' quite generally have one meaning on which they refer to book tokens and another meaning on which they refer to book types. Of course this does mean that strictly speaking there is no straightforward answer to the question 'what does "book" refer to *simpliciter*?' But that fact doesn't force us to reject an externalist semantics any more than the phenomenon of ambiguity does....

Yet the lack of a 'straightforward answer' is precisely the problem. Ambiguity effectively marks the single morphophonemic form as a property of distinct lexical items *because* they don't copredicate (*inter alia*); that is, because the meanings are distinct, the item has two unrelated semantic profiles. With polysemy, there is a single lexical item that does support copredication, which appears to oblige us to ask what its single meaning is, which then leads us to an absurd ontology. We can, as King seems to suggest, avoid the absurd ontology by not asking what the item's meaning is *simpliciter*. But we still want to know what the item's meaning is, and whatever it is, it appears not to be univocally referential. It is not enough, in short, to defuse the problem by saying that 'book' doesn't refer to a single bizarre kind of thing, but refers instead to *X*, *Y*, and *Z*, which are all ontologically kosher, for we want to know how the single item can simultaneously or selectively refer to *X*, *Y*, and *Z*.

In the anaphora cases, at least, an answer might be available:

The natural thing to say here is that when a pronoun is anaphoric on a polysemous noun where the noun is interpreted with polysemous meaning M_1, the pronoun can be interpreted with polysemous meaning M_2 of the antecedent noun, at least in cases where M_1 and M_2 are 'sufficiently close' meanings. (King 2018, 780)

Two problems arise here. Firstly, this is just a description of the phenomenon; we want to know how the anaphoric pronoun (and ellipsis) can be both referentially dependent on an antecedent nominal *and* have a different interpretation from it. Secondly, this kind of solution (such as it is) gives no indication of how it could generalize to cases where there are not two items, anaphoric pronouns or whatever. In (5c), for example, it is dilapidated schools that are happy, and so the intended content can't be finagled into one that states that schools are happy and schools are dilapidated.

c. *Context sensitivity*. Another natural move, indicated by some of King's reasoning, is to consider polysemous nominals to be context sensitive, taking variable values across variable contexts. In copredicative constructions, however, two or more values would have to be simultaneously assigned, which is radically unlike context sensitivity in other cases. Moreover, the values standard context-sensitive items take are drawn from an indefinite range of entities of a specific kind (times, locations, persons, etc.). Polysemy, again, works differently. There is a very small number of senses that pick out entities that are not of the same kind (e.g., populations and buildings). Liebesman and Magidor (2017) offer a spin to the basic idea of context sensitivity by treating a polysemous nominal as referentially univocal, but capable of activating different properties depending on context. Thus, 'book', having a physical book as a referent, can be construed as referring to a purely informational entity in context, by way of the physical book's having an informational property. The spin helps, but not in the right way. Again, copredication involves different construals being simultaneously activated relative to distinct predicates. Thus, even with context, we would still lack a univocal referent. Two other problems are also significant.

First, since 'book', referring to a physical object, can be construed as referring to an informational entity, and 'book', referring to an informational entity, can be construed as referring to a physical one, far from its being the case that 'book' has a univocal referent, its putative referent is wholly indeterminate. Secondly, in copredication it is typically not the context that activates a sense of a polysemous nominal but the predicate.

d. *Let there be strange objects*. We might now be tempted to think that no technical fix will do, and revert to a Devitt-like position, but without the insouciance. In the spirit of Gaskin's (2021) 'ontological generosity' one could think that cities *just are* things that are populations and areas and buildings, etc.; books just are things that are physical and informational; schools just are things that are buildings and pupils and institutions; and so on.

Of course, such queer objects are conjured up precisely to provide a univocal referent for the relevant nominals, and in the present context it simply begs the question to presume that provision of a univocal semantic value suffices for a kosher ontological status. Still, park this problem, for even if we let there be the requisite queer objects, they are not suitable referents for polysemes. The real problem is that polysemes can have their senses not only simultaneously activated, as in copredication, but also selectively activated by a single predicate. In the case of copredication, it is at least a prima facie not implausible idea that the referent of the nominal might be a complex queer object; but when the nominal has a single predicate, the other senses of the nominal are excluded or, at any rate, non-essential. Thus:

(6) a. The book is dramatic.
    b. The school is happy.
    c. London flooded.

We don't want 'book' in (6a) to refer to a thing that is both physical and informational, for it can be true with no relevant physical book being dramatic. Similarly, (6b) can be true if the school buildings have been flattened (the school goes online), and (6c) can be true if the population of London has disappeared. It won't even do, then, for aspects or parts of the putative queer object to be selected as relevant to the referents of the nominal, for the other parts can be entirely absent, not merely not currently relevant.

The general problem here is that while we might be encouraged to conjure up strange objects to accommodate copredication, such objects are precisely not what we want as referents when the polysemous nominal occurs non-copredicatively.

e. *Logical form.* If faced with unwanted ontological commitment, one is free to venture a logical form for the offending construction that lacks the commitment. I have not the space to explore the issue fully, but two related problems bear emphasis. First, it is not enough to construct some or other logical form that lacks the relevant commitment; the logical form must interpret natural-language syntax, if it is to record the semantics of the natural-language sentences. That we can, say, paraphrase so that it is explicit that we are talking about books and schools or whatever in different respects need not be in dispute when considering copredication. The real issue is whether any such paraphrase is actually supported by the syntax of the sentence.[18] Secondly and correlatively, copredication can arise via any means of predication

---

[18] A natural move, for example, would be to render copredicative constructions as clausal conjunctions:

(i) a. The school is happy and dilapidated.
    b. The school is happy and the school is dilapidated.

The two tokens of 'school' can now receive distinct interpretations relative to their respective predicates. No such approach will generalize, of course, because one can have:

(ii) The dilapidated school is happy.

Worse, (ib) is not in fact licensed by (ia). The understood subject of *dilapidated* in (ia) must be the very same subject of 'happy', so positing another token of 'school' gets the interpretation wrong. Syntactically, the right interpretation is catered for by the second predicate's having a covert PRO subject that is (adnominal, relative clause, verbal and adjectival phrases, etc.). It is certain, therefore, that the proposed gambit of fashioning a logical form will result in a diversity of analyses, which renders the endeavour ad hoc; that is, why should every form of predication reflect an unobvious semantic structure that precludes a univocal referent for nominals just when the interpretation is copredicative? For example, a nominal with an adjoined relative clause will somehow have different logical forms between cases where the matrix predicate issues in copredication and cases where it doesn't.[19]

f. Finally, one might think that the apparent coherence of copredication is in fact illusory: the cases are *stricto dictu* ontologically incoherent, but we don't notice because we robustly associate the sentences with a coherent proposition, albeit not one the sentence semantically expresses. Now I think that such a position is in fact highly plausible (Collins 2023). In the present dialectic, however, this position is of no help, for, if true, the upshot is that semantics characteristically offers up ontological incoherence. The putative illusion, that is to say, is not that an ungrammatical sentence is grammatical or even that a sentence is meaningful when it is not; rather, the sentence is perfectly kosher save for the fact that, unrecognized by us, it describes a situation or event that can't possibly occur.

5.6 Truth after All

The story so far details a significant and general rift between semantics and how we reckon the world to be; further, there is no natural-language vocabulary that peculiarly expresses what we really take there to be. Even so, we can, it seems, speak truthfully. We may eschew a far-reaching error theory as a response, for it doesn't respond to the right phenomenon. The principal question is *not* how we might assign a truth value, even falsity, in the face of a scepticism about ordinary objects, but why we take what we say to be true even when it is made evident that a univocal referent would be an absurdity. The point is vivid with fiction. We take all kinds of fictive statements to be true even when we know they are fiction and we unequivocally reject

---

referentially dependent on the overt 'school'. The PRO item works in a similar way to a bound variable, and so cannot take on an interpretation independent of its antecedent.

[19] For example, the syntax and semantics of the subject should be the same across both of these cases:

(i) a. The book, which is heavy, is brown.
    b. The book, which is heavy, is dramatic.

Only the second is copredicative, however.

the existence of, say, cartoon characters. One natural move would be to reject truth-conditional semantics, but I am assuming throughout that the semantics is otherwise acceptable, so the rejection wouldn't amount to any kind of resolution of the problem, just as rejecting a true premise to avoid a paradox isn't any kind of victory.

The next variation would be to finagle a non-world-involving notion of truth. Another move would be to try better on the ontology and be a bit liberal on the amount and kind of 'abstract artefacts' we admit (Thomasson 2014). To the contrary, I think the only thing we need to give up is the tight connection between semantics and ontology; we do not need to play around with either the semantics or the concept of truth, and nor do we need to be liberal about artefacts. Before telling a positive story in this direction, let me first signal why we shouldn't be so much as tempted by the two moves just flagged.

First, then, why should we not be tempted by a plurality of notions of truth, including one that allows us to demur on the relevant ontological commitments? The simple problem is that truth is a univocal concept across the relevant constructions, much as existence is (Azzouni 2010).[20] This is not to say that we can't 'engineer' a new concept for some or other purpose, but, as we shall see, there is no need to, for the univocal notion of truth caters for the cases before us, i.e., truth is not relevantly ontologically committing. The key bit of evidence for the univocity of truth is that it is utterly indifferent to the content to which it is ascribed. Suppose, for example, that one wants to have a non-ontologically committing notion for truth for fiction, but a committing one for non-fiction. What is one supposed to say about (7b) following from (7a)?

(7) a. It is true that Putin is Russian and it is true that Batman is American.
　　b. It is true that Putin is Russian and Batman is American.

Not only should (7b) not follow, if there are distinct concepts of truth in play in (7a), it should be semantically anomalous, but it is fine (true, in fact). One might suggest that *true* is polysemous between committing and non-committing senses, and so (7a) is copredicative. That thought, though, is hardly obvious. For one thing, if (7b) is copredicative, we must be able to specify the relevant selective relation between the clauses and the senses of

---

[20] The adjective *true*, of course, is polysemous with respect to the different kinds of nominals it may modify (*true friend*, *true likeness*, *true line*, etc.). It appears not to be ambiguous, for in each case some standard is maximally satisfied. We presently have the single kind of case in mind where truth is predicated of a clause.

the putative polyseme. Yet this we cannot do, for being fictional is not a feature of a clause; being fictional is a piece of world knowledge, not lexically or syntactically encoded. There are various ways of seeing this. For example, Smith and Jones arguing about what firearm Bond uses are not talking past each other if Smith benightedly thinks that Bond is a real spy. More starkly, one may wonder whether Homer is real or even if Shakespeare is, but here one is not wondering about the meaning of the names; indeed, since we might well never know whether Homer is real, it would appear, on the present view, that we might never know the meaning of the name.

The second move entertained above was to render the apparently absurd ontology resulting from copredication as 'abstract artefacts'. One is free, of course, to be more or less liberal in what to treat as an 'abstract artefact'. That aside, there are two problems with the view.

First, we simply don't recognize the would-be artefacts. So, there is a certain naturalness in thinking of fictional characters, pieces of music, money, football clubs, and endless other things as artefacts. The problem copredication poses is how to have distinct conceptions or senses be selectively or simultaneously activated while retaining the notion of a univocal referent. In this light, to answer: 'It is an abstract artefact' labels the problem rather than answers it.[21] Secondly, positing abstract artefacts is otiose: we can say all we want to say without recourse to them. All we lose is a univocal referent that attracts our ontological commitment, but that is no loss, as we shall now see.

5.6.1 Truth without Ontological Commitment

So, the left-over issue is how to understand truth, if the truth-conditions of a sentence appear to specify an ontology we reflectively renounce. As we just saw, an expansive error theory is off the table, as are various other remedies. What the responses hitherto have in common is the goal to have semantics and

---

[21] The issue, of course, goes back to Aristotle's *aitia*, and the different ways of accounting for a thing, as substance, form, purpose, and effect, as well as his more general hylomorphism. As regards cities, at least, Aristotle says:

> A city belongs to the order of 'compounds', just like any other thing which forms a single 'whole', while being composed, none the less, of a number of different parts. (*Politics*, III, 1274b38)

Here, Aristotle is thinking of a city as simply a population of citizens under a constitution or lawful organisation. See Moravcsik 1975 for a general take on *aitia* that influenced Chomsky (2000) and Pustejovsky (1995) on the complexity of lexical items. Unlike Aristotle, the claim here being made is not an ontological one about the complexity of the things to which our items refer, but rather a claim about the complexity of the ways in which we may refer using a single item.

ontology intimate, so that what there is can be read off truth conditions. This is what we shall have to give up; it will prove surprisingly easy.

The central thought of contemporary truth-conditional approaches is that semantics details relations between language and the world, symbol and thing; it does not merely relate symbol to symbol. After all, if semantics is what a competent speaker knows (in some sense), then to know that one symbol type relates to another symbol type is not yet to know what either means. Still, if semantic specifications do relate the symbolic to the non-symbolic, it remains unclear what fragment of the non-symbolic our specification specifies.

To start with, consider an easy case:

(8) 'Mad dogs and Englishmen are always hungry' is true iff mad dogs and Englishmen are always hungry.

In one sense, such homophonic equivalences are always true and do give the truth conditions of the target sentence, but only indeterminately. The sentence needs to be disambiguated syntactically (does 'mad' scope over the nominal conjunction or just 'dogs'?). What, then, is supposed to happen on the right-hand side to match the disambiguation? Some notation or paraphrase is required in the language we use in order to speak of the world to reflect the syntactic differences that the bare surface form of the target language elides. But now it is obvious that there is no specification that is a pure proxy for the world itself, as if we could drag the dogs and Englishmen themselves into the semantics. Any 'canonical notation' not heir to the ambiguity or vagaries of the target language must itself be underwritten as somehow *really* ontologically committing, at least if we want semantics and ontology to be intimate in the imagined way, but we have seen that it is wholly unobvious how this might be achieved. There appears, in short, to be no linguistic signature of ontological commitment.

Consider fiction under some first-order notation:

(9) a. 'Donald Trump is American' is true iff $(\exists x)[x = \text{DT} \wedge \text{American}(x)]$.
    b. 'Donald Duck is American' is true iff $(\exists x)[x = \text{DD} \wedge \text{American}(x)]$.

If one follows Quine, the thing to say here is that the notation makes it clear that (9b) is false, for there is no suitable value for 'x'. Yet that doesn't follow at all without some prior stipulation over what goes into a domain of quantification, which cannot be provided in such a way as to be constrained or even informed by the semantics of the language one is trying to specify.[22]

---

[22] One might consider there to be *characters* as abstract artefacts, which serve as values for 'x'. This brings its own problems, however, not least that a twin-track approach to in-fiction and out-fiction faces

Turning to copredication and polysemy, we know the *kind* of thing we want to say:

(10) 'Bill painted a door and walked though it' is true iff $(\exists x)[\text{Door}(x) \wedge \text{Painted}(\text{Bill}, x_{[\text{material}]}) \wedge \text{Walked-through}(\text{Bill}, x_{[\text{portal}]})]$.

This labels the problem, though, for we are no better off in understanding how a univocal value for 'x' can be both material and a portal. What is required is a variable whose values are individuated relative to the predicates (cf. Asher 2011). Our concern at the moment, though, is not getting the semantic structure right, but understanding how the world might be in order to render copredications true.

A simple expedient is to think that semantics is just no sure guide to how the world is. This is consistent with the thought that the truth conditions an adequate theory specifies are apt to cover a range of circumstances that count as an instance of the specification, though the semantics does not underwrite what 'counts as' counts as; for that, you would need to appeal to the circumstances at hand and adduce essentially worldly knowledge. So, go back to simple cases:

(11) a. 'There is milk in the fridge' is true iff there is milk in the fridge.
b. 'The car is red' is true iff the car is red.

Taking a leaf from Travis 2008, we know that there are lots of different ways for milk to be in the fridge. A spilt drop wouldn't normally count as milk being in the fridge, but it might if one is OCD. Similarly, red cars are those normally with only relevant bodywork red, but a red interior might count, as might a car that merely looks red in a certain light (for the purposes of photography), or even one wholly red from top to bottom, inside and out (a piece of conceptual art). So, it is not so much that the cases in (11) and innumerable others are wrong or even ambiguous like (8); rather, how the world is to render a sentence true is just not semantically specified. Austin (1950) recognized this early and analysed truth in terms of what he called two kinds of 'conventions' relating a sentence and the world. 'Descriptive conventions' relate sentences types to types of situation, while 'demonstrative conventions' relate tokens (statements involving a type) with particular situations. The 'convention' label is misleading, at least for my purposes.[23] The crucial point is

---

a copredication problem in the guise of constructions like *Bond kills at will but remains as popular as ever* (a character is popular, created, makes money for producers, etc., but only *in* the stories does he kill or drink martinis). See Collins 2021.

[23] I assume that Austin spoke of conventions because he presumed that linguistic meaning was ultimately conventional. If we reject this presumption, Austin's distinction still holds. Furthermore,

only that general competence with a sentence (whether underwritten by convention or not) does not suffice to determine whether a specific situation is one under which a token of the type would be true. A further condition must obtain fixing whether the prevailing situation is one that would count as making true the token of the type. Here, too, it is misleading to talk of 'convention', save that one can't treat any situation as making true any sentence; but there is considerable flexibility. At any rate, you need both to have truth, for the circumstances that might render a token true do not admit of generalization in a way that would guarantee that the type is true no matter what the particularity of the situation. For example, if the interior of a relevant car is red, it does not follow that the type *The car is red* is true, for another token of the type might be false for a speaker who is concerned with bodywork.

We can now think of a semantic theory as specifying properties of sentence types syntactically individuated, not tokens. The types are assigned truth conditions, but these conditions do not translate into determinate ways the world can be that would render the sentence true from one circumstance to another. It is merely that the circumstances that would render the sentence tokens true can be described in terms of the general truth conditions, just as various distinct kinds of cars can be said to be red in general, even if there is nothing that counts as red as such which they all have in common. The morals here provide answers to how fictions and copredications can be true without any offending ontological commitment.

Thus, for fiction, what renders true a token of *Holmes is smart* is a set of complex circumstances involving stories and cultural transmission, knowledge of which can vary between speakers and circumstances, but the truth conditions for the sentence type need make no reference to such varying circumstances, and it can be treated on a par with *Einstein is smart*. So, the semantic competences of someone who thinks Holmes was a real individual and another who knows he is a fiction are relevantly the same. Where they differ is in the respective beliefs about what would render the sentences true. People can thus be confused, in this regard, and go badly wrong in the world, not because they misunderstand their language (although that can otherwise happen, of course), but because they are mistaken about what would make their claims true.

---

it is somewhat misplaced to speak of demonstrative conventions, for there is no convention at all concerning how the prevailing situation of an utterance might fix what one is speaking about.

Copredication works the same, save for in more general terms. The truth conditions for copredications involve a specification of a univocal door or London or whatever. What makes the relevant copredications true, however, cannot match the specification, for there are no queer objects, much as fictions can be true even though there is no Holmes or Donald Duck. A situation that would render true *Bill painted the door and walked though it* would involve both a material object that can be painted and also a portal, with the former being a movable barrier to the latter. But that is not what a truth-conditional semantics tells you. To be sure, one could insist that only a theory that specified such a situation should count as truth-conditional. If this desideratum is to be taken seriously, it must be shown that such conditions actually compositionally reflect the syntax of the sentence type; otherwise, the position I am putting forward wins out, for it is in line with a compositional interpretation that reflects the syntax. Without further ado, the understanding of how the world is that renders the sentence true is, therefore, not part of semantics.

Much more could be said in both articulation and defence of this position, but such a sketch will have to suffice.

5.7 In Conclusion: A Harmless Idealism

We started by considering a thin sense of idealism whereby semantics tells us what there is. I have challenged this view by arguing that the world as semantics specifies it is of a granularity that does not fix truth in any robust way; semantics leaves it open what in the world makes truths true. In particular, there is no special vocabulary, not even the concept of truth, that allows us to read off what there is beyond what we take ourselves to be talking about in the most unreflective disquotational sense. Absent reflection, we simply treat the world as consisting of the entities of which we speak. Upon reflection, however, we can readily discern that language dissembles in the form of generating a conflict between the univocity of truth conditions and an independent take on the kind of entities we reckon there to be. It is in this sense that the thin idealism traditional conceptions of semantics offer is mistaken.[24]

---

[24] My thanks go to Richard Gaskin, for many useful criticisms and suggestions, and Michael Devitt, Paul Pietroski, and Michael Glanzberg. This work was funded by Ikerbasque via the project HORIZON-MSCA-2022-COFUND-101,126,600-SmartBrain3.

References

Aristotle. 1995. *Politics*. Trans. E. Barker (Oxford: OUP).
Asher, N. 2011. *Lexical Meaning in Context: A Web of Words* (Cambridge: CUP).
Austin, J. L. 1950. 'Truth', *Proceedings of the Aristotelian Society*, supp. vol. 24, 111–28.
Azzouni, J. 2004. *Deflating Existential Consequence: A Case for Nominalism* (Oxford: OUP).
Azzouni, J. 2010. *Talking about Nothing: Numbers, Hallucinations, and Fictions* (Oxford: OUP).
Azzouni, J. 2017. *Ontology without Borders* (Oxford: OUP).
Carnap, R. 1934. *Logische Syntax der Sprache*. English translation by A. Smeaton, 1937. *The Logical Syntax of Language* (London: Routledge and Kegan Paul).
Chalmers, D. 2009. 'Ontological anti-realism', in D. Chalmers, D. Manley, and R. Wasserman (eds), *Metametaphysics: New Essays on the Foundations of Ontology* (Oxford: OUP), 77–129.
Chomsky, N. 2000. *New Horizons in the Study of Language and Mind* (Cambridge: CUP).
Cinque, G. 2010. *The Syntax of Adjectives: A Comparative Study* (Cambridge, Mass.: MIT Press).
Coffa, A. 1991. *The Semantic Tradition from Kant to Carnap* (Cambridge: CUP).
Collins, J. 2021. 'The diversity of fiction and copredication: An accommodation problem', *Erkenntnis* 86, 1197–1223.
Collins, J. 2022. 'Natural language quantification is not polysemous', *Synthese* 200, 1–26.
Collins, J. 2023. 'Copredication as illusion', *Journal of Semantics* (https://doi.org/10.1093/jos/ffad014).
Collins, J. and Rey, G. 2023. 'Laws and luck in language: Problems with Devitt's conventional, common-sense linguistics', in A. Fairweather and C. Montemayor (eds), *Linguistic Luck: Safeguards and Threats to Linguistic Communication* (Oxford: OUP), 88–123.
Davidson, D. 1980. *Essays on Actions and Events* (Oxford: OUP).
Davidson, D. 1984. *Inquiries into Truth and Interpretation* (Oxford: OUP).
Devitt, M. 2010. *Putting Metaphysics First* (Oxford: OUP).
Devitt, M. 2021. *Overlooking Conventions: The Trouble with Linguistic Conventions* (Berlin: Springer).
Dummett, M. 1993. *Origins of Analytical Philosophy* (London: Duckworth).
Fine, K. 2009. 'The question of ontology', in D. Chalmers, D. Manley, and R. Wasserman (eds), *Metametaphysics: New Essays on the Foundations of Ontology* (Oxford: OUP), 157–77.
Frege, G. 1884. *Grundlagen der Arithmetik* (Breslau: Koebner, 1884; repr. ed. C. Thiel, Hamburg: Felix Meiner, 1988).
Gaskin, R. 2021. *Language and World: A Defence of Linguistic Idealism* (London: Routledge).
Glanzberg, M. 2014. 'Explanation and partiality in semantic theory', in A. Burgess and B. Sherman (eds), *Metasemantics: New Essays on the Foundations of Meaning* (Oxford: OUP), 259–92.
Gregory, P. 2020. 'Quine's deflationary structuralism', in F. Janssen-Lauret (ed.), *Quine, Structure, and Ontology* (Oxford: OUP), 96–116.
Hirsch, E. 2011. *Quantifier Variance and Realism: Essays in Metaontology* (Oxford: OUP).
Hofweber, T. 2016. *Ontology and the Ambitions of Metaphysics* (Oxford: OUP).
Hylton, P. 1990. *Russell, Idealism, and the Emergence of Analytic Philosophy* (Oxford: Clarendon).
King, J. 2018. 'W(h)ither semantics! (?)'. *Nous* 52, 772–95.
Kripke, S. 1980. *Naming and Necessity* (Oxford: Blackwell).
Lewis, D. 1970. 'General semantics', *Synthese* 22, 18–67.
Liebesman, D. and Magidor, O. 2017. 'Copredication and Property Inheritance', *Philosophical Issues* 27, 131–66.
Moravcsik, J. 1975. '*Aitia* as a generative factor in Aristotle's philosophy', *Dialogue* 14, 622–38.
Pustejovsky, J. 1995. *The Generative Lexicon* (Cambridge, Mass.: MIT Press).
Quine, W. V. O. 1953. *From a Logical Point of View* (Cambridge, Mass.: Harvard University Press).
Quine, W. V. O. 1960. *Word and Object* (Cambridge, Mass.: MIT).
Quine, W. V. O. 1992. *From Stimulus to Science* (Cambridge, Mass.: Harvard University Press).
Russell, B. 1905. 'On Denoting', *Mind* 14, 479–93.

Schaffer, J. 2009. 'On what grounds what', in D. Chalmers, D. Manley, and R. Wasserman (eds.), *Metametaphysics: New Essays on the Foundations of Ontology* (Oxford: OUP), 347–83.
Sider, T. 2011. *Writing the Book of the World* (Oxford: OUP).
Thomasson, A. 2014. *Ontology Made Easy* (Oxford: OUP).
Travis, C. 2008. *Occasion-Sensitivity* (Oxford: OUP).
Williamson, T. 2013. *Modal Logic as Metaphysics* (Oxford: OUP).

6

Metaphysics First or Language First

The Notion of a Single Object

Friederike Moltmann

6.1 Introduction

The notion of a single object or of being one is an important notion in metaphysics, and it is presupposed by any account of the notion of number in the philosophy of mathematics.[1] The notion of being a single object contrasts with that of being a mere plurality, a plurality 'as many', as well as with the notion of mere 'stuff' or, as it is somewhat misleadingly called, a 'portion' or a 'quantity'.[2]

In philosophy, attention has generally been focused on the notion of an object as such, rather than that of a single object.[3] There are two approaches concerning the notion of an object (as such). A metaphysics-first view takes objects to be given independently of language (and often leads to scepticism concerning whether language involves reference to objects at all). The second, language-first view takes the notion of an object to be defined on the basis of language, as in the Fregean definition according to which an object is what a referential noun phrase (NP) may stand for.

The notion of a single object has received much less attention than the notion of an object as such. The notion of a single object has a particularly obvious linguistic reflection, in the use of singular count NPs in English and the use of numeral classifiers in certain languages such as Chinese. In general, the use of a singular count NP is required for attributing number-related properties to an object. The use of a singular count NP is *in general*

---

[1] I would like to thank Richard Gaskin for extensive comments on a previous version of this chapter, which has also benefited greatly from the audience of the Philosophy of Mathematics Seminar in Pavia, especially Andrea Sereni and Silvia de Toffoli, as well as from comments by John Collins.

[2] The term 'quantity' for the elements in the extension of mass nouns is due to Cartwright 1970; see also ter Meulen 1981. 'Quantity', however, is a singular count noun and thus necessarily unable to stand for the same things as a mass noun, as will be discussed.

[3] An exception is Priest 2015, who gives an in-depth philosophical discussion regarding the notion of being one (but only in contrast to being many (pluralities as many), not to being neither one nor many (stuff)).

accompanied by the obtaining of worldly unifying conditions in respect of the relevant object. But this is not *invariably* so: we also find a range of uses of singular count categories that define single entities *without* such worldly unifying conditions being in place. In these cases, the choice of a count or non-count category appears arbitrary, or at least not grounded in the obtaining of worldly conditions. Linguists have referred to this phenomenon as 'grammaticized individuation' (Rothstein 2017) or 'language-driven ontology' (Moltmann 2021). Philosophically such cases seem particularly suited to an application of linguistic idealism, according to which, as applied here, single objecthood ought to be strictly shaped by our linguistic access to entities, not found in the world independently of that access. This means that the way in which the property of being a single object is conveyed in natural language should be viewed as the product of a mental/linguistic faculty, rather than as a mind- and language-independent property of objects. The salient fact here is that there is a range of linguistic devices whose *sole* purpose is to convey unity, and in fact to *impose* unity. There are two general approaches to the content of the mass–count distinction in natural-language semantics: the extension-based approach (which goes back to Quine) and the integrity-based approach (which can be traced to Aristotle). Neither of them, I will argue, captures the notion of a single object in its generality.

In the next section I will outline the general background regarding the relation between language and reality, where we may distinguish three views: first, what one might call the 'naïve view' of the relation between language and reality; second, more recent and still very common stances of scepticism regarding that relation, in particular Chomskyan scepticism (I will propose a way of addressing some of the Chomskyan examples); third, a re-emerging interest in connecting language and reality, such as Peacocke's (2019) project of the primacy of metaphysics and Gaskin's (2021) project of linguistic idealism. The present contribution examines a particular case to which linguistic idealism applies especially well, without necessarily endorsing the more radical view as such. As will be pointed out later on in the paper, the linguistic facts are actually complex, displaying multiple layers of absence or presence of single objecthood and requiring us to distinguish between *conceptually driven* and *syntactically driven oneness*.

6.2 Background: The Relation between Language and Reality

This chapter bears on the very general topic of the relation between language and reality. Briefly, three broad views can be distinguished concerning how language relates to reality. On an older, naïve view, which is at least that of ancient and medieval metaphysics and philosophy of language, but also of many philosophers afterwards (including Frege), language mirrors reality and is accordingly a guide to ontology. Frege's (1884) definition of an object (in a linguistically updated version) is a particularly clear manifestation of that view:

(1) Frege's definition of an object
An object is what a referential NP may stand for.

I will get back to the Fregean definition shortly.

Since the mid-twentieth century, there has been a significant shift towards a different view of the relation between language and reality. Given the wealth of derivative and suspect objects that natural language seems to introduce with its referential terms (typical students, windows, holes, flaws, problems, homes, etc.), many philosophers, taking metaphysics to be about what there really is, have turned away from language as a guide to ontology, focusing on foundational metaphysics instead without appeal to language, which on their view does not 'carve nature at its joints'.

Some linguists have also adopted a sceptical stance towards the relation of language to reality, most notably Chomsky (1986, 1998).[4] According to Chomsky, natural language abounds in referential NPs that fail to stand for objects when used by a speaker. For Chomsky, typical students, windows, holes, flaws, problems, and homes cannot be objects in the real world. One argument for this view, which Chomsky along with a significant literature following him deploys, appeals to apparently contradictory property attributions that entities such as towns, colleges, windows, books, and houses display (Pustejovsky 1995; Collins in this volume). Thus, a book can be both interesting and heavy; one can enter through a window, but the window can also be replaced; a town can be destroyed, yet remain once it has been rebuilt.

Chomsky's scepticism hinges on a particular presupposition regarding how reality is to be understood, namely as a (mainly) mind-independent physical domain containing entities that meet standard conditions of individuation.[5] These conditions include having a single location in space at a time and displaying consistency of property attributions. But recent developments in metaphysics provide responses to at least some of the challenges to referentialist semantics discussed in the literature. These responses include theories of

---

[4] See also Pietroski 2017, and Collins in this volume.
[5] Chomsky in fact extends his scepticism even to merely conceived objects as what a referential NP may stand for: even those could not actually be viewed as objects, on his view (Chomsky 1998, 17).

ontologically dependent objects, minor objects, and mind-dependent objects, plenitudinous or permissive conceptions of reality, theories of grounding that permit different levels of reality, and theories of possible, nonexistent, and fictional objects. Given such developments, a wealth of possibly highly derivative objects can no longer be regarded objectionable as such: we now have ontological theories regarding at least a good part of the examples that originally gave rise to scepticism about the connection between language and reality; these theories do not always adopt standard conditions of object individuation, of course.

Let us take an example that itself raises the issue of unity, though in a way that is orthogonal to the mass–count distinction, as we will see (Section 6.4.2). This is the widely discussed example of the noun 'book', or more generally that of an artifact that permits multiple physical realizations. A referential NP with 'book' as its head permits apparently inconsistent property attributions, such as being interesting (a property of contents) and being heavy (a property of material objects), and these attributions may even occur in a single conjunction:

(2) The book is heavy and interesting.

Assuming that properties of material objects and of contents cannot be had by the same 'real' entities, the conclusion of Chomsky and many other linguists following him is that 'the book' in (2) cannot stand for a single, 'real' object. A number of researchers thus take 'the book' to be polysemous, standing for both a content and a material object, or else to stand for a merely conceptual object. There are various proposals concerning how such a polysemy is possible with a conjunctive predicate as in (2), for example the view that book stands for an underspecified conceptual object, such as a dot object in the sense of Pustejovsky (1995), that is to say, an entity that will be mapped onto a specific object when the relevant predicate is evaluated. Other arguments for the apparent polysemy of 'book' are based on the two different ways of counting books: as contents ('The exam is about only one book of Tolstoy, *War and Peace*'), and as concrete copies ('There are three books on the shelf'). Furthermore, whereas the location of a particular concrete copy seems unproblematic, the book as an information object could not share that location, since it is abstract and thus lacks a location in space; moreover, it could not have multiple locations—the locations of all the material copies at the time.[6]

---

[6] See Liebesman and Magidor 2017 for further discussion of the counting problem with 'book' and an account of the apparent polysemy of 'book' based on principles of property inheritance.

Contemporary metaphysics does not generally share the presupposition of linguists that reality divides into the material and the abstract. Metaphysicians rather have long recognized artifacts as mind-dependent objects that as such can bear both properties appropriate to material objects and content-related properties imposed by an act of creation (Ingarden 1931; Thomasson 1999). And proposals have been advanced to deal with the counting and the location problems. One of these proposals is Fine's (1999, 2020) notion of variable embodiment. Fine takes a variable embodiment to be an object that comes with a 'form', which is a function mapping times to material manifestations of the object at those times. Thus, a book considered as a variable embodiment comes with a (partial) function mapping times at which the book exists to pluralities of concrete copies of the book. The concrete copies not only have a material constitution, but also a content, just like concrete artifacts in general. The book itself will inherit its location at a given time from its manifestation at that time, and thus it may come out multiply located—which need not be considered problematic. When counting a book, either the variable embodiment as such is counted or its manifestations at relevant times. Fine's notion of a variable embodiment thus provides a way of unifying objects that come with multiple realizations.

There is another argument, not discussed in the literature, to the effect that artifactual nouns like 'book' stand for single objects, rather than being polysemous, standing, in a way, for pluralities of content-based and material things. The argument is that for artifacts there are generally predicates that can hold only of the 'entire' object, not the material object or the content as such. For books a case in point would be:

(3) The book appeared last year.

Material objects do not 'appear' in the same sense, and contents do not appear either. Other predicates applying only to the book 'as a whole' are 'was reprinted several times', 'sells well' and 'was on the bestseller list' (disregarding e-books).[7]

There is one case in which predicates of artifacts could not be viewed as introducing properties of the associated concrete physical (or mental) object or of the information object: these are predicates applied to entities like requests and decisions, which are non-enduring products of acts of requesting and deciding, as Twardowski (1911) would say, that is, artifacts that lack a material realization (see also Ulrich 1976; Moltmann 2019). A request can be

---

[7] Further arguments against polysemy have been put forward by Brody and Feinman 2024.

'fulfilled', but neither an act nor a proposition can be 'fulfilled'. A decision can be 'carried out'; but neither a (mental) act nor a proposition can be 'carried out'.

Contemporary metaphysics no longer presents a univocal picture of reality as a physical domain containing objects individuated in terms of their unique spatio-temporal location. Instead, it recognizes a rich panoply of various sorts of ontologically dependent objects; more generally it recognizes different levels of grounding, as well as mind-dependent and social objects of various sorts; not to mention views involving even more permissive or plenitudinous conceptions of reality.[8]

There has also been a renewed interest in establishing a close connection between language and reality. Thus Peacocke (2019) advocates the primacy of metaphysics, arguing that the metaphysics of a domain is involved in the explanation of the meaning of sentences concerning that domain. Peacocke's view is a metaphysics-first view, based on the assumption of a language- and mind-independent reality consisting of domains of objects and their properties. By contrast, Gaskin (2021) advocates a linguistic idealism according to which, roughly, reality is shaped throughout by our linguistic access to it. Gaskin's view is a language-first view, in the sense that reality is partly constituted by how we describe it through language. The contribution of this chapter falls within a language-first view, without, though, necessarily endorsing the radical version presented by Gaskin.

6.3 The Notion of a Single Object

We can now turn to the main topic of this chapter, the notion of a single object. Let us first review Frege's notion of an object, repeated below:

(4) <u>Frege's definition of an object</u>
An object is what a referential NP may stand for.

Here I have replaced Frege's 'name' by 'referential noun phrase (NP)', a notion well-established in linguistics. Definite and indefinite NPs may be referential NPs, but whether an occurrence of an expression in a sentence is a referential NP depends also on its syntactic position as well as on whether the predicate is existence-entailing ('exist', 'think about', 'imagine' are not existence-entailing;

---

[8] For the latter see Hawthorne 2006; Eklund 2008; Schaffer 2009.

'tree', 'house', 'sleep', 'run' are existence-entailing). A further criterion for status as a referential NP is support of anaphora. Here care needs to be taken to distinguish ordinary pronouns that can be used anaphorically ('it', 'he', 'she') and special NPs, such as 'that' and 'the same thing', which can be used with a reifying force, as we will see (Section 4.2).

As mentioned, Frege's definition of an object does not define the notion of a single object, but just the notion of an object, a 'being', as one may say. That is because on Frege's definition, semantic values of definite mass and plural NPs come out as objects as well. Definite plural and mass NPs as in (5b, c) are generally considered referential NPs of the very same sort as singular count NPs as in (5a):[9]

(5) a. The house is on fire.
    b. The students collaborate.
    c. The water is in the bottle.

Philosophers when discussing Frege's definition of an object generally take that definition to define single objects. In fact, contemporary semantic analyses of definite plural and mass NPs generally just treat their semantic values as single entities. This holds for extensional mereological theories of the semantics of plurals and mass nouns (Link 1983; Ojeda 1993; Champollion and Krifka 2016), as well as non-extensional, integrity-based mereological theories (Moltmann 1997, 1998). On both sorts of semantic theories, the definite NP 'the students' stands for the sum of the contextually relevant set of students and the NP 'the water in the bottle' for the maximal portion of water in the bottle. For the semantics of plurals, this contrasts with plural logic, which posits genuine plural variables for pluralities ('as many') (see McKay 2006; Yi 2005, 2006; Oliver and Smiley 2013; Moltmann 2016). For mass nouns, it contrasts with a recent proposal to use genuine mass variables for the quantities, distinct from individual variables (McKay 2016). See Section 6.5.

Extensional mereology takes the semantic values of singular count, plural, and mass NPs to be (single) entities in three domains each ordered by its own part relation: the count-noun-specific part relation applying to individuals ('subatomic parts'), the plural-specific part relation applying to sums of individuals, and the mass-specific part relation applying portions or quantities, which are the entities taken to be in the extension of mass nouns:

---

[9] For an overview of linguistic research on the mass–count distinction, see Doetjes 2012 and Pelletier and Schubert 2012. For empirical, especially crosslinguistic research on the mass–count distinction, see the edited volumes of Moltmann 2019 and Filip 2021.

(6) a. The domain of individuals: $(D, <)$, where $<$ represents the count-noun-specific part relation
   b. The domain of pluralities: $(SUM_{<p}(D), <_p)$, where $<p$ represents the plural-specific part relation
   c. The mass domain: $(M, <_m)$, where $<_m$ represents the mass-noun-specific part relation

Here $SUM_{<p}(D)$ is the closure under sum formation of the domain D, with respect to the plural-specific part relation. On this account, pluralities and quantities are treated as single entities on a par with individuals, even though three distinct domains with their category-specific part relations are distinguished. The same holds for the integrity-based theory of Moltmann (1997, 1998), which does not need to distinguish between three different part relations for individuals, pluralities, and quantities.

The problem with mereological semantic theories of plurals and mass nouns is that the semantic values of definite plural and mass NPs do not semantically act as single objects or as 'one'.

Let us first go through some of the standard criteria for the mass–count distinction. One important criterion for singular count nouns is that they come with a plural; mass nouns don't. Equally important is the applicability of cardinal and ordinal numerals to count nouns, but not mass nouns:

(7) a. the first house, one house, a number of houses
   b. * the first wood, * one wood, * a number of wood

A related criterion is the applicability of number-related predicates such as 'is one of them' or 'are numerous', which are strictly excluded with mass NPs:

(8) a. Joe is *one of* the children at this school.
   b. The students are *numerous*.

(9) a. ??? The rice was one of the meals offered in the evening.
   b. ??? The rice was numerous, so everyone got a portion.

One question that the criteria of the applicability of number-related modifiers and predicates leaves open is whether they are based on syntactic or semantic selection. The mass–count distinction, after all, could just be on a par with gender in languages like German, involving relatively arbitrary category selection that serves the purpose of syntactic agreement (Bale and Gillon 2021).

But there are number-related linguistic phenomena relating to the mass–count distinction in English that can hardly be viewed as a matter of syntactic agreement. One of them is the applicability of verbs of counting, listing, and ranking, that is, verbs describing cardinal- and ordinal-number-related actions (Moltmann 1997, 2016). It can be observed that predicates like 'count', 'list', and 'rank' are impossible with mass nouns like 'wood' or 'gold' (even in a situation in which there are clearly distinct piles of wood or gold); by contrast, 'count' is not that bad with collective NPs like 'class', on the internal reading (according to which we are concerned with the members of the group rather than the group as a whole), though it is worse with 'orchestra' or 'art collection':

(10) a. John counted/listed/ranked the students.
  b. John (?) counted/?? listed/?? ranked the class.
  b. ?? John counted the wood/gold.
  c. ?? John counted the orchestra/art collection.

The constraints on the application of predicates of cardinal- and ordinal-number-related actions are clearly not syntactic but semantic in nature.

There is another phenomenon relating to the mass–count distinction that can clearly only be semantic in nature, and that is the understanding of existence predicates. (11a) and (11b) can be used to deny the existence of an object, a concrete object in (11a), an abstract object in (11b). Now plural NPs and mass NPs do not permit a reading denying the existence of an object beyond the plurality or the stuff itself (Moltmann 2016):

(11) a. The house Bill mentioned does not exist.
  b. The round circle does not exist.

(12) a. The buildings do not exist.
  b. The set/sum/collection/fusion of the buildings does not exist.

(13) a. The rice does not exist.
  b. The portion/quantity of the rice does not exist.

(12b, 13b) can be used to deny the existence of single entities that are sets, sums, collections, portions, and quantities. By contrast, (12a) and (13a) cannot be used to deny the existence of single entities, 'sums' or 'quantities', as single entities beyond the individuals or the 'stuff' that make them up. That is, (12a) cannot be used by a philosopher, say, to deny the existence of a set, sum, collection, or fusion, unlike (12b). Likewise, (13a) cannot be used to deny the existence of portions or quantities, as entities distinct from the rice itself. Without there being a fundamental semantic distinction, the different ways in which existence predicates are understood could hardly be explained.

The different interpretations of existence predicates show that the distinction between singular count NPs and plural/mass NPs is truly a semantic distinction. A singular count NP refers to a single object whose existence can be denied as a thing beyond what makes it up (material or stuff, individual members).

The most common approaches to the mass–count distinction do not actually capture that distinction, and they come with other serious difficulties. Let us briefly turn to those approaches and their problems.

6.4 Standard Views of the Mass–Count Distinction

Two main approaches in contemporary natural-language semantics to the content of the mass–count distinction can be distinguished, and given the close connection between a singular count noun and the notion of being a single object, there are also two corresponding approaches to the notion of a single object, as opposed to pluralities and quantities: the extensional mereological approach and the integrity-based approach.

6.4.1 The Extensional Mereological Approach

The extensional mereological approach is the most common approach in linguistics, though it goes back to Quine (1960). On this view, single objects are defined as atoms relative to a concept (or predicate), as entities that fall under the concept, but do not have any proper parts that also fall under the concept:

(14) x is a single object = x is an *atom* relative to a concept (predicate) C, i.e., $C(x)$ and for no y, $y < x$, $C(y)$.

What distinguishes singular count nouns from both plural nouns and mass nouns is that all elements in the extension of singular count nouns are atoms.

The extensional mereological approach makes use of distinct part relations for the domains of individuals, pluralities, and quantities. The extension of a plural noun N_{pl} is defined as the closure under sum formation (with respect to the plural-specific part relation) of the extension of the singular count noun N. Plurals nouns thus can have non-atoms in their extension (pluralities of two or more entities from the extension of the singular noun). Mass nouns are generally contrasted with singular count nouns as not containing atoms in their extension. The latter condition faces a notorious problem, the minimal-parts problem. Thus, the extension of 'water' does contain atoms given that parts of individual H_2O molecules are no longer water; parts of clothing such as buttons are no longer clothing; and certain parts of rice grains are no longer rice.

Weakening the condition characterizing mass nouns by, for example, requiring that mass nouns are not perceived as containing atoms or that mass nouns do not necessarily contain atoms does not help when it comes to obtaining conditions when mass nouns actually apply.[10]

There are other well-known problems for the extensional mereological account. They include the difficulty applying the account to the following types of nouns:

(15) a. Entity nouns: 'entity', 'being', 'thing'
b. Sequence-type nouns: 'sequence', 'line', 'fence'
c. Collection nouns: 'collection', 'sum', 'group'
d. Portion nouns: 'portion', 'quantity', 'amount'
e. Part nouns: 'part'

A part of an entity is still an entity and thus the count noun 'entity' is not atomic, and since the sum of two entities is again an entity, 'entity' is cumulative (Moltmann 1997, 19; 1998, 81). Likewise, a part of a sequence may still be a sequence (Rothstein 2017). Furthermore, a part of a collection may still be a collection, and so for portions and parts.

One may argue that ordinarily definite NPs with a noun of one of these classes as head are used in contexts in which they refer to a unique (often maximal) object in the context. This seems supported by the way uniqueness of the referent is understood in the following examples:

(16) a. The sequence he wrote down is short.
b. The fence he had built is white.
c. The portion of wine in the bottle is small.

In fact, there is a proposal in the literature capturing that generalization about ordinary uses, namely Rothstein's (2017) account of count nouns.[11] Rothstein proposes that count nouns are to be relativized to a contextually given set, so that atomicity will have to obtain just with respect to that set rather than the entire extension of the count noun. This also means that count nouns are type distinct from mass nouns, and it is that type distinction that, on Rothstein's

---

[10] See Pelletier and Schubert 2012 for discussion.

[11] Zucchi and White 2001 address a related issue, the fact that NPs like 'a sequence', 'a twig', etc. do not lead to homogenous predicates that would allow for the application of *for*-adverbials, as in (ia). They also note that 'some peas' does not lead to a homogenous predicate, as in (ib):

(i) a. For two hours, John constructed sequences/ ??? a sequence.
b. ??? For one hour, John ate some peas.

Their formal proposal does not target the mass–count distinction, but rather the interaction with temporal-measure adverbials, and (ib) makes clear that the phenomenon is in fact a distinct one.

account, ensures the selection of numerals (not atomicity as such). The fact, however, is that NPs with a noun of one of the classes in question can also be used so as not to describe atoms relative to a contextually given set. Thus, (17) is perfectly fine semantically:

(17) Looking at this line on the paper, you can see that there are in fact infinitely many lines on the paper.

Natural language as such does not exclude such uses of count nouns, and it is a task for semantic theory to account for them. In fact, the association of the notion of an atom with countability or being a single object is problematic in the first place: even if there are infinitely many lines, they are still *countable* (in the ordinary sense, not, of course, in the set-theoretic sense of 'countable', contrasting with 'uncountable'). Similarly, there is no problem counting subportions, subquantities, parts of fences and walls, etc.

6.4.2 The Integrity-Based Approach

The second approach to the notion of a single object makes central use of the notion of having a boundary, a form, a structure, or some other form of integrity. The notion of form or of an integrated whole goes back to Aristotle and was revived by Simons in his 1987, against the background of the then dominant extensional mereology.[12] Following Simons, the notion of an integrated whole was applied to the mass–count distinction and to a great range of other natural-language phenomena in Moltmann 1997, 1998, and 2016. The integrity-based approach to the notion of a single object says that being one means being an integrated whole (of one sort or another). Of course, an important question is: what is an integrated whole? There are different notions of integrity, which include notions of form, of having a boundary, and of function. As discussed in Simons 1987, it is hard (if it is even possible) to give a general definition of an integrated whole. But a very simple notion of an integrated whole should suffice as an example, namely the notion of an entity consisting of maximally connected parts, an R-integrated whole (Simons 1987).[13] Here we say that, where R' is the transitive closure of R, x is an R-integrated whole if and only if: for any x, y, and z, if $y < x$ and $z < x$, then $yR'z$, and for no y such that $\neg\, y < x$ is there is a $z < x$ such that $yR'z$. A special

---

[12] The notion of form is also central in the work of Neo-Aristotelian metaphysics, for example, Koslicki 2008.

[13] What unifies a whole may also be function or purpose, see Schaffer and Rosen 2017.

case of an entity with maximally connected parts is the sum of entities sharing a particular property, a notion I will come back to later.

An integrity-based account of the content of the mass–count distinction says that count nouns, but not mass nouns, convey properties of integrated wholes such as having a boundary or form. Such an account is found already in cognitive semantics (Langacker 1987). The situation-based variant of the integrity-based approach says that count nouns but not mass nouns convey properties of integrity relative to a situation (Moltmann 1997, 1998).

The integrity-based approach relativized to a situation offers an account of sequence-type nouns: a maximal sequence counts as an integrated whole in a situation not containing any of its proper parts; this is the integrity-based correlate of Rothstein's (2017) account of context-relative atomicity. However, statements like (17) pose the same problem as for the extensional mereological account. Moreover the integrity-based account still faces problems with collection nouns and portion nouns when their application does not require any worldly or perceived integrity, as below:

(18) a. the sum of this pen and the Eiffel Tower
     b. the lower-half portion of the water in the glass
     c. the quantity of wood from which this chair and that table are made

In such cases no worldly or even perceived integrity conditions seem to be required for the referent to count as one.[14]

One might suggest stronger conditions on unity, such as conditions permitting re-identification over time. However, sentences conveying re-identification over time permit mass NPs (Cartwright 1970), as illustrated below:

(19) a. This is the same gold that we looked at yesterday.
     b. This is the same piece/amount of gold that we looked at yesterday.

(20) The very same material was used for the chair and then later for the table.

---

[14] Some of the nouns in (15) ordinarily require (contextually given) integrity conditions to obtain. Thus, the singular count noun 'thing' generally requires that the entities it applies to be integrated wholes of some sort, as illustrated by the following contrast (Moltmann 1998, 87):

(i) a. ?? This thing is apple.
    b. This thing is an apple.

This also holds of the singular count noun *part* ('The sauce is part of the meal', ? ? 'This sauce is a part of the meal').

While the most natural reading of (19a) and (20) is a kind reading of the mass noun (which turns it into a count noun), portion readings of such examples, though harder to get, are not excluded.

One might suggest that a stronger condition could ensure that the object in question is a single object, namely a condition imposing the 'form' or function that goes with variable embodiments. But in fact variable embodiments need not be single objects. For again, mass NPs can stand for variable embodiments, for example, 'faculty', 'medical staff', allowing for predicates comparing manifestations over time:

(21) a. The faculty/medical staff has increased.
b. The organization of the material has changed.

The integrity-based approach also shares certain problems with the extensional mereological approach. Both the extensional mereological approach and the integrity-based approach have difficulties with so-called object–mass NPs such as 'clothing', 'footwear', 'police force', 'faculty'.[15] Object–mass nouns denote, it seems, pluralities of individuals (single things). Yet object–mass nouns pattern with other mass nouns at least in the more syntactic respects (no plural, no selection of count determiners). The choice of object–mass nouns instead of count nouns is to an extent arbitrary, both within a particular language and across languages, as the following alternations in English indicate: 'clothes'—'clothing', 'shoes'—'footwear', 'police force'—'policeman'/'-woman', 'faculty'—'faculty members', a point emphasized by Chierchia (1998, 2015) and Rothstein (2017).

There is an alternative to using singular count nouns for conveying the notion of a single object, namely so-called individuating classifiers (Cheng and Sybesma 2005; Doetjes 2012). Languages such as Chinese that fail to have a syntactic mass–count distinction may use individuating classifiers instead of count nouns. But classifiers are also used in languages with a syntactic mass–count distinction, for example in English 'head of cattle' and 'amount of wine', 'head', and 'amount' act like individuating classifiers.

On the basis of the data given above, we may say that the following generalization holds. For referring to something x as 'one thing', x need not fulfil any conditions of integrity or atomicity whatsoever. Anything can be conceived or referred to as a single thing. Similarly, any plurality of however well-individuated things can be referred to as a mere 'quantity' with a suitable

---

[15] Cohen 2020 shows that object–mass nouns by no means constitute a marginal class. They may in fact be formed in a productive way morphologically, as is the case in French.

mass noun. The use of a singular count noun suffices for picking something out as a single thing or defining something as a single thing.

In fact, this view is further corroborated by the existence of particular devices in at least some languages, which can serve the purpose of singularizing a plurality or quantity. In English we have the noun 'thing', used as a singularizing noun below:[16]

(22) a. John thought of only *one thing*, his children.
  b. John forgot *two things*: the water and the wine.
  c. Joe ate only *two things*, the peas and the nuts.

In (22a) the noun 'thing' introduces a single thing on the basis of a plurality, in (22b) it introduces single things on the basis of two portions, and in (22c) it introduces single things on the basis of two pluralities.

There is also an expression in English that, in one of its uses, has the very opposite effect, namely of dissolving the unity conveyed by a singular count noun. This is the adnominal modifier 'whole' as in the examples below (Moltmann 1997, 2005):

(23) a. The whole collection is expensive.
  b. The collection is expensive.

On the relevant reading 'whole' has the effect in (22a) of stating that each of part the collection is expensive. This reading is not available for (22b), and that is because distributive readings of predicates are generally excluded with NPs referring to single entities.

Recall also that for a range of entities, the choice of an (object-)mass noun or a plural noun appears rather arbitrary, within a language and across languages.

Referring to something as a single entity or not is thus a matter of using a particular linguistic category or expression, rather than picking up on an independently available individuation of an entity as a single thing or not a single thing. This actually matches general intuitions: there does not seem to be anything in the world that renders a piece of clothing a single thing or just 'clothing'. It can be conceived either way. This then supports a linguistic-idealist approach to the notion of a single object: referring to something as a single thing does not mean referring to something through a *language-independent property* of being one, but rather *linguistically introducing* something *as* a single thing. Being one does not require any constitutive conditions, albeit it often does go along with them. Being an integrated whole facilitates being conceived

---

[16] See Moltmann 2022 on the 'reifying' force of special quantifiers like 'one thing'.

and referred to as one, but it is not either a necessary or a sufficient condition for that to succeed.

There are some semantic processes for which integrity (of a particular sort) and being a single object align. For example, the choice of count or mass nominalizations of verbs generally depends on the *Aktionsart* of the verb, rather than being arbitrary (Barner, Wagner, and Snedecker 2008). Another example is the meaning of 'time' as a classifier for events: when applied to non-telic verbs, 'time' generally selects maximal temporally continuous states/activities as countable event units (Moltmann 1997, ch. 5):

(24) a. John slept a few times today.
 b. Joe lived in Paris a few times in his life.

Integrity aligned with countability can also be achieved by the use of descriptions.

(25) John ate the chocolate and the honey. He ate them/both quickly.

'Them' and 'both' in (25) pick out maximally connected quantities based on sharing a property, quantities that count as single entities.

Conversely, there are places in natural-language semantics where lacking integrity and not being a single object align. One such phenomenon, the semantic process going along with the conversion of certain count nouns into mass nouns, has been called 'the universal grinder' (Pelletier and Schubert 2012). Thus, turning the count noun 'apple' ('many apples') into a mass noun 'apple' ('more apple') goes along with the loss of integrity:

(26) a. Joe put more apples into the salad.
 b. Joe put more apple into the salad.

But the existence of such semantic processes does not mean that single objecthood and integrity as such coincide.

6.5 Consequences for Semantic Theory

What does the distinction between objects that are one, objects that are many, and objects that are neither one nor many mean for formal semantics? The question has been addressed in the literature, but mainly for the case of the distinction between plurals and singular count nouns. Thus, a number of philosophical logicians have argued against the mereological account of plurals according to which definite plurals stand for sums (or sets). They have instead maintained that definite plurals involve genuine plural reference, reference to several entities at once. This goes along with the use of genuine plural variables in plural logic, variables that may take as values several entities at once (Yi 2005, 2006; McKay 2006; Oliver and Smiley 2013). There has been much less formal work on mass nouns in that respect, except for McKay 2016, who proposes a logic for mass reference and quantification, involving terms specifically for reference to 'stuff', as distinct from the singular terms for single entities, including quantities.

We have seen that whether something is referred to as a single object or not is to some extent arbitrary. This leaves two options concerning the way in which we conceive of reality itself. First, one may adopt a plenitudinous conception, according to which reality consists of both the single object and the same thing lacking unity. Second, one may adopt a version of linguistic idealism, according to which being one is imposed through the use of language, such as by the use of a singular-count category or numeral classifier. There is one piece of support in favour of the latter. This is the generalization that reference to single objects without the use of a singular count noun or classifier is basically impossible. That, however, is not what one would expect if the world itself made available single objects as readily as it made available their correlates lacking single objecthood. After all, definite descriptions can be incomplete and need not convey all of the essential properties of the intended referent. If a single object were just as much available as its non-single counterpart, then a definite description should be able to pick out a single object when just the information about its being a single thing was missing. But that is impossible: a mass NP in general cannot be used to refer to a single thing, as the discussed examples show. This indicates that single objecthood is introduced, not selected. That is, uses of count nouns and classifiers introduce unity; they do not pick it up. Here linguistic idealism comes in: the notion of a single object is not grounded in reality, but in language/the mind. Linguistic idealism provides an explanation of why the mass–count distinction displays what has been called 'grammaticized individuation' (Rothstein 2017) or a level of 'language-driven ontology' (Moltmann 2021).

6.6 Complications: Multiple Levels

We have seen that count-noun uses and uses of classifiers set up entities as single things, in part, but not always, based on conditions of integrity. The linguistic facts, however, are more complex than we have indicated so far. Natural-language semantics displays not just a single level of language-driven ontology, but multiple levels. In particular, individuation conveyed by language may take place at the conceptual as well as at the lexical level, allowing for mismatches between the two levels. This is part of a more general grammatical–conceptual divide, mismatches of individuation displayed by grammar and by lexical content, which appear in a range of linguistic phenomena (Copley and Roy 2022).

One example of the involvement of the two levels with respect to the notion of unity are object–mass nouns such as 'furniture', 'police force', 'faculty'. Object–mass nouns are mass nouns syntactically, yet they appear to stand for single entities, 'composing entities', as I will call them. There are generally count nouns available for the composing entities (even if of a more specific sort: 'chair', 'table' for 'furniture'). With object–mass nouns the mass category does not erase the level of countability of the composing entities. But object–mass nouns themselves do not permit numeral modifiers:

(27) a. * many furniture/police force/faculty
     b. * The furniture is numerous.

The countability of the composing entities is apparent in various ways. One of them is the marginal applicability of predicates of counting:

(28) ? John counted the furniture/the police force/the faculty.

Predicates of counting, though, become less acceptable if the mass noun conveys overall structure or function:

(29) a. ?? Mary counted the décor/the furnishing.
     b. ?? Joe counted the content of the bowl.

'Décor' and 'furnishing' can be object–mass nouns, if what they apply to is composed of well-individuated entities. 'Content' and 'target' are relational nouns and describe their referent in relation to another entity, and their referent may be composed of well-individuated entities. Yet predicates of counting are difficult to apply. Obviously, the reason is that these mass nouns convey weak conditions of overall integrity (involving, say, distribution or function) which makes the composing entities less accessible. Note that singular count nouns hardly accept predicates of counting, including relational nouns as in (30b):

(30) a. ?? John counted the orchestra.
     b. ?? Mary counted the target of the flashlight/the topic of conversation.

Another way in which the countability of the composing entities of object–mass nouns matters involves quantitative comparison:

(31) There is more furniture in this room than in that room.

The comparison in (31) appears to be based on counting, rather than on measuring volumes. That means that the composing entities have a countable status even though no count noun has been used, and that countability can be established at a conceptual level beneath the countability conveyed by syntactic categories or functional expressions (classifiers). How is this fact to be understood? Concepts may convey properties defining integrated wholes, and these may, but need not, attribute the additional property being one. 'Furniture' describes collections of integrated wholes, and in the context of (31) those integrated wholes count as single things. Yet that will not suffice for the application of numerals.

There is another range of cases where countability is established at a conceptual level, not by the use of a singular count category, and that is syntactic categories that lack a mass–count distinction, such as verbs, *that*-clauses, and predicates (Moltmann 1997). In general, in these cases, natural language chooses mass quantifiers and numeral classifiers, rather than treating the category in question as either mass or count depending on conceptual content. This is illustrated for event quantifiers below:

(32) a. John fell three times /* three.
     b. John slept three times/* three.

(33) Mary fell too much during practice, but not as much as Sue.

Even though a mass quantifier is used in (33), its evaluation is based on counting events, not measuring them.

Another case of a mismatch is the German quantifier 'beides' ('both'). 'Beides' applies to pluralities of two only, yet syntactically it is singular and can apply only to an antecedent that is mass, such as a conjoined mass NP, not a plural NP. 'Beides' below applies to two maximal portions as countables, like 'thing', but unlike 'two things' in (22b), 'beides' stays singular:

(34) Hans trank das Wasser und den Wein. Er hat beides (sing.)
     schnell getrunken.
     'John drank the water und the wine. He drank both quickly'.

'Beides' here relates to two portions that count as single entities due to the fact that they are described as maximal portions falling under the property given by the description and thus count as integrated wholes. The mass status of 'beides' and its antecedent is further supported by the fact that 'beides' in (34) can be replaced by 'das beides' ('that both'). 'Das' is a mass pronoun syntactically, taking 'das Wasser und den Wein' as its (mass) antecedent.

To sum up, natural language displays unity at different levels: at a conceptual level, at the level of the use of descriptions, and at the level of syntactically imposed unity (through the use of singular count nouns or numeral classifiers). Conceptually conveyed unity enables the application of predicates like 'count' and comparatives based on counting; description-based unity enables, for example, the application of German 'beides'; and syntax-driven unity enables the application of numerals and of such predicates as 'numerous' and 'is one of them'. While unity, when it is conveyed syntactically, is strict, conceptual meaning and definite non-singular descriptions may, but need not, be connected to unity. When they are so connected, unity is added to conditions defining integrated wholes.

Mismatches in countability at different linguistic levels pose a significant challenge for a formal semantic composition. If they require positing multiple ontologies at once, then, it seems, standard compositional semantics has to be significantly revised.

6.7 Conclusion

The more linguistics and the natural sciences have developed, the more the connection of language to reality seems to have become obscure. Philosophers and linguists alike tend to presuppose a conception of a mind-independent reality that is remote from what appears to be reflected in natural language, leading Chomsky and other linguists to the view that referential NPs do not serve to pick out objects at all. Linguistic idealism sheds a very different light on the issue. If reality is shaped throughout by our linguistic access to it, apparent discrepancies between language and reality are to be attributed to the level or type of language, rather than a general disconnect between language and reality. This chapter has not endorsed linguistic idealism and its consequences for debates about natural-language semantics as such. Its aim has rather been to show that the notion of a single object needs to be understood as a notion imposed by the use of natural language (including possibly its conceptual or descriptive level), rather than being found in reality as such. The fact that the notion of being a single object in natural language so obviously applies without conditions of integrated wholes being in place supports the idea of a unity-conveying mental faculty rather than one of a language- and mind-independent property. Language displays unity as linguistically imposed even if at a conceptual level it generally aligns with real (worldly) integrity. In particular, unity is a notion that is not strictly dependent on worldly or even merely perceived conditions of integrity being in place. The notion of a single object thus gives a particularly striking piece of support for linguistic idealism.

References

Barner, D., Wagner, L., and Snedeker, J. 2008. 'Events and the ontology of individuals: verbs as a source of individuating mass and count nouns', *Cognition* 106, 805–32.
Bale, A. and Gillon, B. 2021. 'Re-examining the mass-count distinction', in F. Moltmann (ed.), *Mass and Count in Linguistics, Philosophy, and Cognitive Science* (Amsterdam: Benjamins), 13–36.
Brody, G. and Feiman, R. 2024. 'Polysemy does not exist, at least not in the relevant sense', *Mind and Language* 39, 179–200.
Carrara, M., Arapinis, A., and Moltmann, F. (eds) 2016. *Unity and Plurality. Logic, Philosophy, and Semantics* (Oxford: OUP).
Cartwright, H. 1970. 'Quantities', *The Philosophical Review* 79, 25–42.
Champollion, L. and Krifka, M. 2016. 'Mereology', in P. Dekker and M. Aloni (eds), *Cambridge Handbook of Semantics* (Cambridge: CUP), 369–88.
Cheng, L. and Sybesma, R. 2005. 'Classifiers in four varieties of Chinese', in G. Cinque and R. Kayne (eds), *The Oxford Handbook of Comparative Syntax* (Oxford: OUP), 259–92.
Chierchia, G. 1998. 'Plurality of mass nouns and the notion of "semantic parameter"', in S. Rothstein (ed.), *Events and Grammar* (Dordrecht: Kluwer), 53–103.
Chierchia, G. 2015. 'How universal is the mass/count distinction? Three grammars of counting', in A. Li, A. Simpson, and W. Tsai (eds), *Chinese Syntax in a Cross-linguistic Perspective* (Oxford: OUP), 147–75.
Chomsky, N. 1986. *Knowledge of Language. Its Nature, Origin, and Use* (Westport Ct. and London: Praeger).
Chomsky, N. 1998. *New Horizons in the Study of Language and Mind* (Cambridge: CUP).
Cohen, D. 2020. 'Activewear and other vaguery: A morphological perspective on aggregate-mass', in F. Moltmann (ed.), *Mass and Count in Linguistics, Philosophy, and Cognitive Science* (Amsterdam: Benjamins), 37–60.
Copley, B. and Roy, I. 2022. 'A dual ontology across the grammatical/conceptual divide', in L. Stockall et al. (ed.), *For Hagit: A Celebration. Festschrift for Hagit Borer* (QMUL Occasional Papers in Linguistics 47), 1–6.
Doetjes, J. S. 2012. 'Count/mass distinctions across languages', in C. Maienborn, K. v. Heusinger, and P. Portner (eds), *Semantics: An International Handbook of Natural Language Meaning, Part III* (Berlin: De Gruyter), 2559–80.
Eklund, M. 2008. 'The pictures of reality as an amorphous lump', in T. Sider, J. Hawthorne, and D. W. Zimmerman (eds), *Contemporary Debates in Metaphysics* (New York: Blackwell), 382–96.
Filip, H. (ed.) 2021. *Countability in Natural Language* (Cambridge: CUP).
Fine, K. 1999. 'Things and their parts', *Midwest Studies in Philosophy* 23, 61–74.
Fine, K. 2020. 'The identity of social groups', *Metaphysics* 3, 81–91.
Frege, G. 1884. *Die Grundlagen der Arithmetik* (Breslau: Koebner).
Gaskin, R. 2021. *Language and World: A Defence of Linguistic Idealism* (London: Routledge).
Hawthorne, J. 2006. 'Plenitude, convention, and ontology', in J. Hawthorne, *Metaphysical Essays* (Oxford: OUP), 53–70.
Ingarden, R. 1931. *Das Literarische Kunstwerk* (Halle: Niemeyer).
Koslicki, K. 2008. *The Structure of Objects* (Oxford: OUP).
Liebesman, D., and Magidor, O. 2017. 'Copredication and property inheritance', *Philosophical Issues* 27, 131–66.

Link, G. 1983. 'The logical analysis of plurals and mass nouns', in R. Baeuerle et al. (eds), *Semantics from Different Points of View* Berlin: Springer), 302–23.
McKay, T. 2006. *Plural Predication* (Oxford: OUP).
McKay, T. 2016. 'Mass and plural', in M. Carrara et al. (eds), *Unity and Plurality* (Oxford: OUP), 171–93.
Langacker, R. 1987. *Foundations of Cognitive Grammar* (Stanford: SUP).
Moltmann, F. 1997. *Parts and Wholes in Semantics* (New York: OUP).
Moltmann, F. 1998. 'Part structures, integrity, and the mass-count distinction', *Synthese* 116, 75–111.
Moltmann, F. 2005. 'Part structures in situations: The semantics of *Individual* and *Whole*', *Linguistics and Philosophy* 28, 599–641.
Moltmann, F. 2016. 'Plural reference and reference to a plurality. Linguistic facts and semantic analyses', in M. Carrara et al. (eds.), *Unity and Plurality. Philosophy, Logic, and Semantics* (Oxford: OUP), 93–120.
Moltman, F. 2017. 'Partial Content and Expressions of Part and Whole. Discussion of Stephen Yablo: Aboutness', *Philosophical Studies* 174, 797–808.
Moltmann, F. 2019. 'Attitudinal objects. Their importance for philosophy and natural language semantics', in B. Ball and C. Schuringa (eds), *The Act and Object of Judgment* (London: Routledge), 180–201
Moltmann, F. (ed.) 2019. *Mass and Count in Linguistics, Philosophy, and Cognitive Science* (Amsterdam: Benjamins).
Moltmann, F. 2021. 'Levels of ontology and natural language: The case of the ontology of parts and wholes', in J. Miller (ed.), *The Language of Ontology* (Oxford: OUP), 181–211.
Moltmann, F. 2022. 'Names, light nouns, and countability', *Linguistic Inquiry* 54, 117–46.
Ojeda, A. 1993. *Linguistic individuals* (Stanford: CSLI Pubications).
Oliver, A. and Smiley, T. 2013: *Plural Logic* (Oxford: OUP).
Peacocke, C. 2019. *The Primacy of Metaphysics* (Oxford: OUP).
Pelletier, J. and Schubert, L. 2012. 'Mass expressions', in F. Guenthner and D. Gabbay (eds), *Handbook of Philosophical Logic*, 2nd edn, vol. 10 (Dordrecht: Kluwer), 249–336.
Pietroski, P. 2017. 'Semantic internalism', in J. McGilvray (ed.), *The Cambridge Companion to Chomsky* (Cambridge: CUP), 196–216.
Priest, G. 2015. *One: Being an Investigation into the Unity of Reality and of Its Parts, Including the Singular Object Which Is Nothingness* (Oxford OUP).
Pustejovsky, J. 1995. *The Generative Lexicon* (Cambridge, Mass.: MIT Press).
Quine, W. v. O. 1960. *Word and Object* (Cambridge, Mass.: MIT Press).
Rothstein, S. 2017. *Semantics for Counting and Measuring* (Cambridge: CUP).
Schaffer, J. 2009. 'What grounds what?', in D. Chalmers, D. Manley, and R. Wassermann (eds), *Metametaphysics* (Oxford: OUP), 347–83.
Schaffer, J. and Rosen, D. 2017. 'Folk mereology is teleological', *Nous* 51, 238–70.
Simons, P. 1987. *Parts: a Study in Ontology* (Oxford: Clarendon Press).
Ter Meulen, A. 1981. 'An intensional logic for mass terms', *Philosophical Studies* 40, 105–25.
Thomasson, A. 1999. *Fiction and Metaphysics* (Cambridge: CUP).
Twardowski, K. 1911. 'Actions and Products. Some Remarks on the Borderline of Psychology, Grammar, and Logic'. In J. Brandl and J. Wolenski (eds.): *Kazimierz Twardowski. On Actions, Products, and Other Topics in the Philosophy* (Amsterdam: Rodopi), 103–32.
Ulrich, W. 1976. 'An alleged ambiguity in the nominalizations of illocutionary verbs', *Philosophica* 18, 113–27.
Yi, B.-Y. 2005. 'The logic and meaning of plurals. Part I', *Journal of Philosophical Logic* 34, 459–506.
Yi, B.-Y. 2006. 'The logic and meaning of plurals. Part II', *Journal of Philosophical Logic* 35, 239–80.
Zucchi, S. and White, M. 2001. 'Twigs, sequences and the temporal constitution of predicates', *Linguistics and Philosophy* 24, 187–222.

7
Linguistic Instrumentalism

John A. Keller and Lorraine Juliano Keller

7.1 Introduction

It is widely taken to be a truism that in order for the meaning of an expression to be x, x must exist.[1] Call this *the Constraint*. Given the Constraint's neutrality about what meanings *are*—concrete objects, properties, relations, intensions, ideas, etc.—it seems difficult to deny. The Constraint merely insists that that the set of meanings is a subset of the domain of (existing) things. Platitudinous as it might sound, the Constraint has disquieting implications. If we suppose that meaningful expressions must have meanings,[2] the Constraint entails that the meaningfulness of our language requires semantics to be aligned with ontology. If the ontology presupposed by the semantics of our language turns out to be incorrect, our utterances will be rendered largely meaningless.[3] This isn't just an abstract possibility: there are many false ontologies and only one true one, and it is unclear what would guarantee that semantics tracks the true one. But the possibility that semantics presupposes a false ontology is vertigo-inducing: the meaningfulness of our thought and talk seems to hang by a thread, if it's hanging at all.

---

[1] This idea is ubiquitous. Searle (1969, 77) says 'Whatever is referred to must exist.' Williamson (2007, 20) defends the stronger claim that 'What there is determines what there is for us to mean.' And Szabó's 'First Dogma about Meanings' is that 'An expression is meaningful if and only if there is a semantic value m... and there is a relation R ... such that the expression bears R to m' (2013, 35).

[2] This is not uncontroversial: see Quine 1960 and Jubien 2001. The Constraint applies most straightforwardly to 'entity-assigning' meaning theories, but it applies to other semantic theories as well: for example, it says that the meaning of an expression can only be this pattern of use or that inferential role if those patterns and roles exist.

[3] We assume here that meaningless expressions can't be constituents of meaningful sentences, but an alternative view is that sentences containing meaningless expressions have existent but incomplete meanings: 'gappy propositions' (Braun 1993). But even if gappy propositions would save most sentences from meaninglessness, they wouldn't save them from truth-valuelessness, since gappy propositions aren't true or false. And the claim that most sentences might turn out to be truth-valueless isn't much less disquieting than the claim that they might turn out to be meaningless.

7.1.1 Satisfying the Constraint

Call the problem of finding a guarantee that semantics and ontology are aligned—and thus that the Constraint is satisfied—*the Puzzle*. There are three main approaches to solving the Puzzle:

Meaning Magnetism: Ontological reality determines linguistic ontology. (Sider 2011)
Linguistic Idealism: Linguistic ontology determines ontological reality. (Gaskin 2021)
Supernatural Design: Linguistic ontology and ontological reality align by design.[4]

One might think we have left out an appealing option: *Easy Ontology* views that trivialize alignment by making ontology maximally permissive (Meinong 1960; Thomasson 2015). Easy Ontology views come in different flavors. The more plausible versions don't make ontology *too* permissive, but for that reason don't solve the Puzzle: linguistic ontology contains a menagerie of exotic and arguably impossible objects that only appear in *maximally* permissive accounts of ontological reality. On the other hand, maximally permissive views solve the Puzzle only by postulating implausibly exotic and extravagant ontologies. But there's a deeper problem with this approach: 'first-order' Easy Ontology views are just specific metaphysical theories, no more likely to be correct than any other. The fact that a possible metaphysical theory would satisfy the Constraint isn't any sort of *guarantee* that the Constraint is satisfied, and so doesn't solve the Puzzle. But 'second order' Easy Ontology principles that *guarantee* that the Constraint is satisfied must ultimately reduce to one of the other approaches: recherché counterexamples aside, if X and Y are non-accidentally correlated, then X depends on Y, Y depends on X, or X and Y depend on Z.[5] So, it is to assessing those initial three approaches that we now turn. As we'll see, there is a real worry that these approaches generate more puzzles than they solve.

To begin with, Supernatural Design doesn't have much to recommend it: invoking *God* to solve the Puzzle would be a radical and unpopular move, and prominent supernaturalist positions contradict Supernatural Design anyway (recall the tower of Babel). Solving the Puzzle with a radical and unpopular

---

[4] Something like this view seems to have been held by the *Conimbricenses* (Doyle 2001, 140; Ashworth 2015, 158–9).
[5] In fact, Thomasson's view is best interpreted as a form of linguistic idealism.

version of a radical and unpopular view doesn't actually seem like much of a solution at all.

Meaning Magnetism is an interesting view, and there are influential arguments for it, but there remain deep concerns. On Ted Sider's development of the view, languages have a 'metaphysical semantics' that is quite different from their 'linguistic semantics'. These are not proposed as being two sides of the same coin. For example, linguistic semantics needs to be integrated with other psychological and linguistic theories (e.g., syntax), whereas metaphysical semantics doesn't (2011, 113). But that leaves the relationship between metaphysical semantics and linguistic semantics obscure, and the project of guaranteeing that they are appropriately aligned (such that the truth-conditions they assign determine the same set of worlds) seems not much different from the project of solving the Puzzle in the first place.

In addition, it is worth noting that solving the Puzzle would require a very strong form of Meaning Magnetism indeed.[6] If such a strong form of meaning magnetism is correct, it is all but guaranteed that the semantic theories we actually develop will be mistaken. According to Meaning Magnetism, the *true* ontology determines the ontology of language. But our semantic theories are unlikely to presuppose the true ontology unless we know the true ontology, and that seems rather doubtful given the history of ontological theorizing. In any case, for reasons that will become apparent, the falsity of our best semantic theories is grist to our mill, insofar as it suggests that an anti-realist attitude towards semantics is appropriate.

The last option—Linguistic Idealism—is, as Richard Gaskin himself puts it, 'quite a startling view' (this volume, 24). It would require a radical revision of our conception of the world and our place in it. As Gaskin (this volume, 24) says, 'Human beings are only a tiny and insignificant bit of reality, and yet it is a condition on there being such a thing as reality in the first place—a reality for humans to have evolved in—that it be linguistically intelligible to them. There is a sense in which, notwithstanding Copernicus, planet Earth is the centre of the universe after all.'

Even if we manage to reconcile ourselves to its radical anthropocentrism, the ontological implications of Linguistic Idealism are unsettling. When it comes to abstracta, Gaskin (2021, 169) admits that, 'whatever can consistently exist, does exist'. We would say 'is forced to admit', but Gaskin seems untroubled,

---

[6] One might think that Meaning Magnetism only comes into play to settle edge cases that only philosophers care about. But if the *prima facie* mismatch between semantics and ontology is large, Meaning Magnetism will have to point reference towards meanings that are very 'unintuitive': for example, 'trees' refers to simples arranged treewise, or to ideas of trees, etc.

'For clarity's sake, let me [say] that I see no problem with countenancing the existence of various "silly" (as they have unjustly been called) abstract objects that are often thought to put the kibosh on any policy of ontological generosity: here I am thinking of such objects as, well, sakes and kiboshes' (172). This is a radical ontological view. Things get even worse if, as seems plausible, Gaskin will be forced to admit inconsistent or impossible objects into his ontology. After all, many expressions appear to denote impossible objects if they denote anything at all. Gaskin handles problematic cases of this type by distinguishing between 'genuine names' and 'descriptive names',[7] and arguing that what's denoted by descriptive names for *impossibilia* are not impossible and hence unreal concrete objects, but perfectly real (and hence possible) *concepts of impossibilia*: concepts that actually and hence possibly exist but are not possibly instantiated. Worries about such 'conceptualist' approaches to semantics aside (Kripke 1980), it is unclear that this is a fully general solution, since Russell's Paradox shows that some (purported) concepts, such as the concept of non-self-instantiation, cannot possibly exist. If such a concept existed, would it instantiate itself? Either way, contradiction looms.[8] And of course, there's no guarantee that the true ontology will end up containing concepts at all. (See Machery 2009 for an argument that it won't.)

7.1.2 Rejecting the Constraint

These brief remarks are not intended to be a refutation of Linguistic Idealism—far from it. *Every* attempt to solve the Puzzle has radical implications.[9] But if the only options for ensuring the satisfaction of the Constraint are radical,

---

[7] It's not clear that this distinction can do the work it's being asked to, unless we stipulate that empty names must be descriptive names. Gaskin (2021, 105) says, 'when we discover that [a] name is empty we may decide that, really, it is and was all along a descriptive name'. But there's no 'internal' linguistic difference between empty and non-empty names. (Linguistic analysis doesn't reveal that 'Vulcan' is empty.) So, if empty names must be descriptive names, the world is intruding on semantics in a significant way—a form of Meaning Magnetism—rather the opposite order of influence than the one Gaskin wants! Gaskin is of course alive to this worry (2021, 105–10), but his response, in short, is to accept the implication but draw a distinction: the sense in which language determines reality is *transcendental*, whereas the sense in which reality determines (semantic facts about) language is merely *empirical*. We leave an evaluation of this reply to the reader.

[8] See B. Russell 1980 and Gaskin 2021, 35–8, for a response.

[9] Anscombe (ignoring Supernatural Design) says, 'So now it looks as if either the grammar corresponded to something of the object, its real essence, which it has whether there is language or not, or the "object" were itself dependent on language. The first is like the suggestion made by Plato in the *Cratylus* [that the "logical shape" of words derives from the essence it expresses—akin to Meaning Magnetism]; the second, if it applies through and through, I call "linguistic idealism"' (1981, 113). She goes on to say, 'It is enormously difficult to steer in the narrow channel here: to avoid the falsehoods of idealism and the stupidities of empiricist realism' (1981, 115).

perhaps we might consider rejecting it—also a radical move, we admit, but perhaps the least radical of the bunch. In this chapter we explore the prospects for doing just that: for rejecting the Constraint and holding that claims like 'the meaning of *x* is *y*' can be *correct* even if they are not true, and in particular even if there is no such thing as *y*.

More generally, we want to explore a form of anti-realism about linguistics according to which linguistic theories and principles can be correct without being true. Call this view *Linguistic Instrumentalism*. Van Fraassen (1980, 12) defends a form of *global* scientific anti-realism, according to which 'science aims to give us theories which are empirically adequate; and acceptance of a theory involves a belief only that it is empirically adequate'. We don't think *that's* true: we believe plenty of our scientific theories, and scientists do too. We are, in fact, realists about much of science and pretty much all of mathematics.[10] But we are only realists about *much* of science: *some* scientific theories (the ideal gas law is a notorious example) are clearly only aiming to be instrumentally useful, and accepting them involves a belief only that they are instrumentally useful. (For now, think of being instrumentally useful as a matter of making true predictions.) So, one can heartily reject *global* scientific anti-realism while accepting *restricted* or *local* forms of anti-realism about selected scientific disciplines or theories. Linguistic Instrumentalism is such a restricted form of anti-realism: '*linguistic* science aims to give us theories which are instrumentally useful; and acceptance of a *linguistic* theory involves a belief only that it is instrumentally useful'.

7.1.3 The Plan

This chapter is exploratory. Much has been written on the subject of global scientific realism and anti-realism, and some has been written on realism and anti-realism concerning specific aspects of linguistic theory,[11] but little has been written on the subject of realism and anti-realism about linguistics in general, but *only* linguistics. Our aim here is to clarify Linguistic Instrumentalism, canvas some of the 'big picture' reasons supporting it, and to knit together

---

[10] We're also realists about morality, metaphysics, and logic. We're realists about pretty much anything it is reasonable to be a realist about. It was thus shocking to discover that we found anti-realism about linguistics plausible. But we argue below that linguistics is genuinely more amenable to anti-realism than other subjects.

[11] For example, Rosen 1990 explicitly advocates anti-realism about possible worlds, Ludwig 2002 explicitly advocates anti-realism about T-sentences, and Ball 2018, Schwarz 2018, and Yalcin 2018 defend anti-realist-esque claims about semantics.

some of the arguments for anti-realism about isolated parts of linguistic theory into a more general argument for Linguistic Instrumentalism. We are not yet convinced of the truth of Linguistic Instrumentalism, but we *are* convinced that it merits further consideration.

7.2 Clarifications

The view we are exploring is complicated and confusing. The way the terms 'realism' and 'anti-realism' are used is complicated and confusing. The different ways linguists conceive of linguistics makes talking about linguistics complicated and confusing. Clarifications are in order.

7.2.1 Linguistics

Linguistics is standardly defined as the scientific study of language, and disagreements about the nature of linguistics can be understood as disagreements about whether languages (qua the proper target of linguistic theorizing) are physical, psychological, or abstract (see, e.g., Katz 1985a, 11; Ball and Rabern 2018, 33–4; Pitt 2018, 9). *Nominalist* approaches (e.g., Bloomfield 1936) take linguistics to be the study of fundamentally *physical* entities such as sound waves and inscriptions. *Conceptualist* approaches (e.g., Chomsky 1965) take linguistics to be the study of *psychological* entities such as concepts and psychologically realized rules or grammars. Finally, *Platonist* approaches (e.g., Katz 1985b) take linguistics to be the study of *abstract* entities such as sentence-types and abstract rules or grammars.

We favour an ecumenical approach: by our lights, the study of language involves the study of physical, psychological, *and* abstract entities, and how they relate to one another (compare Santana 2016). This ecumenical perspective is clearly *descriptively* correct, in the sense that the work done in linguistics departments includes the study of the physical, psychological, and abstract aspects of language.

Many linguists favour a less ecumenical *prescriptive* approach according to which much of what goes on in linguistics departments is not *proper* linguistics. For example, Chomskyans think that linguistics 'should aim to express just what is "essential" to natural language' (Chomsky 1966, 537). We don't want to debate how to define or delineate the boundaries of linguistics, and doing so is not required for our purposes. We think that anti-realism is true of 'Chomskyan linguistics' and of (most or all) other 'narrow' conceptions of linguistics as well as linguistics broadly conceived. But the specific way anti-realism is manifested will depend on one's account of linguistics. We discuss *some* such specifics below; here we simply assume that linguistics includes everything done in (most top) linguistics departments.

7.2.2 Correctness

We introduced Linguistic Instrumentalism as the view that linguistic principles can be correct without being true. But what do we mean by 'correct'? The concept is best grasped by example. Consider a mathematical anti-realist who thinks that all mathematical claims are untrue. Most such anti-realists will admit that some untrue mathematical claims are better than others. There is an important sense in which it is *better* to endorse '2 + 2 = 4' than to endorse '2 + 2 = 14'. There is *something* right about '2 + 2 = 4', and pretty much *nothing* right about '2 + 2 = 14'. Intelligent and informed people say things like '2 + 2 = 4', but not '2 + 2 = 14'. And so forth. Even if untrue, '2 + 2 = 4' is still 'good' in an important sense.

Similarly, if you are an anti-realist about colour, and think all colour attributions are untrue, you will likely admit that there is still an important sense in which 'apples are red' is *better*, or more right, than 'apples are blue'. If you are a moral anti-realist and think all moral attributions are untrue, there is still an important sense in which 'murder is wrong' is better, or more right, than 'murder is obligatory'. Etc.

Everybody needs a way of sorting 'good' claims from 'bad' ones. Realists sort by (objective) truth; anti-realists sort by some other method. We are using 'correct' as a label for the category of 'good' claims. Different views yield different accounts of correctness. For realists, correctness is (objective) truth. For van Fraassen, it is empirical adequacy. For instrumentalists, it is usefulness. For cultural relativists, it is popularity. As the name suggests, Linguistic Instrumentalism is the view that correct linguistic claims are those that are *useful*. (We explain this notion of usefulness below.)

7.2.3 Correct Rules?

But does it make sense to talk of linguistic principles as being true? Such principles are often (presented as) *rules*, and rules are plausibly not truth-apt.

The claim that correct rules needn't be true would then be trivial. But even if rules aren't truth-apt, they may have truth-apt *commitments* (presuppositions, entailments, etc.). For example, Reiland (2023) argues that while rules are not truth-apt, they have contents that are. More generally, all manner of non-truth-apt expressions (questions, imperatives, etc.) have truth-apt commitments. For example, regardless of whether the rule 'Do what Zeus commands' is truth-apt, it has a (false) truth-apt presupposition: that Zeus exists.

To avoid repeating the clunky phrase 'not true, or has non-true commitments', we will use 'not true' (and 'untrue') in an extended sense to cover both truth-apt things that are not true ('Snow is green'), and non-truth-apt things that have non-true but truth-apt commitments ('Do what Zeus commands').

7.2.4 Realism and Anti-realism

Linguistic Instrumentalism is a form of anti-realism about linguistics. On standard accounts, realism about a domain d requires:

> *Objectivity*: Facts in d are mind-independent: they do not depend in any non-trivial way on human mental activity (beliefs, desires, hopes, etc.).
> *Truth-aptness*: Discourse in d is truth-apt: it aims at truth and can be evaluated for truth and falsity (unlike, say, discourse in fictional or theatrical domains). In short, correctness = truth.[12]

As noted above, anti-realist views about a domain d correspond with views about what (other than objective truth) makes theories in d correct. For example, van Fraassen's Constructive Empiricism holds that science only aims to produce theories that are true of *observable* reality, and so correct scientific theories can fail to be true *tout court* (since they may be false of *un*observable reality). Such theories—or at least theorists' attitudes towards them—are thus not truth-apt.

---

[12] Similar accounts of realism are common: see, for example, Boyd 1983 and J. A. Keller 2014. Such accounts typically include a third condition, *Transparency*, according to which discourse in d has a transparent interpretation. Consider someone who claimed that moral statements expressed mathematical truths, and hence were objective and truth-apt. We wouldn't call such a person a moral realist, and we need something like Transparency to rule that out. But for reasons outlined in Keller 2014, 15–17, the requirement is difficult to formulate precisely.

7.2.5 Linguistics Is Different

To see why Linguistic Instrumentalism might be plausible even to those who, like ourselves, are realists in other domains, note how much less objective linguistics is than (most) other sciences: for example, if competent speakers believe that 'x' is grammatical and means y in L, then 'x' *is* grammatical and *does* mean y in L. The grammaticality and meaning of expressions just aren't things competent speakers could be wrong about. Likewise with pronunciation, etc. This is as mind-dependent as things get. The contrast with sciences like physics and biology is striking.

While it is uncontroversial that relatively superficial linguistic facts such as that 'x' is grammatical and means y in L are mind-dependent, we nonetheless think it is useful to draw attention to this point in the context of comparing linguistics with the other sciences vis-à-vis realism. But the deeper and more interesting reason to endorse Linguistic Instrumentalism derives from the *non-truth-aptness* of many fundamental linguistic theories and principles.

7.2.6 Laws, Principles, and Theories

We said above that we disagreed with Constructive Empiricism because we think science often *does* aim to produce theories that are true *tout court*. (Not always. Perhaps not usually. But often.) Nevertheless, we compared Linguistic Instrumentalism to a *restricted* version of Constructive Empiricism. But that was actually just a useful simplification: Linguistic Instrumentalism is something much *stranger*.

Terms like 'law', 'principle', and 'theory' are used by linguists in a systematically ambiguous way to refer to both what is being theorized about as well as our theories about it. For example, Chomsky (1965, 25) uses 'the term "theory" ... with a systematic ambiguity, to refer both to the child's innate predisposition to learn a language of a certain type and to the linguist's account of this'. Using terms in a systematically ambiguous way seems liable to cause confusion, so we won't. There is a standard distinction between *laws* and *law statements*: roughly, laws govern and explain the behaviour of things, and (correct) law statements state or express laws in verbal form. But talk of laws of linguistics is strained, so we'll use the term 'principles' to refer to 'linguistic laws'—the things that govern and explain linguistic behaviour (including the operations of the language faculty)—and 'theories' to refer to statements of those principles. This distinction is important, since saying that linguistic *theories* can be correct without being true is very different from saying that linguistic *principles* can be correct without being true. The idea that linguistic *theories* can be correct without being true is a relatively familiar kind of *wordy* anti-realism, *à la* Constructive Empiricism, while the idea that linguistic *principles* can be correct without being true is a relatively unfamiliar kind of *worldly* anti-realism.

7.2.7 Worldly Anti-realism

But what, exactly, *is* worldly anti-realism? Realism was glossed above in terms of objectivity and truth-aptness. Objectivity straightforwardly applies to both principles and theories: 'fact' is another one of those systematically ambiguous words that has both a wordy and a worldly meaning. But the above account of 'truth-aptness' only applies to theories. Still, the core idea behind truth-aptness—that correctness is truth—can be generalized to cover principles. Worldly anti-realism only makes sense in cases where what is being theorized about—the *target* of our theorizing—is something that can be untrue: something truth-apt, or with truth-apt presuppositions. Principles fit this description. Accordingly, the generalization of truth-aptness to linguistic principles is the idea that linguistic principles—the principles *actually* governing and explaining linguistic phenomena—must be true. One might, however, wonder how the principles actually governing and explaining linguistic phenomena could *fail* to be true. After all, principles are linguistic *laws*, and it's generally taken to be *analytic* that laws are true.

The idea that laws must be true has been famously challenged by Nancy Cartwright. On her view (Cartwright 1983), *the laws of nature themselves lie*, and so correct, fully accurate, statements of those laws may lie as well. Here's a simple illustration. Assume that that $F = ma$ (force equals mass times acceleration) is an *actual* law of physics: a principle governing and explaining the behaviour of physical objects. On a Cartwrightian view,[13] this could be the case even if it isn't *true* that force equals mass times acceleration. So, *that F = ma* could be a false law. The law statement '$F = ma$' would also be false, since it's false that $F = ma$. But '$F = ma$' would be a fully accurate—not just empirically adequate—statement of an actual law. Theorists might be aiming to *literally* state a law, and *succeeding*, but nonetheless say something (correct but) untrue. Hence it is not an objection to this view—unlike many forms of

---

[13] Cartwright says things along these lines, but her view is complicated. The aspect of her view that we're focusing on is similar to the one emphasized in G. K. Russell 2023.

anti-realism—that it doesn't *seem* to theorists that they are engaging in pretence or some other non-truth-apt form of discourse. Someone who asserts '$F = ma$' succeeds in literally and accurately describing a law, just as someone who asserts 'Bilbo found a magic ring' succeeds in literally and accurately describing *The Hobbit*. What they assert is nonetheless untrue. The problem, in both cases, is that what they are literally and accurately describing is not itself true.

This view rejects truth-aptness (for both theories and principles) and is thus anti-realist, but the fundamental source of the anti-realism isn't the theory (law statement), or the intentions of the theorizer, but the world (the law or principle itself). Indeed, the deviation from truth-aptness in the case of *theories* can easily be remedied: even if '$F = ma$' is false, 'it's a law that $F = ma$' is true. (Likewise with 'In *The Hobbit*, Bilbo found a magic ring'.) Call law statements like '$F = ma$' *unadorned* and law statements like 'it's a law that $F = ma$' *adorned*. On this view, whether correct law *statements* (theories) are true or false will depend on how they are formulated: on whether they are adorned or unadorned. Hence (in part) the focus on the claim that the laws themselves are false.

We don't agree with Cartwright's view of science any more than we agree with van Fraassen's: it's hard for us to wrap our heads around the idea that the actual laws of physics, for example—the principles actually governing and explaining physical phenomena—are false. But while we reject Cartwright's view as an account of science *in general*, we think it is surprisingly plausible as an account of linguistics: the linguistic principles that actually explain the linguistic facts and govern linguistic behaviour plausibly have false presuppositions, and hence do not accurately describe the phenomena they explain. They are, in short, correct but untrue. As Cartwright might put it, *the laws of linguistics lie*.

7.2.8 Linguistic Correctness

But if the fundamental theories and principles of linguistics don't aim at truth, what *do* they aim at? Instrumentalism replaces questions about whether a theory or principle is *true* with questions about whether it is *useful*. But to know whether linguistic theories or principles are useful, we have to know what they are used *for*. What is the use or purpose of language (and linguistic *principles*), and what is the use or purpose of linguistic *theories*? The details are matters of dispute among linguists, but there is *some* agreement about the broad outlines.

Human beings have thoughts and desires they would like to communicate.[14] Language facilitates this. Call the contents or meanings of complete thoughts and sentences 'meanings$_S$'. If I am thinking a thought with meaning$_S$ p, I can communicate that to you by producing sounds, signs, or marks ('utterances') that you interpret to mean p. For this to work in a general and efficient way, there must be mutually recognized systematic *principles* for associating utterances with meanings$_S$ (in context). Linguistic *theories* are attempts to state those principles. But, and this is the crucial point, those principles do not need to be *true* in order to fulfil their function: in order to enable us to efficiently and systematically associate meanings$_S$ with utterances.

This brings us to an important clarification. We are happy to say that utterances have meanings$_S$, and that it is the job of linguistics to systematically pair utterances with meanings$_S$. But we think the linguistic machinery used for systematically pairing utterances with meanings can do its job even if it presupposes a false ontology and is thus untrue. Hence, we are sceptical about subsentential meanings, syntactic structures, and all the rest of it. We are realists about utterances and meanings$_S$, but not about what comes in between.

If we think of the language faculty as *computing* the meanings$_S$ of utterances in context, what matters is only that the computational principles they use *work*—whether they deliver the right results—not whether they're true. And computational principles *can* work while being untrue. Using the heights of shadows to compute the heights of objects obviously doesn't require thinking that shadows actually exist any more than computing the number of deadly sins by putting them in 1–1 correspondence with the seven dwarves requires thinking that there are dwarves.

Alternatively, we might think of linguistic principles as being used by hearers to *predict* what speakers are thinking given the utterances they produce, and by speakers to *predict* what utterances will enable them to be understood. It is uncontroversial that false principles can reliably make true predictions, and so if linguistic principles are in the business of prediction, that would make anti-realism about them more plausible than anti-realism in other more descriptive domains. Regardless of whether linguistic principles are used for computation or prediction, the fact that they have a practical *use*—unlike, say, the laws of physics—makes anti-realism about them more plausible than anti-realism about physics. Other sorts of scientific *theories* clearly have uses (such as prediction and explanation), and one of the main motivations for *wordy*

---

[14] While this is widely accepted, Chomsky (2017, 87–8) (in)famously dismisses the claim that communication is a central function of language, holding instead that language is fundamentally an instrument of thought.

anti-realism about those theories derives from that fact. But here we are talking about laws (principles), not law statements (theories), and it's unclear what it would mean to say that the laws of physics have a practical use.

Another alternative would be to say that linguistic principles are *instructions* for pairing meanings$_S$ with utterances (cf. Pietroski 2018). But instructions with false presuppositions can do their job, whether they're instructions for computing a solution, getting from *A* to *B*, writing a college essay, or assembling a desk. This is, we think, obvious upon reflection: outside of the philosophy room, non-literal speech is *de rigueur* (with certain exceptions like computer programming). I can successfully explain how to fly from Rome to Reggio Calabria by saying, 'Fly south along the coast until you get to the tip of the boot'; instructions for how to build a desk might make reference to such ontologically suspect entities as 'left sides', 'right sides', 'holes', etc. If instructions had to be literally true in order to be effective, nothing would get done! Or at least, nothing would get done if instructions weren't written by lawyers or philosophers. That's clearly false.

The claim that untrue linguistic principles can 'do their job' is the strangest part of Linguistic Instrumentalism, so it's worth dwelling on the point. Here's an analogy. In blindfold chess, the participants play the game 'in their heads' (without a chessboard or pieces). But it remains *correct* to talk of pieces having a location on the board, players moving their pieces on the board, and capturing, gaining, and losing those pieces by saying things like 'B8 to A6'.[15] That's a sort of wordy anti-realism. But the rules governing, or instructions for playing, blindfold chess are just the rules or instructions for chess: they mention pieces, the board, etc., even though none of those things are actually there. And that's perfectly fine! Playing blindfold chess is, in fact, a way of playing chess. The standard chess rules *correctly* apply to blindfold chess, even though they don't *literally* apply, and even though the state descriptions to which they appeal (e.g., white's king being in such-and-such position) don't actually *obtain*. The point of the rules is to enable play, and the rules do that regardless of whether they literally describe the play they enable. That's a sort of worldly anti-realism.

The chess example illustrates an important point. Anti-realism is not a blank cheque. Van Fraassen says that acceptance of a theory *t* involves a belief only that *t* is empirically adequate. If so, the belief that *t* is empirically adequate is nonetheless truth-apt, and so is correct only if it is true. On van Fraassen's view, *t* is only correct if '*t* is empirically adequate' is true. On instrumentalist views, *t* is only correct if '*t* is useful' is true. *Every* claim about boards and

---

[15] In standard notation, move the piece on B8—Black's knight at the start of the game—to A6.

pieces in a game of blindfold chess is untrue, and *many* are also incorrect. So, correctness isn't trivial to come by: *something* must be true for, for example, 'White has three pieces on the board' to be correct in a game of blindfold chess. It just isn't that White has three pieces on the board.

7.3 Structures

According to the conception of linguistics outlined in Section 7.2.8, what makes the core linguistic subdisciplines (semantics, syntax, morphology, and phonology) *core* subdisciplines (unlike, say, neurolinguistics or sociolinguistics) is the fact that they are essential for the systematic association of utterances with meanings$_S$. (Recall that we are using 'utterances' to refer to physical sequences of sounds, movements, and marks.) Syntax is essential because it determines which utterances are 'in' the language and thus eligible to be assigned meanings$_S$ in the first place (ungrammatical 'utterances' like 'Dog cat chased' don't have meanings$_S$), and because the syntactic structures it assigns to utterances are required for semantic processing. Morphology and phonology are needed—in conjunction with syntax—for identifying the meaningful constituents of utterances. That is essential because the *identities* and *meanings$_S$* of utterances are functions of their syntax and the identities and meanings of their meaningful parts.[16]

We allow that *some* linguistic subdisciplines, such as corpus linguistics, aim at truth. Linguistic Instrumentalism is a view about the *core* linguistic subdisciplines: semantics, syntax, morphology, and phonology. We canvassed some of the 'big picture' reasons supporting Linguistic Instrumentalism in Section 7.2; here we focus on fine-grained considerations supporting Linguistic Instrumentalism in phonology, morphology, and syntax. (We reserve discussion of semantics for Section 7.4.) Call the things to which we attribute phonological, morphological, and syntactic properties/structures *sentences*. In broad and sketchy outline, the case for instrumentalism about phonology, morphology, and syntax is given by *The Argument*:

1. The actual morphological, phonetic, and syntactic *principles* governing the language faculty attribute morphological, phonetic, and syntactic

---

[16] While morphology, phonology, and syntax are distinct sub-disciplines, they cannot be pursued in total isolation: how a sentence should be divided up into meaningful parts depends on morphological, phonetic, and syntactic considerations.

properties or *structures* to sentences. So do (typical/unadorned formulations of) linguistic *theories* that state or describe those principles.
2. Sentences do not have the morphological, phonetic, or syntactic properties or structures attributed to them by the abovementioned principles (and theories).

So, 3. Morphological, phonetic, and syntactic principles and theories are untrue (because not truth-apt).

The Argument seems valid: if the actual *principles* governing language and underlying linguistic competence are (correct but) untrue, that would establish *worldly* linguistic anti-realism. It would follow that unadorned *statements* of those principles are (correct but) untrue. That would establish *wordy* linguistic anti-realism. But is The Argument sound? To support its premises, we must show that morphological, phonetic, and syntactic principles attribute properties to sentences that they do not have. Our initial arguments assume that sentences are utterances—physical sounds, movements, or marks—but we argue in Section 7.3.5 that a parallel argument goes through on Conceptualist and Platonist assumptions.

7.3.1 Phonology

We begin with phonology.[17] Phonologists and phoneticians have long recognized that the speech stream does not present hearers with a set of discrete, articulated sounds, let alone words; instead, hearers perceive features in the acoustic stream that are not really there. One example is the phenomenon of categorical perception. Experiments have confirmed that humans, chinchillas, monkeys, and rats perceive non-existent sharp differences in streams of sound that differ along a continuum: hearers perceive discrete differences between phones (sounds), even in cases where a computer manipulates a phone so that it continuously changes from, for example, /ba/ to /da/ (Adger 2019, ch. 6). Hearers also perceive non-existent spaces between words, even in cases of languages with no writing systems and languages like Mandarin whose writing systems do not use discrete units for phonemes (sets of phones that make

---

[17] Phonology, the study of sound patterns in a language, is standardly taken to deal with speech sounds as discrete, psychological entities. Phonetics, the study of how speech sounds are produced, is concerned with speech sounds as continuous, physical entities. The distinction between phonology and phonetics has been (and, to some extent, still is) fraught, with some historically prominent linguists (e.g., Saussure, Trubetzkoy, and Hjelmslev) arguing that phonetics is not part of linguistics proper (Zsiga 2020, ch. 2).

morphemic or lexical distinctions within a language). Another example is the well-documented phenomenon of phonetic illusion, which Edward Sapir studied in speakers of various languages, including Paiute, Sarcee, and English. Sapir's English-speaking phonetics students transcribed non-existent glottal stops, influenced by internalized rules about the pronunciation of American English (Zsiga 2020, 13). A further example of phonetic misrepresentation is provided by experiments showing that Japanese speakers, influenced by rules forbidding consonant clusters, report hearing non-existent vowels in the midst of consonant clusters: for example they hear [ebzo] as [ebuzo] (Dupoux et al. 1999, 14). Finally, it is well known that transcriptions of phones into the International Phonetic Alphabet vary considerably.

The upshot is that the way hearers represent the speech stream differs significantly from how it actually is: the acoustic signals produced by speakers do not have the phonetic forms attributed to them by hearers. It's *possible* to posit something outside of the minds of language-users that has the phonetic features attributed by the language faculty, but it's not plausible. As Chomsky says,

> Communication could then be described in terms of such (partially) shared entities, which are easy enough to construct: take '*a' to be the singleton set {a}, or {3, a}; or if one wants a more realistic feel, some construct based on motions of molecules. With sufficient heroism, one could defend such a view, though no one does, because it's clear that we are just spinning wheels. (2000, 129)

The evidence thus strongly suggests that *nothing* outside of the minds of language-users has the phonetic structure they impute to the sound stream.[18] Phonetic structure is being *projected onto* the acoustic stream by hearers. While the acoustic stream is experienced and processed *as if* it were segmented into discrete phones, the reality is that it is continuous and unsegmented. As phonologist Elizabeth Zsiga (2020, 29) writes, 'if segments didn't exist, we would have to invent them'. Indeed.

The anti-realism here is fundamentally worldly and only derivatively wordy. It is the language faculty itself, in its interface with the sensorimotor system, that is misrepresenting the acoustic stream. But despite this misrepresentation, or perhaps even because of it, the language faculty is able to do its job effectively. The *actual* principles governing the language faculty are *eo ipso* correct,

---

[18] For simplicity, we've focused on spoken language in this passage, but the same points apply to signed and tactile languages, mutatis mutandis.

regardless of whether they mispresent the sound stream. Of course, whether this worldly anti-realism percolates up into our linguistic theories will depend on whether the 'law statements' in those theories are adorned or unadorned. Either way, the worldly anti-realism remains.

7.3.2 Morphology

Morphology is the study of the forms of words.[19] Lexemes, the fundamental units of the lexicon, are abstract representations that include all inflected forms of a word: for example, there is one lexeme associated with the forms 'sing', 'singing', and 'sung'. While it's true that language-users *represent* distinctions between phonemes, morphemes, and lexemes, in the sense that such distinctions affect how they produce, respond to, and understand spoken, written, or signed speech, it's doubtful that anything outside of their minds has the features language-users are representing—that is, the syntactic, semantic, and functional properties by which (e.g.) morphemes are distinguished. Language-users are responding to sounds, signs, and inscriptions (we assume), but physical tokens do not have the relevant semantic and syntactic properties. For example, consider a scrap of paper with 'IS' inscribed on it. Is the inscription the numeral '15'? Or the English word 'IS'? Or is the paper perhaps upside down and it's the Spanish word 'SI'? Or—if the inscription bled through and we're looking at the wrong side—could it be the approximately-equal sign '≃'? The properties of the inscription itself do not settle the matter.

And of course, spoken morphemes are ultimately composed of phonemes, which are sets of phones. We saw above that phonetic phenomena themselves are illusions of a sort—they are projected onto the acoustic stream by hearers. The acoustic stream itself is not actually divided into phones. But phones are the ultimate building blocks of (spoken) morphemes. The result is that the structures they compose (morphemes, etc.) 'would seem to be enormous and intricate buildings resting on—nothing. Or, if there turned out to be something, this would be entirely accidental' (Rey 2006, 250). The principles governing the language faculty attribute properties to parts of utterances, but those parts don't actually have those properties and may not actually exist. But, as before, the principles governing the language faculty are *eo ipso* correct, and likewise with unadorned statements of them. They are just not true.

---

[19] Morphemes are the smallest linguistic constituents that have a meaning or function: for example, the suffix '-m'—a morpheme that marks the accusative case in 'whom'—has a function but not a meaning.

7.3.2.1 Wordy Morphological Anti-realism

The fact that linguists generally assume that expressions have their meanings and other linguistic properties *necessarily* provides strong support for anti-realism about current linguistic practice: this is an idealized assumption that is clearly false of expressions in actual human languages. We don't deny that this idealization is theoretically useful, but it *is* an idealization: linguistics isn't (primarily) in the business of uncovering necessary truths. The meanings of natural-language expressions—and of the sentences in which they appear— are at least largely contingent and empirical matters. This way of individuating expressions and indeed languages for the purpose of theorizing is strong evidence that that theorizing is not being undertaken in a wholly realist vein. While this is mere wordy anti-realism that doesn't seem to have a worldly correlate, we think it is worth pointing out since, as Yalcin (2014, 35) says, it is 'standard in syntax and semantics'.

It is worth stressing that there is a *lot* of merely wordy anti-realism in linguistics. According to Williamson (2018, 21), 'As we learn ever more of the extraordinary complexity underlying even the most ordinary conversations, philosophers of language and linguists may have to rely increasingly on a model-building methodology.'[20] Models proceed by way of *idealization*, and 'To say that it is good often to proceed by way of idealization is to argue that sometimes, in thinking about the world, truth isn't what you need.... [A]n idealization is a useful untruth' (Appiah 2017, xii). Linguistic theorizing by way of model-building is not truth-apt.

Such merely wordy anti-realism is not our focus because there is a fair amount of merely wordy anti-realism—including idealization and model-building[21]—in most scientific disciplines, and adjudicating whether there is proportionately more in linguistics would be difficult and not particularly interesting. Even more importantly, merely wordy anti-realism doesn't dissolve the Puzzle. The Puzzle isn't about the alignment of our current or even ultimate semantic *theories* with the true ontology, but about the alignment of the semantic *principles* actually governing natural languages with the true ontology.

---

[20] This perspective is explicitly defended in Yalcin 2018 and only a bit less explicitly in Ball 2018.
[21] We know it is controversial to claim that modelling is an anti-realist enterprise: if you disagree feel free to substitute 'non-truth-apt' for 'anti-realist'.

7.3.3 Syntax

Finally, consider syntax, and in particular the sort of tree structure commonly used to represent the syntax of sentences like

(W) John seems to Bill to want to help himself.[22]

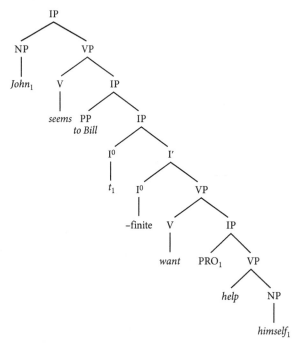

Call this structure '(S_W)'. One argument for syntactic instrumentalism is that (S_W) contains 'empty' categories—trace (t_1) and PRO_1—that, as Rey (2006, 245) puts it,

> indicate a node in the tree that for one reason or another has no [constituent] attached to it, for example, because [a constituent] has been 'moved' to a different node in some 'transformation' of the sentence, and/or needs to be co-indexed with elements at other nodes: thus t_1 is co-indexed with *John*, PRO, and with *himself*, capturing the fact that the subject of *want* and *help* are both *John*, and not *Bill*.

We have worries about the non-metaphorical meaning of 'moved' and 'transformed', but our fundamental concern is that utterances don't seem to instantiate anything like (S_W). Intuitively, (W) is supposed to instantiate the

---

[22] We borrow this example from Rey (2006, 245).

structure (S_W), but no physical utterances—neither the string of marks that appears to the right of '(W)' above nor the sequence of sounds one would produce if one read it—actually instantiates (S_W). Indeed, given that (S_W) contains empty categories, it's unclear what it would mean for something to instantiate it. Only things with three sides can instantiate a triangular structure. Does something instantiating (S_W) need to have 14 elements? At first glance, yes; but since trace (t_1) and PRO_1 are empty, 14 seems like too many. Yet how could something with less than 14 elements instantiate (S_W)? That sounds about as plausible as saying that something with two sides could instantiate a triangular structure.

But set that worry aside. The fact that utterances don't have the syntactic structures posited by our syntactic theories is entailed by the existence of structurally ambiguous utterances (strings that can be associated with more than one syntactic form). For example:

(K)   I killed the king with a knife

can be associated with

(S_{K1}) $[_{TP}[_{NP}I\ [_{VP}killed\ [_{NP}the\ king][_{PP}with\ [_{NP}a\ knife]]]]]$ (I killed the king by using a knife)

or with

(S_{K2}) $[_{TP}[_{NP}I\ [_{VP}killed\ [_{NP}[the\ king][_{PP}with[_{NP}a\ knife]]]]]]$ (I killed the king who was wielding a knife).

This sort of structural ambiguity is pervasive. Utterances thus do not have the syntactic structures attributed to them by the linguistic principles governing our language faculties and explaining linguistic competence. But, to repeat, those principles are *eo ipso* correct. They are thus correct but untrue. Likewise with unadorned statements of them.

7.3.4 Non-physical Sentences

Our argument so far has assumed that sentences are utterances: physical entities. But what if sentences are mental or abstract entities, as Conceptualists and Platonists hold? Let's grant for the sake of argument that such entities exist, in addition to physical utterances. Call physical sentences 'sentences$_P$', abstract sentences 'sentences$_A$', and mental sentences 'sentences$_M$'. Might sentences$_A$ or sentences$_M$ *be* or at least literally *have* syntactic structures like (S_W), as well as phonetic and morphological structure? Could such a view vindicate phonological, morphological, or syntactic realism?

Consider first the view that sentences are sentences$_A$. One obvious worry about that view is a version of Benacerraf's problem: there are too many candidates among abstract entities for playing the role of sentences and no principled way of choosing from among them (Benacerraf 1965).[23]

But there is a more fundamental problem with using sentences$_A$ to vindicate realism. Think about the poverty of the stimulus argument (Chomsky 1965, 30–1). A key premise of that argument is that the stimuli language learners encounter are compatible with a wide variety of possible grammars (sets of linguistic principles). That's true if stimuli are sentences$_P$ (utterances) like (W), but much *less* true if they are sentences$_A$, or indeed *anything* that literally has a tree structure.[24] Call the tree *diagram* above '(D)'. If our stimuli included tree-diagrams like (D)—if, say, that were how English was written—then our (written) stimuli *wouldn't* be compatible with (such) a wide variety of grammars. (D) contains much more grammatical information than (W). So, anyone who thinks the poverty of the stimulus argument is onto something cannot think that our stimuli are things like (D). But in any case, we obviously *don't* communicate using tree diagrams like (D), or indeed anything that is or has a rich tree structure. Evidence for the obvious is provided by the lamentable but indisputable fact that there are, in reality, structurally ambiguous utterances like (K). One can insist that utterances like (K)—our structurally ambiguous stimuli—are not genuine sentences. The cost of this move is that it would make genuine sentences irrelevant to communication. As Rey argues, abstract objects like numbers earn their keep by being indispensable to physics, but the syntactic structures of sentences (like sentences themselves) 'have no role to play independently of our representations of them' (2006, 250).

Rey is a Conceptualist and seems to be suggesting that sentences$_P$ are just as irrelevant as sentences$_A$: that it's sentences$_M$ that matter for linguistics. But the same considerations regarding the poverty of the stimulus apply to sentences$_M$. *If* sentences$_M$ have rich syntactic tree structures, they cannot be among our stimuli (given that our stimuli are impoverished). Of course, sentences$_M$ plausibly have a significant role to play in language comprehension and production. They are certainly not linguistically irrelevant. But the idea that sentences$_M$—or sentences$_A$ for that matter—are among our stimuli is deeply implausible. Just as children cannot hear (or see) abstracta, nor can

---

[23] See King (2007, 47) and L. J. Keller (2019).

[24] Of course, our stimuli would still be impoverished by not including (many) 'negative' (ungrammatical) examples. See Rey (2020, §1.3).

they hear (or see) the constituents of their interlocutors' minds. In any case, forget The Argument, and consider *The Argument**:

1*. The actual morphological, phonetic, and syntactic *principles* governing the language faculty attribute morphological, phonetic, and syntactic *properties* or *structures* to sentences$_P$. So do (standard formulations of) linguistic *theories* that state or describe those principles.

2*. Sentences$_P$ do not have the morphological, phonetic, or syntactic properties or structures attributed to them by the above-mentioned principles (and theories).

So, 3. Morphological, phonetic, and syntactic principles and theories are untrue (because not truth-apt).

The soundness of The Argument*—assuming it is valid—only requires that phonetic, morphological, and syntactic structures are attributed to sentences$_P$, and that sentences$_P$ don't have them. Perhaps such structures are *also* attributed to sentences$_M$ and sentences$_A$, and perhaps they *do* have them. That would do nothing to undermine The Argument*.

It does not matter for The Argument* what sentences are. Let them be sentences$_A$, or sentences$_M$, or tree diagrams, or actual trees for that matter. The fact remains that linguistic principles guide us, or our language faculties, to attribute phonetic, morphological, and syntactic structures to sentences$_P$ like (W) and (K). In so doing, they are attributing structure that is not actually there. But of course, the linguistic principles governing our language faculties—the principles explaining and enabling linguistic competence—are *eo ipso* correct. They are thus correct but untrue. Likewise with unadorned statements of those principles. Hence, premises (1*) and (2*) of The Argument* are true, thus establishing Linguistic Instrumentalism with respect to morphology, phonetics, and syntax.

The claim that we represent utterances or at least sentences$_P$ as having properties they do not have, and treat them as if they did, is a form of *projectionism*: we (or our language faculties) are *projecting* such properties onto the world. Such 'projection' talk is not uncommon in linguistics and philosophy of linguistics.[25] Since projectionism is a form of anti-realism, this buttresses our claim that morphology, phonetics, and syntax involve a form of worldly anti-realism.

---

[25] For example, in the course of defending the claim that sentences and words are mental entities, McGilvray (1998, n. 19) says, 'What about the offended complaint: "But we hear words issuing from another person's mouth, and surely other people's mouths are outside the head!" The same, however, is true of colours, and they too are inside the head. We need a projectivist account here.'

7.4 Semantics

Let's reorient ourselves. What, exactly, do we need an instrumentalist semantics to do? According to the Constraint, the meaning of an expression can only be x if x exists. The Constraint makes meaningfulness beholden to ontology in a way that has seemingly sceptical implications. The Puzzle was to find a way to ward off scepticism by *guaranteeing* that the Constraint was satisfied. But since every *solution* to the Puzzle raised puzzles of its own, we've been exploring the idea that instead of solving the Puzzle, we should *dissolve* it: reject the Constraint and hold that the meaning of an expression *can* be x even if x fails to exist. More broadly, we have been exploring the prospects of Linguistic Instrumentalism, a broad form of anti-realism about linguistics.

Linguistic Instrumentalism allows that there are utterances and meanings$_S$, but is instrumentalist about everything in between.[26] Linguistic principles systematically pair utterances with meanings$_S$, such that given an utterance we can compute its meaning$_S$, and given an expressible meaning$_S$, we can compute an utterance that expresses it. Very broadly, Linguistic Instrumentalism is the view that the principles pairing utterances with meanings$_S$ can be successful—can reliably enable the systematic pairing of utterances with meanings$_S$—even if they are untrue.[27] This *helps* dissolve the Puzzle, since many proposed principles for pairing utterances and meanings$_S$ presuppose implausible ontologies. If the ontological presuppositions of linguistic principles had to be true for them to 'work', there would be a real worry that they *didn't* work, and hence that most of our thought and talk was meaningless. Linguistic Instrumentalism alleviates that worry by holding that linguistic principles can do their job of pairing utterances with meanings$_S$ even if they have false ontological presuppositions. It *insulates* linguistics from ontology.

7.4.1 The Decoupling Objection

One might worry that insulating linguistics from ontology is ill-advised: that Linguistic Instrumentalism dissolves the Puzzle only by decoupling language and reality, rendering utterances devoid of truth-conditions and thus compatible with any state of the world whatsoever. Call this *the Decoupling Objection*.

---

[26] It is neutral on the *nature* of meanings$_S$: perhaps they're propositions, or thoughts, or truth-conditions, or whatever.

[27] Compare Grice's 'ontological Marxism', where he defends commitment to 'queer' entities so long as they 'help with the housework' and 'are not detected in illicit logical behaviour' (1975, 30–1).

It is widely held to be a datum that competent speakers of a language L are able to recognize the truth-conditions of sentences in L, and that a desideratum on semantic theories is to explain that fact. For example, Stanley (2001, 41) says that it is a constraint on semantics that 'we are able smoothly to grasp the truth-conditions of novel... sentences on the basis of our familiarity with their parts'; but the claim is ubiquitous.[28]

Aristotle would insist that there must be at least a *grain* of truth in this common consensus, and so there is. Competent speakers must recognize the truth-conditions of sentences—but only in a shallow and superficial sense. Linguistic competence enables speakers to recognize *some* facts about truth-conditions, and it is a constraint on semantics that it should explain how. Language and reality are not *completely* decoupled. But linguistic competence only requires speakers to recognize *shallow* facts about truth-conditions, and emphatically *doesn't* require speakers to recognize *philosophically interesting* facts about truth-conditions, if, indeed, it is true that ordinary assertions *have* philosophically interesting truth-conditions. So, language and the fundamental nature of reality are *largely* decoupled. This is what allows the Puzzle to be dissolved. Such significant but incomplete decoupling is both plausible and desirable. The reason it is *desirable* is that it dissolves the Puzzle. But explanation is required to see why it is *plausible*. The challenge, as Stanley (2001, 44) puts it, it to 'give a successful account of how we could assign ontologically innocent truth-conditions to ontologically promiscuous discourse'.

7.4.2 Instrumentalist Semantics

The two leading traditions in semantics are inspired by the pioneering work of Donald Davidson (1967a) and Richard Montague (1970). In what follows we present a simplified 'toy' semantic theory in each of these traditions and explicate the role of instrumentalism therein.

7.4.2.1 Davidsonian Semantics

Davidsonian approaches to semantics minimize the assignment of entities as meanings. Instead, there are meaning *axioms* for subsentential expressions which systematically entail meaning *theorems*—T-sentences; statements of truth-conditions—for whole (declarative) sentences. Sentences are thus

---

[28] See, for example, Heim and Kratzer 1998, 1; Jacobson 2014, 21; Yalcin 2014, 20; King 2018, 784, etc. Radical Contextualists might object, holding that we need pragmatics to derive (full) truth-conditions (Cappelen and Lepore 2005). We do not mean to dismiss Radical Contextualism, but we are assuming for the sake of argument that semantics assigns truth-conditions. If it doesn't, that just makes The Decoupling Objection easier to answer.

not paired with propositions but assigned (typically homophonic) truth-conditions without any sort of propositional intermediary. To get the flavour of this approach, consider the following meaning axioms and the truth-condition they generate:

(DR)   The name 'Pegasus' refers to Pegasus.
(DP)   For any name N, 'N flies' is true iff the referent of N flies.
(DTC) 'Pegasus flies' is true iff Pegasus flies.

Because Davidsonian approaches minimize the assignment of entities as meanings, there is relatively little opportunity for ontology to be misaligned with semantics. But only *relatively* little: (DR) (classically) entails that Pegasus exists.[29] It seems that ontology must cooperate with Davidsonian semantics by supplying referents for names and other singular terms. While this may be a problem—not all sentences containing empty names seem meaningless—it is a relatively *limited* problem. If we could be assured that most names weren't empty, it might not be worth worrying about. But we *can't* be assured that most names aren't empty. Compositional nihilism entails that pretty much all names are empty, organicism entails that the names of inorganic things are empty, etc. (van Inwagen 1990). Davidsonian semantics thus remains hostage to ontological fortune.

7.4.2.2 Davidsonian Instrumentalism

Or at least apparently: while some Davidson*ians* adopt non-classical 'free' logics to skirt the problem of empty names (Sainsbury 2005), Davidson himself seemed to think that such manoeuvres were unnecessary:

> words, meanings of words, reference, and satisfaction are posits we need to implement a theory of truth. They serve this purpose without needing independent confirmation or empirical basis.... [Satisfaction and reference are] notions we must treat as theoretical constructs whose function is exhausted in stating the truth conditions for sentences. (Davidson 1977, 254–5)

This sounds amenable to instrumentalism:[30] the linguistic principles ('meaning axioms') for singular terms are *useful* for systematically generating truth-conditions for sentences, but they can do that while being untrue. Once sentential truth-conditions (meanings$_S$) have been generated, the ladder of reference can be kicked away. This sort of view, if tenable, is exactly what we

---

[29] Further developments of Davidson's approach plausibly generate further commitments: domains of quantification need to be populated, perhaps with events in addition to individuals (Davidson 1967b), etc.

[30] Talk of Davidson's (flirtation if not consummation with) instrumentalism is ubiquitous: see, for example, Williams 2013.

are looking for: a way of generating meanings$_S$ without generating ontological commitments in the process.

But what about the ontological commitments of meanings$_S$ themselves? Common sense requires that semantics place *some* constraint on the truth-conditions of sentences, but dissolving the Puzzle requires that constraint to be *shallow*: largely or wholly neutral with respect to questions of abstruse metaphysics. Disquotational truth-conditions satisfy this joint desideratum nicely. Consider:

(S) 'Snow is white' is true iff snow is white.

(S) rules out a lot: it allows us to make firm judgements about the truth-value of 'snow is white' in many cases. But (S) is largely or wholly metaphysically *neutral*. The truth-conditions it gives seem compatible with any account of the metaphysics of colour or the ontology of snow. As Davidson claims, 'The theory reveals nothing new about the conditions under which an individual sentence is true; it does not make those conditions any clearer than the sentence itself does' (1967a, 311).

What we know when we grasp Davidsonian truth-conditions is shallow and philosophically uninteresting. If you took high-school German, you know that 'Smith weiß, dass Jones einen Ford besitzt' is true iff Smith knows that Jones owns a Ford. That's a useful piece of information, but it doesn't tell you anything *philosophically interesting* about the conditions under which 'Smith weiß, dass Jones einen Ford besitzt' is true. After all, if you knew what those conditions were in a philosophically interesting sense, you'd be a famous epistemologist (cf. J. A. Keller 2015, 117).

But what about 'Pegasus flies'? Just how robust a grasp of the truth-conditions of 'Pegasus flies' does competence require? Not very: after all, competent speakers don't *have* a robust grasp of those truth-conditions. We know the relevant 'facts on the ground', as it were, regarding Pegasus. But if we had to bet our lives on whether 'Pegasus flies' were true, we'd be terrified. Some competent speakers think 'Pegasus flies' is false, since 'Pegasus' doesn't refer. Some think it's true, since 'Pegasus' refers to a flying creature of fiction. As competent speakers, we grasp (DTC). But that 'reveals nothing new', as Davidson puts it, about the conditions under which 'Pegasus flies' is true. Our grasp of those conditions is shallow and metaphysically neutral.[31]

---

[31] The main text suggests that (possibly untrue) meaning axioms are used to derive true meaning theorems (statements of truth-conditions). But (DTC) itself may not be metaphysically neutral, since it arguably entails the existence of Pegasus, or at least of something that flies iff 'Pegasus flies' is true. Perhaps, then, (DTC) is false. It is nonetheless correct: grasping it enables us to determine the truth-value of 'Pegasus flies' in many circumstances. (E.g., 'Pegasus flies' is false in circumstances where Pegasus is an existent but non-flying horse.) Note that we can clearly *use* non-truth-apt conditions for sorting:

Note that this isn't just a point about *Davidsonian* truth-conditions. It's a point about our actual grasp of truth-conditions. As a matter of empirical fact, that grasp is very shallow, just as required for dissolving the Puzzle. The distinction between shallow-linguistic and deep-metaphysical truth-conditions is intuitive, although rarely drawn.[32] As Sarah-Jane Leslie says, metaphysical truth-conditions:

> should not be mistaken for semantically derived truth conditions. . . . [If] a dispositionalist theory of color is correct, . . . 'Bob is red' . . . is true if and only if Bob is experienced as red by standard observers in standard conditions. This is a specification of the circumstances in the world that must obtain for 'Bob is red' to be true. Such a specification does not tell us anything about the semantically derived, compositionally determined truth conditions for 'Bob is red', however. . . . It is in no way part of semantic competence to recognize that the truth of 'Bob is red' entails that there exist standard observers. . . . This is not plausibly a semantic entailment, but merely a metaphysical one. The semantic truth conditions for 'Bob is red' may well be no more than Red(Bob). This respects the compositional structure of the sentence. . . . For this reason, and others, it is very often desirable to simply disquote individual expressions when giving semantic truth conditions. Any further analysis of individual expressions very often belongs to metaphysics rather than to semantics. . . . (2008, 43–4)

7.4.2.3 Logical Form

A close cousin to the Decoupling Objection is the concern that semantics should ground competent speakers' knowledge of the *logical forms* of expressions.[33] Logical form in this sense is at least conceptually distinct from LF; it refers to the 'formal' properties of utterances or meanings$_S$ in virtue of which they stand in (formal) logical relations (entailment, consistency, etc.).

If competent speakers knew the logical forms of expressions, it would be reasonable to think that semantics must explain that. But they don't, so it isn't. Competent speakers must recognize trivial analytic entailments, such as that 'Gabriel is short' entails 'Gabriel is not tall'. But they don't *have to* recognize the logical forms of expressions, because they *don't* recognize the logical forms

---

for example, I can reliably (albeit imperfectly) determine what things satisfy the condition 'bigger than Bilbo'.

[32] Similar *distinctions* are defended in King 2002, Williams 2010, and Sider 2011, and similar *views* are defended in Johnson 2007, Szabó 2013, Glanzberg 2014, and Yalcin 2018.

[33] We take this to be a plausible explication of the common claim that semantics grounds speakers' knowledge of 'entailment facts' (Yalcin 2014, 20; King 2018, 784).

of expressions. 'Translating' ordinary sentences into the regimented idiom of logic is non-trivial even for trained philosophers, much less ordinary speakers. The logical forms of, for example, 'It's raining', 'Pegasus does not exist', and 'Izzy believes that Pegasus flies' remain highly controversial.[34]

Given this, we focus in what follows on the plausibility of instrumentalism about semantic *principles* without worrying about the truth-conditions or entailments of the meanings$_S$ those principles generate.

7.4.2.4 Montague Semantics

To get a sense of how Montagovian theories work, consider the following toy semantics:

(MR) $[[\text{Pegasus}]] = \text{Pegasus}$

(MP) $[[\text{flies}]] = \text{the } f \text{ such that for any } x, f(x) = \begin{cases} 1, & \text{if } x \text{ flies} \\ 0, & \text{otherwise} \end{cases}$

(MS) $[[\text{Pegasus flies}]] = [[\textit{flies}]]([[\textit{Pegasus}]]) = \begin{cases} 1, & \text{if Pegasus flies} \\ 0, & \text{otherwise} \end{cases}$

Understanding this requires a little unpacking. '$[[x]]$' denotes the semantic value of x. Here, the idea is that $[[\text{Pegasus}]]$ is an entity and $[[\text{flies}]]$ is a function from entities to truth-values. Truth-values—truth and falsity—are typically identified with 1 and 0. The function $[[\text{flies}]]$ thus maps entities that fly to 1 and entities that don't to 0. (MR) and (MP) thereby generate (MS), the meaning$_S$ of 'Pegasus flies'. Our toy semantics entails that $[[\text{Pegasus flies}]]$ is 1 or 0, depending on whether Pegasus flies. But that individuates meanings$_S$ much too coarsely: there are only two of them! Non-toy versions of Montague semantics identify meanings$_S$ with *intensions*: functions from possible words to truth-values, or more typically their characteristic sets. Thus, $[[\text{Pegasus flies}]]$ would be the set of worlds at which Pegasus flies:

(IMS) $[[\text{Pegasus flies}]] = \{w: [[\text{flies}]]^w([[\text{Pegasus}]]^w) = 1\}$
$= \{w: \text{Pegasus flies @ } w\}.$

Montague semantics essentially *identifies* meanings$_S$ with truth-conditions.[35]

---

[34] See J. A. Keller 2015, L. J. Keller 2019, King 2002, and Szabó 2012 for discussion.

Because on this view semantic values are things, there appears to be abundant opportunity for ontology and semantics to misalign. Our toy semantics appealed to (purported) ordinary entities like Pegasus, functions, and truth-values; (IMS) adds possible worlds to the mix, and typical non-toy theories add times, events, degrees, kinds, situations, and vectors (see Rett 2022).

7.4.2.5 Montagovian Instrumentalism

How plausible is instrumentalism about Montagovian semantics? Can we use Montagovian principles to pair utterances (or, really, the outputs of phonological and morphological processing) with meanings$_S$, and then kick away the ladder once we're done? There is evidence that Montagovian *theorizing* is not generally undertaken in a realist vein. The identification of truth-values with 1 and 0 is a tell: whatever truth and falsity are, they aren't 1 and 0! Sometimes the anti-realism is explicit, as when Pauline Jacobson says 'There is little, if any, reason to choose between the unary rule and the silent lexical item approach; they ultimately may just be different metaphors for the same thing' (2014, 123–4).

More generally, theorizing in this tradition exhibits a sort of reckless indifference to ontology. This seems like strong evidence that the resulting theories are not intended to be truth-apt. For example, Derek Ball counsels against ontological scruples in semantic theorizing in his response to a version of Benacerraf's dilemma for the semantics of gradable adjectives:

> Semantics is said to be the study of meaning. If we took a formal semantic theory to be making a claim about what meanings are (identical to)—for example, that the meaning of *tall* is a function from individuals to sets—then the proliferation of candidates would be a problem and formal semantics would be in trouble. But that should not be our attitude. (2018, 389)

Similarly, Zoltan Szabó writes:

> Linguists want to say what the meanings of various expressions are without having to say too much about them. The situation resembles that of the mathematician: she wants to say enough about the number 2 to prove that its square root is irrational, but not so much as to take sides in the metaphysical debate among Platonists, intuitionists and formalists. The aim is to present a set of minimal commitments. (2013, 39)

---

[35] Note that this truth-condition—'Pegasus flies' is true @ w iff Pegasus flies @ w—is just as shallow as the Davidsonian truth-condition discussed above.

Semantic theorizing in the Montagovian tradition thus seems not only compatible with instrumentalism, but (often) to *be* instrumentalist.³⁶ Of course, this is mere *wordy* anti-realism. How plausible is it that there is a worldly analogue? At least somewhat. We argued in Section 7.2.8 that linguistic principles *can* do their job of associating utterances with meanings$_S$ even if they are untrue.³⁷ Given that, it's plausible that that's how they *do* do their job. Language is, we assume, the product of evolution. Evolution cares about *efficiency*, not truth—and there is almost always a trade-off between them. This at least suggests that we should not expect evolved linguistic principles to have only true presuppositions.

7.4.2.6 Mathematical Meanings

We have said that we are realists about mathematics. Some hold that formal semantics in the Montagovian tradition *is* basically just math (Pickel 2019). Does Linguistic Instrumentalism thus conflict with mathematical realism? We don't think so. Linguistic Instrumentalism allows that *some* linguistic theories are truth-apt. So if formal semantics turned out to be truth-apt, that wouldn't necessarily be an objection. But we don't think formal semantics *is* truth-apt. Formal semantics might be *basically* just math, but it isn't *just* math: it's mathematical operations on atomic meanings (the meanings of morphemes). And so, if atomic meanings don't exist, formal semantics will have false ontological presuppositions.

Let's see how all of this fits together. Hearers are presented with 'utterances'—relatively undifferentiated and 'fuzzy' sequences of sounds, movements, or marks—something like an auditory version of

(U) **pegasusflies**

On standard views, phonological and morphological principles assign (project onto) (U) structure that it doesn't have, generating something like the following (mis)representation of (U)

(R1) Pegasus flies.

Syntactic principles then assign (project onto) (U) further structure, and *lexical* semantics assigns (plausibly non-existent) lexical semantic values, thus generating a 'richer' (mis)representation of (U):

---

³⁶ See Ball 2018, Schwarz 2018, and Yalcin 2018 for fairly explicit arguments to this effect.
³⁷ Note that Davidsonian and Montagovian semantic *theories* both work—both associate utterances with meanings$_S$—regardless of their truth.

(R2) $[[\text{flies}]]^w \left([[[\text{Pegasus}]]^w \right)$.

Finally, *compositional* semantics computes the function in (R2), yielding something like

(IMS) $\{w: \text{Pegasus flies} @ w\}$.

We are realists about utterances like (U) and truth-conditions like (IMS)—and about meaning$_s$ more generally—but instrumentalists about the attributions/projections involved in the intermediate steps between them: about the correctness of representations like (R1) and (R2). That is, we think representations like (R1) and (R2)—and the linguistic principles that generate them—are (often) correct but untrue. The mathematical step to (IMS) doesn't involve attributions or projections, and so we are happy to be realists about that. We are neutral on whether there *is* such a mathematical step—this is just one common picture—but if there is we have no beef with realism about it.

We have also argued that speakers' grasp on truth-conditions like (IMS) is shallow and largely metaphysically neutral. (Likewise with their grasp of logical forms.) Thus, Linguistic Instrumentalism minimizes potential conflicts between the ontology and the truth-conditions of anodyne utterances—and the ontological commitments of the linguistic principles governing them.

Our view is not entirely novel. Rey (2020) defends a similar picture—he is sceptical about the existence of words, syntactic structure, subsentential semantic values, etc.—but his *interpretation* of the picture is quite different. Because Rey is a linguistic *realist*, he endorses a conglomerate of murky and implausible ontological and ideological theses about 'intentional inexistence' in order to make sense of his picture. It seems preferable to simply acknowledge that linguistic principles can be correct—*useful* for generating (shallow) truth-conditions—without being true.

7.5 Conclusion

We end with a note of possible *rapprochement*. Wittgenstein (1929, 164–5) famously said that 'we can draw no conclusions—except very vague ones—from [grammatical form] as to the actual logical form of the phenomena described'. Gaskin *contrasts* this realist sentiment with Linguistic Idealism, according to which there is no question of our 'having to worry', in general, that an object 'perhaps does not exist': if my language is meaningful—and the criteria for that are internal to the language-game itself, a matter of whether the signs I purport to employ do indeed have use—then whatever objects my words can be interpreted as referring to *eo ipso* exist. For to say that my words refer to objects is just another way of saying that these words are indeed meaningful. (this volume, 14–15)

We, on the other hand, take these sentiments to be perfectly compatible, and hope the congruence between these passages and what we've argued here is as striking to the reader as it is to us. The idea that linguistic principles should be evaluated 'internally' is a core component of Linguistic Instrumentalism, but also of Linguistic Idealism. We are drawn to anti-realism about linguistics because we wish to maintain a robust realism about both metaphysics and our ordinary thought and talk. Perhaps Gaskin would say that our realism is merely *empirical*, perfectly compatibly with some sort of *transcendental* idealism. We brushed aside the distinction between empirical and transcendental realism above (in n. 7) because, frankly, we can make neither head nor tail of it. We take the inability to make sense of that distinction to be a mark of a true realist. But perhaps Gaskin would argue that it is instead the mark of a true transcendental idealist. *Whereof one cannot speak thereof one must be silent*.[38]

References

Adger, D. 2019. *Language Unlimited* (Oxford: OUP).
Anscombe, G. E. M. 1981. *From Parmenides to Wittgenstein* (Cambridge: CUP).
Appiah, A. 2017. *As If: Idealization and Ideals* (Cambridge, MA: Harvard University Press).
Ashworth, E. J. 2015. 'Medieval theories of signification to John Locke', in M. Cameron and R. Stainton (eds), *Linguistic Content: New Essays in the Philosophy of Language* (Oxford: OUP), 156–75.
Ball, D. 2018. 'Semantics as measurement', in D. Ball and B. Rabern, *The Science of Meaning: Essays on the Metatheory of Natural Language Semantics* (Oxford: OUP), 381–410.
Ball, D. and Rabern, B. 2018. *The Science of Meaning: Essays on the Metatheory of Natural Language Semantics* (Oxford: OUP).
Benacerraf, P. 1965. 'What numbers could not be', *The Philosophical Review* 74, 47–73.
Bloomfield, L. 1936. 'Language or ideas', *Language* 12, 89–95.
Boyd, R. 1983. 'On the current status of scientific realism', *Erkenntnis* 5/19, 45–90.
Braun, D. 1993. 'Empty names', *Nous* 27, 449–69.
Cappelen, H. and Lepore, E. 2005. *Insensitive Semantics* (Oxford: Blackwell).

---

[38] Wittgenstein (1922, 23). Thanks to the Saint Joseph's University Friday Reading Group, the Rutgers Metaphysics Reading group, and to Derek Ball, Bryan Pickel, Jeff Speaks, and especially Richard Gaskin for helpful comments and discussion. They should not be held accountable for any of the many deep flaws we are sure this paper contains.

Cartwright, N. 1983. *How the Laws of Physics Lie* (Oxford: OUP).
Chomsky, N. 1965. *Aspects of the Theory of Syntax* (Cambridge, MA: MIT Press).
Chomsky, N. 1966. 'Explanatory models in linguistics', in E. Nagel, P. Suppes, and A. Tarski (eds.), *Studies in Logic and the Foundations of Mathematics* (Amsterdam: Elsevier), 44, 528–50.
Chomsky, N. 2000. *New Horizons in the Study of Language* (Cambridge: CUP).
Chomsky, N. 2017. *On Language* (New York: The New Press).
Davidson, D. 1967a. 'Truth and meaning', *Synthese* 17, 304–23.
Davidson, D. 1967b. 'The logical form of action sentences', in N. Rescher (ed.), *The Logic of Decision and Action* (Pittsburgh, PA: University of Pittsburgh), 81–95.
Davidson, D. 1977. 'Reality without reference', *Dialectica* 3, 247–58.
Doyle, J. P. 2001. *The Conimbricenses: Some Questions on Signs, Translated with Introduction and Notes* (Milwaukee: Marquette University Press).
Dupoux, E., Kakehi, Y., Hirose, Y., Pallier, C., and Mehler, J. 1999. 'Epenthetic vowels in Japanese: A perceptual illusion?', *Journal of Experimental Psychology: Human Perception and Performance* 25, 1568–78.
Gaskin, R. 2019. 'From the unity of the proposition to linguistic idealism', *Synthese* 196, 1325–42.
Gaskin, R. 2021. *Language and World: A Defense of Linguistic Idealism* (New York: Routledge).
Glanzberg, M. J. 2014. 'Explanation and partiality in semantic theory', in A. Burgess and B. Sherman (eds), *Metasemantics: New Essays on the Foundations of Meaning* (Oxford: OUP), 259–92.
Grice, H. P. 1975. 'Method in philosophical psychology: From the banal to the bizarre', *Proceedings and Addresses of the American Philosophical Association* 48, 23–53.
Heim, I, and Kratzer, A. 1998. *Semantics in Generative Grammar* (Malden, MA: Blackwell).
Jacobson, P. I. 2014. *Compositional Semantics* (New York: OUP).
Johnson, K. 2007. 'The legacy of methodological dualism', *Mind and Language* 22, 366–401.
Jubien, M. 2001. 'Propositions and the objects of thought', *Philosophical Studies* 104, 47–62.
Katz, J. J. 1985a. *The Philosophy of Linguistics* (Oxford: OUP).
Katz, J. J. 1985b. 'An outline of platonist grammar', in J. J. Katz, *The Philosophy of Linguistics* (Oxford: OUP), 17–48.
Keller, J. A. 2014. 'Theological anti-realism', *Journal of Analytic Theology* 2, 13–42.
Keller, J. A. 2015. 'Paraphrase, semantics, and ontology', in K. Bennett and D. Zimmerman (eds), *Oxford Studies in Metaphysics* 9 (Oxford: OUP) 89–128.
Keller, L. J. 2019. 'What propositional structure could not be', *Synthese* 196, 1529–53.
King, J. C. 2002. 'Two sorts of claim about "logical form"', G. Preyer and G. Peter (eds), *Logical Form and Language* (Oxford: OUP), 118–31.
King, J. C. 2007. *The Nature and Structure of Content* (Oxford: OUP).
King, J. C. 2018. 'W(h)ither semantics!(?)', *Noûs* 52, 772–95.
Kripke, S. 1980. *Naming and Necessity* (Cambridge, MA: Harvard University Press).
Leslie, S. J. 2008. 'Generics: Cognition and acquisition', *Philosophical Review* 117, 1–47.
Ludwig, K. 2002. 'What is the role of a truth theory in a meaning theory?', in J. K. Campbell, M. O'Rourke, and D. Shier (eds), *Meaning and Truth: Investigations in Philosophical Semantics* (New York: Seven Bridges Press), 142–63.
Machery, E. 2009. *Doing without Concepts* (New York: OUP).
McGilvray, J. 1998. 'Meanings are syntactically individuated and found in the head', *Mind & Language* 13, 225–80.
Meinong, A. 1960. 'The theory of objects', in R. M. Chisolm (ed.), *Realism and the Background of Phenomenology* (Glencoe, IL: Free Press), 76–117.
Montague, R. 1970. 'English as a formal language', in B. Visentini et al. (eds), *Linguaggi nella Società e nella Tecnica* (Milan: Edizioni di Communita), 189–224.
Pickel, B. 2019. 'Structured propositions in a generative grammar', *Mind* 128, 329–66.
Pietroski, P. 2018. *Conjoining Meanings: Semantics without Truth Values* (Oxford: OUP).
Pitt, D. 2018. 'What kind of science is linguistics?', in C. Behme and M. Neef (eds), *Essays on Linguistic Realism* (Amsterdam: John Benjamins Publishing Company), 7–20.
Quine, W. V. O. 1960. *Word and Object* (Cambridge, MA: MIT Press).

Reiland, I. 2023. 'Regulative rules: A distinctive normative kind', *Philosophy and Phenomenological Research*, 2 July 2023, 1–20 (https://doi.org/10.1111/phpr.13008).
Rett, J. 2022. 'A typology of semantic entities', D. Altshuler (ed.), *Linguistics Meets Philosophy* (New York: CUP), 277–301.
Rey, G. 2006. 'The intentional inexistence of language—but not cars', in R. Stainton (ed.), *Contemporary Debates in Cognitive Science* (Oxford: Wiley-Blackwell), 237–55.
Rey, G. 2020. *Representation of Language: Philosophical Issues in a Chomskyan Linguistics* (Oxford: OUP).
Rosen, G. 1990. 'Modal fictionalism', *Mind* 99, 327–54.
Russell, B. 1980. 'Correspondence with Frege', in G. Frege, *Philosophical and Mathematical Correspondence* (Chicago: University of Chicago Press), 130–1.
Russell, G. K. 2023. 'How the laws of logic lie', *Episteme* 20, 833–51.
Sainsbury, R. M. 2005. *Reference without Referents* (Oxford: OUP).
Santana, C. 2016. 'What is language?', *Ergo* 3, 501–23.
Sapir, E. 1921. *Language* (New York: Harcourt).
Schwarz, W. 2018. 'Semantic possibility', in D. Ball and B. Rabern (eds), *The Science of Meaning: Essays on the Metatheory of Natural Language Semantics* (Oxford: OUP), 361–80.
Searle, J. 1969. *Speech Acts* (New York: CUP).
Sider, T. 2011. *Writing the Book of the World* (New York: OUP).
Stanley, J. 2001. 'Hermeneutic fictionalism', *Midwest Studies in Philosophy* 25, 36–71.
Szabó, Z. G. 2012. 'Against logical form', in I. G. Preyer (ed.), *Donald Davidson on Truth, Meaning, and the Mental* (Oxford: OUP), 105–26.
Szabó, Z. G. 2013. *Problems of Compositionality* (Hoboken: Routledge).
Thomasson, A. L. 2015. *Ontology Made Easy* (New York: OUP).
van Fraassen, B. 1980. *The Scientific Image* (Oxford: OUP).
van Inwagen, P. 1990. *Material Beings* (Ithaca: Cornell University Press).
Williamson, T. 2007. *The Philosophy of Philosophy* (Oxford: OUP).
Williamson, T. 2018. 'Model-building as a philosophical method', *Phenomenology and Mind* 15, 16–22.
Wittgenstein, L. 1922. *Tractatus Logico-Philosophicus*, C. K. Ogden (trans.) (London: Kegan Paul).
Wittgenstein, L. 1929. 'Some remarks on logical form', *Proceedings of the Aristotelian Society*, Supplementary Volume 9, 162–71.
Williams, J. R. G. 2010. 'Fundamental and derivative truths', *Mind* 119, 103–41.
Williams, J. R. G. 2013. 'Reference', in E. Lepore and K. Ludwig (eds), *A Companion to Donald Davidson* (Oxford: Wiley-Blackwell), 264–86.
Yalcin, S. 2014. 'Semantics and metasemantics in the context of generative grammar', in A. Burgess and B. Sherman (eds), *Metasemantics* (Oxford: OUP), 17–54.
Yalcin, S. 2018. 'Semantics as a model-based science', in D. Ball and B. Rabern (eds), *The Science of Meaning: Essays on the Metatheory of Natural Language Semantics* (Oxford: OUP), 334–60.
Zsiga, E. 2020. *The Phonetics/Phonology Interface* (Edinburgh: Edinburgh University Press).

8
Abstract Objects and the Philosophy of Language

William Stirton

8.1 The Question

The purpose of this chapter is to consider whether there can be a good argument for the existence of abstract objects which proceeds through considerations in the philosophy of language alone. There may be good arguments for the existence of abstract objects which do not so proceed. For example, one argument, associated with the name of Quine above all, is that our best total theory of the world cannot avoid a commitment to abstract objects.[1] This sort of argument rests on considerations from the philosophy of science. Other philosophers have argued for the existence of abstract objects on the ground that, when the notion of perception is properly understood, it becomes clear that we can perceive abstract as well as concrete objects.[2] This sort of argument rests on considerations in the philosophy of perception and therefore is not purely linguistic.

In contrast to these last two kinds of argument, some philosophers have claimed that reflection on the conditions necessary for a language to function as a language is enough to show that some expressions must refer to abstract objects. According, for example, to Gaskin's linguistic idealism, every meaningful expression has a referent which is very often, though not always, abstract (2021, 100 and *passim*) and understanding the expression consists in being acquainted with its referent (2008, 41). An argument for the existence of abstract objects which proceeds through the philosophy of language alone shall henceforth be called a 'linguistic argument'.

---

[1] The merits of this sort of argument are debated in depth in a recent collection (Falguera and Martínez-Vidal 2020) with contributions from both supporters and opponents.

[2] See Husserl 1921, Investigation VI, chs 6–8, and Maddy 1980.

Limitations of space and of the author's competence make it impractical to try to establish what, in general, an abstract object is. Throughout the following, natural numbers will be the kind of abstract object that is mainly under discussion.

A number of the linguistic arguments that have been put forward will receive detailed attention in Sections 8.4–8.6 below. Sections 8.2 and 8.3 are devoted to arguing for some preliminary theses which underlie the criticisms made in Sections 8.4–8.6. The verdict in each case is not that the argument clearly fails but that it can be accepted only at the cost of undertaking some fairly strong commitment. In two cases, for example, acceptance of the argument requires a commitment to the solvability of Frege's *Julius Caesar Problem*, about which more will be said in Section 8.3 below. Whether the Julius Caesar Problem can be solved has been the subject of a prolonged and lively debate which promises to continue for some time yet; the present chapter will not try to adjudicate it.[3]

8.2 Theories of Truth

In contrast to Gaskin, some philosophers have argued that reference to abstract objects on the part of certain expressions is necessary, not for sentences in general to be as much as meaningful, but certainly for some sentences to be true.

The leading examples are Wright (1983, 8) and Hale (1987, 11),[4] who have defended the following argument for the existence of abstract objects:

(1) If a singular term *t* occurs in a true atomic sentence which is free of intensional idioms, then *t* denotes some object;

(2) Some singular terms, which can only denote abstract objects if they denote at all, do occur in true atomic sentences which are free of intensional idioms;

(3) *Therefore* some singular terms denote abstract objects.

It is with premiss (1) that we are concerned in the first instance. (1) is not exactly a theorem of any particular theory of truth (as it generalizes over *all* sentences in *all* languages) but it can be regarded as a meta-claim about

---

[3] Wright 1983, §xiv, and Hale and Wright 2001, ch.14, have tried to solve the problem, while I (in Stirton 2003, 2016) have criticized their proposals. Wright 2020, 314–15, has in turn replied to my objections.

[4] The argument presented in the text is an amalgamation of slightly different arguments presented by Wright and Hale respectively. The basic shape of the argument is indebted more to Hale but the formulation of the premisses incorporates qualifications made by Wright 1983, 8, and 171 n. 4. See also Hale and Wright 2001, 8.

satisfactory theories of truth: if a theory of truth is going to be satisfactory, then there are sentences to which it cannot assign a truth-condition capable of being satisfied unless it also assigns a denotation to every singular term occurring within these sentences.

It will be argued in Sections 8.3 and 8.5 below that the weakest point of the argument is premiss (2), so relatively little turns on whether (1) is true. For what it is worth, a reasonable case for (1) can be made along the following lines. 'Singular term' and 'object' are both technical terms. It follows that everyone who uses these terms should use them in accordance with (at least reasonably) clear and sharp rules for their use, whether these rules have been set up by themselves or by some earlier writer. If (1) be rejected, the correct use of 'object' is no longer as firmly anchored to the correct use of 'singular term' as it would be if (1) were in force; and I am not aware of any proposals, on the part of philosophers who would like to reject (1),[5] that could replace it.

Theories of truth have been important for the philosophy of language because many philosophers have thought that an informative analysis of what it is to understand some natural language L must, or at least can, make reference to the idea of a theory of truth for L. Supporters of this thesis will be called *truth-conditional theorists*. They are far less numerous now than they were in the 1980s, as the philosophical community has grown increasingly aware of difficulties in the way of making true wide-ranging generalizations about the conditions for an utterance to be true or false. Just how devastating the difficulties are is a disputed matter.[6] At all events, it is hard to see that a strong opponent of the systematizing tendency in the philosophy of language is likely to be a strong supporter of linguistic arguments. Truth-conditional theorists still exist (Borg 2004, §1.1.1; Glüer 2012) and some of the philosophers to be discussed here (Wright 1983, 72–3;[7] Gaskin 2021, §4 and §7) are among them. All the philosophers to be considered here endorse (1) and therefore presumably feel confident of their ability to identify at least some, entirely general, necessary conditions for an atomic sentence to be true. So I will assume that someone deploying linguistic arguments is likely to be a truth-conditional theorist.

It will be useful to fix some terminology. If Th is a theory of truth of the most familiar kind and s a sentence of its object-language containing no indexical elements, then Th will contain exactly one theorem of the shape

---

[5] Such as Lambert 1983, especially ch. 6.
[6] See Recanati 2005 and Borg and Fisher 2022 for overviews of the range of positions that have been taken up.
[7] See also Wright 1986, especially ch. 9.

(4) s is true iff ...,

where what stands in place of the dots contains no expression referring to s or its parts and no semantic terminology ('true', 'refers', 'satisfies') not already in s. Such a theorem is called a *T-theorem* (sc., of *Th*) and, when s is fixed, *the T-theorem for s*. In a theory of truth of the simplest kind, still assuming that s contains no indexical expressions, what stands in place of the dots in (4) will be a sentence of *Th* synonymous with s. As to what a T-theorem for a sentence s which does contain indexical expressions might look like, an example is (9) below.

Truth-conditional theorists are agreed that, for a theory of truth to be of much use for the philosophy of language, it has to do more than generate a true T-theorem for every sentence of the object-language. One further desideratum is that, even when what stands in place of 's' in (4) is an atomic sentence, that instance of (4) should not simply be postulated as an axiom but should be deducible from axioms of the theory which state semantic properties of singular terms and predicates occurring in s. Now this desideratum is somewhat in tension with another thesis which truth-conditional theorists also endorse: that it should be possible for all speakers of a natural language L to *know* (perhaps in some unusual or etiolated sense of 'know') the axioms and rules of a theory of truth for L. The tension is due to the fact that, although it is plausible enough that anyone who can speak L implicitly knows, or at least would easily recognize the truth of, any *T-theorem* for a sentence of L,[8] there is considerably more awkwardness in maintaining that they know the propositions expressed by axioms containing highly technical words like 'denotes' and 'satisfies'.[9]

Those truth-conditional theorists who accept that there is a difficulty here have tackled it in a variety of ways. Perhaps the most sophisticated is Davies's *structural constraint* (henceforth SC) which, for theories of truth with object-language L, is formulated as follows:

> If, but only if, there could be speakers of L who, having been taught to use and know the meanings of sentences (of L) $s_1, \ldots, s_n$ (and so, *inter alia*, to know the truth conditions of $s_1, \ldots, s_n$), could by rational inductive means go on to use and know the meaning of the sentence s (and so, *inter alia*, to know the truth condition of s), then a theory of truth for L should employ in the

---

[8] Difficulties caused by semantic paradoxes are rather tangential to the concerns of the present chapter.
[9] Wright 1986, ch. 6, explains both why truth-conditional theorists sometimes want to hold both these theses and why there is some difficulty in holding them both at once.

canonical derivations of truth-condition-specifying biconditionals for $s_1, \ldots,$ s_n resources already sufficient for the canonical derivation of a biconditional for s (1981, 138).

This seems sufficiently strong to rule out the kind of theory of truth that would simply take the T-theorem for s as an axiom.

It is with the 'only if' part of the *SC* that we are mainly concerned. If Davies is right, a theory of truth could potentially be faulted for trying to break up atomic sentences more finely than the *SC* allows. Even if Davies is wrong, the main point is that he was at least grappling with a genuine difficulty: anyone who wants to endorse a theory of truth that finds a finer articulation within atomic sentences than the *SC* warrants has to produce some argument to justify doing so. This general principle will be called the *structural limitation principle*. Why it is important will become clear in the next section. To state the principle explicitly: for any sentence s of the object-language L, if s means that p, then there is a limit to the number of distinct axioms in a theory of truth for L, if that theory of truth is to be of any use for the philosophy of language, that should have to be posited in order to make possible a deduction that s is true iff p. That limit is determined by the *SC* if the *SC* is true; if the *SC* is false it is determined by some general principle which has to be argued for.

To a large extent, the structural limitation thesis is already plausible to common sense. English contains expressions like 'for my sake' and 'for your sake'. It is, to say the least, hard to see what advantage someone who tries to learn the meaning of 'sake' on its own has over someone who learns 'for the sake of X/for X's sake' as an indissoluble unit.[10]

8.3 The Julius Caesar Problem

For any one-place sortal predicate $\ulcorner P(x) \urcorner$, the intended meaning of the singular term $\ulcorner Nx: P(x) \urcorner$ is that it denotes the number of things that satisfy $\ulcorner P(x) \urcorner$. It is clear that stipulating the meaning of $\ulcorner Nx: P(x) \urcorner$ in this way is legitimate only to the extent that it is legitimate to assume that there are such things as numbers. The question therefore arises whether there is a way of explaining the meaning of expressions of the shape of $\ulcorner Nx: P(x) \urcorner$ (henceforth: *N*-terms) in such a way that the property of denoting numbers can be seen to follow from

---

[10] I take this to show that a good theory of meaning will not assign any semantic value to 'sake'. Gaskin disagrees, arguing that there are such objects as sakes (2021, 172). I will argue in the next section that this could be so only if the word 'sake' occurred in other contexts besides 'for the sake of X/for X's sake'. For more on the structural limitation principle, see n. 11.

the way their meaning is explained, as opposed to being blatantly assumed by the meaning-explanation.

A putative way (Wright 1983, 104; Hale and Wright 2001, passim) of explaining the meaning of *N*-terms is to stipulate that the universal closure (formed by binding the predicate-variables *F* and *G*) of the second-order formula

(5) $Nx: Fx = Nx: Gx \leftrightarrow \exists A[\forall x(Fx \to \exists!y(Gy \land Axy)) \land \forall x(Gx \to \exists!y(Fy \land Ayx))]$

shall be true. Frege (1950, §§65–7) raised the question whether, by stipulating the universal closure of (5), it would be possible to give the second-order functional expression *Nx* its intended meaning, which is that it denotes a function taking sortal concepts to the number of things falling under them. He returned a negative answer and his reason for doing so was the *Julius Caesar Problem*.

Frege's argument can be divided into two parts. The title 'Julius Caesar Problem' is more appropriately given to the first part alone, which goes as follows. It can be conceded to the philosopher who wants to use (5) as a definition that stipulating the universal closure of (5) to be true fixes a truth-condition for every sentence of the shape ⌜*Nx: Fx = Nx: Gx*⌝. However (Frege objects) it does nothing to fix a truth-condition for sentences of the shape ⌜*Nx: Fx = t*⌝, where *t* is not an *N*-term. From the point of view of a truth-conditional theorist, it follows that no reason has been given for thinking that such a sentence has any truth-value or any sense either.

At this point, there are two counter-objections that someone might be tempted to raise against Frege's objection. One turns on the fact that a sentence of the shape of ⌜*Nx: Fx = Nx: Gx*⌝ has the identity-sign in its middle. According to this counter-objection, any sentence of the shape of ⌜*s = t*⌝ has a truth-condition, which can be described by saying that the sentence is true if *s* and *t* denote the same object and false otherwise. So a sentence of the shape of ⌜*Nx: Fx = t*⌝, whatever *t* may be, cannot fail to have a truth-condition.

This counter-objection errs in overlooking the possibility that the use of the identity-sign in the left hand side of instances of (5) might be a *mis*use. There is nothing to prevent anyone from taking any expression of any language, combining it with other expressions in order to form a sentence and stipulating a meaning for that sentence without regard to the normal meanings of its component expressions. To do this is to introduce a new ambiguity into the language, which is the sort of thing a careful philosopher wants to avoid. Philosophers who want to stipulate the universal closure of (5) to be true have to show that they are not doing exactly that.

To be fair, it has to be acknowledged that there is one school of philosophers—the neo-Fregeans—who have made a serious attempt to show this. They have argued (see footnote 3 above) that someone to whom a stipulation of the universal closure of (5) is presented can quite rationally work out the truth-condition of ⌜$Nx: Fx = t$⌝, for at least a good sample of singular terms t that were in the language prior to the introduction of Nx. Whether the neo-Fregeans (who, on the present issue, are at odds with the historical Frege) are right about this is a question that cannot be pursued here. In view of the arguments they have presented, however, I believe they would agree with me that the facile counter-objection currently under consideration is not good enough to defuse the Julius Caesar Problem.

A somewhat similar counter-objection turns on the fact that (5) makes use of the expression ⌜Nx⌝, which has the syntactic form of a second-order functional expression. Someone pressing this counter-objection might urge that, since ⌜Nx⌝ *is* a second-order functional expression, it must denote a total function, so that every N-term must denote an object and every sentence of the shape ⌜$Nx: Fx = t$⌝ must have a truth-condition. The answer to this counter-objection is that it does not follow simply from the syntactical form of ⌜Nx⌝ that stipulating the universal closure of (5) gives ⌜Nx⌝ the meaning appropriate to a second-order functional expression. That the stipulation gives it such a meaning needs to be argued, not assumed.

The verdict on the first half of Frege's argument, therefore, is that while a case can perhaps be made that stipulating the universal closure of (5) fixes a truth-condition for sentences of the shape ⌜$Nx: Fx = t$⌝, there is no easy way to make it.

The second half of Frege's argument applies the principle of structural limitation to the conclusion of the first half. If the stipulation of the universal closure of (5) is all that we have to go on in trying to work out the truth-conditions of sentences of the shape of ⌜$Nx: Fx = t$⌝, then N-terms just do not occur in a sufficiently wide range of meaningful contexts to justify counting them as genuine singular terms.[11] If ⌜$Nx: Fx$⌝ and ⌜$Nx: Gx$⌝ do not function as genuine singular terms in ⌜$Nx: Fx = Nx: Gx$⌝, then ⌜$Nx: Fx = Nx: Gx$⌝ would be more perspicuously rewritten to show that it is really composed

---

[11] This is admittedly an over-interpretation of what Frege explicitly wrote about the Julius Caesar Problem, but on the other hand something like the principle of structural limitation does operate in his *Grundgesetze* (1893/1903). In the appendix on Russell's Paradox (II, 255) he considered the possibility of treating class-names as mere *Scheineigennamen*, arguing that an expression which looks like a singular term is a mere *Scheineigenname* if the range of contexts in which it can intelligibly occur is very narrow.

not of two singular terms flanking the identity-sign but of a second-order relational expression with the first-order predicates F and G inserted into its argument-places. In that case, a good theory of truth should not assign denotations to N-terms. So, one possible linguistic argument has been scotched already.

At this point it would be good to forestall a possible misunderstanding. If someone sees any merit in maintaining that there are *some* values of t such that the string of words $\ulcorner Nx\colon Fx = t\urcorner$ has no truth-value, perhaps even that it does not make sense, they can do so without rejecting the argument that has just been presented. All that that argument requires is that, in order for N-terms to be genuine singular terms and therefore to be candidates for denoting objects, there should be a *reasonable selection* of singular terms t which are not N-terms, with the property that $\ulcorner Nx\colon Fx = t\urcorner$ does make sense. What sort of set of terms constitutes a reasonable selection is determined by the SC, or whatever someone wishes to put in its place.

Two questions arise in passing. One is whether, if stipulating the universal closure of (5) did give N-terms a meaning appropriate to genuine singular terms, they would also denote objects. The second is whether the objects they then denoted would be abstract. If we accept (1), the answer to the first question has to be affirmative. As to the second, it has been technically demonstrated (Wright 1983, §xix) that, from (5), the existence of infinitely many objects follows by second-order logic; and there would be something very uncomfortable about thinking that the existence of infinitely many *concrete* objects could be known a priori.

The Julius Caesar Problem, at least as it is understood here, does not arise for someone who is prepared to accept the existence of numbers *in advance of* making any claims about the truth-conditions of sentences which appear to make reference to them. However, even a thinker of this kind might feel some puzzlement over the truth-values of sentences like '2 = Julius Caesar'. Such sentences, which imply identity between what are normally taken to be two objects of radically different kinds, are called *cross-categorial identifications*. Perhaps the commonest view about them, defended by Hale and Wright (2001, 394) and Linnebo (2018, ch. 9), is that they are all false, but Lowe (2009, 2) has argued (or at least claimed) that they do not even make sense. At all events, questions about cross-categorial identifications are to be distinguished from the problem that was presented earlier in this section as the 'Julius Caesar Problem'. This will be important in Section 8.6 below.

8.4 Gaskin's Linguistic Idealism

Gaskin[12] (2008, §§7–8; 2021, §14) has shown that at least two relations between words and things, either of which might be called 'reference', have been the object of philosophical attention over the millennia. He calls them *suppositio* and *significatio* respectively. In the case of proper names and singular demonstrative phrases, *suppositio* very often coincides with *significatio* (2008, 74–5, 123) but they are always distinct in the case of sentences, predicates, definite descriptions, and the majority of kinds of linguistic expression that one comes across. A definite description, for example, has a descriptive concept, in Russell's sense, as its *significatio* (2008, 79) whereas its *suppositio*, when the latter exists at all, is the object (if any) which satisfies the description. It should be clear from this that definite descriptions and genuine names need to be sharply distinguished (2008, §15).

When Gaskin is expounding his own philosophy, he uses 'reference' always to mean *significatio*. What this technical term means is explained as follows:

> [T]he object of reference of an expression is just that thing which an adequate theory of meaning for the language in question specifies as what understanders need to think of, and what it suffices for them to think of (so long as they think of the relevant object *as* the meaning of the relevant item of language), in order to count as understanding the expression in question. Or, to put it in Russellian terms: the object of reference of an expression is just that thing (concrete or abstract) with which it is necessary and sufficient for an understander to be acquainted in order to count as understanding the expression in question (2008, 41).[13]

If there are entities with the property that to understand an expression is to be acquainted with, or think about, one of these entities, then it is hardly disputable that many of them will be abstract. Two people who are light years apart can think the very same proposition or grasp the very same concept. If so, then propositions and concepts cannot be minds or mental contents

---

[12] I am very grateful to him for extensive discussions in correspondence of the topics tackled in this section, which saved me from misrepresenting his position in more than one respect.

[13] Cf. Gaskin 2021, 87, where *significatio* is defined as 'what an understander has to think about in order to count as understanding a linguistic expression'. In other contexts, Gaskin adds that in order to understand an expression I need not only to be acquainted with its referent but also to be acquainted with the referent *as* the referent of the expression, for example: 'acquaintance with [the referents of] simple concept-expressions—and acquaintance with them *as* the referents of their corresponding expressions—will then be what an understanding of those concept-expressions consists in' (2021, 90).

(in the sense of contents of just *one* person's mind). There would be almost equally huge difficulties with taking them to be any kind of material object. So, if Gaskin is right, the existence of abstract objects will be a necessary condition of language's functioning at all.

The foregoing definition of *significatio* entails that that there is no such thing as understanding a name which has no referent. Gaskin concludes, quite reasonably, that there is simply no such thing as a name which has no referent, as the possibility of understanding a name is essential to its functioning as a name (2008, 247). It must be recognized, however, that the referent of a *descriptive* name (a concept introduced by Evans: 1982, 35–6) is a descriptive concept and therefore not what is ordinarily called 'the referent' (2021, 104). Another qualification is that demonstrative phrases have a sort of meaning which can be grasped even in the absence of a referent. This aspect of meaning is called, following Kaplan, their *character* (2008, 171 n. 202).

For Gaskin, the character of a demonstrative phrase is not part of its sense but a separate aspect of its meaning (2008, 171 n. 202). He distinguishes two notions of sense—the epistemological and the semantic notions—of which only the latter has much relevance to the philosophy of language (2021, 85–6). The semantic concept of sense is elucidated with the remark that 'to grasp a sense is to cognize the referent that the sense presents—and the sense must present a referent, indeed must present the very referent that it does present' (2021, 99). When we work with this conception of sense, the meaning of a demonstrative phrase cannot be exhausted by its sense. If it were, there would be no such thing as understanding a demonstrative phrase when it is not being used to refer to anything and little room for an explanation of how the expression functions when it *is* being used to refer to something. Suppose I hear someone say 'That spider is a *tegenaria agrestis*.' Enthused at the prospect of seeing a *tegenaria agrestis*, I look at the speaker to see if the speaker is looking or pointing towards any particular spatial region. If they are, I then look at that region, hoping to catch a glimpse of a spider. Only at the point in time (if there is one) when I see one particularly salient spider in the region do I recognize the speaker's referent and therefore it is only then that I grasp the sense which 'that spider' has on that particular occasion of use. On the other hand, there must be something I have grasped about the meaning of 'that spider' that directs me in my search for the referent and that something is what Kaplan and Gaskin call the *character* of the phrase.

If demonstrative phrases have both a character, which is invariant from occasion to occasion, and (in favourable circumstances) a sense, which can vary from one occasion of use to another, why should something similar not be said about proper names?

Like a demonstrative phrase, a personal proper name (at least, as names are normally individuated) can be used on different occasions to refer to different people. When I hear a fairly common name like 'Richard', I have to work out somehow, of all the Richards I know, which one, if any, is being referred to. It is at least fairly natural to conjecture the following:

(6) For every person's name N and every situation S in which N is used to perform a speech-act, there is an aspect of the meaning of N, which might as well be called its 'character', such that I must take account both of that aspect and of the details of S in order to work out whom N refers to in S.

If we work with Gaskin's conception of sense (2021, 99, quoted above), it is not until that question (whom does N refer to in S?) is answered that I have grasped the sense the name N has in S.

A terminological point should be made here. Gaskin (2008, 62) allows that *distinct* expressions may be phonologically and morphologically identical. One way in which two names might be counted as two despite being phonologically and morphologically identical would be through having distinct referents. If names are to be individuated in this way, it follows that as soon as I know which name N is I *eo ipso* know whom it refers to. But if we want to understand 'name' in this way, (6) only needs to be reformulated using different terminology: the letter 'N' should be taken to range not over names but over classes of homonymous names.

It is the obvious resemblances between demonstrative phrases and proper names that tempt some of us to endorse (6). But of course there are differences too. Whereas, when I hear the phrase 'that spider' I can, at least under favourable circumstances, establish which spider is being referred to by understanding the phrase and looking for a spider, the identities of the bearers of any given personal name are fixed in the main not by the name's connotations but by arbitrary decisions made by the bearers' parents. This fact makes it tempting to endorse:

(7) When I hear a person's name N being pronounced by someone making a statement, I do not know who is being referred to unless I either
(a) am acquainted with the referent (perhaps through having had them introduced or pointed out to me) as a bearer of N; or (b) know a definite description which picks out the referent.

From (7) and

(8) When someone uses the personal name N in the course of a statement, I do not understand the statement unless I know whom the name N, in the context of that statement, refers to

it is possible to construct an argument that I can understand N as a strict (i.e., non-descriptive) name only if I am acquainted with at least one of its bearers. We are also close to having an argument that I come to understand N precisely through being introduced to or shown the relevant bearer of the name. This conclusion is incompatible with (6): according to the present argument, there is nothing about the meaning of N which I can be said to grasp prior to my first encounter with one of its bearers.

This argument is vitiated by a failure to distinguish two kinds of understanding, which I will call *linguistic understanding* and *speech-act understanding* respectively. The objects of linguistic understanding are strings of words, including sentences; the objects of speech-act understanding are speech-acts or utterances, including statements. Whether someone linguistically understands a sentence or not depends on how good their knowledge of the language is and nothing else. For example, suppose I find in *Teach Yourself German* an exercise which runs 'Translate the following sentence into German: Hans is coming to my house tomorrow.' If I manage to produce a synonymous German sentence, as far as linguistic understanding is concerned, that provides pretty good evidence that I understand perfectly both the English original and the German translation. No one would accuse me of lack of linguistic understanding because I do not know who Hans is, which day 'tomorrow' refers to or whose house is being mentioned. There is no answer at all to these questions.

Understanding a speech-act, by contrast, is (at least if the speech-act is an assertion) knowing what information the speaker conveys or what the speaker commits herself to. If someone makes an actual statement by saying 'Hans is coming to my house tomorrow', in order to know these things I do need to know who Hans is, who the speaker is and what day 'tomorrow' refers to.

One reason for thinking this distinction has to be drawn is that the question whether I understand sentence S can arise even when S has not (within my experience, at least) been used to perform any speech-act at all, as in the 'Hans' example.

If the distinction is sound, the argument based upon (7) and (8) suffers from equivocation. Premiss (8) is plausible only if 'understand' is understood to mean speech-act understanding whereas, for the conclusion to be true without qualification, 'understand' in the conclusion has to mean *any* kind of understanding.

A second reason for rejecting the argument based upon premises (7) and (8) is that the conclusion is incompatible with (6); but (6), considered by itself, is highly plausible. We often do hear a name being pronounced by someone performing a speech-act and successfully work out which person the speaker is referring to. How this happens is a distinctly non-trivial question, especially in the case where both speaker and hearer are acquainted with several people who share the name. Should the hearer take it that, of all these common acquaintances, the speaker is referring to the one whom he refers to with the greatest frequency? Or the one whom he mentioned most recently? Or the one who was most recently in the presence of both speaker and hearer? None of these suggestions is either obviously right or obviously wrong and this rather supports the conjecture that the actual conventions governing the use of people's names are quite complicated. Someone learning their native language has to internalize these conventions, something we generally succeed in doing at a fairly early age.[14] In addition, proper names have what might as well be called 'connotations': someone familiar with a language will know that certain names in it are men's names, others are women's names, others are names of cities (and so on), and some fall into more than one of the foregoing classes. Knowledge of the connotations of a name and the conventions governing its use is something independent of, and something that can be had prior to, becoming acquainted with any of the name's bearers. The thesis that someone does not *in any sense* understand a proper name unless they are acquainted with at least one of its bearers is therefore to be rejected.

Gaskin (2021, 167) takes numerals, when used as nouns, to be descriptive names rather than strict names and the foregoing conclusion therefore has no *immediate* relevance to whether he has a good argument for the existence of numbers. What it does entail is that there is no true universal principle to the effect that, if a word means something to a community of language-users, all members of the community must be acquainted with at least one possible referent of the word. Such a principle cannot then be used to support the conclusion that numerals have to refer to something. The only way to support such a conclusion is to bring forward an argument that concerns

---

[14] It is the job of philosophers and linguists to make them explicit. This is a task that Evans (1982, chs. 9–11) can be regarded as having made a start on. If his treatment is even roughly on the right lines, it makes clear how complicated the conventions are.

concept-expressions (or at least some sub-class of them which is large enough to include all numerals) specifically and this is something Gaskin does not do.

It is relevant at this point to ask why a theory of meaning needs to make use of the concept of reference at all. Gaskin believes that it is needed in connection with *every* kind of expression whatsoever. The clearest explanation I can find for his taking this line is a passage in which, after arguing that all subsentential expressions are equally unsaturated, he continues:

> [I]f *all* words ... are uniformly unsaturated, it seems that we may as well say that they are all names referring to objects. At least, we shall have to say either that all words are names referring to objects or that none are, and it is obscure what the point of selecting this latter option could be: the notions of name and object would in that case be deprived of application (2008, 196).

This is somewhat hasty. One of the reasons philosophers have traditionally been more inclined to speak of 'referring to an object' in connection with certain expressions—especially proper names (in the ordinary sense) and singular demonstrative phrases—than with others is that it is expressions in the former class that are most clearly capable of changing their reference from context to context. It is very difficult to set up a theory of truth for an object-language containing demonstrative phrases without making use of the idea of reference. For example, a T-theorem for 'this wine is rancid' might go:

(9) 'This wine is rancid', as spoken by speaker l at time t, is true iff there is wine which l refers to at t using the phrase 'this wine' and it is rancid.

To formulate a T-theorem for 'this wine is rancid' that makes no use of the notion of reference is, to say the least, not easy. For example, it will not do to replace 'wine which l refers to ...' with 'wine which is nearer to l than any other wine' or 'wine l is pointing to', for reasons that are obvious enough.

Are predicates in any similar position? While there certainly are indexical predicates like 'is here' and predicates constructed from proper names like 'is Napoleonic', the most obvious way to make sense of these is to think of them as synonymous with other predicates containing a demonstrative phrase or proper name: 'is in this place', 'is in the style of Napoleon'. The r.h.s. of a T-theorem for a sentence containing 'is here' will then include a phrase like 'is in the place which the speaker is referring to'.

If a case is to be made that a theory of truth needs to ascribe reference to predicates themselves, as well as to proper names and indexical expressions that occur within predicates, that case will have to proceed along different lines. Travis (2019, 223) has argued that the chemical constitution a liquid needs to have for the predicate 'is lager' to be true of it can vary from context to context. Someone who accepts this claim might deduce from it that the reference of 'is lager' varies from context to context, just like a proper name or demonstrative phrase. But this conclusion, even if possible, is hardly compulsory. An alternative diagnosis of the phenomena would be to say that the predicate 'is lager' denotes the same property in all contexts but that what an object needs to be like to count as *having* the property varies from context to context. Or, better still, we could dispense with the idea of reference to properties, which does not seem to be helping much, and simply say that what an object needs to be like in order to count as *satisfying* the predicate varies from context to context.[15]

Even if it is true that the predicate 'is lager' denotes different properties on different occasions of use, the properties differ from each other only slightly, which is not something that can be said about the possible referents of a demonstrative phrase. Whereas a would-be theory of truth that generated the T-theorem

(10) 'This wine is rancid' is true iff this wine is rancid

would be hopeless, it is not clear that a theory of truth cannot deal with atomic predicates of the object-language simply by correlating them with predicates in the language of the theory, as in:

(11) For any singular term a, $a \frown$ 'is lager' is true iff any referent of a is lager.

That is, any context-dependence in a predicate of the object-language is simply carried across to the matching predicate in the language of the theory of truth. In any case, if it is true (as Travis probably thinks) that the semantic properties of *every* expression are context-dependent, it is futile to expect the language in which a theory of truth is presented to be free of context-dependence.

It would be inappropriate to take leave of linguistic idealism without addressing what Gaskin says specifically about numbers. He takes numerals, as descriptive names, to be not genuine names but lightly disguised definite descriptions (2008, 71; 2021, 167). Someone familiar with standard treatments of definite descriptions will likely take these claims to imply that a perspicuous formalization of

---

[15] It seems to me that Travis himself takes the view that saying predicates denote properties is a permissible position rather than an irresistible one: 'If we do say [that predicates denote properties], we must also say ... that there are, or may be, things which, on some occasions for judging, count as having the property and on others do not' (1997, 98).

(12) 2 is a finite cardinal number

would be, in a notation used by Evans (1982, 58),

(13) Ix [TWO(x), x is a finite cardinal number],

where ⌜TWO(x)⌝ and ⌜x is a finite cardinal number⌝ are first-level predicates. Discussion of what ⌜TWO(x)⌝ means will be postponed for a few lines. ⌜$Ix[\Phi(x), \Psi(x)]$⌝ is a second-order predicate which takes two one-place first-order predicates as arguments and binds the variable x occurring in their argument-places. What in (13) is the equivalent of the noun '2' as it occurs in (12)? Perhaps nothing is the exact equivalent but the best candidate would be

(14) Ix [TWO (x), $\Psi(x)$]

which takes just one one-place first-order predicate as argument. One way of stating the truth-condition of (13) is to say that it is true iff exactly one object satisfies both the first-order predicates and no object satisfies the first but not the second. Given that (12) is true (for everyone except nominalists) and assuming that (13) is a good formalization of (12), what then is the one object that satisfies both ⌜TWO(x)⌝ and ⌜x is a finite cardinal number⌝ in order to make (13) true? It certainly has to be a finite cardinal number and the obvious suggestion is that it is 2. The predicate ⌜TWO(x)⌝ would then be a predicate that is satisfied by 2 and nothing else.

All this is unexceptionable, even boring, but the remarkable twist in the story is that Gaskin takes a number to be not the satisfier of the predicates in an expression like (13) but the *referent* of an expression like (14), considered as a whole (2021, 168). Given certain commonplace assumptions (not all of which, admittedly, are accepted by Gaskin: more on this below) it is possible to derive a contradiction from the claim that (14) refers to a number. The commonplace assumptions are:

(15) For any n, a predicate of level $n + 1$ in Frege's hierarchy of levels refers to a concept of level $n + 1$.

(16) Each individual number has a level lower by 1 than the concept of a number.

(17) For any n, ⌜x is a number⌝ is a predicate of level $n + 1$ iff (14) is a predicate of level $n + 2$.

Assume that (14) is a predicate of level $n + 2$. If (14) refers to a number, then, by (15), that number is located at level $n + 2$. By (16), the concept of a number is then located at level $n + 3$, whereas by (17) together with (15) and the assumption it ought to be located at level $n + 1$. The standard view on levels is that an expression cannot *without being ambiguous* occur at more than one level, though this is one of the standard assumptions Gaskin rejects (2008, §52).

It might be thought that the contradiction is better avoided not by rejecting this standard assumption about levels but by holding that a number is not the *referent* of an expression like (14) but the sort of thing that makes (13) true, by satisfying the predicates ⌜TWO(x)⌝ and ⌜x is a finite cardinal number⌝, and is therefore of lower level than them. Perhaps it is, but is such a position entirely compatible with linguistic idealism? The question arises what sort of linguistic expressions, if any, on the position envisaged just now, could actually *refer* to numbers. If we say that it is not even *possible* for such expressions to exist, we have abandoned linguistic idealism, which holds that 'whatever exists is nameable' (2021, 56). We could, alternatively, argue that, because numbers exist and have a level—say, n—lower by 1 than the concept of a number, it *must* therefore also be possible for expressions of level n to refer to them. But to argue like this is make inferences from the nature of reality to the nature of language, whereas some formulations of linguistic idealism, with its 'language-driven approach to ontology' (2021, 166), imply that one should only argue in the opposite direction from that.

If the coherence of Gaskin's theory can be saved by saying that an expression can belong to more than one level, a slight variation on this would be to replace (16) with a rival principle:

(18) Each individual number has a level higher by 1 than the concept of a number.

One way to defend (18) would be to hold that, if the concept of a number has level $n + 1$, the individual numbers have both level n and level $n + 2$. (16) and (18) would then both be true.

A final twist in the story is that Gaskin has argued (2008, ch. 4) that the Fregean hierarchy of levels is no more defensible than a rival 'anti-Fregean' hierarchy. The anti-Fregean hierarchy can be thought of (roughly) as derived from the Fregean hierarchy by shifting monadic concept-expressions from Frege's first level to the new zeroth level, moving the former inhabitants of Frege's zeroth level to the new first level, and then by making various consequential adjustments that need not concern us here (2008, §49). It might be thought that adoption of the anti-Fregean classification of entities, by itself, entails (18): if numbers are at level 0 in the Fregean hierarchy and the concept of a number at level 1, then on the anti-Fregean scheme of things the concept of a number is located at level 0 and the individual numbers at level 1. But to think this is to forget that an expression like (14) cannot be located at a level lower than 2 in the Fregean hierarchy, which entails by (15) that numbers (in Gaskin's view) cannot either. In the process of forming the anti-Fregean hierarchy out of the Fregean one, it is only the two lowest levels that are permuted, so if numbers have level ≥ 2 in the Fregean hierarchy and if (16) is true of it, (16) is true of the anti-Fregean hierarchy too. So acceptance of (18) goes beyond the commitments incurred simply by adopting the anti-Fregean hierarchy.

There is therefore a way, perhaps two ways, in which the coherence of Gaskin's theory of numbers might be saved. Either of these ways involves rejecting some very widespread assumptions. Whether rejecting these assumptions is itself a coherent policy is unfortunately not a question that can be discussed in the space available, but it should be of interest that their rejection is not only permitted but unavoidable if the coherence of Gaskin's theory of numbers is to be saved.

8.5 Hale and Wright's 'Fregean Argument'

One way to defend premiss (2) of the Hale–Wright argument (see Section 8.2) is to argue that the universal closure of (5) is true when N is understood as carrying the meaning it acquires when that very sentence is viewed as a definition of N. As we saw in Section 8.3, sustaining this position requires solving the Julius Caesar Problem. Another way is to hold that (2) should be accepted by default, on the ground, perhaps, that it seems acceptable to common sense and no strong reasons for not accepting it have ever been given.

It certainly *seems* that there are plenty of true sentences in natural languages which corroborate (2), for example '2 + 2 = 4'. The difficulty is to be sure that there is a way of construing this sentence according to which it simultaneously is true and also contains singular terms. It is possible to hear it not as a statement of a relationship between two individual objects called '2' and '4', but as a generalization, which might be formalized as

$$\forall F \forall G (\neg \exists z (Fz \wedge Gz) \rightarrow \exists_2 x Fx \rightarrow \exists_2 x Gx \rightarrow \exists_4 x (Fx \vee Gx)).$$

This formula, which will from now on be called simply 'the generalization', contains no singular terms and does not, in any obvious way, imply the existence of numbers.

Given suitable definitions of the numerically definite quantifiers $\exists_2$ and $\exists_4$, the generalization becomes a truth of logic. It can also be experimentally tested, by counting. If anything is indisputably true, it is. But it does not follow that '2 + 2 = 4' is. That sentence is, I believe, ambiguous. When taken as a statement of a relationship between two individuals called '2' and '4' respectively, it is not so clear how it can be tested. In a way, it can, if you accept the following two principles,

(19) If 2 + 2 = 4, if nothing is both an *F* and a *G*, if the number of *F*'s is 2, and if the number of *G*'s is 2, then the number of things that are an *F* or a *G* is 4,

(20) The number of *F*'s is *n* iff there are *n* *F*'s (or, in symbols, iff $\exists_n xF(x)$),

since (19) and (20) together entail a conditional that has '2 + 2 = 4' as its antecedent and the generalization as its succedent. But it is unlikely that anyone not already convinced of the existence of numbers could accept (19) and (20), whereas the purpose of this chapter is to consider whether there are any non-question-begging arguments for the existence of numbers.

The claim that '2 + 2 = 4' is ambiguous might be mistaken. If it is, this could be demonstrated by showing that everyone who understands that sentence actually *always* understands it as a singular statement. This would require that an empirical test for whether a speaker of English understands a word as, logically speaking, a singular term should be set up and that there is no possible use of '2 + 2 = 4' in which the numerals fail that test. But if this should happen, the question whether the sentence is true then arises. The reasons for thinking that the generalization is true are not relevant, since, in the situation under consideration, we have agreed that '2 + 2 = 4' is not, on any construal, synonymous with the generalization.

For what it is worth, I do not believe that ordinary speakers always hear '2 + 2 = 4' as a singular statement. Suppose, for the sake of argument, that it is one and that the Dummett–Wright–Hale definition of 'singular term'[16] is roughly on the right lines. Then ordinary speakers must always be willing to endorse the inference from '2 + 2 = 4' to 'Something is such that it plus 2 is equal to 4'. I would be surprised if ordinary speakers would *never* hesitate to endorse this inference. It would, moreover, not be surprising if 'Two plus two makes four' came into English usage through a process which seems to have happened elsewhere too (as in 'Slow and steady wins the race') of substantives

---

[16] See Dummett 1973, ch. 4; Wright 1983, §six; Hale 1987, ch. 2; Hale and Wright 2001, chs 1–2.

being dropped from a sentence and the adjectives qualifying them coming to be used as if they were themselves substantives. The original sentence would have been 'Two things plus two things make four things'. In any case, for reasons given in the last paragraph, nothing vital turns on these empirical questions.

8.6 Linnebo's Base and Extended Languages

The main problem raised by (20) was how to justify the inference from the r.h.s. of an instance of (20) to the l.h.s. It is akin to the problem of how to justify the inference from the r.h.s. of an instance of (5) to the l.h.s. The neo-Fregeans tried to legitimize this inference by stipulating that the l.h.s. always has the same truth-value as the r.h.s., and we have seen that this proposal, while not clearly unviable, leads to the Julius Caesar Problem. But perhaps it is possible to explain the meaning of an instance of the l.h.s. of (5) without *either* simply stipulating that it has the same truth-value as the corresponding instance of the r.h.s. *or* assuming at the outset that N-terms denote—and explain it, moreover, in a way that makes the truth of the instance follow from the explanation. Some recent work by Øystein Linnebo seems to me to be trying to do more or less that.

His defence of abstract objects is presented in an article (2009) and his book *Thin Objects* (2018), especially chapter 8, where he considers in detail how a community of people who to begin with refer only to concrete objects can make the transition to referring to one kind of abstract object, namely letter-types.

The initial language of the community, in which only concrete objects are referred to or quantified over, is called L_0 (2018, 137). It is assumed that every sentence of L_0 has a determinate truth-condition and that L_0 contains an equality-sign = as well as a two-place relational expression ~ with the property that $a \sim b$ is true when and only when a and b are equiform letter-tokens (i.e., as we would put it, although the speakers of L_0 would not, when a and b are instances of the same letter-type). We are asked to imagine that the members of the community advance to speaking a language L_1 which includes L_0 but contains, in addition, a functional expression § which is not in L_0, a new equality-sign $=_1$ not to be confused with =, and a number of new predicates. The language L_1 is two-sorted: the variables and constant singular terms of L_0 constitute one sort of singular term in L_1 while there are variables of a second sort in L_1, which, along with singular terms formed using §, constitute the class of singular terms that belong to L_1 but not L_0. There are two kinds of equation in L_1: those of the shape ⌜$a = b$⌝, where a and b are singular terms of the first sort; and those of the shape ⌜$a =_1 b$⌝, where a and b are singular terms of the second sort. Identity-sentences in which the identity-sign is flanked by singular terms of different sorts are, for the duration of chapter 8, not permitted (2018, 137–8).

The discussion from this point on proceeds in two stages. First, Linnebo describes (2018, 138–40) how the community may start using L_1 as if ⌜§a⌝, where a denotes a letter-token, denoted the type exemplified by the token which a denotes. Secondly, he considers (2018, 140–51) whether we should then say that the members of the community are *really* referring to letter-types, i.e., to abstract objects of a certain kind, or whether they are only talking *as if* there were such things.

In the first stage, the community is envisaged as coming to use sentences of L_1 that are not already in L_0 as if they were following certain fairly precise rules. The formulation of these rules makes use of the metalinguistic relation *assertible of* which relates formulae of L_1 containing n free variables of the first sort to n-tuples of objects that can be referred to in L_0. The three most important of the rules (2018, 139) are:

(21) A formula ϕ of L_0 is assertible of objects $o_1, o_2,..., o_n$ iff it is true of them according to the intended interpretation of L_0;

(22) The atomic formula ⌜§$x_1 =_1$ §x_2⌝ is assertible of objects o_1, o_2 iff $o_1 \sim o_2$;

(23) The formula ⌜Vow*(§x)⌝ is assertible of o iff o is a vowel-token.

Special attention should be paid here to (22), which bears a certain resemblance to (5). There are considerable differences, nonetheless, between Linnebo's procedure and that of the neo-Fregeans. He envisages (22) not as a principle that is necessarily actually presented to the speakers of L_0 (although it could be that) but rather as a metalinguistic generalization about when they will consider a sentence of the shape of ⌜§$a =_1$ §b⌝ to be assertible (2018, 156).

Because of the provisional ban on mixed identity-sentences, there is no need for the time being to specify when a formula of the shape of ⌜§$x_1 =_1 x_2$⌝ or ⌜§$x_1 = x_2$⌝ is assertible of any two objects (objects, that is, that can be referred to in L_0).

The rules (21)–(23) concern simple formulae of L_1. Regarding the assertibility-conditions of composite formulae, Linnebo merely remarks:

To complete the characterization of the assertibility-conditions, it remains only to specify how the connectives and quantifiers are handled. Here there are no surprises: we adopt the obvious compositional clauses. (2018, 140)

As far as quantifiers are concerned, this perhaps leaves a little too much to the reader's guesswork.[17] On p. 151, Linnebo cites ⌜$\exists y_1.\text{Vow}^*(y_1)$⌝ as an example of a quantified sentence of L_1. Perhaps the most obvious way of defining its assertibility-condition is to say

(24) ⌜$\exists y_1.\text{Vow}^*(y_1)$⌝ is assertible (absolutely) iff the formula ⌜$\text{Vow}^*(\S x)$⌝ is assertible of some object o that can be referred to in L_0.

where the r.h.s. is true (by (23)) iff o is a vowel-token.

The most interesting part of Linnebo's discussion of the community that advances from speaking L_0 to speaking L_1 is his consideration (2018, 140–51) of the question whether they are really referring to, and quantifying over, abstract objects after they have made the transition. He concludes that they are. I would like to argue now that some of the conditions needed to justify this conclusion are missing.

The discussion of Section 8.3 above defended the need to distinguish between an expression's being a *genuine* singular term and its merely bearing a superficial syntactic resemblance to one. A possible strategy for Linnebo to adopt would be to begin by arguing that terms of the shape of ⌜$\S a$⌝ are genuine singular terms and then appeal to (1) to support the conclusion that they also denote objects. He certainly stipulates (2018, 137) that there are individual constants proper to L_1. As I argued in Section 8.3, though, the status of an expression as a genuine singular term cannot be ensured by a mere stipulation: it has to follow from the way its meaning is explained. Just as with ⌜$Nx: Fx = Nx: Gx$⌝, it can be asked whether an expression like ⌜$\S x_1 =_1 \S x_2$⌝, when certified by (22) as assertible of objects o_1, o_2, is a genuine equation with genuine singular terms flanking the identity-sign $=_1$ or merely a syntactically misleading way of saying $o_1 \sim o_2$. The reasons given in Section 8.3 for thinking that truth-conditions have to be discerned for at least some equations of the shape ⌜$Nx: Fx = t$⌝ operate again here: this time the question is whether Linnebo's explanations enable us to work out when an equation like ⌜$\S x_1 =_1 x_2$⌝ or ⌜$\S x_1 = x_2$⌝ is assertible of a pair of objects.

---

[17] Assertibility-conditions for formulae of L_1 are defined in a more logically standard way in appendix 8A (2018, 154–5) but, as far as quantified sentences are concerned, that appendix adds nothing to the treatment in the main text.

Linnebo does not follow this strategy. Throughout chapter 8, he treats equations like ⌜$§x_1 =_1 x_2$⌝ and ⌜$§x_1 = x_2$⌝ as ill-formed. His actual strategy appears to be to argue first (2018, 151) that an existential statement like ⌜$∃y_1.\text{Vow}^*(y_1)$⌝, as used by speakers of L_1, can be true. Only in chapter 9 (2018, 170) does he consider the question which pairs of objects an equation like ⌜$§x_1 =_1 x_2$⌝ or ⌜$§x_1 = x_2$⌝ might be assertible of.

There is something unsound about trying to argue that ⌜$∃y_1.\text{Vow}^*(y_1)$⌝ can be true without first arguing that terms of the shape of ⌜$§a$⌝ are genuine singular terms. At least, this is so if the symbol ∃ in ⌜$∃y_1.\text{Vow}^*(y_1)$⌝ is supposed to have the meaning of the usual existential quantifier, as opposed to being something that just happens to look like it. The definite article in 'the usual existential quantifier' is admittedly not quite appropriate, as two rather different explanations of its meaning—objectual and substitutional—are found in the literature. If we want ⌜$∃y_1.\text{Vow}^*(y_1)$⌝ to be true in the substitutional sense, we need to argue that there is a genuine singular term t of L_1 such that ⌜$\text{Vow}^*(t)$⌝ is assertible. This is precisely what Linnebo opts not to do. On the other hand, if ⌜$∃y_1.\text{Vow}^*(y_1)$⌝ is supposed to be true with ∃ functioning as the standard *objectual* existential quantifier, the explanation (24) of the assertibility-condition of ⌜$∃y_1.\text{Vow}^*(y_1)$⌝ would have to feature quantification (in the r.h.s.) over a domain containing vowel-types, which is something that (24) does not do.

The last three paragraphs amount to an argument that Linnebo should have solved the Julius Caesar Problem before concluding that ⌜$∃y_1.\text{Vow}^*(y_1)$⌝ is true. If he could solve the Julius Caesar Problem, there would then be little ground for doubting that ⌜$∃y_1.\text{Vow}^*(y_1)$⌝ is true. A defence of (1) would be needed, but I believe that (1) is defensible (see Section 8.2 above).

It may sound perverse to accuse Linnebo of neglecting the Julius Caesar Problem: he devotes a whole chapter (ch. 9) to a problem which he calls 'the Julius Caesar Problem'. But the problem he tackles there is distinct from the problem that was so called in Section 8.3 above. The problem of Section 8.3 was posed in the formal mode, as the problem of showing that enough has been said about the meaning of N-terms to justify regarding ⌜$Nx: Fx = t$⌝ as either true or false. The problem Linnebo tackles in chapter 9 is posed as a question about objects: 'Is the natural number 3 identical to the Roman emperor Julius Caesar?' (2018, 159). The reason I avoided this style of formulation is that it presupposes that 3 exists, whereas at the end of chapter 8 we still have not been presented with a satisfactory argument for the existence of *any* abstract object. Linnebo seems to have thought he could conclude that there are abstract objects before tackling the Julius Caesar Problem; the burden of the last four paragraphs was to argue that he really needed to solve the Julius Caesar Problem first.

There is a minor objection, which should be mentioned in passing, to the idea that anything like (24) can capture the standard meaning of ∃. If someone wished to formalize the sentence

(25) There are vowel-types of which no token exists,

and did so quite naively, thinking of ∃ as the obvious symbol to use whenever 'There are' or 'exists' has to be formalized, the result would probably be

(26) $\exists y_1 \left(Vow^*(y_1) \land \neg \exists z (y_1 =_1 §z) \right).$

Someone with a liberal attitude to uninstantiated universals would say that (25) (and therefore (26) too, when read in the naïve way) is true. If there are uninstantiated universals, then presumably there are among them a multitude of vowel-types which have never been tokened. On the other hand, (26) entails ⌜$\exists y_1 \neg \exists z(y_1 =_1 §z)$⌝ and, if we try to state the assertibility-condition of this last formula in accordance with the same principle as that according to which (24) states the assertibility-condition of ⌜$\exists y_1.Vow^*(y_1)$⌝, the assertibility of ⌜$\exists y_1 \neg \exists z(y_1 =_1 §z)$⌝ would seem to require that there be an object o of which ⌜$\neg \exists z(§x =_1 §z)$⌝ is assertible, which is logically impossible. So (24) seems to be based on an understanding of ∃ which entails there cannot be uninstantiated universals. Perhaps there are none, but it is tendentious to recommend a reading of ∃ according to which the idea that there are uninstantiated vowel-types cannot even be coherently formalized.

8.7 Conclusion

Even if the foregoing attempt to pour cold water on linguistic arguments is judged a success, it should not give any comfort to nominalists. There are still avenues available for people who want to defend linguistic arguments. Moreover, as emphasized in Section 8.1, there may be good arguments for the existence of abstract objects which are not linguistic arguments. Finally, and most important of all, whether there are any good arguments *against* the existence of abstract objects is, as far as this chapter and its author are concerned, still a wide open question. As often in philosophy, a great deal depends on who is expected to shoulder the burden of proof.

References

Borg, E. 2004. *Minimal Semantics* (Oxford: OUP).
Borg, E. and S. Fisher 2022. 'Semantic content and utterance context: A spectrum of approaches', in P. Stalmaszczyk (ed.), *The Cambridge Handbook of the Philosophy of Language* (Cambridge: CUP), 174–93.
Davies, M. 1981. 'Meaning, structure and understanding', *Synthese* 48, 135–61.
Dummett, M. A. E. 1973. *Frege: Philosophy of Language* (London: Duckworth).
Evans, G. 1982. *The Varieties of Reference*, ed. J. H. McDowell (Oxford: OUP).
Falguera, J. L. and C. Martínez-Vidal (eds) 2020. *Abstract Objects: For and Against* (Synthese Library 422) (Cham: Springer Nature).
Frege, G. 1950. *The Foundations of Arithmetic*, tr. J. L. Austin (Oxford: Blackwell).
Frege, G. 1893/1903. *Grundgesetze der Arithmetik*, 2 vols (Jena: Hermann Pohle).
Gaskin, R. 2008. *The Unity of the Proposition* (Oxford: OUP).
Gaskin, R. 2021. *Language and World: A Defence of Linguistic Idealism* (New York and London: Routledge).
Glüer, K. 2012. 'Theories of meaning and truth-conditions', in M. Garcia-Carpintero and M. Kölbel (eds), *The Continuum Companion to the Philosophy of Language* (New York: Continuum Publishing), 84–105.
Hale, B. 1987. *Abstract Objects* (Oxford: Blackwell).
Hale, B. and C. Wright 2001. *The Reason's Proper Study* (Oxford: OUP).
Husserl, E. 1921. *Logische Untersuchungen*, 2nd edition (Tübingen: Max Niemeyer), 3 volumes.
Lambert, K. 1983. *Meinong and the Principle of Independence* (Cambridge: CUP).
Linnebo, Ø. 2009. 'Frege's context principle and reference to natural numbers', in S. Lindström et al. (eds), *Logicism, Intuitionism and Formalism (Synthese Library 341)* (Springer), 47–68.
Linnebo, Ø. 2018. *Thin Objects: an Abstractionist Account* (Oxford: OUP).
Lowe, E. J. 2009. *More Kinds of Being* (Chichester: Wiley–Blackwell).
Maddy, P. 1980. 'Perception and mathematical intuition', *Philosophical Review* 89 (1980), 163–96.
Recanati, F. 2005. 'Contextualism and literalism: Some varieties', in G. Preyer and G. Peter (eds), *Contextualism in Philosophy* (Oxford: OUP), 171–96.
Stirton, W. 2003. 'Caesar Invictus', *Philosophia Mathematica* (series III) 11, 285–304.
Stirton, W. 2016. 'Caesar and circularity', in P. Ebert and M. Rossberg (eds), *Abstractionism* (Oxford: OUP), 37–49.
Travis, C. 1997. 'Pragmatics', in B. Hale and C. Wright (eds), *A Companion to the Philosophy of Language* (Oxford: Blackwell), 87–107.
Travis, C. 2019. 'Their work and why they do it', in E. Marchesan and D. Zapero (eds), *Context, Truth and Objectivity* (New York and London: Routledge), 205–47.
Wright, C. J. G. 1983. *Frege's Conception of Numbers as Objects* (Aberdeen: Aberdeen University Press).
Wright, C. J. G. 1986. *Realism, Meaning and Truth* (Oxford: Blackwell).
Wright, C. J. G. 2020. 'Replies', in A. Miller (ed.), *Logic, Language and Mathematics* (Oxford: OUP), 277–432.

9
Mathematics and the Limits of Language

Silvia Jonas

9.1 Introduction

The question that connects the essays in this volume is whether and to what extent the world might depend for its nature and constitution on language. While the commonsense view is arguably that the world is entirely independent of language, and notwithstanding the downfall of idealism as a central philosophical doctrine in the twentieth century, there has recently been increasing interest in the possibility that language and/or thought may not only be a descriptive device, but may in fact play a constitutive role in the formation of the world (Bloor 1996; Gaskin 2019; Hofweber 2023). *Linguistic idealism* is the view that some facts of reality depend for their existence on our linguistic practices, for example by figuring in or being identical to true and false propositions (Gaskin 2021, x). In the introduction to this volume, Gaskin, for example, describes this relationship as a transcendental 'asymmetrical dependence of world on language', due to which 'the world is constituted by language in the following sense: worldly structures mirror linguistic structures at the deepest level and as a matter of their essence.... It is because *language*—and that ... means ultimately if not immediately *human* language— is the way it is that the world is, in broad terms, the way *it* is'; consequently, 'for the world to exist it must be expressible (this volume, 23).'

In this chapter, I offer a mathematical perspective on the question of linguistic idealism in order to challenge the claim that for the world to exist it must be expressible. More precisely, I investigate the question whether linguistic idealism is a plausible position for mathematics by examining the extent to which language is constitutive of the mathematical cosmos and of our epistemic access to it. I start from the assumption that mathematical knowledge depends on linguistic formulability, with the consequence that whatever mathematical insight cannot be formulated does not count as knowledge. On the basis of three examples I then draw a distinction between mathematical knowledge and mathematical understanding, and I argue that the latter does not bear such a close connection to language as the former. The first example, logical consequence, is used to demonstrate that understanding the deductive validity of a mathematical argument is ultimately non-propositional. The second example, Gödel's second incompleteness theorem, serves to show that understanding the consistency of mathematics is independent of there being a (set of) propositions proving this consistency. The third example, Cramér's random model of the prime numbers, shows that our understanding of the distribution of the prime numbers is independent of there being a proposition explaining why the distribution is the way it is. Based on these examples, I then argue the following: while on the one hand, there is a sense in which the existence of the mathematical cosmos quite obviously depends on language (since we cannot perceive mathematical structures through our senses; the only way the mathematical cosmos can manifest itself to us is through language), the fact that mathematical understanding is independent of linguistic formulability shows, on the other hand, that we do have a language-independent access to mathematics, which in turn suggests that the anterior existence of the mathematical cosmos was a prerequisite for the development of mathematical language, just as the anterior existence of the physical world was a prerequisite for the evolution of human language.

9.2 Mathematical Knowledge and Formulability

Let's start with mathematical knowledge and its connection to linguistic formulability. I shall assume that, in the mathematical realm, whatever insight cannot be formulated, i.e. brought into propositional form, does not count as a state of knowledge. The reasons for this assumption are epistemological rather than mathematical considerations. There is wide agreement that mathematical knowledge must meet the same criteria as knowledge about other, non-abstract realms—say, knowledge about physical facts. In fact, some theories of knowledge—notably Goldman's 'causal' theory of knowledge (Goldman 1967)—were criticized because they failed to accommodate mathematical knowledge. Today the most extensively discussed theory of knowledge is the 'JTB' account, according to which knowledge consists of justified true belief (JTB) plus some additional component such as safety, warranted assertibility, or reliability, which is intended to block Gettier cases (cf. Ichikawa and Steup 2018, for a comprehensive overview). On the JTB account, A knows that p iff (1) p is true, (2) A believes that p and

(3) *A* is justified in believing that *p* (where the justification should have been conferred in a way that is not vulnerable to Gettier cases). What is immediately noticeable here is that the objects of knowledge are taken to be *propositions*. Propositions, or propositionally formed derivatives like assertions, are taken by many to be the primary bearers of truth. Given that truth is a fundamental condition for knowledge according to the JTB account, and assuming that the primary bearers of truth are propositions, the account implies that we can know only propositions. Other prominent theories of knowledge, such as Williamson's 'knowledge first' account, according to which the concept of knowledge is not analysable into more fundamental terms (Williamson 2000), also imply that knowledge is knowledge of propositions, or conversely, that whatever does not have propositional form cannot be an object of knowledge. Hence, if mathematical knowledge is modelled on one of the standard accounts of knowledge, it is justified to assume that whatever cannot be formulated does not count as an object of knowledge.

Of course, not everyone agrees with the idea that all knowledge is propositional. Building on Ryle's initial argument from regress (Ryle 1949), 'anti-intellectualists' have come up with numerous objections against the idea that all knowledge is propositional 'knowledge-that'. Rather, they argue, some forms of knowledge cannot be expressed propositionally, but only manifest themselves in a person's knowing how to do something: riding a bike, playing the violin, etc. (cf. Pavese 2022, for a comprehensive overview). However, while many of the arguments for knowledge-how as a *sui generis* epistemological category are convincing, it is implausible to think that mathematical knowledge is best thought of as a version of knowledge-how that cannot be translated into knowledge-that. For what would be the specific ability manifesting a person's mathematical know-how if not coming up with ever more true mathematical *propositions*? It is thus plausible to conceive of mathematical knowledge as propositional, which is to say that the objects of mathematical knowledge are propositions and that states of mathematical knowledge are linguistically expressible.[1]

---

[1] One might object here that perhaps some mathematical propositions cannot be expressed but only known, so that a subject could be in a state of inexpressible mathematical knowledge. I am not convinced that such epistemic states are best described as states of knowledge that have an ineffable proposition as their object, chiefly because I am not convinced that the concept of an ineffable proposition is coherent. For example, if propositions are taken to be our primary truth-bearers and our theory of truth is deflationist, then there can be no ineffable propositions because truth on the deflationist picture implies expressibility. If ineffable propositions are supposed to be ineffable because they express irreducibly subjective points of view ('perspectival facts' such as what it is like to be a bat or to see red; cf. Nagel 1974; Jackson 1982), then this either leads to a contradictory or fragmented picture of

9.3 Mathematical Knowledge vs Mathematical Understanding

In the following three sections, I will argue that mathematical understanding is different from mathematical knowledge in this respect. Using three mathematical examples, I show that the epistemic state of mathematical understanding is not necessarily propositional and therefore, unlike states of knowledge, not necessarily linguistically expressible. This, in turn, will lead me to the conclusion that we do have language-independent access to the mathematical cosmos, that a language-independent mathematical cosmos grounds mathematical language, and consequently, that the doctrine of linguistic idealism is implausible.

9.3.1 Logical Consequence

The first example to illustrate my claims concerns logical consequence, or more precisely, basic logical laws. I will take *modus ponens* as my example and argue that we understand the truth of basic logical laws even though it is impossible to come up with a proposition that explains or justifies why the derivation is true. The conclusion I draw from this example is that, unlike mathematical *knowledge*, mathematical *understanding* is non-propositional because there is no proposition that expresses why basic logical derivations are true.

Let's start the argument. It should be noted that the point about *modus ponens* is not new but receives a new meaning in the context of the discussion of linguistic idealism and the distinction between mathematical knowledge and understanding. In his well-known dialogic paper 'What the tortoise said to Achilles' (Carroll 1995 [1895]), Lewis Carroll implicitly suggests that justification of deductively valid reasoning is ultimately impossible because it is impossible to justify fundamental logical principles like *modus ponens*. Achilles tries to convince the tortoise that the inference from premise (1) $p \to q$ and premise (2) p to the conclusion q is valid. The tortoise is unwilling to accept this and claims that such an inference would require an additional premise (3), namely $((p \to q) \land p) \to q$. Achilles concedes the point, then tries to convince the tortoise to accept the inference to conclusion q based on premises (1)–(3). The tortoise refuses this as well, claiming that such an inference would require yet another premise (4), namely $((p \to q) \land p \land ((p \to$

---

reality. For an extensive dicussion of the concept of ineffable propositions, cf. Jonas 2016, Ch. 4. See also Moore 1997 for a number of arguments against ineffable propositions.

$q) \wedge p) \rightarrow q) \rightarrow q$. And so forth, leading into an infinite regress of yet additional premises. The punchline here is of course that the truth of basic logical laws like *modus ponens* cannot be demonstrated by proof, so strictly speaking basic logical laws are unjustified. One either understands that the inference is valid or one doesn't. If someone fails to see the validity of *modus ponens*, adding auxiliary premises does not help because, to the '*modus ponens* sceptic', the inference from such a new set of premises to the conclusion would be just as much in need of justification as the original set of premises was—and would use the very rule that we are trying to justify. Frege, too, picks up on the issue:

> As to the question why and with what right we acknowledge a law of logic to be true, logic can respond only by reducing it to another law of logic. Where this is not possible, it can give no answer. (Frege 1903, XVII)[2]

For Frege, basic logical laws 'neither need nor admit of proof' (Frege 1988, 4)—their truth is self-evident and forces itself on anyone capable of understanding their meaning.[3]

What are the relevant conclusions to be drawn from this example? First, we understand and acknowledge the truth of basic logical laws like *modus ponens* even though their truth cannot be demonstrated by proof or by any other form of propositionally expressible reasoning. From this follows, second, that our understanding of logical consequence is non-propositional because there is no proposition that expresses why basic logical derivations are true. And this in turn means, third, that understanding a mathematical fact X (e.g., that *modus ponens* holds) is independent of the existence of a proposition expressing that understanding. Hence, there is a fundamental difference between mathematical *knowledge*, which is by definition propositional, and mathematical *understanding*, which, in cases like the one just discussed, can be non-propositional.

Before I proceed to my next example, I would like to address a possible objection against the distinction I have just drawn between mathematical knowledge as always propositional and mathematical understanding as not necessarily propositional. Someone might say that our understanding of logical consequence, though non-propositional, might still constitute knowledge,

---

[2] 'Die Frage nun, warum und mit welchem Rechte wir ein logisches Gesetz als wahr anerkennen, kann die Logik nur dadurch beantworten, dass sie es auf andere logische Gesetze zurückführt. Wo das nicht möglich ist, muss sie die Antwort schuldig bleiben.' (my translation)

[3] For an extensive discussion of the concept of non-propositional knowledge in the context of Frege's logicism, see Jonas 2016, Ch. 6.4.

namely a particular kind of knowledge-how that enables us to reason logically. This also seems to be what Gilbert Ryle had in mind when he wrote:

> Knowing a rule of inference is not possessing a bit of extra information but being able to perform an intelligent operation. Knowing a rule is knowing how. It is realized in performances which conform to the rule, not in theoretical citations of it. (Ryle 1945, 7)

If understanding logical consequence is a case of knowledge-how, so the objection could continue, then mathematical understanding is, after all, a kind of knowledge and so the purported distinction between mathematical knowledge and mathematical understanding collapses.

The response to such an objection is the following: the relevant distinction between mathematical knowledge and understanding lies with their respective connection to propositionality (and therefore language), not with the label 'knowledge'. One might call understanding of logical consequence a case of knowledge-how, but the important point would still be that it is fundamentally different from knowledge that, say, the sum of angles of a triangle is 180 degrees, in that it is non-propositional and therefore inexpressible in language.[4] What marks the distinction between the epistemic state of understanding and the epistemic state of knowledge is the in-principle possibility of linguistic expression, which is given in the case of knowledge and not necessarily given in the case of understanding (nor in the case of knowledge-how; cf. Jonas 2016, and Pavese 2022).

In this section I have argued that understanding logical consequence is non-propositional and that a distinction is thus to be drawn between mathematical knowledge and mathematical understanding: mathematical knowledge is always, at least in principle, linguistically expressible, whereas mathematical understanding is, at least in some cases, linguistically inexpressible. I will now proceed to my second example.

9.3.2 The Consistency of Mathematics

My second example concerns our understanding of the consistency of mathematics. Specifically, I will argue that we understand that mathematics is consistent even though it is impossible, according to Gödel's second incompleteness

---

[4] For a comprehensive treatment of ineffability and the various kinds of ineffable knowledge, see Jonas 2016.

theorem, to prove this. The conclusion I draw from this example is that understanding a mathematical fact X is independent of the existence of a proposition proving that X is true.

Let's begin with a very rough sketch of the implications of Gödel's two incompleteness theorems (cf. Gödel 1938), whose fundamental results had significant implications for modern logic. Roughly speaking, the theorems delineate what can and cannot be proved in formal mathematical systems. A formal system is a structured framework consisting of axioms and rigorously defined rules of inference based on which new theorems can be created. The foundational set of axioms in this context must be finite or, at the very least, decidable, meaning that there must be an algorithmic method to decide whether a given statement is an axiom of the system or not. Also for the rules of inference it must be possible to ensure the validity of a rule's application, so that it becomes possible to determine for any finite sequence of formulas whether it constitutes a valid derivation given the axioms and the rules of inference of the system in question. A formal system can be said to be complete when, for any statement in its language, it can either prove the statement or its negation. And consistency means that there exists no statement for which both the statement itself and its negation can be derived within the system.

Gödel's first incompleteness theorem then states that in any consistent system that can handle basic arithmetic, there are statements that can't be proved true or false within that system—any such system is therefore incomplete. The second incompleteness theorem says that, if such a system is indeed consistent, it cannot prove its own consistency—meaning that for any consistent system containing basic arithmetic it is impossible to prove that the system is indeed consistent. One such system is Peano arithmetic (PA), the theory of the natural numbers defined by the five axioms given in 1889 by the Italian mathematician Giuseppe Peano. PA is a very important, perhaps the most important, formalization of the natural numbers. Another such system is Zermelo–Fraenkel set theory (ZF, or ZFC if the Axiom of Choice is included), which is widely considered the standard foundation for mathematics because the set-theoretic universe described by its axioms is so comprehensive that all mathematical objects and arguments can be expressed in its language, and every mathematical theorem can be logically deduced from its axioms using nothing but first-order logic. Gödel's second incompleteness theorem thus implies that it is impossible to prove the consistency of the most important theory of the natural numbers and of the standard foundation of mathematics—an earth-shattering result that has occupied logicians and mathematicians since the 1930s.

So much for a rough sketch. However, it is important to mention that most mathematicians tend to assume the consistency of mathematics in spite of Gödel's theorem. The consistency of a set of axioms is standardly demonstrated by showing that it has a model, that is, that there exists a structure that satisfies all the axioms. For example, it can be proved in ZFC that the set of natural numbers ℕ constitutes a model of Peano arithmetic. So, provided that we independently believe in the consistency of and assumptions made by ZFC, mathematicians have good reasons to believe in the consistency of PA, Con(PA) for short. Nevertheless, ZFC is strictly *stronger* than PA, and Gödel's theorem tells us that it is impossible to prove the consistency of PA and other relevant systems in strictly *weaker* systems.[5] So Gödel would not have been impressed by a consistency proof for PA in ZFC (and at any rate, there is no consistency proof for ZFC). Gerhard Gentzen came up with a proof of Con(PA) that is carried out in a system that is neither weaker not stronger than PA, but equally strong (for the different versions of Gentzen's proof, see Gentzen1969). Although there is some controversy over the status of Gentzen's proof (cf. Chow 2019, for an excellent non-technical overview), it settled the question of the consistency of PA for most mathematicians. The consistency of ZFC, the foundation of all mathematics, however, remains unproved for the reasons spelled out in Gödel's second incompleteness theorem, though it is widely assumed.[6]

Again we can ask what relevant conclusions we can draw from this example. The first conclusion is that mathematicians understand and acknowledge the consistency of fundamental areas of mathematics such as PA and ZFC even though the consistency of those axiom systems cannot be formally proved in those systems. From this follows the second conclusion that our understanding of the consistency of mathematics is non-propositional because there is no proposition that expresses why, say, ZFC is consistent. This, in turn, demonstrates again the fundamental difference between mathematical knowledge and mathematical understanding. But, moreover, we can draw a third conclusion, namely that understanding a mathematical fact X (such as the consistency of mathematics) is independent of the existence of a proposition expressing the grounds of my understanding.

---

[5] It is for this reason that Gödel's theorem effectively ended Hilbert's programme.

[6] The development and study of large cardinal axioms, which introduce concepts of 'large' infinite cardinals beyond those directly describable in the standard ZFC axioms, can be seen, in part, as a response to the question of consistency of ZFC.

Before I proceed to my third example, I would like to address a possible objection again. Someone might argue that what I have been describing in this section is not *understanding* but *assuming*: in the absence of examples proving the opposite, mathematicians assume, rather than understand, the consistency of mathematics, just as they assume the truth of certain axioms and then go on to prove theorems based on those assumptions. Yet assuming and understanding are two completely different things.

My response is that, in specific cases, assuming is in fact not as different from understanding as one might at first think. To *assume X* means to accept X as true without trying to prove or justify X on the basis of more fundamental principles. To *understand X* is, at least in some cases, to acknowledge the truth of X even in the absence of a proof of X or a proposition explaining or justifying why X is true. To say that assuming and understanding are in some cases not very different from one another may seem counter-intuitive at first, given that we can *assume* pretty much anything for the sake of argument, whereas we can certainly not *understand* anything for the sake of argument. But this counter-intuitive flavour disappears as soon as we realize that there are two different types of assumption. One type of assumption is purely *stipulative*: we assume X, Y, and Z for the sake of argument, no matter how outlandish X, Y, and Z may be, and see which conclusions we can draw by applying our accepted laws of inference. For example, we could assume (stipulatively define) that 'Krokkoks are mammals with beaks and scales'. From this assumption, we could infer that 'Krokkoks have scales', but we wouldn't have learned much about the real world. Another type of assumption is *descriptive*: we assume X, Y, and Z because it fits the known facts and there are no known or even possible scenarios in which X, Y, and Z do not hold. This second type of assumption tries to get at 'the way things really are', rather than just postulating 'fictitious facts' for the sake of further inference. Assuming the consistency of mathematics is one example of this type of assumption; assuming the validity of *modus ponens* is another. This latter type of assumption is, I submit, similar, if not identical, to understanding.

9.3.3 Cramér's Random Models of the Primes

My third example concerns number theorists' understanding of the distribution of the prime numbers within the set of natural numbers. I will illustrate a particular method of gaining new insights into their distribution that involves the use of statistical models. The conclusion I draw from this example is that understanding a mathematical fact X is independent of the existence of a proposition that explains why X is true.[7]

Number theory is the branch of mathematics that studies the properties of whole numbers. One of the most important topics of investigation in number theory concerns the prime numbers, and specifically their distribution within the set of the natural numbers. The reason for mathematicians' interest in the distribution of the primes is that a better understanding of it is necessary to settle some of the oldest and most notorious conjectures in number theory, jointly called *Landau's Problems*. The best-known of those is *Goldbach's conjecture*, first formulated in 1742, which asks whether every even natural number is the sum of two primes. The *Twin Prime conjecture*, first formulated in 1849, asks whether there are infinitely many pairs of primes of the form $(p, p + 2)$. There is also *Legendre's conjecture* from 1797, which asks whether for every n there exists a prime p between n^2 and $(n + 1)^2$. And there is the fourth Landau conjecture, first formulated in 1760, which asks whether there are infinitely many primes p of the form $p = n^2 + 1$. What is so remarkable about these problems is that they are both formidably simple (one can understand what they are about even with only a high-school background in mathematics) and formidably intractable (hundreds of years have passed and no solutions are in sight).

In order to answer these questions, mathematicians need a better understanding of the distribution of the primes in the natural numbers. This, however, has proved extremely difficult to attain because the prime number series exhibits no discernible pattern. Euclid proved around 300 BCE that there are infinitely many primes, and thanks to the independent proofs of Jacques Hadamard and Charles Jean de la Vallée Poussin in 1896, we have a rough idea of the asymptotic density of the prime numbers up to n, namely that the number of primes up to n approaches $\frac{n}{log(n)}$: their so-called *Prime Number Theorem* states that $\pi(n) \sim \frac{n}{log(n)}$, where $\pi(n)$ is the prime counting function and $log(n)$ is the natural logarithm. Unfortunately, knowing this much about the density of the prime numbers is not enough to settle the notorious conjectures.

However, in 1932 the Swedish mathematician Harald Cramér had the ingenious idea to tackle the question of the prime number distribution with statistical means. From the *Prime Number Theorem*, explained above, we can infer that every natural number n has a probability of $\frac{1}{log(n)}$ of being prime

---

[7] This section draws heavily on D'Alessandro 2022, who discusses Cramér's random models of the primes and the function field model of the integers as two examples of unrealistic models in mathematics.

(because $\frac{\frac{n}{\log(n)}}{n} = \frac{1}{\log(n)}$). Cramér's idea then was to construct models of what one might call 'quasi-primes' up to n by independently picking each $n > 2$ with probability $\frac{1}{\log(n)}$. Put differently, one creates a subset of the natural numbers, where each number greater than 2 is independently selected to be included with a probability of $\frac{1}{\log(n)}$. The quasi-primes of the models thus constructed have the same asymptotic density within the natural numbers as the real primes, which makes it plausible to anticipate that other statistical and distributional characteristics of the actual prime number sequence will also resemble those found in the model. And since the statistical properties of distributions with strong independence properties (like the quasi-primes) are easier to study than those of distributions without such properties (like the actual primes), statistical models have become a standard method for number theorists to investigate the distribution of the prime numbers. Working with statistical models of quasi-primes, mathematicians were able to (a) confirm known facts, (b) generate support for existing conjectures, and (c) motivate entirely new conjectures about the distribution of the primes. For example, mathematicians consider the fact that the four Landau conjectures hold for the quasi-primes to be a very strong indication that also hold for the actual primes. As D'Alessandro (2022) points out: 'Each of these hypotheses was suspected to be true before the advent of the Cramér model. But the results from the model served to increase mathematicians' confidence, in some cases significantly.' In fact, as Terence Tao, arguably the most distinguished number theorist alive, writes: 'the models are so effective ... that analytic number theory is in the curious position of being able to confidently predict the answer to a large proportion of the open problems in the subject, whilst not possessing a clear way forward to rigorously confirm these answers!' (Tao 2015). In addition to these achievements, statistical models can be used for 'providing a quick way to scan for possible errors in a mathematical claim (e.g. by finding that the main term is off from what a model predicts ...); gauging the relative strength of various assertions (e.g. classifying some results as "unsurprising" [and] others as "potential breakthroughs" ...); or setting up heuristic barriers ... that one has to resolve before resolving certain key problems' (Tao 2015). D'Alessandro (2022) summarizes the implications of these examples as follows: 'In view of this list of uses, benefits and insights, I conclude that number theorists have gained significant understanding from Cramér-type models.'

However, there are also crucial differences between quasi-primes and actual primes. For example, unlike actual primes, a quasi-prime can be even or can have a direct successor that is quasi-prime as well. Moreover, each

Cramér prime is chosen independently of all others, whereas the actual primes are not random, given that the primeness of the actual primes is dependent on the laws of arithmetic. Calling Cramér's models 'idealizations' of the prime numbers (in the sense of abstractions that omit inessential details) is therefore not correct, given that the models involve 'an explicit and extensive misrepresentation of its subject matter', with 'no prospect of "de-idealizing"... without discarding the model framework entirely' (D'Alessandro 2022).

Again, we can ask about the relevant conclusions to be drawn from this example. The first conclusion is that Cramér's random models of the prime numbers have significantly increased mathematicians' understanding of the distribution of the primes among the natural numbers. As D'Alessandro (2022) discusses in detail, this is the case even though those models are *unrealistic* in the sense that they irremediably distort central properties of the objects they are about. The understanding those models provide is not based on novel *explanations* about the distribution of the prime numbers because there are neither ontic nor counterfactual dependence relations that hold between the quasi-primes of Cramér's models and the actual primes and that are revealed through the models. The second conclusion, which follows directly from the first, is that the understanding generated by random models of the prime numbers is non-propositional because there is no proposition that expresses why the distribution of the actual primes is such-and-such, given an analogous distribution of the quasi-primes. The third conclusion I draw from this is, again, more general, namely that the object of mathematical understanding (such as the distribution of the prime numbers) is independent of the existence of a proposition expressing it.

9.4 Implications

I have discussed three mathematical examples and argued that the epistemic states of understanding involved in each case as well as the objects of those epistemic states cannot be expressed propositionally. I take these examples to imply that linguistic idealism is implausible at least for these cases because there simply are no propositions available to constitute expressions of those particular 'parts' of mathematical reality that are the objects of the respective epistemic states. There *is* a mathematical reality, or cosmos, that constitutes the object of our understanding in each of the three cases I discussed, and the state of understanding puts us into direct epistemic contact with the mathematical cosmos. But it is not the case that for every 'part' or 'aspect' of mathematical reality, there is a corresponding proposition that expresses it. The mathematical cosmos is constituted of mathematical objects and structures, not by propositions.

Gaskin (2021, Ch. 8) considers a different kind of mathematical example, which he calls 'mathematical indefinability', and argues that linguistic idealists can solve the problem with a 'split-level' move. The problem of mathematical indefinability is that some mathematical objects, notably objects of transfinite set theory, 'are too complicated, for example too randomly assembled, for a language—any language—to pick them out individually and determinately, and name them' (2021, 241). Gaskin acknowledges this as a genuine worry for linguistic idealists but argues that it can be solved by distinguishing between ontological levels, a basic and a derived one. The basic ontological level is constituted by ordinary propositions whereas the derived ontological level is inhabited by 'unnameables and indescribables'. The propositions of the derived level then 'emerge' from the propositions of the basic level: in this way, the propositions of the basic level manage to reach 'into the realms of the unnameable and indescribable'. The general picture is, then, that 'language makes everything, but it does so in stages, and while its earlier creations cannot outrun its expressive resources, its later ones can'—'the derived level really is derived: it depends asymmetrically on the basic level: we have a generative, hierarchical structure, so that linguistic idealism, though not true at the derived level, does hold at the basic level, on which the derived level depends' (2021, 242).

I see two problems with this approach. The first one is that the concept of 'emergence' remains very vague. In what sense of the word is it the case that 'indefinable' mathematical objects 'emerge' out of the clearly expressible propositions of the basic level? A plausible way of thinking of 'emergence' in the context of propositions would be that emerging propositions are somehow explanatorily connected to the propositions of the basic level, for example by following deductively from, being implied by, or being made more probable by a prior set of propositions. But clearly this cannot be what is meant here, given that the propositions on the derived level are about categorically indefinable mathematical objects. So I am not sure that the concept of derived, inexpressible propositions emerging out of basic, expressible propositions can give us anything but a metaphorical grasp on what would be needed to make the split-level strategy work.

The second problem is that the solution wouldn't work even if we could give a suitably precise meaning to the word 'emergence'. The reason is that, in light of recent developments in foundational set theory (cf. e.g., Hamkins 2012 and Antos et al. 2015), the mathematical cosmos plausibly consists of a plenitude of mutually incompatible universes (the collection of which is sometimes called the set-theoretic 'multiverse') rather than just one large, internally coherent universe. As a consequence, it has become significantly more difficult to justify ontological commitment to all mathematical objects, including those of higher set theory, and the reason for this is precisely that we lack sufficient explanatory connections between the mathematical objects on the 'basic' (applied) level and the objects of higher set theory (cf. Jonas 2023).

Yet even if solutions could be found for those issues, the mathematical objections formulated in this chapter would not be solved by them. The reason is that the examples discussed above illustrate that mathematical understanding exceeds linguistic formulability. There need not always be a proposition that expresses the object of my understanding. Put differently, what an understander needs to cognize in order to count as understanding need not be a proposition.

9.5 Objection

I would like to conclude the chapter by addressing a potential objection to my construal of understanding as a direct, not propositionally expressible epistemic relation between a subject and the object of understanding, namely that my argument confuses 'expression' with 'explanation'. Someone might argue that the linguistic idealist's claim that everything can be expressed does not entail that we ought to be able to explain or give reasons for everything. In some cases there might be no reason. Take for example the fact that there is something rather than nothing. This fact is perfectly expressible by the proposition 'There is something rather than nothing.' However, it might be a brute fact that there exists something rather than nothing, i.e. a fact of which there is no explanation, just as it might be a brute fact that *modus ponens* is valid, that mathematics is consistent, and that the prime numbers are distributed the way they are. If so, then it is no surprise that there are no propositions that express *explanations* of those facts: there simply is no explanation and hence no corresponding proposition. And if there is no proposition there, then there is nothing to express, so no deficit on language's part that it doesn't express it, and certainly no deficit on linguistic idealism's part.

My response to this is that for the linguistic idealist, unlike for the commonsense realist, claiming the non-existence of a proposition expressing X is equivalent to claiming the non-existence of a fact X, which has implausible ontological consequences. Applied to our three mathematical examples, it means that claiming that there is *no proposition* explaining the reasons for *modus ponens*, the consistency of mathematics, or the distribution of the prime numbers respectively is equivalent to claiming that there is *no fact of the matter* grounding *modus ponens*, the consistency of mathematics, or the distribution of the prime numbers. And this has undesirable consequences.

Take the consistency of mathematics, for example. There are good reasons to believe that mathematics is consistent, even though we know, thanks to Gödel, that proving the consistency of any axiom system strong enough to contain arithmetic (e.g., ZFC) within that system itself is impossible. Of course we can utter the natural-language proposition 'Mathematics is consistent', but that is an entirely different proposition from the provably impossible proposition (or more accurately: string of propositions) proving the consistency of ZFC within ZFC. A natural, realist way of making sense of this situation is to think (a) that there is a mathematical cosmos out there, (b) that this cosmos exists independently of our language, and (c) that mathematicians use mathematical language to describe this cosmos, knowing full well that some of its properties cannot be captured in it.

But how can the linguistic idealist make sense of this situation, given her belief that reality is essentially propositionally expressible? I see two options. The first would be to say that Gödel's theorem shows that there simply *is* no proposition to express, hence no fact of the matter regarding mathematics' consistency.[8] This is an implausible conclusion because it would lead to confusion about the very fabric of mathematical reality. For the linguistic idealist, the absence of a consistency *proposition* must mean that there is no *fact* of the matter regarding the consistency of mathematics 'gluing' together its parts into an interconnected, coherent whole: the mathematical cosmos would be a body of propositions for which it was unclear whether it is unified, fragmented, or contradictory and thus, whether it is ontologically stable. Note that this worry is a direct consequence of the linguistic idealist's assumption that 'for the world to exist it must be expressible'. The worry does not arise on the commonsense assumption that mathematical reality exists independently of our language because on this picture, what ensures the unity, interconnectedness

---

[8] Note that the natural-language proposition 'Mathematics is consistent' is not an adequate replacement for a string of propositions proving the consistency of ZFC within ZFC; its content is very different from the content of the provably impossible string of propositions proving the consistency of ZFC within ZFC. Moreover, as a natural-language sentence, it is not part of mathematical reality.

and coherence of reality is reality itself—a reality made up of objects and structures.

A second option for the linguistic idealist would be to say that there does indeed exist a string of propositions proving, say, the consistency of ZFC within ZFC, but that this string of propositions is ineffable. This move might block the worry about a fragmented mathematical cosmos,[9] however at the cost of introducing the questionable concept of ineffable propositions (see footnote 1).

My general point is that, in order to ensure a single, unified reality, the linguistic idealist must assume that for any (arbitrarily chosen) true proposition p_1, there must be a proposition p_2 whose content explains the contents of p_1, thereby linking or joining it with the rest of the linguistic facts that constitute the world. It is plausible to assume that there are explanatory propositions for most propositions (e.g., for all propositions expressing ordinary empirical facts). Yet, as I hope I have managed to show, it is not plausible to assume that there are explanatory propositions for *modus ponens*, the consistency of mathematics, and the distribution of the prime numbers.

9.6 Conclusion

In this chapter, I have offered a mathematical perspective on the question whether linguistic idealism is a plausible position for mathematics by investigating to what extent language is constitutive of the mathematical cosmos and of our epistemic access to it. After drawing a distinction between mathematical knowledge and mathematical understanding, I argued that the latter is not necessarily linguistically expressible whereas the former must, at least in principle, be linguistically expressible. I used the example of logical consequence to demonstrate that understanding the deductive validity of an argument is ultimately non-propositional. I used the example of Gödel's second incompleteness theorem to show that understanding the consistency of mathematics is independent of there being a (set of) propositions (e.g., a proof) expressing this consistency. I used the third example, Cramér's random model of the prime numbers, to argue that our understanding of the distribution of the prime numbers is independent of there being a proposition explaining why the distribution is the way it is. Based on these examples, I then argued that

---

[9] Although I have doubts that it ultimately does because it is questionable whether an ineffable proposition can play the connecting role that it would have to play to ensure the unity, interconnectedness, and coherence of mathematics.

there is a sense in which the existence of the mathematical cosmos both does and does not depend on language. On the one hand, since we cannot perceive mathematical structures through our senses, the only way the mathematical cosmos can manifest itself is through language. On the other hand, the fact that mathematical understanding is independent of linguistic formulability shows that we do have a language-independent access to mathematics, which in turn suggests that the language-independent existence of the mathematical cosmos was a prerequisite for the development of mathematical language, just as the anterior existence of the physical world was a prerequisite for the evolution of human language. Linguistic idealism, from a mathematical point of view, is not a plausible position.

References

Antos, C., S.-D. Friedman, Honzik R., and Ternullo C. 2015. 'Multiverse conceptions in set theory', *Synthese* 192, 2463–88.
Bloor, D. 2018. 'The Question of Linguistic Idealism Revisited', in H. Sluga and D. Stern (eds), *The Cambridge Companion to Wittgenstein*, 2nd edn. (Cambridge: CUP), 332–60.
Carroll, L. 1995 [1895]. 'What the tortoise said to Achilles', *Mind* 104, 691–93.
Chow, T. Y. 2019. 'The consistency of arithmetic', *The Mathematical Intelligencer* 41, 22–30.
D'Alessandro, W. 2022. 'Unrealistic models in mathematics', *Philosophers' Imprint* 23: 27. https://doi.org/10.3998/phimp.1712.
Frege, G. 1962 [1903]. *Grundgesetze der Arithmetik, begriffsschriftlich abgeleitet* (Volume II) (Hildesheim: Olms).
Frege, G. 1988. *Die Grundlagen der Arithmetik* (Hamburg: Meiner).
Gaskin, R. 2019. 'From the unity of the proposition to linguistic idealism', *Synthese* 196, 1325–42.
Gaskin, R. 2021. *Language and World. A Defence of Linguistic Idealism* (London: Routledge).
Gentzen, G. 1969. Copyright page. In M. Szabo (ed.), *The Collected Papers of Gerhard Gentzen*, Volume 55 of *The Collected Papers of Gerhard Gentzen* (Amsterdam: Elsevier), iv.
Gödel, K. 1938. 'The consistency of the axiom of choice and of the Generalized Continuum Hypothesis', *Proceedings of the National Academy of Sciences of the United States of America* 24, 556–7.
Goldman, A. 1967. 'A causal theory of knowing', *The Journal of Philosophy* 64, 357–72.
Hamkins, J. D. 2012. 'The set-theoretic multiverse', *The Review of Symbolic Logic* 5, 416–49.
Hofweber, T. 2023. *Idealism and the Harmony of Thought and Reality* (Oxford: Oxford University Press).
Ichikawa, J. J., and Steup, M. 2018. 'The analysis of knowledge', in E. N. Zalta (ed.), *The Stanford Encyclopedia of Philosophy* (Summer 2018 ed.), Metaphysics Research Lab, Stanford University.
Jackson, F. 1982. 'Epiphenomenal qualia', *The Philosophical Quarterly* 32, 127–36.
Jonas, S. 2016. *Ineffability and Its Metaphysics: The Unspeakable in Art, Religion, and Philosophy* (New York: Palgrave Macmillan).
Jonas, S. 2024. 'Mathematical pluralism and indispensability', *Erkenntnis* 89, 2899–923.
Moore, A. 1997. *Points of View* (Oxford: Oxford University Press).
Nagel, T. 1974. 'What is it like to be a bat?', *The Philosophical Review* 83, 435–50.
Pavese, C. 2022. 'Knowledge How', in E. N. Zalta and U. Nodelman (eds.), *The Stanford Encyclopedia of Philosophy* (Fall 2022 ed.), Metaphysics Research Lab, Stanford University.

Ryle, G. 1945. 'Knowing how and knowing that: The presidential address', *Proceedings of the Aristotelian Society* 46, 1–16.
Ryle, G. 1949. *The Concept of Mind* (Chicago, IL: Chicago University Press).
Tao, T. 2015. 'Probabilistic models and heuristics for the primes', 254A, supplement 4.
Williamson, T. 2000. *Knowledge and Its Limits* (Oxford: Oxford University Press).

10
Isomorphism and Idealism

Michael Morris

10.1 Some Linguistic Inferences

Here is a rule of a familiar kind about an English sentence:

(SsR)　The sentence 'Shaftesbury is hilly' is true if and only if Shaftesbury is hilly.

Here is a fact about Shaftesbury:

(S1)　Shaftesbury is hilly.

If you know both the rule and the fact, you can immediately draw the following conclusion:

(S2)　The sentence 'Shaftesbury is hilly' is true.

This looks as if it is a significant inference, because it seems that you could know the fact about Shaftesbury which (S1) states—that is, you could know that Shaftesbury is hilly—without knowing either the rule (SsR) or the fact about an English sentence which (S2) states, and you could know the rule (SsR) without knowing either the fact about Shaftesbury which (S1) states or the fact about an English sentence which (S2) states. For example, it seems that a monolingual French-speaker could properly be described as knowing that Shaftesbury is hilly without knowing either that the English sentence 'Shaftesbury is hilly' is true if and only if Shaftesbury is hilly, or that the English sentence 'Shaftesbury is hilly' is true; and in beginning to learn English, it seems that such a monolingual French-speaker could properly be described as coming to know that the English sentence 'Shaftesbury is hilly' is true if and only if Shaftesbury is hilly, without yet knowing either that Shaftesbury is hilly or that the English sentence 'Shaftesbury is hilly' is true.

There are similar inferences which concern subsentential expressions. Here is a rule about an English name:

(SnR)　The thing called by the name 'Shaftesbury' is Shaftesbury.

Here is a fact about a thing which you might know in virtue of having lived in Shaftesbury all your life:

(Sn1) This place is Shaftesbury.

If you know both the rule and the fact about the thing, you can immediately draw the following conclusion:

(Sn2) This place is the thing called by the name 'Shaftesbury'.[1]

And we can do something similar with predicates. Here is a rule about an English predicate:

(SpR) The predicate 'x is hilly' is true of something if and only if that thing is hilly.

Here is a fact that might strike you about a place you find yourself in:

(Sp1) This place is hilly.

If you know the rule and the fact about the place, you can immediately conclude:

(Sp2) The predicate 'x is hilly' is true of this place.

These two inferences seem to be significant in the same way as the first one is.

9.2 The Issue

There is a widespread view that language and world are, in some sense, isomorphic. One expression of that view is this:

(Syn) Language is syntactically structured and the world has a corresponding structure, a quasi-syntax.

Another is this:

(Sjoi) To fundamental linguistic predicates there correspond fundamental categories in reality (fundamental language carves reality at its (reality's) joints).

Suppose (just for a moment) that (Syn) and (Sjoi) are true. The question arises: are they true because language matches the world (a realist view) or because the world (the world we speak about, at least) matches language (an idealist view)?

---

[1] This inference is only likely to strike us as establishing new knowledge if the fact stated in (Sn1) is known through a foreign language, or in some such circumstance as that in which Kripke's Pierre finds himself in Kripke 1979. The interesting question is whether that makes it a special case: my remarks in the last section have some bearing on this.

I think that if we were faced with that choice, we should be idealist. But I don't want to be idealist, so I don't want to be faced with that choice. So I want to reject the claim of isomorphism—I want to reject anything like (Syn) and (Sjoi). To be able to do that we need to understand what the claim of isomorphism really amounts to. What is it for the world to have a quasi-syntax, which is somehow a counterpart to the syntax of language? What is it for there to be fundamental categories in reality?

I think the answers to questions of this kind are quite abstract, and the key to them is provided by linguistic inferences like the ones I've just presented.

10.3 McDowell and the Given

One way to see the connection between inferences like those and some form of isomorphism thesis is through John McDowell's treatment of what he calls the 'Myth of the Given'.

McDowell is, on the face of it, interested not in the relation between language and the world, but in that between judgement and the world. His focus is sometimes on the relation between judgement and *experience*, but this is only because he thinks (McDowell 1996, 27):

> Experience enables the layout of reality itself to exert a rational influence on what a subject thinks.

The way this works is that, when things work well, experience is a matter of being open to the layout of reality (McDowell 1996, 26), and such experience then provides us with a rational constraint on our judgement.

McDowell interprets this rational constraint in a particular way (1996, 7):

> [W]e cannot really understand the relations in virtue of which a judgement is warranted except as . . . relations such as implication or probabilification.

It seems clear from this that the relations he has in mind are inferential relations. The idea seems to be that he and those who accept the 'Myth of the Given' agree that judgements have to be capable of being inferentially justified by experience—to put it simply, that experience must be able to provide a premise in an inference whose conclusion is that a judgement is correct—although they disagree about the way experience has to be for that to be possible. McDowell insists that 'the relations in virtue of which a judgement is warranted' have to be understood as 'relations within the space of concepts', because the relations in question, 'relations such as implication or probabilification', 'hold between potential exercises of conceptual capacities'; whereas someone who accepts the 'Myth of the Given' thinks 'the space of justifications or warrants ... extends more widely than the conceptual sphere', to include, at the experience end, 'non-conceptual impacts'.

He makes clear what he takes this to mean (McDowell 1996, 6):

> The idea [of the 'Myth of the Given'] is that when we have exhausted all the available moves within the space of concepts, all the available moves from one conceptually organized item to another, there is still one more step we can take: namely, pointing to something that is simply received in experience. It can only be pointing, because *ex hypothesi* this last move in a justification comes after we have exhausted the possibilities of tracing grounds from one conceptually organized, and so articulable, item to another.

That assumed implication, 'conceptually organized, and so articulable', means that the idea of 'conceptual organization' which is in play here is clearly the idea of being in some way isomorphic with language: on McDowell's view, experience seems to come with something like a quasi-syntax, and to be in some way already categorized; and since experience is, if things go well, openness to the layout of reality, reality too must come with something like a quasi-syntax and be in some way already categorized. It looks as if McDowell is here committing himself to something like (Syn) and (Sjoi).

And he does it because of an assumption he seems to share with what he calls the 'Myth of the Given': that judgements are inferentially justified by experience. This seems to me an assumption which it's plausible to think lies at the heart of the idea of the Given: the Given is supposed to be something which settles issues. To do that, it must have two properties: first, it must be something which is, in some way, independent of the particular point that is at issue; and secondly, appeal to it must be decisive. Deductive inferences clearly provide us with the second property, provided the premises are secure; and the security of the premises is at least enhanced when we are appealing to something which has the first property—something which is independent of the issue at hand. The fact that McDowell agrees on this second point with the position he calls the 'Myth of the Given' makes it natural to ascribe to him a belief in some sort of Given: he too seems to think, in effect, that the world provides us with a premise of an inference whose conclusion is that some judgement is correct.

McDowell is also committed to a kind of Given which has the first property—some sort of independence of the particular point that is at issue.

He describes the coherentist response to the Myth of the Given as leaving us with a 'frictionless spinning in the void' (1996, 11). Some kind of independence is required of anything which is to provide friction. What this amounts to may need to be characterized differently on different conceptions of the relation between thinking and the world, but it looks as if on an inferential model, of the kind which McDowell shares with the Myth of the Given, we need at least this: we need it to be possible in principle to acknowledge the given, the independent ground of judgement, without already making the judgements which are supposed to be grounded on it. In this way, we can understand McDowell saying that his view 'makes room for a different notion of givenness' (1996, 10).

We seem to be able to take the following thought from McDowell: the world can only supply a premise in an inference whose conclusion is that a judgement is correct if the world has the same form as judgement. And it looks as if, on his view, having the same form as judgement is having the same form as language.

10.4 What Is the Inference?

As we have seen, McDowell is ostensibly concerned with the relation between judgement and the world, and only indirectly with language (because judgement has the same form as language). In fact, however, I think the issue here is ultimately just one about the relation between language and the world.

McDowell seems to think that the world has to supply the premise of an inference whose conclusion is that some judgement is correct. What inference could it be?

He says that 'In experience one finds oneself saddled with content' (1996, 10). He then wants to allow that judgement is 'spontaneous', or free—that is, in some sense, up to the subject. So he says (1996, 11):

> How one's experience represents things to be is not under one's control, but it is up to one whether one accepts the appearance or rejects it.

This suggests that the inference which McDowell has in mind is something like this:

(M1) It seems to me, on the basis of looking, that Shaftesbury is hilly; *so*
(M2) Shaftesbury is hilly.

(M1) might be taken to probabilify (M2), since things are generally as they seem. We have here something which is a bit like an inductive inference; but there is room for the subject to question whether things really are as they seem to be, so there is space for freedom of judgement.

Unfortunately, it is not plausible that anything like (M1) represents the content of perceptual experience in the ordinary case, and McDowell himself can hardly think it does. McDowell conceives of experience as 'openness to the layout of reality', and takes himself to be entitled to that characterization at least in part because he allows that in experience one 'takes in ... *that things are thus and so*' (1996, 26). If what one 'takes in' in the ordinary case had the form of (M1), all that we could ordinarily be said to 'take in' would be some fact about its *seeming to* me that things are thus and so. And this would hardly present experience as 'openness to the layout of reality'.

We might then think experience could present us with this premise instead:

(M1*) Shaftesbury is visibly hilly.

But now we should ask whether 'visibly' here expresses part of what experience presents—the idea would be that the visibility is part of the experience—or just the way experience presents what it presents (when we're in Shaftesbury, looking, say). If it's the latter, and experience supplies us with a premise of inference at all, the premise it supplies must be just this:

Shaftesbury is hilly.

That is a premise we have encountered before, as (S1). But if that were the premise, then it seems the inference would have to be this:

(S1) Shaftesbury is hilly; *so*
(M2) Shaftesbury is hilly.

And the problem with this is that it's hard to see how we can preserve what is crucial to the idea of the Given. We may recall that two properties were essential to the Given: first, it must be something which is, in some way, independent of what is at issue; and secondly, appeal to it must be decisive. Certainly, appeal to (S1) is decisive in its support for (M2): no premise could necessitate its conclusion more obviously. But that decisiveness is bought at the cost of the premise's independence. It might be that McDowell would hope to secure the right kind of independence by insisting that (S1) represents what is experienced, not what is judged, and by claiming that such experience is independent of judgement (see McDowell 1996, 9–11). Unfortunately, this way of securing the independence of what (S1) supplies undermines the claim to decisiveness which the idea of the Given needs. The hope is that an inference such as that from (S1) to (M2) might supply a certain necessity to the conclusion, something which will settle the issue at hand. But the necessity of inference is conditional: commitment to the conclusion of an inference is only required of us if we are already committed to its premises. It is hard to see how commitment to (M2) can be forced on us without commitment to (S1); but commitment to (S1) is already commitment to (M2), which of course prevents (S1) representing a properly independent step.

So much for the suggestion that 'visibly' in (M1*) expresses just the way experience presents what it presents, rather than part of what the experience itself presents. But what if 'visibly' in (M1*) expresses part of what the experience presents? Understood in this way, the inference from (M1*) to (M2) presents quite an attractive picture of a kind of inference we might make on the basis of perceptual experience. Unfortunately, it's not clear that it can do the work that McDowell needs it to do, if what we're concerned with is the justification of judgement in general by the world. For his own version of the idea of the Given, McDowell needs an inference which shows a judgement to be justified by experience. If the inference in question has anything like the form of those which we've been considering so far, it needs to take us from what experience delivers—the way the world is, if things go right—to judgement. That means that he needs an inference in which judgement appears for the first time at the stage of the conclusion. But part of the problem we've just found with the inference from (S1) to (M2) now recurs: the inference from (M1*) to (M2) is only compelling—only an issue-settler of the kind the Given is supposed to provide—for someone who is committed to (M1*)—only, in effect, for someone who *judges* (M1*). So judgement needs already to have come in at the first step of the inference.

In order to meet that point, while still keeping the premise independent of the conclusion, it is tempting to change the form of the inference, and replace (M2) with something like this:

(M2**)   It is correct to judge that Shaftesbury is hilly.

If we do this, we no longer have an inference which might be thought to copy the order in which information comes to the mind: instead, we have one which explains the justification of a perceptual judgement retrospectively, as it were, from a position after the judgement has been made. This seems to give us a theory of the way in which judgement is answerable to the world which is a kind of shadow of an account we might offer of the way in which language is answerable to the world, which rests on linguistic inferences like those I began with. The idea would be that in acquiring concepts we learn rules for their use:

this would be the analogue to learning rules for the use of words. And these rules for the use of concepts would generate rules for making judgements, of something like this form:

(SjR)   It is correct to judge that Shaftesbury is hilly if and only if Shaftesbury is hilly.

And this, of course, is a counterpart to the linguistic rule (SsR).

10.5 The Problem

But this shadow theory is a sham, and the explanation of the answerability of judgement to the world which it provides is empty. There is a key difference between the inference from (S1) to (S2), on the one hand, and that from (S1) to (M2**), on the other. I will first present the difference, and the problem it presents for the idea that (S1) might express the grounds which the world provides for (M2**), in outline, before looking in more detail at the crucial steps.

Here is the outline. (S2) presents the justification for using the sentence 'Shaftesbury is hilly', and it is apparently grounded in a premise, (S1), whose content, it is assumed, can be accepted without yet using that very sentence (for example, by a monolingual French-speaker). But while (M2**) presents the justification for judging that Shaftesbury is hilly, what is presented as its ground—(S1) again—cannot be accepted without in effect making that very judgement. This is because (S1) cannot figure as the ground of a judgement in an inference without itself being endorsed. And what is endorsed when the content of (S1) is judged is nothing other than the judgement that Shaftesbury is hilly. But to endorse the judgement that Shaftesbury is hilly is in effect to judge that the judgement that Shaftesbury is hilly is correct. That is, to endorse what is expressed in (S1) is in effect to make the judgement expressed in (M2**). The inference still goes through, of course, but for the wrong reason: not because (S1) provides an appropriate justification for (M2**), but because one cannot accept (S1) without already in effect having accepted (M2**).

That is the problem in outline. Now let us look at the key steps in this presentation of it:

(a) (S1) cannot figure as the ground of a judgement in an inference without itself being endorsed;

(b) To endorse (S1) is already in effect to make the judgement expressed in (M2**);

(c) If (b) is true, (S1) cannot provide the right kind of justification for (M2**).

It is crucial for (a) that (S1) is meant to figure as the ground of a judgement in an inference which yields that judgement as its conclusion. At its heart is a certain conditionality of inference: in the case of a valid deductive inference, you must accept the conclusion *if* you accept the premises. But an inference is compelling *only* for someone who accepts the premises. The inference from (S1) to (M2**) is meant to capture the rational constraint to which our judgement is subject, but it will only do so if it is assumed that (S1) is accepted.[2] I take it that there is no significant difference between acceptance and endorsement: if you accept (S1), you must endorse it. It is just that the notion of endorsement makes it clear that in accepting a judgement you are committed to thinking that it is correct.

That takes us on to (b). I have carefully avoided saying that endorsing (S1) is already actually making the judgement expressed in (M2**): instead, I am claiming merely that endorsing (S1) is *in effect* making the judgement expressed in (M2**). There is therefore no obvious risk of a regress of higher-order judgements of the form 'It is correct to judge that...', whether or not such a regress would be vicious. The idea is rather this: (M2**) is no more than an expression of—a making explicit of—the endorsement of (S1). This is because endorsing something is just taking it to be correct (or otherwise valuable).

It is worth noting here the difference between the role played by (SjR) in the argument from (S1) to (M2**), on the one hand, and that played by (SsR) in the argument from (S1) to (S2), on the other. (SsR) is a genuinely non-redundant premise, supplying substantive information about the meaning of the English sentence 'Shaftesbury is hilly'. Without it, the inference from (S1) to (S2) would not be valid.[3] But (SjR) is strictly unnecessary in the inference from (S1) to (M2**), even if it helps in the formal regimentation of that inference into a familiar kind of pattern. (M2**) follows from (S1), just in virtue of the meaning of the words used (not quoted) in it, and (SjR) does no more than spell out explicitly that this is so.

---

[2] This is the source of what I think is the central difficulty with McDowell's account of experience as somehow both 'receptive' (passive) and 'spontaneous' (active). He claims that 'conceptual capacities are drawn on *in* receptivity' (McDowell 1996, 9), which I think is an attempt to have his cake and eat it. It seems to me just a fudge over the status of (S1) in the rational constraint of judgement by experience.

[3] I am assuming here that there is something epistemic about validity (it's not just modal, for example): even if we understand the meaning of sentences to be essential to them (as I am inclined to do) nobody could come to know (S2) on the basis just of knowing (S1)—they would also need to know (SsR). In any case, I think it is an epistemic notion that the idea of the Given needs.

And so to (c). The claim is that if the point just made is good, we cannot see the inference from (S1) to (M2**) as an instance of the grounding of judgement in the world which is necessary to make judgement answerable to the world in the first place. The problem is that the use of (S1) in the argument is not sufficiently independent either of judgement in general, or of the judgement of the correctness of (S1) in particular. (S1) cannot represent the world's constraint on judgement, because it can only play the role it has to play in this inference if it is itself endorsed—and that endorsement is tantamount to judgement, and so not a constraint on judgement. And it cannot provide a constraint on the higher-order judgement that (S1) itself is correct, because that higher-order judgement is no more than a making explicit of the commitment already accepted in accepting (S1).

So it seems that the inference from (S1) to (M2**) cannot be the inference McDowell needs for his view—an inference from what is present in perception to some further judgement. And that means that none of the three supposed inferences we have considered—the inference from (M1) to (M2), the inference from (S1) to (M2), and the inference from (S1) to (M2**)—can do the job which McDowell requires. In fact, it seems that the only kind of inference which allows the world as it presents itself in perception to supply immediately a premise for some further judgement, and which is at all relevant to the issues here, is the kind exemplified by the move from (S1) to (S2), in linguistic inferences of the kind I began with. And that means that the only way of making sense of McDowell's claim that the content of perceptual experience is conceptual is as a view about language.

10.6 The Linguistic Given

The view about language which McDowell's position seems to end up having to be can be thought of as a commitment to a certain kind of idea of the Given: as something given for language, rather than for judgement. Let's call this the idea of the Linguistic Given. A form of this position which follows the spirit of McDowell's own view seems to have two core commitments:

(G1) The world itself can supply a premise in an inference whose conclusion is that the use of a sentence (or other expression) is correct;

(G2) (G1) can only be true if the world itself is linguistically organized (where linguistic organization is the explicitly linguistic counterpart to the conceptual organization which McDowell actually appeals to).

We can imagine a new kind of 'Myth of the Linguistic Given'—perhaps the secret Myth which the original Myth really depended on—which accepts (G1) without accepting (G2).

This idea of the Linguistic Given is a response to a problem which is parallel to the one which McDowell's own kind of appeal to the Given is designed to dissolve. The question is: how can our language be answerable to the world? For if our use of words is not answerable to the world, it's hard to see how we could describe the world. The key thought is that our use of words can only be answerable to the world if it can, in principle, be justified by the world. And then the idea of the Linguistic Given is offered as what is required for it to be possible for the use of words to be justified by the world. It is worth isolating the key assumptions here. First, there is the following claim about the possibility of describing the world:

(D) It is only possible to describe the world if the use of words can be justified by the way the world is.

And then there is the assumption which links that to the idea of the Linguistic Given:

(SG) The use of words can only be justified by the way the world is if (G1) is true.

10.7 Tarskian Framing

That last piece of reasoning makes it seem as if we get to the idea of the world being isomorphic with language by considering a deep philosophical problem. That is certainly true, but there is a way of ending up in the same position which seems to depend on more everyday, more mundane considerations, even if we have to start some way away from the everyday to explain their true location.

The linguistic inferences I began with will obviously recall Tarski: the rules they depend on look as if they are colloquial versions of the kind of thing which occupies a central position in Tarski's account of truth (Tarski 1956). In these contexts, we sometimes forget Tarski's concern with truth: he was looking for a way of specifying the truth or falsity of every sentence of the languages he was interested in. (His particular concern was to do that without falling foul of the liar paradox, but we can leave that to one side here.) His interest in the rules of which things like (SsR) are the colloquial counterparts was that they put one in a position to specify the truth or falsity of the sentences they concern.

If we bear that in mind, we can introduce the idea of what I will call a *Tarskian framing* of a language, which I will define as follows:

(TF) A *Tarskian framing* of a language provides
(i)   A *semantic theory* for that language which
(ii) Puts one in a position, given epistemically favourable circumstances, immediately to determine the truth or falsity of every sentence in the language.

And I take a semantic theory for a language to be defined, in general, as follows:

(ST) A *semantic theory* for a language assigns meanings to subsentential expressions in the language in such a way as to permit the derivation of an assignment of meaning for every sentence of the language.

It is clear from (TF) that a semantic theory which is part of a Tarskian framing for a language will be a truth-theory for that language: that is, the assignments of meaning to whole sentences which are derived within it will be assignments of truth-conditions. And the idea will be to allow it to be possible, given epistemically favourable circumstances, for there to be a linguistic inference of the sort exemplified in the move from (S1) to (S2) for each sentence in the language. We can link the idea of a Tarskian framing for a language to the issues which lie behind the idea of a Linguistic Given by saying that a Tarskian framing for a language is, in effect, a semantic theory with a particular goal: the goal is to provide a specification, for each sentence, of how the world might justify its use.

This brings out something about semantic theories which might not otherwise be obvious. What a semantic theory assigns to each expression as its meaning or semantic value is something whose presence, when recognized, will immediately and decisively justify the use of that expression. (At least, it will justify the use as *correct*—even if it does not ensure that it is appropriate in all respects.) Someone who knows that this place is Shaftesbury will be immediately and decisively justified in calling the place 'Shaftesbury', given the rule (SnR). Someone who knows that a place is hilly will be immediately and decisively justified in using the adjective 'hilly' to describe it, given the rule (SpR). And someone who knows that Shaftesbury is hilly will be immediately and decisively justified in using the sentence 'Shaftesbury is hilly', given the rule (SsR). The immediacy and decisiveness of the justification in each case is the immediacy and decisiveness of an elementary deductive inference. The whole point of a semantic theory is to assign to each expression a semantic value the recognition of whose presence will bring the correct use of that expression within the range of an elementary deductive inference.

10.8 Two Approaches to Semantic Theories

Rosanna Keefe (2000, 49–61) makes a useful distinction between two ways of viewing theories of vagueness, which we can apply to semantic theories more generally. She characterizes it as a distinction between *modelling* and *realist* approaches, but given the role of the issue of realism here, I will characterize it as a distinction between *modelling* and *literalist* approaches. The *modelling* approach treats the construction of a semantic theory as an attempt to produce a toy version of a language, whose expressions have a toy version of linguistic meaning. The idea is to produce something which is thoroughly intelligible in a way that perhaps only a toy can be, but which is nevertheless as life-like as possible: the idea is to constrain the toy expressions so that they behave as similarly as possible to the real expressions of a real language. The *literalist* approach, by contrast, treats the construction of a semantic theory as an attempt to produce a true and literal description of a real language. The semantic values which a semantic theory assigns to expressions are supposed to be the real meanings of those expressions, and the relationships between the semantic values of different expressions are supposed to be the real relationships of the real meanings of those expressions.

There are obvious differences between these two approaches. On the literalist approach, any difference between the behaviour of an expression as predicted by a semantic theory and the behaviour of the real-language expression which it represents is a potentially decisive fault in the theory: it is something which needs somehow to be explained away if the theory is to be maintained. On the modelling approach, on the other hand, there is no expectation of exact similarity of behaviour, so a certain divergence is tolerable, provided the toy language is itself neatly comprehensible, and the comparisons which it offers with the real language are illuminating. Again, on the literalist approach, it is natural to think that there ought ideally to be one best semantic theory—the one which actually describes the real language correctly[4]—whereas the modelling approach can easily allow different theories to

---

[4] Although the assumption that there is one best theory is commonly made in science, and in the philosophy of logic, it is famously put in question by indeterminacy arguments—most obviously those for the thesis of the 'inscrutability of reference' see Quine 1960, ch. 2, and Davidson 2001b.

be roughly equally good, and as good as any theory could be, if they model different aspects of the behaviour of a real language well.

Sometimes people adopt different attitudes to different theories: one theory perhaps is illuminating when understood in the modelling way, while another looks closer to the truth when considered in the literalist way. And many people think that we are at least some distance away from any plausible theory for a whole real language towards which anything like the literalist approach would be reasonable. But it is common to think that we should aim for a semantic theory which could be understood in the literalist way: after all, why should we be content with anything less?

This assumes that there could be a theory which did truly describe the real meanings of the expressions of a real language. What would have to be true for there to be such a theory? Clearly, the semantic values assigned by the theory to the expressions of a language would have to be the real meanings of those expressions. And for them to be the real meanings of expressions which we understand, they must stand in a relation to us which makes sense of our coming to understand those expressions—that is, makes sense of them being the meanings which we come to understand those expressions to have.

This is naturally understood to have a particular consequence if the semantic theory is presented as part of what I have called a Tarskian framing for a language: the semantic values assigned to sentences must be the real truth-conditions of those sentences, and they must be the things (so to speak) which we recognize as being assigned to those sentences when we come to understand them. Sentences are true or false in virtue of the way the world is, so the real truth-conditions of sentences will be ways the world is or might be. And if these ways the world might be are to be the things which we recognize as being assigned to those sentences when we come to understand them, it is at least natural to think they must be things which we can in principle recognize as present independently of understanding the sentences in question.[5]

There are two general kinds of account which we can give of our coming to understand a language which meet this requirement. One—the more traditional approach—begins with subsentential expressions, perhaps individual words. On this view, what we learn first are rules like (SnR), for proper names,

---

[5] This isn't strictly required: it's possible that the things can be both ways the world itself might be, and also such that they can only be recognized by someone who can understand a particular set of sentences (rather than just, for example, some sentences or other, in some language or other); but we get an account which is a better fit for the everyday idea that words are arbitrary signs, which I'll turn to in the next section, if we suppose that what is meant by sentences can in principle be recognized independently of those very sentences.

or (SpR), for predicates (though we can imagine someone suggesting a more basic rule for adjectives which looks more like the rule for proper names, and which is then transformed in a standard way to generate a rule for predicates like (SpR)). The idea here is that we learn that *this* is the word for *that*, where '*that*' points to some item in the world which is available in principle to someone as they begin to learn the language. Rules for sentences—rules like (SsR)—are then strictly derived from this. Something like this kind of view is probably everyone's first theory of language-learning: the Augustinian picture which Wittgenstein uses at the beginning of the *Philosophical Investigations* is one famous expression of it.

The other approach begins with sentences. We come across someone using a whole sentence, and take them to be saying something which is correct in the circumstances. We then look to the world to see which particular way the world is might be that in virtue of which this sentence is correct. We take it that *this sentence* is correct *now*, or *here* (where '*now*' and '*here*' are ways of getting at the circumstance which makes the sentence correct). Gradually we piece together assumptions of this kind, which give us—at least provisionally—rules which specify the truth-conditions of sentences, rules like (SsR). We then construct a theory to explain the systematic connections between these rules for sentences. The theory we construct presents the best explanation of the sentences' having the truth-conditions they do as being that those truth-conditions are derivable from rules for subsentential expressions, which recur in different combinations in many sentences—rules such as (SnR) and (SpR). This is the kind of approach made famous in Davidson's theory of radical interpretation (e.g., Davidson 2001a).

Whether we start with individual words or with sentences, the important point for our purposes is that the aspects of the world which we recognize in learning a language are also, on this natural understanding of a literalist approach to Tarskian framings, the things which are assigned to linguistic expressions as their meanings. But we have seen that this relation of assignment involves assigning to each expression something the recognition of whose presence will bring the correct use of that expression within the range of an elementary deductive inference. It is something the recognition of whose presence justifies the use of the expression in question immediately and decisively. That is to say, a literalist approach to Tarskian framing commits one to the idea of what I have called the Linguistic Given.

I suggested earlier that a natural form of the idea of the Linguistic Given—a form to be found underlying McDowell's view—involves a commitment to these two claims:

(G1) The world itself can supply a premise in an inference whose conclusion is that the use of a sentence (or other expression) is correct;

(G2) (G1) can only be true if the world itself is linguistically organized (where linguistic organization is the explicitly linguistic counterpart to the conceptual organization which McDowell actually appeals to).

A literalist approach to Tarskian framing commits us to (G1). This is because the relation of assignment requires what is assigned in a semantic theory to be something which can figure as a premise in an inference whose conclusion is that the use of the relevant linguistic expression is correct; and a literalist approach to Tarskian framing requires what is assigned to be part of the world.[6]

But we can easily see that a literalist approach to Tarskian framing also commits us to something which might be offered as a non-metaphorical interpretation of (G2). A Tarskian framing provides, not just isolated truth-conditions, but a complete semantic theory for a language, which enables us to assign a truth-condition to every sentence of the language, no matter how many there are. The number and interdependence of the sentences ensures that these truth-conditions are linked together in a structure which is constituted by the fact that they are all derivable from rules for subsentential expressions—rules like (SnR) and (SpR). Since truth-conditions are the things in virtue of which sentences are true, when they are true, and sentences are true in virtue of the way the world is, this structure which links the truth-conditions is a structure which can, in some way, be found in the world. Moreover, on a literalist reading of a Tarskian framing, it has to be a structure which can be found in the world as it might in principle present itself to someone learning a language. That looks as if it is all that might be meant by saying that the world itself is linguistically organized. That is, it looks as if what it is for the world itself to be linguistically organized is for the world itself to supply a premise in an inference to the conclusion that the use of a given expression is correct, for every expression in a language the truth-conditions of whose sentences are linked together in this kind of way.

---

[6] This is for the case of inferences whose conclusion is that the use of a *sentence* is correct, as required for (G1): but it also holds for the case of assignments to at least some subsentential expressions—for example, those involved in such inferences as from (Sn1) to (Sn2) or (Sp1) to (Sp2), which I considered at the outset.

10.9 A Mundane Redescription

I said that there was a way of ending up with the idea of the Linguistic Given, in very much the form in which McDowell is committed to it, as a result of pursuing more everyday, more mundane considerations than those which McDowell is concerned with. The path I have just presented, leading through semantic theories and Tarskian framings, might not seem to be much more everyday or mundane than McDowell's way. But there is a very simple way of redescribing slightly less technically what I have just presented.

What we need in order to get to the idea of the Linguistic Given is nothing more than the idea that words are arbitrary signs, with the proviso that what they are signs for are things in the world. What emerged in the presentation of Tarskian framing is that the kind of assignment which is involved there is the assignment to an expression of a language of something the recognition of whose presence brings the correctness of the use of an expression within the range of an elementary deductive inference. Such an inference settles the correctness of the use immediately and decisively, in the way that the idea of the Linguistic Given requires. But a little thought about what is involved in treating words as arbitrary signs reveals, I think, that to treat words as arbitrary signs is just to regard them as things whose real meaning is given to them by some kind of assignment. If what they are signs for are things in the world, then it is natural to think that their real meanings are things the recognition of whose presence justifies their use immediately and decisively in the way that the idea of the Linguistic Given requires. In effect, pursuing a literalist approach to a Tarskian framing for a language, on its most natural understanding, is just pursuing in a more theoretical way the ordinary idea that the words of that language are arbitrary signs for things in the world.

10.10 How to Avoid Idealism

I said at the beginning that I think that if we are forced to accept that language and the world are somehow isomorphic, it is better to be idealist rather than realist. But since I think it is better not to be idealist, I think it is therefore better to find a way to avoid accepting that language and the world are somehow isomorphic. I think we are now in a position to offer some confirmation of both of those judgements, as well as the outline of an account of how to avoid accepting that language and the world are somehow isomorphic.

First, once we recognize that the isomorphism thesis is only really intelligible as a way of spelling out the idea of the Linguistic Given, we can see that it is quite hard to motivate independently of idealism. The reason is that the motivation for the idea of the Linguistic Given is epistemological: it is rooted in the desire for a certain kind of debate-settler, an immediate and decisive justification for a view. The aim is to compel us to judge in a certain way on the basis of something which is not itself a matter of judgement. Insisting that the world must be a certain way for epistemological reasons of this kind is already an idealist move: there is therefore automatically some tension in any view which insists on an isomorphism between language and the world, while trying to take a realist view of the world.

The same problem arises in general for realist views which take literalist approaches to logic or semantics, while choosing their logic or semantics for epistemological or pragmatic reasons. And there is no reason to accept literalism about semantics, anyway. The important thing here is not to think that the modelling approach is somehow second-best. Rather, the whole point of the modelling approach is that you are able to focus on the real areas of difficulty and puzzlement by deliberately tidying up what can be tidied up. In semantics, the aim will in general be to assign as semantic values things which are themselves reasonably clearly individuated and well-understood: then the complications of real language will be exposed more clearly for what they are. The goal here is to see what assignments we need to make in order to mimic the real behaviour of real words. That task precisely does not involve raising questions about what it is to assign a semantic value to an expression: it is central to the project that we do not worry about that here. And in fact, the task requires the relationship between the assignment and the behaviour to be as simple as possible. When we are concerned about the behaviour of an expression, given an assignment, the behaviour we are concerned with is fundamentally whether we would count the expression as well or badly used, including correctly or incorrectly, across a number of dimensions, in as full a range of contexts as possible. We are concerned with conditional questions of the form 'If it had that value, rather than some other, would it be being well or badly used here?' We are precisely not concerned with issues which arise over what it would be for it to have any such value at all. This is what ensures that what is assigned in the assignment of a semantic value is bound to be something the recognition of whose presence is just a step of elementary deductive inference away from justifying the use of the expression in question. But by the same token it seems also to ensure that there is no good reason to adopt the literalist approach to semantics, since adopting the literalist approach consists in assuming that a relationship which is set up to be as simple as possible for one specific purpose is in fact the same as the relationship which really obtains between language and reality, when it is unclear that the latter relationship was established for any purpose at all.

Next, it is clear that one thing we need to do if we are to avoid idealism, is to reject the idea that the world itself provides the kind of decisive justification for our use of words which the idea of the Linguistic Given wants it to. This does not mean that it provides no justification for our use of words: it is just that it does not provide a kind of justification for judgements about the correct use of words which forces such judgements on us on the basis of something which is not itself a matter of judgement.

What we need to reject is the idea that something independent of judgement can force judgement in the way inference can, and the judgement still be justified. There is no unjudged first step in an inference. This does not stop the world justifying judgements about the use of words: it is just that the justification does not work by the pressure of an inference from a position outside judgement. There is an alternative story to tell: that we learn how to use words directly, in case-by-case confrontations with the world; and then, in virtue of that knowledge, that we simply judge that they are used correctly here, and incorrectly there. These judgements are not arbitrary, because our knowledge of how to use words is precisely knowledge of how to make these judgements. But the pattern of the cases on the basis of which we make those judgements need not be discernible independently of the judgements themselves.[7] We need to remember an obvious point here: the fact that something is a matter of judgement does not mean that it is a matter of opinion.

This alternative story seems true to life. It seems to us that our use of words is indeed a matter of judgement, and is never forced on us by something which is not itself a matter of judgement. I think the phenomenon of vagueness would make this seem phenomenologically obvious—had it not been that too many heavy boots have tramped over that particular terrain for too long. I think it is impossible to make phenomenological sense of a judgement about the correct use of a vague term being forced on us by something which is not itself a matter of judgement. Whenever we use such a term, the grey areas are always visible in the periphery of our vision, as it were, and we make our judgements about particular cases in the light of their location relative to those grey areas.

---

[7] It is striking that this is harmonious with McDowell's own view elsewhere, particularly in ethics: e.g., McDowell 1985.

And something akin to vagueness looks as if it arises for a very wide range of terms—at least every empirical term, for example.

I have said that rejecting the idea that the world itself provides the kind of decisive justification for our use of words which the idea of the Linguistic Given hopes for does not mean that the world provides no justification at all for our use of words. Can this claim really be upheld? It seems to run against one of McDowell's main arguments for his view of the relation between judgement and the world. He claims that if we suppose that judgement is constrained by something non-conceptual, we have to think of the relevant constraint as an 'alien force' delivering a 'brute impact' (McDowell 1996, 8). And this means that we have to think of the constraint as providing 'exculpations where we wanted justifications'. An exactly parallel argument looks as if it could be made against the idea that the use of language can be justified by a world which does not itself have the form of language.

The key to answering this objection is to note that exculpatory constraints differ from justificatory constraints not just in their character, but also in what they constrain. An exculpatory constraint—a constraint of brute or alien force—makes something *happen*; a justificatory constraint makes something *right* or *good*. So what we have to make sense of is the world making a use of language correct, or explaining the correctness of a use of language, even if it does not itself have the form of language. And this can be done quite simply, by making sense of such formulations as these, given that a sentence's being true is a way of its being in order, or good:

(J1) The sentence 'Shaftesbury is hilly' is true because Shaftesbury is hilly;
(J2) The fact that Shaftesbury is hilly makes the sentence 'Shaftesbury is hilly' true.

If uses of language can be justified by the world, even if the world does not itself have the form of language, then in particular the *unquoted* uses of the sentence 'Shaftesbury is hilly' in (J1) and (J2) can be justified by the world, even though the world does not itself have the form of language. That is to say, those unquoted uses in (J1) and (J2) may describe the way the world is, even though the world does not itself have the form of language. And that means that formulations like (J1) and (J2) can themselves be used to describe the way that uses of language can be justified by the world, even though the world does not itself have the form of language: they show that uses of the quoted sentence are correct in the real-world circumstances described by the unquoted uses of the same sentence.

What this shows is that *if* uses of language can be justified by the world without the world itself having the form of language, *then* formulations like (J1) and (J2) can be descriptions of how the world justifies uses of language without itself having the form of language. Such formulations cannot prove to a sceptic that uses of language really are justified by a world which does not have the form of language, but they show how that possibility can be made sense of. In particular, they show that the justification of language by the world does not require us to point beyond the articulable (compare McDowell 1996, 6), even if the world does not have the form of language: the alternative view which I'm sketching here holds precisely that in language we articulate a world which does not itself have the form of language.

In the same spirit, holding that the world does not itself have the form of language does not mean that it is an amorphous blob: the world has all the shapes and articulations we might naturally think it does—except that it does not have the form of language. But since for the world to have the form of language is for it to be such as to provide the premises for decisive, debate-settling inferences, there is no obvious non-idealist reason for thinking that the world should have the form of language.

Perhaps it might be thought that the view I've sketched can't really show the character of the justification of language by the world, since it seems to have very little to say about it. But again, this looks as if it's requiring that the world fit some kind of epistemological demand—in this case, for a satisfying explanation—which seems to beg the question in favour of idealism. And linguistic idealism surely faces challenges of its own on this score—for example, in providing an account of the learning of a first language which is even coherent.

Finally, we need to consider again the way in which we understand the kind of linguistic inference I began with. We had a rule about an English sentence:

(SsR)   The sentence 'Shaftesbury is hilly' is true if and only if Shaftesbury is hilly.

And we had a fact about Shaftesbury:

(S1)   Shaftesbury is hilly.

Knowing both the rule and the fact, we were able immediately to draw the following conclusion:

(S2)   The sentence 'Shaftesbury is hilly' is true.

I noted that this looks like a significant inference, because it seems that you could know the fact about Shaftesbury which (S1) states—that is, you could know that Shaftesbury is hilly—without knowing either the rule (SsR) or the fact about an English sentence which (S2) states, and you could know the rule (SsR) without knowing either the fact about Shaftesbury which (S1) states or the fact about an English sentence which (S2) states. And I gave as an example the case of a monolingual French-speaker who could properly be described as knowing that Shaftesbury is hilly without knowing either that the English sentence 'Shaftesbury is hilly' is true if and only if Shaftesbury is hilly, or that the English sentence 'Shaftesbury is hilly' is true. Suppose that a monolingual French-speaker started to learn English: it seems they could properly be described as coming to know that the English sentence 'Shaftesbury is hilly' is true if and only if Shaftesbury is hilly, without yet knowing either that Shaftesbury is hilly or that the English sentence 'Shaftesbury is hilly' is true.

Now suppose this monolingual French-speaker—let us call her *Colette*—comes to know that Shaftesbury is hilly. She is properly described as knowing that Shaftesbury is hilly, and that the English sentence 'Shaftesbury is hilly' is true if and only if Shaftesbury is hilly, in virtue of her understanding and acceptance of French sentences which are well translated by (S1) and (SsR).[8] And in virtue of that understanding of those French sentences, she is able to make an inference which is properly translated as the inference from (S1) to (S2) on the basis of (SsR). For her, that inference is indeed a significant inference, which lays out an advance in her knowledge.

But Colette's inference is, fundamentally, an inference in French. It cannot be an inference which ordinary English-speakers perform. It cannot be that on the basis of which an ordinary English-speaker's use of the sentence 'Shaftesbury is hilly' is justified. If we accept the idea of the Linguistic Given, then we can imagine an ordinary English-speaker 'taking in', in some way, in perception, something of which (S1) is a kind of translation. On this view, there is still room for the inference from (S1) to (S2) on the basis of (SsR) to be a significant, knowledge-advancing inference, even for an ordinary English-speaker, and for it to be the basis of an ordinary English-speaker's use of the sentence 'Shaftesbury is hilly' being justified. But if we do not accept the idea of the Linguistic Given—if we do not accept that there is an isomorphism between language (or at least English) and the world—it is not clear that we can make sense of this. The only way in which (S1) could present itself to an ordinary

---

[8] I assume here that someone does not cease to be a monolingual French-speaker just in virtue of knowing (in French) *one* rule like (SsR). Alternatively, one could take Colette to be an *otherwise* monolingual French-speaker.

English-speaker as something which could be used in an inference is precisely as something whose use is justified by (S2) on the basis of (SsR). That is, for an ordinary English-speaker, the inference seems to have to run the other way.

Here is another way of putting that. If we reject the idea of the Linguistic Given, and with it the idea that there is an isomorphism between language and the world, then coming to learn a first language will be coming to possess a disposition to recognize *non-inferentially* that uses of expressions of that language are correct or incorrect, simply on the basis of the way the world presents itself as being in experience.

At this point it is unclear that there is much more that we can do to explain the way in which the use of language is justified by the world. That may feel unsatisfying; but that sense of dissatisfaction is not itself a good reason to move back into an acceptance of the Linguistic Given and with it the view that there is an isomorphism between language and the world. It could only be a good reason if thinking that it would be explanatorily satisfying were a good reason for believing that the world is a certain way. But as we have seen, only an idealist could think that was a good reason.

References

Davidson, D. 2001a. 'Reality without reference', in D. Davidson, *Inquiries into Truth and Interpretation*, 2nd ed. (Oxford: OUP), 215-26.

Davidson, D. 2001b. 'The Inscrutability of Reference', in D. Davidson, *Inquiries into Truth and Interpretation*, 2nd ed. (Oxford: Oxford University Press), 227-42.

Keefe, R. 2000. *Theories of Vagueness* (Cambridge: CUP).

Kripke, S. 1979. 'A puzzle about belief', in A. Margalit (ed.), *Meaning and Use* (Dordrecht: Reidel), 239-83.

McDowell, J. 1985. 'Values and secondary qualities', in T. Honderich, (ed.), *Morality and Objectivity* (London: Routledge), 110-29.

McDowell, J. 1996. *Mind and World*, 2nd ed. (Cambridge, Mass.: Harvard University Press).

Quine, W. V. 1960. *Word and Object* (Cambridge, Mass.: MIT Press).

Tarski, A. 1956. 'The concept of truth in formalized languages', in A. Tarski, *Logic, Semantics, Metamathematics: Papers from 1923 to 1938* (Oxford: OUP), 152-278.

11

Representation, Alien Languages, and Linguistic Idealism

Matti Eklund

11.1 Alien Languages and Alien Metaphysics

Here is a question that strikes me as very deep and interesting: what kind of alien languages can there be, if any?[1]

By *alien language* I here mean a language that is different from familiar languages when it comes to semantics, which is so through being structurally different from familiar languages, and which is different more specifically in having a type of expression or a mode of composition not found in familiar languages. I focus on semantic differences as opposed to, for example, syntactic differences, in part because they are what is relevant to metaphysics. I stress structural differences, since the differences I am concerned with are not merely differences with respect to what objects and properties the languages have expressions for. And while some seemingly exotic languages could be different from familiar ones through lacking something that familiar languages have, the languages I want to focus on have added alien elements.

Why take an interest in the question whether there are alien languages? One kind of reason for doing so might be a general interest in the nature of representation. If one is interested in what kind of phenomenon representation is, one does well to consider not only the systems of representation that happen to be employed but also what other possible systems of representation there are. But what I will focus on here is metaphysics. So let me describe why the question of alien languages is of relevance to metaphysics. While philosophers working on metaphysics of course have defended very different theories of the world, their theories very much share the following basic structure: there are objects and they are certain ways and stand in certain relations. This basic structure, one might note, mirrors the structure of familiar languages as we

---

[1] In Eklund 2024 I discuss this question at length.

take them to be. We take the logical forms of familiar sentences to be such that those sentences contain singular terms, predicates of various adicities, and of course also connectives and quantifiers. Objects correspond to singular terms, ways things might be correspond to 1-place predicates, and ways in which things might be related correspond to n > 1-place predicates. There is a striking structural similarity between how we take languages to be and how we take the world to be. There seems to be a tacit reliance on a view—call it *the reflection view*—given which the structure of the world matches the structure of the languages we use.

One might ask sceptical questions about the reflection view. For example, it is not unreasonable to suspect that we take the world to have the structure we take it to have only because we employ the kind of language we employ: we use language built around sentences with familiar structure, for example singular term–predicate structure, we process information about the world using such tools, and as a result we see the world as having corresponding object–property (and objects-in-a-relation) structure.

Attending to this possibility also illustrates what an alien language might be. I introduced the notion of an alien language in abstract terms. But one kind of language that would be alien in the sense at issue is a language whose simple sentences are built up from something different from singular terms and predicates.

If there are alien languages of the kind at issue one can ask: might the world's structure be such that it is better captured by an alien language of that kind than by a familiar language.

Are there alien languages of the kind described? Well maybe so and maybe not. I won't attempt to settle that issue here. I will critically assess some considerations against the contention that there are, but I will not attempt to make a positive case.[2]

Even if there are alien languages, the question about metaphysics remains separate. In principle, there could be alien languages of the kind indicated while still there are independent reasons why the structure of the world can only be represented by familiar, non-alien languages and the reflection view is right. There could be good reasons why alien languages are not a good guide to metaphysics. And even if there cannot be alien languages of the kind indicated, that of course does not mean that the world has structure of the kind suggested by familiar languages. Another possibility is that the world's structure is such that it cannot be captured by any language at all, but is ineffable.

---

[2] However, in my 2024 I defend the idea.

Yet another possibility is that the world does not have 'structure' in the special sense indicated at all.

In this chapter, I won't get into much more detail than I have so far about what alien languages might be. And again, I won't attempt to reach a verdict on whether alien languages really are possible. My aim will be more limited and more modest: I will relate the issues regarding alien languages that I have mentioned to the question of *linguistic idealism*. As Richard Gaskin (2019) describes it, linguistic idealism is the view that 'the general structure of the world is asymmetrically dependent on a metaphysically (though not historically) prior fact about language'.[3] In general terms: the world has a structure which is metaphysically dependent on (something about) language. In various writings, Gaskin uses variations of the formulation that 'reality is a precipitate of language', and that is clearly in the same spirit.[4] The label 'linguistic idealism' has been used in other ways as well, but except where flagged I will here use 'linguistic idealism' as just indicated.

There are connections, obviously, between linguistic idealism and the considerations regarding alien languages and the structure of the world that I have presented. One immediate idea might be that given a certain simple form of linguistic idealism, it is not a live possibility that the world has alien structure. The thought would be this. We use language with familiar, non-alien structure. Given linguistic idealism, the structure of the world is dependent upon language. Given the most straightforward form such dependence can take—if we use language with a certain kind of structure, then the world must have structure that corresponds to the structure of our language—we can immediately conclude that, correspondingly, the world has familiar, non-alien structure. The reflection view is right. In another way, linguistic idealism and alien structure might still fit well together. The idea would be that given linguistic idealism, the world can easily have alien structure so long as alien languages are possible. All we need to do is to speak an alien language. On a non-idealist view where the world has its structure independently of what kind of language gets employed, things may seem more unforgiving.

The considerations just presented can be problematized. For one thing, even assuming that the structure of the world is dependent on language, that does not have to mean that the structure of world is dependent on *the language we speak*. The structure of the world could, for example, instead be dependent

---

[3] Gaskin 2019, 1325. (Quoted from the abstract for the article.)
[4] See, e.g., Gaskin 2019, 1325; 2021, vii.

on *what possible languages there are*. For another thing, it could be that the world's structure depends on language in something other than what I called the 'straightforward' way.

In what follows I will further explore the connections between linguistic idealism and the possibility of alien languages. Much of my discussion will take the form of a critical look at Gaskin's recent work on linguistic idealism. The reasons are two. First, Gaskin's discussions are the most prominent contemporary discussions of this view. Second, as we will see, specific themes that come up in Gaskin are such that the question of alien languages is highly relevant to them. While the explicit focus is on Gaskin, the aim is to make general points about the relationship between linguistic idealism and the issue of the possibility of alien languages. My aim is not a systematic exposition of Gaskin's view—many elements of his overall philosophical view will not be discussed—but only to bring up those themes that seem to me to be the most germane to my overall topic.

To put my cards on the table: I don't find linguistic idealism to be an attractive view. But my aim here will not to assess the view, but rather precisely to make points about the relationship between linguistic idealism and the possibility of alien languages.

11.2 Gaskin and Transcendentalism

Gaskin has discussed the issue of linguistic idealism in several places. It comes up in his book *The Unity of the Proposition* (2008), and it is of course a main theme in his book *Language and World: A Defence of Linguistic Idealism* (2021). But for much of my discussion I will focus on his article 'From the Unity of the Proposition to Linguisic Idealism' (2019). The reason is simple: the specific defense of linguistic idealism found in that article naturally invites questions about the possibility of certain kinds of alien languages.

In the course of his 2019 argument for linguistic idealism, Gaskin distinguishes between what he calls *empiricism* and *transcendentalism*. Both these views take as given that there is some sort of significant correspondence between the structure of the world and the structure of language. Empiricism is described as the view that this is so because the structure of language depends on the structure of the world (2019, 1334). As we will see, Gaskin also takes empiricism to entail that it is a contingent fact that the language we use is able to represent the world. According to transcendentalism '[l]anguage is competent because it *has to be* competent, and this for logical or metaphysical, not empirical, reasons. Anything that language could not describe would not be a world; the possibility of a world that is not representable by language can be ruled out a priori' (2019, 1334). Gaskin here speaks of 'competence' but it is clear from his discussion that what is at issue is what elsewhere in the article he calls *omnicompetence*: the ability to represent everything.

Transcendentalism obviously does not entail linguistic idealism, given that it does not say anything about what is dependent on what, but Gaskin still thinks that transcendentalism provides support for the view. One possible argument for linguistic idealism based on transcendentalism is that linguistic idealism provides the best explanation of the truth of transcendentalism. ('Why is there this guarantee that language competently represents the world, in the sense at issue?'—Because the way the world is, is determined by the way language is.) It may be useful to compare some views given which transcendentalism but not linguistic idealism is true. First, the world might be in a relevant sense *shapeless*—it may be an 'amorphous lump'—and as a result be such that sentences with any kind of semantic structure can successfully represent it. If the world is necessarily shapeless and this is something that can be ascertained a priori, then transcendentalism is true given this view, whether or not the world is the way it is because of language, as the linguistic idealist would have it. Second, the world might be, in a sense, maximally *rich* in structure: no matter what structure the sentences of some language might have, there is structure corresponding to such sentences. So long as this is so necessarily and this can be ascertained a priori, then transcendentalism is true also given this view, again whether or not the world is the way it is because of language. This all just goes to emphasize that transcendentalism does not immediately entail linguistic idealism. Generally, both empiricism as characterized by Gaskin and linguistic idealism involve claims to the effect that there is a dependence relation between the structure of language and the structure of the world. However, there need be no such dependence, and transcendentalism by itself implies nothing about there being any dependence.

I will pause on the argument for transcendentalism, which clearly is of significance itself whatever the fate of linguistic idealism. There are many questions that can be asked about how exactly how to understand transcendentalism in Gaskin's sense. Let me first remark on, just to set aside, one kind of issue. As characterized, transcendentalism at least involves the claim: It is a priori that necessarily, every way the world can be is representable by language.

This claim by itself is compatible with the idea that it is by synthetic a priori insight that we come to see that every way the world can be is representable by language. Gaskin's talk of 'logical' reasons suggests to me that he has in mind something more specific. But let me not pause on what this something might be. I will simply focus on the claim just isolated.

A different question, one which will occupy me more, is what 'language' means, as used by Gaskin in the characterization of transcendentalism. When Gaskin uses the general 'language', does he mean *every* language? Or *some* language? Or something else? I will address the question what Gaskin means by 'language' in tandem with investigating the argument for transcendentalism that Gaskin offers. Here is that argument, stated in general terms:

Version 1
(1) Language is omnicompetent: no matter how the world is, it can be represented in language.
(2) This can be explained in one of two ways: the empiricist way or the transcendentalist way.
(3) Empiricism, understood as the claim that (1) just happens to be true, is unworkable.
(4) So we should be transcendentalists: it is a priori that necessarily, every way the world can be is representable by language.

Of course, Gaskin says more about his argument than is captured in this first bare bones presentation, but let me introduce details piecemeal.

What is meant by 'language' here? If 'language' meant *all* languages, premise (1) would surely be false. Not all languages are omnicompetent. Two possibilities regarding how instead to understand 'language' immediately suggest themselves. One is that 'language' means our *actual* language; another is that 'language' means *some language or other*. Running the argument with the first of these two ways of construing 'language' yields seeming oddities. How are we to understand the transcendentalism? It sounds odd to say it is a priori that necessarily *our* language has to be omnicompetent, if not all languages are omnicompetent. For if not all languages are omnicompetent, then we are simply lucky to find ourselves in the position that we speak one that is. There certainly is more to say about this and I will return to this in Section 11.3.[5] For

---

[5] A different issue about 'our language' concerns the fact that we do not use only one language. Even one speaker can master several languages. One way to get around this is to treat all languages now used by at least one human as together comprising one master language, and 'our language' is this master language.

now let me just note that it appears more reasonable to understand 'language' to mean *some* language:

Version 2
(1) Language is omnicompetent: no matter how the world is, it can be represented in *some* language.
(2) This can be explained in one of two ways: the empiricist way or the transcendentalist way.
(3) Empiricism, understood as the claim that (1) just happens to be true, is unworkable.
(4) So we should be transcendentalists: it is a priori that necessarily, no matter how the world is, it is representable in some language.

Version 2 seems more reasonable, whatever in the end its proper fate. But it is somewhat hard to see how establishing transcendentalism in the sense at issue in this reconstruction of the argument is relevant to linguistic idealism. Even if there is a guarantee of the kind indicated that the world is representable in some language, it is compatible with the argument that there are languages with different kinds of structure and it is left open just which kind of language the world is representable in. So in what sense is the structure of the world supposed to be dependent on the structure of language?

So far when discussing possible construals of Gaskin's argument I have done so in abstraction from Gaskin's own discussion. Let me now add more detail from that discussion. The added detail will also help with the connection to linguistic idealism. Gaskin speaks of 'language' exhibiting 'function–argument structure' (2019, 1329). The idea is something like that the mode of composition found in language is function application. This idea is sometimes called *Frege's conjecture*.[6] The supposed function–argument structure is paradigmatically exhibited in simple subject–predicate sentences. The subject expresses the argument and the predicate expresses the function. On Gaskin's view, as we will see, one finds subject–predicate structure in all languages.

From Gaskin's discussion it is clear that the claim that language exhibits function–argument structure is important for him. For example, in the abstract for the article, he says 'Language exhibits a function–argument structure, but does it do so because it is reflecting how things are in the world, or does the relation of dependence run in the other direction (or in neither)?' (2019, 1325). The construal of the argument for transcendentalism that

---

[6] See Heim and Kratzer 1998, 13.

we have ended up with so far says nothing about function–argument structure. Here is yet another construal (where 'FA-language' is short for *function–argument language*, and where that in turn is a language whose sentences exhibit function–argument structure):[7]

Version 3
(1) FA-language is omnicompetent in the sense that no matter how the world is, it can be represented in some FA-language.
(2) This can be explained in one of two ways: the empiricist way or the transcendentalist way.
(3) Empiricism, understood as the claim that (1) just happens to be true, is unworkable.
(4) So we should be transcendentalists: it is a priori that necessarily, no matter how the world is, it is representable in some FA-language.

Version 3 hews more closely to Gaskin's actual discussion.

If all languages—all possible languages—are FA-languages, as is Gaskin's view, then the differences between the two last construals of Gaskin's argument are of no consequence. Suppose, however, that not all languages are FA-languages. Maybe there are alien languages of the kind earlier indicated, and some alien languages lack FA-structure. If so, the differences matter. It could be that even if it is metaphysically necessary that the world is representable in some language or other, it is not metaphysically necessary that the world is representable in an FA-language. If languages can have different 'structures'—for example, some are FA-languages and some are not—then even if (somehow) there is a guarantee that the world's structure is representable in some language or other, there needn't be a guarantee that, for some given structure that a language has, the world has that structure specifically. The world could turn out to be one way; it could turn out to be another. But if so, then premise (1) can be resisted. And more generally, there is no reason to think the world's structure is imposed on it by language.

The hypothesis that there are languages with different structures, including non-FA-languages, is not immediately a hypothesis to the effect that there are alien languages. Maybe already some sentences of familiar languages fail to have function–argument structure: witness one natural understanding of

---

[7] Speaking of FA-languages this way in principle slides over a difficulty. Do all sentences of these languages exhibit function–argument structure, or do only paradigmatic ones do? But I am assuming that Gaskin takes all descriptive sentences to exhibit such structure.

sentences like 'it is raining' where 'it' is a mere dummy subject. But while this is a possibility I will for ease of exposition speak as if non-FA-languages are alien in the sense indicated.

Gaskin does have a separate argument for the specific claim that the world is representable in an FA-language. This argument comes up in connection with his rejection of empiricism, premise (3) in my presentation of the argument. Gaskin says,

> the supposition that our confidence in language's competence might be merely inductively based is unacceptable: it makes theoretical room for a scenario in which there is supposedly a stretch of reality to which language does not apply; but if language really does not apply to it, how can it be a stretch of reality? For something to be a stretch of reality there must be a way things are there: but saying that much already involves a minimal application of language, and we are already asserting that the subject–predicate distinction—at least the analytical subject–predicate distinction, if not the grammatical one—applies to our would-be stretch of reality. So the empiricist position is self-undermining: it is obliged to try and make sense of a situation that in fact does not make sense.
>
> ... [T]he problem for our envisaged empiricists is this: they have to be able to make sense of the possibility that there might be a scenario in which things really are a certain way in a region of the world, but in which there is no sentence, or set of sentences, saying that things are that way, so describing that stretch of reality truly. But the minimal sentence 'Things are, in this scenario, a certain way' will itself do the trick of (minimally) describing that stretch of reality, assuming that the reference of the demonstrative is appropriately secured. (2019, 1335)

No matter how the world might be, it is some way or other. But so long as it is some way or other, the 'analytical subject–predicate distinction' applies. We can still represent the world using the 'minimal sentence': things are, in this scenario, a certain way.

Gaskin distinguishes between a 'grammatical' subject–predicate distinction and an 'analytic' one. Roughly speaking, the first is superficial and the latter concerns a deeper level of analysis, what is often called logical form. Gaskin helpfully illustrates, using the example 'Someone killed Kennedy'. 'Someone' is what 'traditional grammar' identifies as the grammatical subject, Gaskin says. But since Frege, there is a tradition of analysing 'someone' as a second-level predicate, and thus to find a deeper level of analysis where this sentence differs in structure from 'Oswald killed Kennedy'.[8] I prefer to speak of a singular term/predicate distinction but will here use Gaskin's terminology.

This argument of Gaskin's does not address the question whether there also can be *non*-FA-languages. Claiming that no matter how some part or aspect of the world can be it is representable in FA-language is compatible with saying that it is also representable in some non-FA-language.

I think that Gaskin's argument for the claim that the world is representable in an FA-language is problematic, both for reasons having to do with details and for more interesting theoretical reasons. First, some reasons having to do with the details. Gaskin's 'minimal sentence' uses indexical and quantificational language. Consider first the 'this' in 'this scenario'. There will be problems with securing a determinate reference for 'this', so that the sentence really says of some specific scenario that things are a certain way in it. And then there is the apparent quantification in 'a certain way'. In what sense do I describe or represent some situation when saying that in that situation things are 'a certain way', as opposed to saying, of some way, that the situation is that way? Compare the exchange: 'Describe the woman you saw!'—'Well, she was a certain way.' Extremely general quantificational characterizations like these are at most degenerate cases of descriptions.

Suppose that possible complications like these can be satisfactorily dealt with. Still, a different complication remains, and I think this complication is more significant. (The label 'complication' is chosen with care. What I go on to argue does not really cast doubt on the thesis that Gaskin defends, that the world is representable in FA-language. Rather, it casts doubt on whether this thesis is strong enough for his purposes. I will get back to this only after having raised the complication at issue.)

Consider first some warm-up exercises. Take the state of affairs represented by the sentence 'Socrates is wise'. One could in principle use an unstructured sentence 'S' to stand for that state of affairs. For example, this sentence might be introduced by stipulation. Then 'S' is true iff Socrates is wise, and moreover, 'S' represents the state of affairs that Socrates is wise. But while 'S' does represent that state of affairs, one may think that 'Socrates is wise' along some relevant dimension does a better job of representing it, having a structure that is parallel to the structure we intuitively ascribe to that state of affairs: corresponding to the object Socrates we have the singular term 'Socrates' and corresponding to the property of being wise we have the predicate 'is wise'.

---

[8] Gaskin 2019, 1332.

Using terminology that is sometimes used for this end, let us say that while 'S' represents the state of affairs in question, only 'Socrates is wise' *perspicuously* represents it.[9] Given a distinction between representation and perspicuous representation, the possibility opens up that even if Gaskin is right that no matter how the world may be it can be represented in FA-language, the world may not always be perspicuously representable in FA-language.

Here is another example illustrating the same idea. Compare the sentences 'Socrates is wise' and 'Socrates instantiates wisdom'. Again we may think the sentences represent the same state of affairs, and again we may think that one of them better reflects the structure of this state of affairs. Whichever it is, that sentence is the one that perspicuously represents the state of affairs in question.

One can certainly reject the distinction between perspicuous representation and merely true representation: I shall get back to this point shortly. But for the time being, I will treat it as in good standing.

If there are alien languages of the kind indicated, and if sentences can represent truly without doing so perspicuously, then it can be the case that a familiar kind of sentence and an alien sentence both represent the same state of affairs, but that there is a separate question which sentence, if any, more perspicuously represents this state of affairs.

The distinction between mere representation and perspicuous representation is relevant for how to think of transcendentalism. I have already distinguished between different transcendentalist theses through distinguishing between different things that might be meant by 'language'. We get a new set of theses through distinguishing between mere representation and perspicuous representation. Even if, no matter how the world may be, it can be represented in an FA-language, it is a different question whether, no matter how the world may be, it can be perspicuously represented in such a language. Consider then the following reasoning:

In addition to FA-languages, there are non-FA-languages.
Some metaphysically possible scenarios are most perspicuously represented by FA-languages and some are most perspicuously represented by non-FA-languages.
So there is no guarantee, regarding any actual scenario, that whichever language we speak will be the kind of language that most perspicuously represents it.

---

[9] See, for example, O'Leary-Hawthorne and Cortens 1995 and Russell 2018. It is a separate task to describe what exactly distinguishes perspicuous representation from non-perspicuous representation.

But then there is no guarantee that our kind of language is the right kind of language for perspicuously representing the world.

This reasoning assumes that there are non-FA-languages. Gaskin rejects that assumption, as we will see. But while the possible existence of non-FA-languages is an interesting issue in its own right, the point I just made does not actually require this assumption. One might instead just argue as follows:

Even if there is a guarantee that an FA-language successfully *represents* the world, there is no guarantee that an FA-language *perspicuously* represents the world.

It could be that no language is such that the structure of its sentences correspond to the world's structure. Perhaps the only representational systems that do so correspond are non-linguistic. Or perhaps the world's structure cannot be perspicuously represented at all.

I said that I was going to describe a *complication* regarding Gaskin's claim that the world is representable by FA-language. I haven't argued that the claim is false. What I have argued is that there is a separate issue of whether an FA-language can perspicuously represent the world. The reason this is a relevant complication is that if there is such a separate issue, then it seems that what matters for, for example, the discussion of linguistic idealism is perspicuous representation. If an FA-language represents the world but another kind of language is what is needed to perspicuously represent the world, then—to relate back to the characterization of linguistic idealism—it would be odd to say that the world's structure is determined by the FA-language. If the world's structure is plausibly determined by any kind of language at all, it would be the kind of language that *perspicuously* represents the world.

As already indicated, one might of course want to reject the distinction between perspicuous representation and mere representation that I have appealed to. It is by no means obvious that this distinction is in good standing. There are two ways to reject the distinction.

One way is through saying that a sentence is true only if its structure matches that of the world in the way that I have said that sentences perspicuously representing the world do. If this is so, a sentence manages to truly represent the world only if it perspicuously represents the world. The bar for truth is high. This view is what Agustín Rayo calls *metaphysicalism* (2013, 5–13). Rayo rejects the view, and I think that it is implausible myself. But suppose metaphysicalism is true. Would this help Gaskin's argument for transcendentalism? I do not see that it does. For given metaphysicalism's strong demands on successful representation, the question arises: why think, given these strong demands on representation, that a sentence like Gaskin's minimal sentence manages to represent the world? In an intuitive sense it may represent the world, but we have left the intuitive sense behind.

Turn then to the other way one might reject a distinction between perspicuous representation and mere representation. One might say that perspicuous representation is a chimera. All there is, is mere representation. If Gaskin takes this line, then he can reject all objections that rely on the supposed distinction, while avoiding the problems that metaphysicalism invites.

But then consider a different problem nearby, a problem that remains even if the distinction is rejected. Even if there is a guarantee that no matter how some stretch of world may be some sentence of an FA-language represents it, what if some sentence of a *non*-FA-language *also* represents this stretch of world? This does not present a problem regarding the omnicompetence of FA-languages, as this has been characterized. It suffices for such omnicompetence that FA-languages *can* represent the world. But if a stretch of world can be represented both in an FA-way and in a non-FA-way, what should we say about the structure of that stretch of world? Given that it can be represented in an FA-way, it seems wrong to say that it is non-FA-structure. Given that it can be represented in a non-FA-way, it seems wrong to say that it is FA-structure.

I have been assuming that there are non-FA-languages. As already noted, Gaskin argues against this possibility. Central to his argument is the distinction between a grammatical and an analytical subject–predicate asymmetry. He notes correctly that one can come up with languages without a grammatical subject–predicate asymmetry, but that in such languages there can still be what he calls an analytical subject–predicate asymmetry. Here's a toy example illustrating the point. There could be a language all of whose sentences consist of names, but which are such that what the sentences express is that the referents of the names are identical. In the sentences of this language—for example 'Mark Samuel'—grammatical subject and predicate cannot be distinguished. But this language still seems to employ an *analytical* subject–predicate distinction: being identical with each other is predicated of the referents of the names, Mark and Samuel.

Gaskin correctly notes that one should not argue from the point that languages may fail to display a grammatical asymmetry of that kind to the conclusion that they may also fail to display an analytical symmetry of that kind. But that does not by itself show that there must always be an analytical subject–predicate asymmetry. Gaskin seems to think that it is plain that all languages must exhibit an analytical subject–predicate asymmetry even if they do not need to exhibit a grammatical subject–predicate asymmetry. And he takes this to entail that all languages must exhibit function–argument structure: they are FA-languages. It is not clear to me exactly what Gaskin takes to support these positive claims. Can there not be languages which even lack an analytical subject–predicate distinction?

One possible thought is that no matter what a given language may be like, it is still possible to analyse it as having 'analytical subject–predicate structure', whence all languages must exhibit such structure. One general question about such a line of thought is: in what sense is it possible to analyse a sentence that way? Distinguish between a weak claim and a strong claim. The weak claim is that such an analysis gets the structure of the sentence sufficiently nearly right that it is serviceable. The strong claim is that this analysis represents the structure that the sentence really has. I can easily see what could be used to support the weak claim, whatever in the end its fate. It is harder to see what would support the strong claim. Here is an example that illustrates the problem with the strong claim. I assume that it is possible to represent the content of a pictorial representation using a set of ordinary subject–predicate sentences. But the conclusion that the pictorial representation in question *thereby* has subject–predicate form would seem to be hasty. Perhaps one might indeed ascribe subject–predicate form to pictorial representation, but not by virtue of this argument alone. Now, pictorial representation is not linguistic, and Gaskin's claim only concerns linguistic representation. But the point is general. The argument that would be too hasty in the case of pictorial representation would be similarly hasty in the case of superficially alien kinds of linguistic representation.[10]

There is another distinction worth drawing. One claim is that a sentence can be analysed (in the strong sense) as having a given kind of structure; a different claim is that it can be analysed (in the strong sense) *only* as having that kind of structure. One theoretical possibility is that a given sentence can have multiple kinds of decomposition. If a sentence can have different decompositions then even if it has subject–predicate structure, or more generally function–argument structure, given one kind of decomposition, it is a further claim that it has such structure under each decomposition.

---

[10] Compare the parallel discussion in ch. 4 of Eklund 2024.

11.3 Languages We Cannot Make Sense Of

Some may think that there are principled problems concerning the idea of there being languages we cannot make sense of. There is, for example, a broadly Davidsonian view to the effect that, somehow or other, there cannot be such languages. Some may find that Davidsonian view attractive, and they may further think that the view rules out alien languages of the kind I have brought up, including non-FA-languages.

One could accept the Davidsonian view described, but think that we can make sense of alien languages of the relevant kind. There are then two claims to keep track of:

(1) There cannot be a language we cannot make sense of;
(2) We cannot make sense of the supposed alien languages of the kind at issue.

Why accept (1) in the first place? Here is one thought one may have. One element of Davidson's own overall view is a kind of interpretivism. What the sentences used by a speaker mean is what a suitable radical interpreter would take them to mean. However, this interpretivism is not by itself sufficient to justify (1). To get to that view one also needs to add that the radical interpreter must not be assumed to have at their disposal linguistic resources we cannot make sense of.

In Davidson's famous paper 'On the Very Idea of a Conceptual Scheme' (1974), a main point is that a theory of meaning for a language must take the form of a Tarskian truth theory, and to state such a theory for a language L one must have the resources to translate the sentences of L into one's own language. But this point on its own yields no more than that to give a theory of meaning for L one needs to be able to translate sentences of L into one's own language. This obviously does not entail that sentences of L *lack* meaning unless one can translate them into one's own language. Again (1) seems unsupported.

So I see no good Davidsonian reason to accept (1). Already this suffices to set aside the Davidsonian line of argument. But what about (2)? Is it really true that we cannot make sense of an alien language? Briefly, I just see no reason why not. In general, we can come to understand new things, including things structured differently from what we are used to. Why would matters be different with languages, and linguistic structure? However, I suppose a Davidsonian would find it natural to understand the question whether we can make sense of an alien language as one of translation: can we translate an alien language into a familiar one? I don't think that is the best understanding. Sometimes we can come to understand things that are genuinely novel and have no equivalent in our earlier conceptual repertoire. But suppose we go along with Davidson and understand the question as one of translatability. Even so I see reason to resist (2). One must keep in mind that translatability can amount to different things. Let a language *L1* be *strictly* translatable into another *L2* if and only if each expression of *L1* can be matched up to an expression of *L2* with the exact same meaning. Let a language L1 be *loosely* translatable into a language *L2* if and only of each sentence of *L1* can be matched up to a sentence of *L2* which has a sufficiently similar meaning that the translation is serviceable: a speaker relying on the translation would get by well enough. Then even if an alien language were not strictly translatable into a familiar language it could well be loosely translatable into one. Is it strict or loose translatabily that goes with making sense of a language? I think the default view must be that it is loose translatability that is relevant, assuming that translatability is what it is relevant to consider in the first place: that is because, for example, it is not obvious that different natural languages—of which we can make good sense—*are* strictly translatable into each other.

Let me now turn from Davidson to Gaskin. Gaskin (2021) marshals some considerations in favour of what I call the broadly Davidsonian view, but his arguments are somewhat different from Davidson's own.

> We find ourselves forced ... into a sort of transcendental anthropocentrism. We can see that there are facts which bees cannot grasp (as well as facts which they can grasp), but the argument which tries to persuade us that, by parity of reasoning, there are or could be facts which we cannot grasp stumbles over a crucial asymmetry between bees and us: the concept of fact belongs to *us*, not to the *bees*. It is *our* concept, a product of *our* language. Symmetry between the bees and us would only be restored if the facts which we supposedly could not grasp but which, say, superbeings could, were governed by their (the superbeings') concept of fact, not ours. But that can never be, for the reason that, to put it crudely, if the superbeings' facts were not also our facts, then they would not be facts at all. We are the ones who call the conceptual shots; after all, we invented the concept of concept. There are thus limits, set by us, on what can count as a concept; similarly, there are limits on what can count as a language, and again those limits are set by us. (2021, 243)

Gaskin goes on to allow that there can be some facts which are 'inaccessible' to us, but those facts are 'constructs of objects and operations that are nameable and describable by us' (2021, 243). Despite the qualification the underlying point still remains: since the concept *concept*, the concept *fact* and the concept *language* are our creations it is we who set the limits on what can fall under these concepts.

One response to Gaskin involves taking seriously the lessons from the arguments for externalism in the philosophy of language and mind. We can introduce a concept by the (implicit) stipulation that it is to apply to whatever belongs to the same natural kind as certain representative samples. Paradigm examples are the concepts picked out by 'water' and 'gold'. Even though natural-kind concepts are our creations, they are creations we throw out into the world, seeing what, possibly beyond our ken, they latch onto. 'Fact' can express a concept that in this regard is like natural-kind concepts.

There are other responses to Gaskin that are not directly related to lessons from the arguments from externalism. Even if these concepts are our creations, surely it does not follow that in order for something to fall under one of these concepts, it must be possible for us to ascertain that it does. To insist otherwise would seem to be to rely on a general assumption that nothing can fall under one of our concepts without its being possible for us to ascertain that it does. This is a verificationist assumption, and I just do not see why it should be taken as plausible, whether generally or in the specific case of language and thought. However, set doubts about the verificationism to the side. Even given the verificationist assumption, alien languages, including non-FA-languages, are not excluded. To use the verificationism to exclude such languages one also needs the assumption that we could not ascertain that something which is in fact a non-FA-language (or would be one if it is a language in the first place) is a language. And just why couldn't we? Imagine first that we come across some creatures using some superficially language-like system. They utter noises to each other in systematic ways and seemingly as a result they engage successfully in cooperative endeavours. Even if we cannot make head or tail of what the expression-like things of their language-like system might mean or even what logical categories they belong to, we can take ourselves to have evidence that they do have meaning (otherwise how can they be so successful?) and that their expressions do belong to some logical categories or other. We can recognize that there is a system to the inscriptions and utterances they produce even if we cannot figure out what this system might be, and even if we are wholly unable to figure this out. This is just like in the case of non-representational physical systems. I can recognize that something I encounter in nature is a 'system' and there is some systematic account of how it works, even if I am completely unable to figure out just how it works. We cannot obtain conclusive verification that this language-like system is a non-FA-language, but we can have good reason to accept such a claim nonetheless.

11.4 The Primacy of the Sentence

Let me now turn to another theme. As mentioned, Gaskin discusses linguistic idealism at length also elsewhere (2008, 2021). The focus there is sometimes on the primacy of the sentence. Let me again quote Gaskin at length:

> There are two approaches [...] which both demand to be recognized, but which may seem to be in conflict with one another: the perspective of linguistic idealism and the perspective of empirical realism. According to the first of these perspectives, sense and reference are essentially *derived* notions. Intelligible symbolic language is the given, and the senses and referents of items of symbolic language are theoretically derived posits, precipitated by a correct account of the meaningfulness of those items: put otherwise, the levels of sense and reference are transcendentally deduced by the semantic theorist as required for a correct theoretical understanding of the meaningfulness of symbolic language. Even before that, the phenomenon of creative language use forces us to find structure and compositionality in language, and in order to model this aspect of language we need to discern fundamental components of meaningful language—the basic building blocks out of which everything else is constructed. Having done that, we proceed to assign semantic values (referents) to the components of language we have discerned and to their combinations. In pursuing this bipartite strategy we will be able to show how the meanings of complex linguistic structures (in the first instance, sentences) are functionally dependent on the semantic values we assign to relatively simple components. *We might put the perspective of linguistic idealism by saying that sentences are the primary datum, and that theoretically posited entities are derived in two directions, horizontally and vertically: horizontally (that is, at the level of symbolic language), we derive the notion of semantically significant parts of sentences (words, phrases, clauses); vertically (descending the semantic hierarchy), we derive the referents of sentences and of their semantically significant parts.* (2008, 42–3. The italicization of the last part is mine.)

There is a focus here on whole sentences, and what I will discuss in this section is how this focus relates to the themes that have come up so far. In the italicized part at the end, Gaskin provides a characterization of linguistic idealism. I will shortly turn to how this characterization relates to the one I have thus far operated with. It should be clear that the relationship is not obvious. But first let me briefly pause on another issue.

I think that the italicized part is ambiguous in a crucial way. Talk of 'posits' can be understood either *epistemically* or *metaphysically*. Understood epistemically, to say that something is a posit is just to say that it is a thing whose existence we have reason to believe in based on other, more immediate data. To say that something is a posit in a metaphysical sense can be understood to mean that it is merely a convenient myth, or, more moderately, that it is metaphysically dependent on non-posits. Either way, to say that something is a posit in a metaphysical sense is to say something about its metaphysical status, as opposed to our reasons for believing in it.

Start with the epistemic understanding. To say that something is a posit in the epistemic sense is not to say anything about its metaphysical status. We may (for example) posit subatomic entities because of how they help explain macroscopic phenomena we observe, while holding that the entities thus posited are as real and fundamental as anything. Such entities are then taken to be posits in the epistemic sense but not in the metaphysical sense. Now to say that semantically significant parts of sentences and their referents are posits in this sense may be made plausible but is hardly relevant to anything worth the label linguistic idealism. The claim may be made plausible: one might start with the view that it is by the use of sentences that we say something, and insofar as we have reason to believe in theoretically significant parts of sentences, and insofar as we have reason to believe that some such parts refer, that is because this helps explain the use and meaning of whole sentences. But that this is the epistemic order of priority says nothing about what is metaphysically dependent on what—in particular, it is compatible with the view that the referents of subsentential expressions come first in the metaphysical order of explanation. But then it says nothing about linguistic idealism, either, as we have hitherto understood that doctrine, following its treatment in Gaskin's 2019 article. Of course, and as mentioned earlier, 'linguistic idealism' has been used as a label for many things. But the substantive point is: no claim about *epistemic* priorities promises to be relevant for any claims about whether 'the general structure of the world is asymmetrically dependent on a metaphysically (though not historically) prior fact about language' (to repeat Gaskin's 2019 characterization of idealism), for such claims are about metaphysical dependence.

Gaskin speaks of what is 'derived' from sentences. That way of speaking has a somewhat epistemic flavour—we come to know of other things on the basis of our knowledge of sentences—but the considerations just presented show that Gaskin's talk of posits still is best understood metaphysically. I assume, then, that the best understanding of this talk is that the 'posits' are real but metaphysically dependent on non-posits. What are we to say about this idea? Note first an unclarity. What exactly is it that the referents of sentences and their semantically significant parts would be metaphysically dependent on? Is it simply *the sentences*, that is, the mere existence of the sentences, or is it the *truth* of the sentences? Gaskin's actual formulation suggests the former. But how could the existence of, for example, Donald Trump be metaphysically determined by the existence of any sentences, including sentences containing the name 'Donald Trump'? An immediate response is that no putative sentence containing the name 'Donald Trump' could be *meaningful* if Donald Trump did not exist: maybe the meaningfulness of a name requires that the name refers. This is a theme in Gaskin's work, for example in his 2021. However, that only establishes a *necessary* connection between Trump's existence and the meaningfulness of the putative sentences. It is a further step to go on to say that Trump's existence depends on the meaningfulness of the sentences and not vice versa. Instead of saying that Trump exists because 'Donald Trump' is meaningful one can for example say that 'Donald Trump' is meaningful because Trump exists.

Turn then to the view that the referents are somehow metaphysically dependent on the *truth* of certain sentences. For example, given that 'Donald Trump is a Presidential candidate' is true, Donald Trump must exist; and moreover, the claim would be, it is because the sentence is true that Trump exists. But again I have questions. What about the truth of sentences in the first place? The natural view is surely that the truth of a true sentence, for example 'snow is white', is not fundamental but depends on what it is about, in this case snow's being white. The point to keep firmly in mind is that to say that is a fundamental fact that a is F is not the same as to say that it is a fundamental fact that 'a is F' is true. It is the latter kind of fact that Gaskin would take to be fundamental, on the interpretation now explored. It is much more plausible to hold that even on the assumption that subsentential parts of sentences and the referents thereof are metaphysically dependent on sentences and their truth, the truth of the sentences is in turn metaphysically dependent on how the world is.

Consider then a supposed idealist view according to which the truth of sentences does depend on how the world is. There is no vicious circularity in such a view, so long as one does not in turn spell out 'how the world is' in terms of facts about reference, such as facts about which entities serve as referents of subsentential parts. But how does this view relate to linguistic idealism as we have discussed it earlier, the thesis that 'the general structure of the world is asymmetrically dependent on a metaphysically (though not historically) prior fact about language'? If one simply understands linguistic idealism as the general thesis that *the world* is dependent on language, there would be an obvious conflict between the view characterized and linguistic idealism. For that general thesis appears to be incompatible with the truth of sentences being dependent on how the world is. But Gaskin's characterization of linguistic idealism leaves wiggle room, given the specific reference to *structure*: the claim is not that the world generally is dependent on language but only that the 'general structure' of the world is. However, that said, the view described still does not make good on Gaskin's quoted claim that 'sentences are the primary datum'. If the truth of sentences is metaphysically dependent on the world that claim is plainly false, understood as a claim about the metaphysical priority of sentences.

11.5 Alien Languages and the Primacy of the Sentence

Return now to the issue of alien languages. To what extent is the possibility of the alien relevant to the linguistic idealism thesis at issue in Gaskin (2008), where the focus is on the thesis of the primacy of the sentence? Insofar as that thesis just amounts to the claim

> (Truth-determination) What sentences are true depends on how the world is, and the truth of sentences in turn determines what the referents of semantically significant parts of sentences are

then the possibility of alien languages of the kind so far considered is hardly relevant at all. The question whether what sentences are true depends on how the world that they are about is seems independent of the question whether there are alien languages, for example non-FA-languages. And the question whether there are non-FA-languages likewise seems independent of the question whether the truth of sentences in turn determines what the referents of semantically significant parts of sentences are. The possibility of such alien languages is only relevant to some more specific theses. For example, consider a possible view that affirms not only the general thesis just stated but also (for example) that the referents of subsentential parts are all and only referents of singular terms and predicates. This view assumes that for all sentences of all possible languages, the only subsentential parts that have referents are singular terms and predicates—and it is relevant to this claim whether some true sentences have other kinds of decomposition.

So far the kinds of alien languages that have been considered are ones that somehow differ from familiar languages at the subsentential level. But if we are taking seriously the idea of alien languages, should we not also consider the possibility of *alternatives to sentences*? Might some possible language be such that instead of sentences, properly assessed in terms of truth and falsity, it has sentences*, properly assessed in terms of truth* and falsity*?

What might such alternatives be? I will here be brief and just indicate a few routes to explore.[11] First, in the literature on truth various theories of truth have been proposed—different correspondence theories, different deflationary theories, and different epistemic and pragmatic theories—and even a theory that fails to describe the truth concept we actually employ can still successfully describe some possible truth-like concept—call it *truth**. One can then envisage languages, and practices of using languages, centred on truth* instead of truth. Second, in the same vein, even if there are good reasons for thinking that truth does not admit of degrees, some possible truth-*like* concept *might* admit of degrees. Even if those who have postulated degrees of truth, for example in attempts to capture the phenomenon of vagueness, fail to adequately represent our actual truth concept, they may successfully describe some possible truth-*like* concept. Third, compare pictures. It is often held that pictures are properly assessed in terms of *accuracy* instead of truth, and that they can be more or less accurate. The standard of correctness for pictures is then something that comes in degrees. Now, pictorial representation is something other than linguistic representation, and even given what is suggested regarding pictures it might be strenuously resisted that the standard of correctness for linguistic representations might be something that comes in degrees. But never mind. Even if there is that difference between pictorial and linguistic representation one can appeal to the example of pictures to make a point related to principles like (Truth-determination). Even if there are true sentences and those sentences have constituents with thus-and-such features, there can be other kinds of correct representations of the world, whether linguistic or not. If those representations in turn have structure one can ask: which structure does the world have—structure corresponding to true sentences? or corresponding to representations of other kinds? or both? This kind of question

---

[11] For further discussion, see ch. 10 of Eklund 2024.

parallels a question I raised earlier, in connection with FA-languages: even if sentences of FA-languages are true and manage to represent the world, what structure should we say the world has if there also are true sentences of non-FA-languages?

11.6 Concluding Remarks

My theme here has been alien languages and linguistic idealism. Specifically, I have brought up some themes from Gaskin's work and discussed how the possibility of alien languages problematizes claims that Gaskin makes. I have not here attempted to mount a full-scale defence of the idea of alien languages (although I have responded to some objections to the idea) but instead focused mainly on what the consequences might be, given that there are such languages. Along the way I have sought to get clearer on what linguistic idealism and some of the arguments for that view should be taken to be.

References

Davidson, D. 1974. 'On the very idea of a conceptual scheme', *Proceedings and Addresses of the American Philosophical Association* 47, 5–20.
Eklund, M. 2024. *Alien Structure: Language and Reality* (Oxford: OUP).
Gaskin, R. 2008. *The Unity of the Proposition* (Oxford: OUP).
Gaskin, R. 2019. 'From the unity of the proposition to linguistic idealism', *Synthese* 196: 1325–42.
Gaskin, R. 2021. *Language and World: A Defence of Linguistic Idealism* (London: Routledge).
Heim, I. and Kratzer A. 1998. *Semantics in Generative Grammar* (Oxford: Blackwell).
O'Leary-Hawthorne, J. and Cortens A. 1995. 'Towards ontological nihilism', *Philosophical Studies* 79, 143–65.
Rayo, A. 2013. *The Construction of Logical Space* (Oxford: OUP).
Russell, J. S. 2018. 'Quality and quantifiers', *Australasian Journal of Philosophy* 96, 562–77.

12
Linguistic Idealism and the Genealogy of Negation

Richard Gaskin

12.1 Negation as Exclusion

According to linguistic idealism, in the version of that doctrine which I favour, the world is constituted by language, in the sense that the shape of worldly structures is, at the deepest level and as a matter of their essence, determined by the shape of linguistic structures. This is a transcendentalist doctrine: of course, the world did not spring into existence with the evolution of human (or any empirical) language; rather, the idea is that for the world to exist it must be expressible—its nature must be describable—in language, the necessity of this relation in turn necessitating an idealistic gloss on the relation between language and the world. A world-describing language need not be human language—it need not even be empirically realized—but it must be accessible to human language and human mindedness in the sense that it is, or would be, mediately if not immediately intelligible to us humans.[1]

In this chapter I am going to argue that the linguistic idealist's case can be helped out by an examination of the way in which negation works. Let us start by asking quite generally: where does negation come from and what is its point? Consider these passages from Wittgenstein's *Big Typescript*:

> How can the word 'not' negate? Well, but do we have a concept of negation other than negation with a sign? Yes, we can think of something like: impediment, rejecting gesture, exclusion. (2005, 87, tr. adapted)

---

[1] See further the Introduction to this volume, Sections 1.4–1.5; more detail in Gaskin 2008 and 2021.

Again:

> If I say [to someone], for example, 'You aren't allowed to come in', then it's natural to accompany these words by stepping in front of the door and holding it closed. But it would not be so obviously natural if I opened the door for him as I uttered those words. As they are understood in this case, these words obviously have something to do with that action. The action is an illustration of the words, so to speak.... (2005, 88–9, tr. adapted)

In the *Philosophical Investigations* Wittgenstein remarks that 'Negation, one might say, is an excluding, dismissing gesture' (1977, I, §550). The idea that at the core of negation we find exclusion is an intuitive one,[2] and it makes a good starting point for our inquiry in the sense that it does not appear to beg any questions in the linguistic idealist's favour.

Quite the reverse, indeed: the thought that negation is, *au fond*, constituted by impediment or exclusion might seem, if anything, to count against any kind of linguistic idealism. The Wittgensteinian passages just quoted might prompt the thought that, insofar as it is a *linguistic* operation, negation takes its cue, so to speak, from *real*—that is, in this context, non-verbal—transactions involving impediment and exclusion. Recently a number of philosophers have explored the idea of grounding negation in *rejection* (or denial),[3] but rejection is usually conceived as being (like denial) a linguistic status, whereas the intuitive idea that Wittgenstein seems to be floating is—unsurprisingly, given his view that 'acting is at the bottom of the language game' (1979c, §204)—that negation might be grounded in *non-verbal* actions of certain sorts.

In fact, it is tempting to expand Wittgenstein's sketch into a conjectural four-stage historical process, as follows. (i) At the first stage, before human beings or any forms of conscious life have evolved, there are present *in rerum natura* brute non-conscious excluding phenomena, as when a boulder stops a fallen tree from rolling down a hillside. (ii) With the evolution of animal life we move to a second stage, at which there occurs a transference of the non-conscious phenomena found in (i) to conscious behaviour. At this second stage one finds intentional gestures of an excluding kind, as when one hunting animal, say, warns a rival away from its booty by displaying a hostile signal like a snarl or a feint attack. (iii) It is then natural to suppose that some of the gestures found in (ii) manage to evolve into a primitive sign-language.

---

[2] It works better than the traditional idea that the essence of negation lies in the idea of separation or division: see on this point Hossack 1990.

[3] See, e.g., Price 1994, 146–9; Smiley 1996; Rumfitt 2000. Cf. Humberstone 2000.

At the pre- or proto-linguistic stage that is then reached, we find a sort of embryonic lingualization of (ii). Humans would have evolved from their non-human ancestors during stages (ii)–(iii). (iv) Finally, we reach a level of sophistication at which the primitive signs of (iii) are replaced, or supplemented, by symbols for negation functioning as elements of a recognizably mature linguistic system of communication.

But this piece of speculative conceptual archeology, though it might appear, assuming it is anywhere near historically accurate, to confront the linguistic idealist with a problem, does not in fact do so. The fable locates the causal origin of linguistic negation in non- and pre-linguistic phenomena, but any incipient awkwardness for linguistic idealism is neutralized by the transcendentalism of that doctrine in the version that I favour. Linguistic idealism, as I understand it, is not concerned to tell a just-so story, with, as it were, a chapter on the historical development of negation just after the one about how the leopard got its spots; the doctrine is interested not in negation's causal but in its metaphysical aetiology. Relatedly, no difficulty resides in the fact that the above fable envisages the existence of what one might call negation *in re*, or real negation: my linguistic idealist is quite happy with the idea of negation *in re*, only insisting that any such real negation has been placed in the world—transcendentally, not empirically, placed there—by language. In fact, in my view linguistic idealism needs to marry up its transcendentalism with a quite radical form of ontological generosity, according to which *all* semantically significant aspects of language have worldly referents. This is because, on the theoretically driven approach to reference that I support, reference is *the* relation that models meaning, so that *any* meaningful expression—the word 'not', for example—has a referent as a matter of course. There is nothing more to the reference enjoyed by a supposedly central case of a referential expression—and in particular there is nothing more to the reference relation that obtains between a proper name and its bearer—than just the *meaningfulness* of the relevant expression; but *that* feature of the expression is shared with *all* semantically significant expressions, including non-nominal parts of speech like the negation operator.[4] So I have no objection to the above genealogy of negation: maybe it does indeed roughly describe how things went in evolutionary terms. But, if it does, for the reasons explained I do not think that it constitutes any embarrassment for linguistic idealism.

---

[4] See Gaskin 2008, esp. §§9, 40, 53; 2021, esp. chs 2–4.

12.2 Symmetries and Asymmetries

Suppose, now, that we accept the intuitive idea that exclusion is essential to negation. That is, suppose we accept that exclusion is essential to negation both when this is thought of as a linguistic operation, and also when we are considering what I above called negation *in re*. Note here that the phrase 'negation as a *linguistic* operation' refers not merely to the *syntactic* but also to the *semantic* properties of negation signs. We need both if we are to capture the idea that exclusion is essential to negation *in verbis*: for clearly as a matter of pure syntax the negation sign does not work in an exclusionary way; or, rather, to the extent that it does it does so only in the sense in which *any* sign so works. It is true of *any* sign that its utterance or inscription excludes the utterance or inscription of another sign, as a matter of physical necessity: token signs are physical entities and so compete with other physical entities for spatial and temporal slots. Hence to identify a *special* sense in which the negation sign is exclusionary we need to adduce its semantics. The question then before us is: which way round does the explanatory relation run between negation *in re* and negation *in verbis*? Does real negation explain linguistic negation, as a realist would maintain, or does it go the other way round, as my linguistic idealist will insist? (Or does neither side have priority?)

Negation inherits important symmetries and asymmetries from exclusion. In any case of exclusion something is excluded; but the excluded thing is, in its turn, an excluder. That is because it is something determinate, and determination of one thing involves exclusion of something else. Negation inherits this feature: as Spinoza said, 'determination is negation'.[5] One manifestation of this symmetry is epistemological: not only could you not grasp the concept (property) of not being blue, say, if you did not also grasp the concept (property) of being blue; it is further the case that you could not grasp the concept (property) of being blue if you did not also grasp the concept (property) of *not* being blue. (Note that, like Frege, I take concepts to be reference-level entities, and as such genuine denizens of the world; unlike Frege, I then identify concepts with properties.)[6] Mastery of the one concept presupposes mastery of the other.[7] But the relevant symmetry is not just epistemological: the concept of being blue could not *exist* if the concept of not being blue did not also exist.

---

[5] Spinoza 1909–12, vol. 2, 370; Armstrong 1997, 200. See also Buchdahl 1961, 167; Ayer 1969, 48.
[6] Gaskin 2021, 89.
[7] There is no vicious circularity here (*pace* De Rizzo 2019, 72), since presupposition is not *in se* necessarily an asymmetric relation: that is, if *A* presupposes *B*, it is not entailed that *B* does not presuppose *A* (see Gaskin 2010, 306–7).

Indeed, there could not be blue *things* if there were not also things that were *not* blue. (Even if all the physical objects in the universe were coloured blue, the abstract objects, such as justice, holiness, the number three, and the concept *blue* itself, would not be.) In this sense, then, there is symmetry between positive and negative.

But alongside this symmetry there is also an asymmetry: the positive is prior to the negative in a constructional sense, since the negative is constructed out of the (ultimately) positive, and some.[8] That ultimately positive thing will, as we have said, be determinate, and therefore, as we have agreed (the Spinoza point), will in its turn be a negation of something. But any sequence of exclusions must ground out in something that is not merely an exclusion. There must be something substantial to say about that ultimate excluded thing, something more than—what will undoubtedly be true—that it is itself an excluder of something (else). One might say that any chain of excluding transactions must terminate in something which, as well as being an *excluded* thing, is an excluded *thing*. This is the ontological counterpart of the point that iterated negations must operate on a positive base—a proposition, for example; a mere sequence of negation signs is not well formed. The asymmetry in question is, we have said, a constructional one. For example, the (negative) concept of not being blue is *constructed out of* the (positive) concept of being blue, plus something more; and the construction goes *that* way round, not the other way. Moving up to the level of language, observe that the asymmetry in question emerges in the fact that if you say that something is blue, although you thereby rule out alternative positive states of affairs, you do not *eo ipso say* what any of these alternatives that you rule out *are*, whereas when you say that something is not blue you *do* say what the ruled-out positive state of affairs is.

Now recognizing this asymmetry does not settle the dispute between the realist and the linguistic idealist in favour of either party. Negation is constructed out of (in part) positivity both at the level of ontology and at the level of language. The construction *in re* and the operation *in verbis* mirror one another: but is the syntactic operation metaphysically prior to the real one, so that (meaningful) syntax is driving ontology, as the linguistic idealist holds?[9] Or does the metaphysical dependence run in the opposite direction, as the realist says, or indeed in neither direction? So much for the asymmetry, but

---

[8] Cf. Wittgenstein 1922, 5.5151, with Black 1964, 280.
[9] But note that I do not subscribe to a syntactic priority thesis in the sense of so-called neo-Fregeanism, which restricts the thesis that ontology drops out of semantics to syntactically nominal items of language in a traditional, narrow sense of 'nominal', one that does not include all words: Gaskin 2008, ch. 4; 2021, §§9, 27–8. I operate no such restriction.

the same aporia arises for the sense in which positive and negative are related symmetrically: we said that, for example, mastery of a positive statement presupposes mastery of its negation, and vice versa; but again, no reason has been offered so far to suppose that (meaningful) syntax takes metaphysical priority over ontology, as the linguistic idealist maintains. In my Introduction I gave a general argument in favour of linguistic idealism; here I wish to reach the same conclusion on the basis of specialized considerations bearing on the nature of negation.

12.3 Blue and Eulb

We have been talking about the positive *versus* the negative, and presupposing that we know what we are talking about; but what exactly is the distinction? Consider here a fantasy devised by A. J. Ayer:

> Imagine a community the members of which are for some reason unconcerned with differences of colour. The only colour of special interest to them is the colour blue, to which they attach a magical significance. For all other colours they use a single word, let us say the word 'eulb' [= 'blue', written backwards]. They also have a word for blue, but because blue things are sacred, the word is never used except in the course of certain ceremonies to which only the initiated are admitted. Children are taught the use of the word 'eulb' ostensively, but not the use of the word which stands for blue. They learn to refer to blue objects, which, let us further assume, they are seldom if ever allowed to see, simply as not being eulb. Thus it is 'eulb' that they regard as the positive predicate; and if they are disposed to be philosophers and iconoclasts it may even be imagined that when, at the initiation ceremony, they are finally taught the use of the word for blue, they protest that this property of blueness to which their elders attach so much importance is not a true universal, that it is nothing but the property of not being eulb. (1969, 51)

Ayer thinks that this scenario poses us a problem—namely that of distinguishing positivity from negativity. There is no *natural* distinction, as the scenario seems to show: blue is no more naturally positive, and eulb naturally negative, than vice versa. So wherein lies the distinction?

Ayer himself makes the tentative suggestion that we might distinguish positivity and negativity in terms of degree of specificity.[10] The idea is that 'blue'

---

[10] Cf. De Rizzo 2019, 61–5, on a similar proposal by Hirsch.

is more specific than 'eulb', and that it is in virtue of this feature that 'blue' counts as positive and 'eulb' as negative. But this solution will not work, not only because it leads to counterintuitive results, as Ayer himself notes (e.g., 'coloured' will count as negative and 'colourless' as positive), but also because in fact 'blue' is *not* more specific than 'eulb', or at least not obviously so: 'blue' already covers a continuum of shades of blue.[11] One might, of course, try to argue that, while the set of shades of blue *merely* has the cardinality of the continuum, the set of shades of non-blue actually has a *larger* cardinality than that of the continuum. But it seems absurd to attempt to distinguish positivity and negativity along any such esoteric lines.

In Ayer's fantasy scenario, eulbness counts, for his hypothesized community, as every bit a positive condition as blueness does in our community: the statement 'That is eulb' counts, for Ayer's community, as being just as positive a statement, and 'That is not eulb' as being just as negative, as 'That is blue' and 'That is not blue' count for us as positive and negative respectively. The fact that 'That is eulb' gets translated into English as 'That is not blue', and that 'That is not eulb' gets translated into English as 'That is blue' has no metaphysical depth; it does not mean that the concept *eulb* is *really* negative, and the concept *blue* really positive, or some such. After all, the translational situation is symmetrical: 'eulb' has a negative translation *in English*; but 'blue' has a negative translation *in Eulbspeak*. And that symmetry is unsurprising, given that (moving to the ontological level) the concept *eulb* simply focuses on a different part of the colour spectrum from the one that is targeted by the concept *blue*. English operates with several divisions (vaguely determined, of course) between named colours, and the meaning of 'red', say, is fixed by inserting a (vague) cut-off point towards the left-hand end of the colour spectrum; speakers of English then say 'We'll call everything to the left of this division "red".' By contrast, Ayer's imagined community operates with only one division, it is placed much further to the right in the spectrum, and the community adds the gloss 'We'll call everything to the left of this point "eulb".' But both English 'blue' and Eulbspeak 'eulb' can be defined directly and positively in terms of ranges of the colour spectrum; neither definition need explicitly invoke the concept of negation. (Of course, since all determination *is* negation, as we have seen, the corresponding concepts *are* implicitly negative, as well as being positive, but that applies equally to both 'blue' and 'eulb'.)

Ayer considers a purely syntactic criterion for distinguishing positivity and negativity, which he rejects (1969, 36–8). But surely the moral of his fable is

---

[11] See Gale 1976, 21–5.

that syntax *does* yield *a* principle of distinction between positivity and negativity.[12] At the level of language, negative sentences are formed by (in the first instance) taking positive sentences and subjecting them to a syntactic operation of negation. This is the linguistic dimension of the constructional asymmetry we mentioned in Section 12.2. There was a mirror image of this asymmetry at the ontological level, and these mirroring asymmetries surely do suffice to distinguish positivity from negativity: at the ontological level negation *in re* is *constructed out of* the ultimately positive; at the linguistic level negation *in verbis* performs a syntactic operation on an ultimately positive base. Given the fact that syntax is mirrored in ontology, the syntactic criterion of positivity is reflected in an ontological such criterion, and similarly for negativity. These criteria, syntactic and ontological, are two sides of the same coin, as it were, and the question we are aiming to settle is which side of the mirroring relation, if either, takes metaphysical priority.

(There is a complication that needs to be mentioned here, concerning what we should say about the ontological level. As a matter of syntax, 'blue' counts as positive in English and 'eulb' counts as positive in Eulbspeak; as we have seen, neither expression needs to be defined explicitly in terms of the operation of negation. Now at the ontological level we must exercise some care in describing what is going on. As an adherent of the so-called identity theory of truth, I identify facts with true propositions, and I maintain that versions of this identity hold at both levels of sense and reference: indeed at the level of reference, which is what concerns us here, my view is that worldly states of affairs, obtaining or non-obtaining, are identical with propositions, true or false respectively, existing at that referential level.[13] Further, propositions at the level of reference can be individuated more or less finely, depending on our occurrent purposes.[14] At the level of finest grain, the proposition *that A is eulb* can count as distinct from—though mutually entailing with—the proposition *that A is not blue*. At that level, it is then straightforward to say that the former proposition is positive and the latter negative. But for many purposes we will wish to individuate propositions less finely; when we do this we in effect put relatively finely individuated propositions into equivalence classes collected under some suitable synonymy relation obtaining at the linguistic level. Following this policy we might regard, for example, the proposition *that A is eulb* and the proposition *that A is not blue* as being the *same* proposition, because

---

[12] Cf. Hommen 2018, 88 and passim.
[13] See Gaskin 2008, ch. 2; 2020; 2021, chs 5 and 6.
[14] Gaskin 2021, ch. 5, esp. §21.

for these purposes we are treating their governing sentences as synonymous. And in respect of that—relatively coarsely individuated—proposition the question 'Is this proposition positive or negative?' lacks a determinate answer. It might be thought that this complication tilted matters in favour of the linguistic idealist; but, much as it might help my case if this were so, I do not think that it is. Even though there are, as we have just noted, levels of abstraction at which there is no ontological determinacy in respect of positivity and negativity—I mean, no determinate answer to the question 'Is this proposition positive or negative?'—it remains the case that at the *basic* level, the level of finest grain, where propositions exactly mirror syntax and so where there *is* a determinate answer to that question, we *still* have to settle whether, for example, it is the negativity of the worldly state of *A*'s being not blue—that is, the true proposition that *A* is not blue—that is driving language—the relevant sentence thus shadowing the reality—or vice versa.)

Now an important point here is that, as the quoted passage makes clear, for Ayer's community the concept *eulb* is *not* the concept *not blue, simpliciter,* but *rather* (translated into English) the concept *coloured but not blue.* It is precisely this *latter* concept that, I have been claiming, is just as positive in Eulbspeak as the concept *blue* is in English. And that is because there is a way of specifying the meaning of 'eulb' without invoking negation: one simply demarcates the visible colour spectrum as far as the (vague) point at which it starts turning blue. The concept *eulb* does not need to be conceived as a negative concept that has been constructed out of something relatively positive; it can count as positive in its own right. By contrast, the concept *not blue simpliciter* is *genuinely* negative in the sense that there would be no means of characterizing it positively, in the way that I have positively characterized Ayer's concept *eulb*—namely as applying to all colour on the spectrum to the left of a certain (vaguely defined) cut-off point near the spectrum's right-hand end. Not merely colours (coloured objects) other than blue (ones), but everything that is not a colour (coloured) at all counts as being *not blue simpliciter*: for example, all abstract objects are not blue *simpliciter*. There is no means of characterizing the rag-bag of things that are not blue *simpliciter* other than in exactly those terms.

If we distinguish the two possible concepts of *non-blue* that are in play as $eulb_A$ ('Ayer's *eulb*'), that is, the concept *coloured but not blue*, and $eulb_B$ ('big *eulb*'), which is the concept *not blue simpliciter*, we can represent the situation pictorially as follows (exaggerating the relative size of the coloured domain for ease of reading):

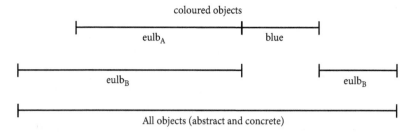

In words: both the class of coloured objects and the class of $eulb_B$ objects are proper subclasses of the class of all objects (abstract and concrete) with a non-empty intersection comprising the objects that are $eulb_A$; the class of all objects divides without remainder into two mutually disjoint subclasses, one comprising those objects that are blue and the other those that are $eulb_B$; this latter class itself divides without remainder into two mutually disjoint subclasses, one comprising those objects that are $eulb_A$ and the other those that are not (either because they are blue or because they are not coloured at all). The concept $eulb_A$ can be defined in positive terms, both in Eulbspeak and in English ('occurring on the colour spectrum to the left of *this* point'); by contrast, the concept $eulb_B$ *really is* negative, in the sense that it *cannot* be defined in positive terms. 'Big' concepts are deeply negative. And the sense in which $eulb_B$ is really negative is, as we have seen, a constructional one: this holds both at the level of ontology and at the level of (meaningful) syntax. But, once again, making that point does not in itself settle the dispute between the linguistic idealist and the realist: it does not tell us which, if either, side of the mirroring relation drives which.

12.4 Negativity Depends on Positivity

The constructional sense in which positivity is prior to negativity yields also an explanatory priority: at the ontological level, for example, a negative concept or state of affairs is explained in terms of the positive correlate that is being excluded. (In that sense, too, while $eulb_A$ can count as positive, $eulb_B$ must come out as negative.) And, at the linguistic level, the point that negation is an *operation* on something else, whereas the positivity of the (ultimate) underlying form, the form that is (ultimately) negated, is not itself an operation but the *basis* for an operation, allows for the possibility that *iterations* of the negating operation may have special and varying effects: in the case of classical negation, for instance, double negations logically cancel out (rather than, for example, reinforcing). There is no analogy to the differential effects of single and double negation—in general: an odd *versus* an even number of applications of the negation operation—in the case of positive statements, precisely because positivity is *not* an operation. We can certainly, if we like, so style positivity as to make it *look like* an operation: we do this when we prefix 'it is the case that ...' to a statement. But this prefix necessarily iterates redundantly, because it is already redundant, whereas 'it is not the case that ...' is a genuine operation, prefixing it makes a palpable difference, and *that* opens up the possibility of non-redundant iteration and of toggling effects.[15] Toggling can in turn be thought of as grounded in negation-as-exclusion: suppose, to revisit one of the examples quoted above from Wittgenstein, that the door is open, and A tries to close it in order to prevent B from entering; then C, an enemy of A and friend of B, comes along and tries to prevent A from closing the door; then D, an ally of A, intervenes in an attempt to stop C from preventing A ...; then E etc. Note that insisting on this feature of negation does not in itself furnish a move against intuitionism or Dummettian anti-realism: the dispute between classical logicians and intuitionists concerns not the meaning specifically of 'not'[16]—so that talk of classical and intuitionist negation is strictly speaking misleading—but the concept of meaning in general, and the question whether our theory of meaning should take a broadly verificationist form. Intuitionists reject the rule of double-negation elimination (DNE) because they read it as, in effect, licensing a transition from $\Box\neg\Box\neg p$ to $\Box p$, where '$\Box$' is interpreted as 'provably'.[17]

If the idea of exclusion is, as I am taking it, essential to negation, we must nuance a point that Wittgenstein makes, when he writes, in pursuit of a fantasy scenario of his own:

> We can easily imagine human beings with a 'more primitive' logic, in which something corresponding to our negation is applied only to certain sorts of sentence; perhaps to such as do not themselves contain any negation. It would be possible to negate the proposition 'He is going into the house', but a negation of the negative proposition would be meaningless, or would count only

---

[15] Cf. Wittgenstein 1979a, 36 (entry for 13.12.1914). It now seems to me that I made a mistake on this point at Gaskin 2021, 211–12, where I argued that, if we imagine a language containing a symbol, say '*', purportedly denoting affirmation, in complementary distribution with another symbol, say '~', purportedly denoting negation, then it is not metaphysically determinate which of '*' and '~' should be correlated at the level of reference with affirmation *in re* and which with negation *in re*. I made this claim quite generally, but I should have restricted its scope to languages without significant iteration of these symbols. As soon as we permit iteration and toggling effects, speakers will exhibit differential reactions to pairs of the form *p/**p and ~p/~~p. Cf. Black 1964, 180–1.

[16] See Wright 1993, 130.

[17] Cf. Priest 2008, 108. Note also that, since $\Box\neg\Box\neg p = \Box\Diamond p$, in the context of the S5 axiom, $\Diamond p \to \Box\Diamond p$, accepting $\Box\Diamond p \to \Box p$ would lead to modal collapse.

> as a repetition of the negation. Think of means of expressing negation different from ours: by the pitch of one's voice, for instance. What would a double negation be like there? (1977, I, §554, tr. Anscombe)

Wittgenstein may be right that the scenarios he here imagines are possible ones, but we must add that, if they do make sense, they do so only to the extent that they allow for the insertion into the relevant speakers' practice of a rule of DNE. That is to say, perhaps there could be a community of language users who, as things stand, have never iterated their negation operator, and would not understand it if someone tried to do so; alternatively, we might imagine a community that iterates negation only in a reinforcing sense ('negative concord'). But, if in either of these communities the sign used for negation really is a sign *for negation*, then the analysis of negation as exclusion predicts that it will be possible to extend or adapt their language-games by introducing the rule of DNE, without losing the original meaning of the uniterated negation sign. In the case of a community that has not iterated negation at all hitherto, the new use will integrate smoothly and conservatively. In the case of a community that already allows iteration of its negation sign, but only for reinforcement purposes, the new use, involving as it does DNE, might either oust their former practice, or sit alongside it in peaceful co-existence. The latter possibility is exemplified by many languages: in English, for example, depending on context, speaker's register, and so on, 'I don't want nothing' can mean either 'I want something' or 'I don't want anything'. For the point is that exclusion just *is* iterable with cancelling effect; prevention is *itself* preventable. These are essential properties of exclusion/prevention, which (genuine) negation, assuming that it is grounded in the idea of exclusion, simply inherits.

Some linguists think that Wittgenstein's fantasy scenario is actually historically accurate, in the sense that the use of an iterated negation operator to reinforce a single negation is more primitive than its cancelling use.[18] Still, even if DNE came on the scene relatively late in the history of language use, as a refined rule found initially only in the salons of the educated, while the many continued as they had always done to iterate negation either not at all or, if so, only in a reinforcing way—even if that is so it remains the case that for a sign to be a negation sign it must, according to the exclusion analysis, allow for the possibility of introduction of a rule of DNE. So

---

[18] See, e.g., Jespersen 1917, 68. In languages which follow 'Jespersen's cycle', negatives may (as in French) initially be reinforced by positives (e.g., 'pas', 'point', 'rien', 'personne', 'mie', 'goutte') which, if they survive, come to be heard as negatives ('Jeo ne dis' ⇒ 'Je ne dis pas' ⇒ 'Je dis pas'), and which can eventually stand on their own as negators ('Qu'est-ce que tu veux?'—'Rien'). See Willis, Lucas, and Breitbarth 2013/2020, vol. 2, Introduction and Part 1, and Hansen's contribution to vol. 1.

we must say about Wittgenstein's hypothetical community that their language makes available a syntactic possibility that they themselves have not yet exploited, but could exploit.[19] Similarly with his idea of pitch-as-expressing-negation: if pitch of voice is genuinely to express *negation*, then the exclusion analysis will insist that the relevant negating operation must in principle be iterable with cancellation effect, perhaps by raising and then lowering the pitch.

The fact that negation is an operation on (ultimately) a positive base is a feature that it inherits from exclusion, which depends, as we saw above, on the prior idea that *something* is being excluded—the something in question being again (in the basic case) a positive state of affairs. (Any excluded state, to repeat, will itself be in turn an excluder—the Spinoza point that positivity always involves negativity—but the ultimate basis of a sequence of exclusion transactions cannot be *merely* an excluder, just as a sentence formed from sheer iterations of the negation operator is not well formed.) When one thinks about such processes as physical hindering and excluding, one sees that they involve positivity in a further respect. It is not merely that they prevent the realization of a positive state of affairs; they also involve the *putting in place* of a positive state of affairs, one that precisely blocks the realization of the prevented state of affairs. So, in Wittgenstein's example, one might arrange for the door to stand in *this* positive position—shut and locked—in order to prevent someone's entering the room. The idea of exclusion, as a real phenomenon, is the idea of one positive situation's *getting in way of* another positive situation. If the door is shut and locked, then—assuming a range of background facts about physical laws, human capacities, implements to hand, social etiquette, and so on—another person *cannot* enter. Equally, of course, if someone *does* enter, the door *cannot* be locked (given the same provisos). And that takes us to the suggestion, common in the philosophical literature, that the essence of negation resides not merely in exclusion but more precisely in *mutual* exclusion, or *incompatibility*. In our scenario, someone's entering the room—that particular positive state of affairs—is *incompatible with* the position of the locked door and the walls—another positive state of affairs (modulo the relevant background facts, as we have said). In a physical sense of 'cannot', you *cannot* have both of those two particular positive states of affairs. This is a physical case of incompatibility, but note that when we speak of incompatibility we are not simply broadening the idea of exclusion to make it two-way,

---

[19] Of course, a community might have *other* reasons for refusing to adopt the rule of DNE: perhaps they are adherents of Dummettian anti-realism. But the point is that a community's objection to DNE, if it has one, must derive not from the semantics of 'not', but from general meaning considerations.

but also making clear that it encompasses not just the physical, but also the metaphysical, conceptual, and logical. This point will be important in due course.

The idea that incompatibility is the core of negation is nicely expressed by Huw Price in a well-known discussion. Suppose you and I are having a conversation about the whereabouts of Fred the cat. And suppose our language contains no sign for negation. We might then end up in such straits as the following:

ME: 'Fred is in the kitchen'. (Sets off for kitchen.)
YOU: 'Wait! Fred is in the garden'.
ME: 'I see. But he is in the kitchen, so I'll go there.' (Sets off.)
YOU: 'You lack understanding. The kitchen is Fred-free.'
ME: 'Is it really? But Fred's in it, and that's the important thing.' (Leaves for kitchen.)

Price continues:

> Your problem is to get me to appreciate that your claims are incompatible with mine. Even in such a trivial case, we can see that it would be useful to have a device whose function was precisely to indicate that an incompatible claim was being made: precisely to deny an assertion or suggestion by somebody else. It seems that this is what negation gives us. (Price 1990, 224)

Of course, the problem in the above conversation is not the trivial one that our *language* has no sign for negation, no way of talking explicitly about incompatibility. You might introduce such a sign and *still* get nowhere with me. The problem is that I have no understanding of the idea of incompatibility: I am hearing 'Fred is not in the kitchen' as merely detailing the particular way in which Fred is in the kitchen, like 'Fred is asleep in the kitchen.'

12.5 Negation and Incompatibility

The idea that negation expresses incompatibility is well summarized in the following passage by Francesco Berto:

> It is difficult to think of a more pervasive and basic feature of experience, than that some things in the world rule out some other things; or that the

obtaining of this precludes the obtaining of that; or that something's being such-and-such excludes its being so-and-so. Not only rational epistemic agents and speakers of natural languages, but also animals, or sentient creatures generally, are acquainted with (in)compatibility. On the cognitive side, incompatibility shows itself in the most basic ability a new-born can acquire: that of distinguishing objects, recognizing a difference between something and something else. On the practical side, we face choices between doing this and that, and to face a choice is to experience an incompatibility:. . . . If the awareness of incompatibility is more primitive than the use of any negation, the primary purpose of uttering a 'not' in the history of the world must have been that of recording some perceived incompatibility and of manifesting it to others,. . . . That the core role of negation in the vernacular is to signal incompatibility is hinted at in [a] passage from the *Sophist* [257bc]. Plato appears to claim that to say of something that it is not such-and-such is to assert that it is different from being such-and-such, 'difference' meaning here some incompatibility: the being so-and-so of the thing rules out its being such and-such, which is different from and incompatible with being so-and-so. (2015, 770)

The passage from Plato's *Sophist* to which Berto alludes is worth looking at in a little more detail. Theaetetus is in dialogue with the Eleatic Stranger:

STRANGER: It seems that whenever we talk about *that which is not*, we are not talking about something contrary (*enantion*) to *that which is*, but only something different (*heteron*) from it.
THEAETETUS: How do you mean?
STRANGER: Well, when we talk about something as being *not large*, do we seem to you to denote *the small* in our expression as opposed to *the equal* (*to ison*)?
THEAETETUS: No indeed.
STRANGER: So when it is claimed that negation (*apophasis*) signifies a contrary, we shall not agree, but concede only this much, that when words for 'not' are prefixed to names that follow them they indicate something *other* than (*tōn allōn ti*) the names, or rather, other than the things that the names uttered after the negation are about. (257b2–c3)

This passage is actually a notorious crux in the interpretation of the *Sophist*, but *one* way of reading it is indeed Berto's, as I shall now explain.

Notice first that Plato does not talk about incompatibility, in glossing the idea of negation, but simply difference. And difference is of course quite different, in general, from incompatibility: being red is a different property from being square, but they are entirely compatible in an ordinary, extensional sense (something can be both red and square). The new-born may indeed, as Berto says, '[recognize] a difference between something and something else', but so far that does not mean that the new-born recognizes any *incompatibility* between something and something else. Why, then, does Berto say that 'difference' in our Platonic passage means 'incompatibility'? Well, this construal is hinted at in the argument that the Stranger uses to motivate his main thesis. He asks Theaetetus: 'When we speak of something as *not large*, does it seem to you that we indicate *the small* rather than *the equal* (*to ison*)?'. By 'the equal' it is not implausible to suppose that 'the middling in size' or similar is meant. So the idea would be that a thing is judged to be small/large/equal by comparison with a standard of reference, itself counting as being of medium size. If that is right, it looks as though the Stranger is getting Theaetetus to agree that 'not large' takes us not simply to a property that is *different* from large—any old different property, such as being malicious or being purple with pink spots or being divisible by seven without remainder—but to a different property in what we might call *the same incompatibility range* (IR).[20] Put in terms of the discussion of Section 12.3, we are being taken not to $egral_B$—*big* not-large, i.e., (falling under) a merely different property from largeness, whether or not incompatible with it—but to $egral_A$—i.e., (falling under) a property other than largeness but *in the same IR*. And now, so long as we stay within the same IR, any different property will do: relative to a given IR, difference *is* the same thing as incompatibility.[21]

We may note here that the idea that properties fall naturally into IRs was crucial to Wittgenstein's abandonment of one of the fundamental themes of the *Tractatus*, namely the doctrine that elementary sentences are all mutually consistent. The retreat was announced in 'Some Remarks on Logical Form' of 1929 (reprinted 1993, 28–35) and elsewhere, as for instance in his discussions with the Vienna Circle:

Once I wrote: 'A sentence (*Satz*) is laid against reality like a ruler. Only the end-points of the graduating lines actually *touch* the object that is to

---

[20] Cf. Kostman 1973, esp. 203–6. Wittgenstein has a similar idea at 1922, §4.0641; 1975, §62. Cf. Gale 1976, 8 with n. 11.

[21] This statement needs to be hedged in obvious ways to exclude counterexamples like red/scarlet, red-or-green/red-or-orange: see De Rizzo 2019, 132–3.

be measured.' [*Tractatus* 2.1511–2.15121] I now prefer to say that a *system of sentences* (*Satzsystem*) is laid against reality like a ruler. . . . It is not the individual graduating lines that are laid against it, but the entire scale. . . . If I say, for example, that this or that point in the visual field is blue, then I know not merely that, but also that this point is not green, nor red, nor yellow, etc. I have laid the entire colour-scale against it in one go. . . . [In the *Tractatus* I thought that] elementary sentences must be independent of one another, that you could not infer the non-existence of one state of affairs from the existence of another. But if my present conception of a system of sentences is correct, it will actually be the rule that from the existence of one state of affairs the non-existence of all the other states of affairs described by this system of sentences can be inferred. (Wittgenstein 1979b/1984, 63–4, tr. adapted)

To put it another way, and continuing with Wittgenstein's example, colour is a determinable which can only be determined once (in respect of the same point in space, at the same time, etc.). Observe an asymmetry (similar to, but not quite the same as, one mentioned in Section 12.2) between positive and negative—between, say, 'it is red' and 'it is not red'. The latter statement does not tell you what colour the thing is, but the former does tell you what colour(s) it is not: at least, the former statement tells you what colour(s) the thing is not in the sense that it *entails* what colours that thing is not (it does not explicitly *state* what colours it is not, the point that was relevant earlier). Assuming that the thing has some colour, 'it is red' entails that it is *not* blue, etc.; but 'it is not red' does not tell you (entail) which of blue, etc., it is. So long as we are restricted to the relevant IR, here that of colours, 'not red' takes you to *one* of the members of that IR other than red, but not to any *particular* one.

In 'Some Remarks on Logical Form' Wittgenstein indicates his retreat from the position he had adopted in the *Tractatus*, as we have noted. But in that article he still wishes to maintain the Tractarian view that no elementary sentences are negative (*TLP* 4.211), so that, in any sense in which there are negative facts (*TLP* 2.05–06), these are simply constituted by the non-existence of elementary positive facts.[22] Hence it is still Wittgenstein's position that elementary sentences cannot stand in contradiction with each other. He therefore has to distinguish contradiction and exclusion:

---

[22] See Brownstein 1973, 43; Anscombe 1996, 30.

> The mutual exclusion of unanalysable statements of degree contradicts an opinion which was published by me several years ago and which necessitated that atomic propositions [i.e., elementary sentences] could not exclude one another. I here deliberately say 'exclude' and not 'contradict', for there is a difference between these two notions, and atomic propositions, although they cannot contradict, may exclude one another. (1993, 33)

Something's being 2m long excludes its being 3m long, but there is no contradiction in the offing between these alternative possibilities since neither of the relevant states of affairs—the thing's being 2m or its being 3m long—is negative: to put it in syntactic terms, the corresponding sentences are all positive; none of them is governed by a wide-scope negation sign.

The construal of negation as incompatibility in effect analyses its origin into several distinct metaphysical stages: a negative state of affairs N—to cast the point in ontological terms—obtains in virtue of the non-obtaining of a state of affairs P; P fails to obtain, in turn, because *another* state of affairs, Q, obtains which *excludes* P; the two states, P and Q, are incompatible, so that, necessarily, if one of them obtains the other does not obtain. (P and Q may themselves be negative, and so on down; though, as we have seen, the process must ultimately be grounded in the exclusion of a positive state of affairs.) I have been operating with the idea that negation traces its origin to exclusion: with the passage just quoted from Wittgenstein in mind, someone might object that the idea of exclusion falls short of that of negation inasmuch as, to put it roughly, in order to exclude P we need merely install *a* state which is a *contrary* of P, not *the* state which is its *contradictory*; but negation imports the contradictory, not merely a contrary, status to what is negated. That is correct. But we can still regard negation as grounded in exclusion because we can think of contradictoriness as *abstracting on* contrariety: not-P is the *weakest* status that excludes P, in the sense that it is entailed by all P-excluding statuses.[23] This incidentally yields an insight into the non-atomicity of negative sentences in the *Tractatus*, a matter on which Russell famously taxed Wittgenstein in correspondence.[24] For in effect negating P takes us to *some* Q—but not any particular Q—incompatible with P; in other words, negation contains a concealed existential quantification or long disjunction.

---

[23] See here Peacocke 1987, 163–4; Wright 1993, 123–4. Note that, in making this move, we depart from the Aristotelian terminological tradition, in which 'contrary' usually means 'contrary-but-not-subcontrary': for present purposes contrariety does not exclude contradiction; rather, I am taking contradiction to be a limiting case of contrariety (see on this point Humberstone 2011, 1165).

[24] Wittgenstein 1995, 121–6.

12.6 Positivity Depends on Negativity

An important point to make here is that talk of incompatibility as the core or basis of negation can be misleading if it is taken to imply an asymmetric relation between the two statuses. It would be quite wrong to suppose that an entailment relation runs only from negation to incompatibility, or to exclusion in general, and not also in the reverse direction. The ideas of incompatibility and exclusion presuppose that of negation just as much as vice versa. (The same applies to denial and rejection.)[25] A basic case of exclusion is defined in terms of the positive state of affairs that is excluded, and in the basic case incompatibility involves the mutual exclusion of positive phenomena; but, no matter how much we stress the involvement of positivity in the relations of exclusion and incompatibility, there is no prospect of an *eliminative reduction* of negation to the positive components of these relations.[26] In general, there is no prospect of reducing negativity to positivity. It is true that an absence is defined in terms of the presence of which it is an absence, that a state of privation is defined in terms of the corresponding state of possession, and that a negation is defined and explained in terms of what it is that is being negated, as we have said: these general asymmetric relations of dependence of negativity on positivity do indeed hold. But equally there are relations of dependence the other way round, in at least two respects.

The first of these is the Spinoza point we have already mentioned. Positive states of affairs are determinations, and determination involves exclusion. It follows that positive states and statuses are at least in part understood in terms of what they exclude, of what they are not. You could not grasp the concept or property of, say, being blue if you did not *also* grasp the concept or property of *not* being blue.[27] The second way in which there is a dependence of positivity on negativity is also relatively familiar: it is the point that it is not possible to give a complete, purely positive description of the world, because any such description would need to deploy the concept *all*, and *that* concept is (or includes) a negative status.[28] Suppose that Theaetetus is sitting (at ground level). Then

(NT)   Theaetetus is not flying

---

[25] *Pace* Price 1994, 146–9.

[26] This is surely Russell's point, at 1956, 213–15, 288–9, against Demos 1917, though admittedly it does not emerge very clearly: Molnar 2000, 74. (For a different reading of Russell, see Brownstein 1973.) It is White's point against Black in Buchdahl's dialogue (1961). See also Hand 1999, 196–7.

[27] Cf. Wittgenstein 1979b, 87; Tennant 1999, 216–18.

[28] Taylor 1952, 441–2; Ayer 1969, 37, 64–5; Armstrong 1997, 200; 2004, 70; Molnar 2000, 80–2; Dodd 2007, 389; Mumford 2021, 158.

is true. What state(s) of affairs must exist to sustain the truth of (NT)? Suppose we try to argue that (NT) can be supported by (all) the positive truths about Theaetetus. Once we purportedly have a list of (all) these positive truths, will (NT) not be entailed by the set of them? Well, only if three conditions are met, *all* negative or importing negativity, namely: (i) we really have collected all the positive truths about Theaetetus, so that any positive truth *not* on our list is *not* about Theaetetus (otherwise we cannot rule out the possibility that 'Theaetetus is flying' is another truth about him which should be added to the list, so that (NT) is false); (ii) 'Theaetetus is flying' is *not* identical with (or entailed by) any item on the list; and (iii) the list is consistent, since we do not want (NT) verified by virtue of *ex contradictione quodlibet*.

Colin Cheyne and Charles Pigden (2006) suggest that we can finesse this latter argument, which, they say,

> relies on the conceit that Theaetetus's positive properties are not incompatible with flying. And this is surely false. It is true that Theaetetus could be flying and sitting (if he were seated in an aeroplane or on a magic carpet for instance), but he could not be sitting as he is—on the ground or a bench in earnest conversation with Socrates—and be flying at the same time. His ground-bound activities are inconsistent with aerial adventures. Thus the big fact (or collection of facts) that we can roughly characterize as Theaetetus as he actually is necessitates the truth of (NT). For if Theaetetus were flying this fact would not exist. (2006, 259)

But surely, one wants to object, the incompatibility between Theaetetus' sitting and his flying (when these concepts are precisified in suitable ways) is a basic—and *negative—fact*, required if the necessity that Cheyne and Pigden want is to obtain. They reply:

> what we are saying is that the existence of certain positive states of affairs—some relatively small and some unimaginably large—is incompatible with the falsehood of certain negative propositions. If the facts or states of affairs exist then the propositions cannot be false. But notice that we are unlike earlier incompatibilists. For us the incompatibility relation holds between (the existence of) certain facts and the falsehood of certain propositions. (2006, 260)

The idea is that the incompatibility between Theaetetus' sitting and his flying obtains between the *fact* that he is sitting and the *proposition* that he is flying.

What we are not allowed to say is that the fact of his sitting is incompatible with the (would-be) *fact* of his flying, and that *that* is why (NT) is true. For to say that would be to let negativity in at the metaphysical ground level: we would have negative facts. This argument depends on recognizing a distinction between facts and (true) propositions, as I do not, but even if we admit that distinction, the case is hopeless. Propositions are components of the world, are they not? So the incompatibility that Cheyne and Pigden are willing to allow, between the fact that Theaetetus is sitting and the proposition that he is flying is an incompatibility between two bits of the world; it is a negative *fact*.[29]

Probably most people accept that *incompatibility* is a negative status, but it has sometimes been mooted that *difference* is a positive concept,[30] and in his *Human Knowledge: its Scope and Limits* (first published in 1948), Russell advanced (1992, 138–42) the curious idea that disbelief is a positive mental state and that difference and dissimilarity are positive conditions:

> Given a single indicative sentence, such as 'this is red', we may have towards it two attitudes, belief and disbelief. Both are 'positive' in the sense that they are actual states of the organism, which can be described without the word 'not'. Each is capable of being 'true', but the 'truth' of a disbelief is not quite the same thing as that of a belief.... If disbelief in 'this is red' is a judgment of perception ... then 'this' must be a colour. It is only in logic or philosophy that we are concerned to disbelieve in the redness of smells or sounds, and such disbelief belongs to a later stage than that which has to be considered in relation to our present problem. I shall therefore assume that when, as a judgment of perception, we disbelieve 'this is red', we are always perceiving that it is some other colour. We may therefore say that a disbelief in 'this is red' is 'true' when it is caused by something having to red the relation of positive dissimilarity.... (1992, 141)

Now, the most favourable case for Russell is, as he implicitly recognizes, the situation that arises *within* a single IR. I am confronted with something blue, let us say, and, at an initial stage, my *belief* that this thing is *not* red gets analysed as (or underwritten by) a *disbelief* that it *is* red. Is this disbelief a positive or a negative mental state? Negative, you would think, given the prefix attaching to the noun 'disbelief'; but at a second stage of analysis Russell then tells us that this state of *disbelief* in the *redness* of the thing is really a state of *belief*

---

[29] For further criticism of Cheyne and Pigden, different from mine, see Parsons 2006.
[30] So, e.g., Black in Buchdahl's dialogue (1961).

in its *blueness*. Does this strategy work? Wittgenstein once remarked that 'it is difficult not to confuse what is not the case with what *is* the case instead of it' (1979a, 33): Russell would protest that he is not *confusing* the two things, but engaging in *analysis*. But the crunch comes at the point where Russell says that, in the above kind of scenario, we are not paying particular attention to the non-identity of a colour and a sound, say—that sort of thing is irrelevant in an ordinary scenario, since 'It is only in logic or philosophy that we are concerned to disbelieve in the redness of smells or sounds, and such disbelief belongs to a later stage than that which has to be considered in relation to our present problem.' Is that right? No; and seeing why it is incorrect will bring us back to the main task of this chapter, which is to make a case for linguistic idealism on the basis of the nature of negation.

12.7 Negation and Linguistic Idealism

In the last section I argued that the idea of incompatibility entails that of negation, and that there is no prospect of reducing negation to pure positivity. Earlier, I agreed with the position of those who think that the idea of negation essentially involves that of incompatibility. So the result is that, at the metaphysically fundamental level, the concepts of negation and incompatibility exist in symbiosis. However, the way in which negation involves incompatibility is subtler than has emerged from the discussion so far, and it is this extra subtlety that brings linguistic idealism into the picture. The basic idea here is this: negation involves incompatibility, which is mutual exclusion, but the idea of exclusion imports that of an IR, for two entities (of whatever sort) exclude one another only *with respect to a particular IR*; now that in turn imports the idea of identity and distinctness of IRs, and we find on examination that (in a way to be spelt out below) *this* idea draws language into its constitution. It is, of course, quite true, as we have said, that at a certain primitive stage in the history of our planet—at a stage before even any form of consciousness, let alone of language, had evolved—exclusion existed as a perfectly good real phenomenon: for example, boulders stopped trees rolling down hillsides. But that fact does not entail that incompatibility is, at the most basic level, a metaphysical *rather than* a linguistic phenomenon, for the reason that I have just indicated, but have yet to expound, namely that the very existence of any kind of exclusion depends on the existence of distinct IRs, and the identity conditions of IRs are set up in an essentially language-dependent way.

Recall Russell's claim that disbelieving in the redness of sounds comes at a 'late' stage of intellectual sophistication, at a stage which is metaphysically posterior to disbelieving in, say, the redness of an item of apparel. Russell would hold, I think, that there is at least a logical stage, and that probably there was also a temporal stage, at which humans can or could be said to disbelieve in the redness of a tunic, but not (yet) disbelieve in the redness of a lion's roar. Note that, even if our humans at this conjectured logico-temporally primitive stage had no language, or only insufficient language, to say anything as sophisticated as 'I disbelieve in . . .', their disbelief could be manifested behaviourally. They might, for example, wear red tunics on certain occasions but not on others: perhaps they realized that this bright colour attracts attention, so is good to wear if one is partying but not if one is hunting. But the idea that disbelieving in the redness of a material object like a garment must be inherently *anterior*, in either a logical or a temporal sense, to disbelieving in the redness of a sound is mistaken. Being able to *say* 'I disbelief in the redness of a lion's roar' is no doubt a developed linguistic achievement, perhaps more advanced than being able to say 'I disbelieve in the redness of this tunic', but the former disbelief can be manifested in behaviour just as much as can the latter, and *is* manifested in human behaviour—this is the crucial point—just as early on, temporally and logically speaking, in the process of acquiring cultural and linguistic sophistication, as the latter, perhaps even earlier. That is because one cannot distinguish between items falling *within* a given IR if one cannot (already, so to speak, or at least coevally) distinguish *between* different IRs. To distinguish between different colours, say, is *already* to know that colours are not sounds or smells.

Hence the concept of incompatibilities within a given IR presupposes the concept of relations of non-identity between IRs. And the concept, crucial to the constitution of negation *in re*, of a range of distinct IRs, the very idea that any one such IR *is not* another IR, involves language. This is because the concept of a range of distinct IRs—or, otherwise expressed, of a range of distinct *categories*—is a matter of *what we talk about*. IRs—categories—are essentially *topics of our discourse*. 'We' and 'our' here refer to possible as well as actual language users, and in this context a phrase like 'what we talk about' presupposes the widest possible indexing, so introduces the idea of what we talk about at any time or in (respect of) any possible world at which language users exist. To say that the idea of *different IRs or categories* is a matter of what we talk about is, then, tantamount to saying that it is a matter of different *actual and possible* topics of discourse. Consider an example. The size range *is not* the colour range: these are non-identical IRs. But the one range does not exclude the other in any ontological, *pre-linguistic* sense: it cannot do that, because then an object could not have both a size and a colour. So what makes it the case that these are *different* ranges? Well, that is a matter of how we talk and what we find intelligible. These categories are *subject matters*; and it is as such—as subject matters—that they are non-identical.

So the linguistic idealist gives the right account of the origin of negation. When people appeal to incompatibility or, more generally, to exclusion as integral to the nature of negation, they generally have low-level exclusions in mind, involving physical objects. And there is, of course, a lot of that sort of exclusion around in the world. But these exclusions and incompatibilities could not have found their way into the world in the first place without category distinctions, without the existence of non-identical IRs, and *those* non-identities have been put there by language. Transcendentally put there, not empirically so, it should be stressed. Non-identity of determinables is more fundamental than incompatibility between the determinates, taken pairwise, falling under a given determinable, because these latter incompatibilities could not arise if there were not non-identical determinables for them to fall under. You might say, then, that non-identity is *the* fundamental form of negation. Interestingly, there is a sense in which Plato anticipated this point in the *Sophist*. In the first instance, according to the Eleatic Stranger, 'not' signifies not contrariety, but mere difference (non-identity). Plato illustrates this point with the non-identity of the 'five greatest kinds' (254b8–257a12), which is in effect the point that we work with different fundamental *categories*, and that these categories are distinct from, but not in all cases contrary to, one another. And when he comes to solve the problem of falsity, the Stranger again operates with a fundamental notion of non-identity. The falsity of 'Theaetetus flies' is analysed as consisting in the non-identity of flying with any of the things which Theaetetus is (or has).[31] There is no question, here, of a reduction of negation to something else—negation is present in the analysans every bit as prominently and essentially as it is in the analysandum—but the idea is that the *basic* form that negation takes is non-identity. Of course, since we are here explicitly analysing falsity, language is already in the picture; my suggestion has been that the non-identity of ontological categories—fundamental to negation *in re*—is *also*, essentially, a linguistic matter.

Note, finally, that this point goes deeper than an important observation about negation that arose in connection with our reflections on 'big' concepts, at the end of Section 12.3. Big concepts stand in relations of incompatibility

---

[31] I am here following the so-called 'Oxford' interpretation of 263b11–12: see Crivelli 2012, 238–40.

to the concepts in terms of which they are defined: so $eulb_B$, for example, is incompatible with *blue*. The IR in question here is the widest possible category, that of all existents (abstract or concrete), and precisely that feature of the situation is that in virtue of which, as we said, $eulb_B$ is *essentially* negative, in the sense that it has *no* positive surrogate; concepts like *blue* and $eulb_A$, by contrast, can be defined in purely positive terms ('colours on *these* parts of the spectrum'). But, though there is no contrasting IR to be set over against—and so to be non-identical with—the IR comprising all existents, the distinction between *blue* and $eulb_B$ nevertheless still depends on the idea of non-identical IRs, because it depends on the concept *blue*, and *that* concept presupposes the idea of distinct IRs—in the first instance it imports the colour range, but then by implication it imports the idea of ranges that are non-identical with the colour range. So even in what one might think of as the extreme, limiting case of incompatibility and exclusion—the case where the relevant IR comprises everything, so that there are no further IRs contributing their non-identity with this one to the intellectual scenario—we still have to invoke the idea of non-identical IRs in order to make sense of things. Big concepts like $eulb_B$ may be *in se* essentially negative in a way that concepts such as *blue* and $eulb_A$ are not, but they still depend for their constitution on such concepts as *blue* and $eulb_A$, and these latter concepts, even if not negative *in se*, still *presuppose* negation as manifested by the non-identity of IRs, which is in turn *constituted by the language-game*. At the most basic level, the phenomenon of negation is linguistic. But then, since positivity needs negativity just as much as negativity needs positivity (Section 12.6), the linguistic nature of negativity rubs off on positivity. Hence, for something to exist, there needs to be language: no language, no world.[32]

References

Anscombe, G. E. M. 1996. *An Introduction to Wittgenstein's Tractatus* (Bristol: Thoemmes).
Armstrong, D. 1997. *A World of States of Affairs* (Cambridge: CUP).
Armstrong, D. 2004. *Truth and Truthmakers* (Cambridge: CUP).
Ayer, A. J. 1969. *Philosophical Essays* (London: Macmillan).
Berto, F. 2015. 'A modality called "negation"', *Mind* 124, 761–93.
Black, M. 1964. *A Companion to Wittgenstein's Tractatus* (Cambridge: CUP).
Brownstein, D. 1973. 'Negative exemplification', *American Philosophical Quarterly* 10, 43–50.
Buchdahl, G. 1961. 'The problem of negation', *Philosophy and Phenomenological Research* 22, 163–78.

---

[32] My thanks to Julio de Rizzo, and to the participants in a Berlin workshop on idealism, for their comments on drafts of this chapter.

Cheyne, C. and Pigden, C. 2006. 'Negative truths from positive facts', *Australasian Journal of Philosophy* 84, 249–65.
Crivelli, P. 2012. *Plato's Account of Falsehood: A Study of the Sophist* (Cambridge: CUP).
Demos, R. 1917. 'A discussion of a certain type of negative proposition', *Mind* 26, 188–96.
De Rizzo, J. 2019. *Reasons Why Not: On the Positive Grounds of Negative Truths* (Berlin: Metzler).
Dodd, J. 2007. 'Negative truths and truthmaker principles', *Synthese* 156, 383–401.
Gale, R. 1976. *Negation and Non-Being* (Oxford: Blackwell).
Gaskin, R. 2008. *The Unity of the Proposition* (Oxford: OUP).
Gaskin, R. 2010. 'Replies to Vallicella, Schnieder, and García-Carpintero', *Dialectica* 64, 2010, 303–11.
Gaskin, R. 2020. 'The identity theory of truth', *Stanford Encyclopedia of Philosophy* (https://plato.stanford.edu/entries/truth-identity/).
Gaskin, R. 2021. *Language and World: A Defence of Linguistic Idealism* (London: Routledge).
Hand, M. 1999. 'Antirealism and falsity', in D. Gabbay and H. Wansing (eds), *What Is Negation?* (Dordrecht: Springer), 185–98.
Hansen, M. 2013. 'Negation in the history of French', in D. Willis, C. Lucas, and A. Breitbarth, 2013/2020: *The History of Negation in the Languages of Europe and the Mediterranean*, 2 vols (Oxford: OUP), 51–76.
Hommen, D. 2018. 'Making sense of negative properties', *Axiomathes* 28, 81–106.
Hossack, K. 1990. 'A problem about the meaning of intuitionist negation', *Mind* 99, 207–19.
Humberstone, L. 2000. 'The revival of rejective negation', *Journal of Philosophical Logic* 29, 331–81.
Humberstone, L. 2011. *The Connectives* (Cambridge, Mass.: MIT Press).
Jespersen, O. 1917. *Negation in English and Other Languages* (Copenhagen: Bianco Lunos).
Kostman, J. 1973. 'False logos and not-being in Plato's *Sophist*', in J. Moravcsik (ed.), *Patterns in Plato's Thought* (Dordrecht: Reidel), 192–212.
Molnar, G. 2000. 'Truthmakers for negative truths', *Australasian Journal of Philosophy* 78, 72–86.
Mumford, S. 2021. *Absence and Nothing: The Philosophy of What There Is Not* (Oxford: OUP).
Parsons, J. 2006. 'Negative truths from positive facts?', *Australasian Journal of Philosophy* 84, 591–602.
Peacocke, C. 1987. 'Understanding logical constants: a realist's account', *Proceedings of the British Academy* 73, 153–200.
Price, H. 1990. 'Why "not"?', *Mind* 99, 221–38.
Price, H. 1994. 'Semantic minimalism and the Frege point', in S. Tsohatzidis (ed.), *Foundations of Speech-Act Theory: Philosophical and Linguistic Perspectives* (London: Routledge), 132–55.
Priest, G. 2008. *An Introduction to Non-Classical Logic: From Ifs to Is*, 2nd edn. (Cambridge: CUP).
Rumfitt, I. 2000. '"Yes" and "no"', *Mind* 109, 781–823.
Russell, B. 1956. *Logic and Knowledge: Essays 1901–1950*, ed. R. C. Marsh (London: Allen and Unwin).
Russell, B. 1992. *Human Knowledge: Its Scope and Limits* (London: Routledge).
Smiley, T. 1996. 'Rejection', *Analysis* 56, 1–9.
Spinoza, B. de, 1909–12. *The Chief Works of Benedict de Spinoza*, ed. R. Elwes, 2 vols (London: Bell).
Taylor, R. 1952. 'Negative things', *Journal of Philosophy* 49, 433–49.
Tennant, N. 1999. 'Negation, absurdity, and contrariety', in D. Gabbay and H. Wansing (eds), *What Is Negation?* (Dordrecht: Springer), 199–222.
Willis, D., Lucas, C., and Breitbarth, A. 2013/2020. *The History of Negation in the Languages of Europe and the Mediterranean*, 2 vols (Oxford: OUP).
Wittgenstein, L. 1922. *Tractatus Logico-Philosophicus* (London: Routledge).
Wittgenstein, L. 1975. *Philosophical Remarks*, ed. R. Rhees (Oxford: Blackwell).
Wittgenstein, L. 1977. *Philosophische Untersuchungen* (Frankfurt/Main: Suhrkamp), tr. G. E. M. Anscombe, *Philosophical Investigations* (Oxford: Blackwell, 1968).

Wittgenstein, L. 1979a. *Notebooks: 1914–1916*, 2nd edn., ed. G. H. von Wright and G. E. M. Anscombe (Oxford: Blackwell).
Wittgenstein, L. 1979b. *Ludwig Wittgenstein and the Vienna Circle*, ed. B. McGuinness (Oxford: Blackwell).
Wittgenstein, L. 1979c. *Über Gewissheit/On Certainty*, ed. G. E. M. Anscombe and G. H. von Wright (Oxford: Blackwell).
Wittgenstein, L. 1984. *Wittgenstein und der Wiener Kreis*, ed. B. McGuinness (Frankfurt/Main: Suhrkamp).
Wittgenstein, L. 1993. *Philosophical Occasions: 1912–1951*, ed. J. Klagge and A. Nordmann (Indianapolis: Hackett).
Wittgenstein, L. 1995. *Cambridge Letters: Correspondence with Russell, Keynes, Moore, Ramsey, and Sraffa*, ed. B. McGuinness and G. H. von Wright (Oxford: Blackwell).
Wittgenstein, L. 2005. *The Big Typescript: TS 213: German–English Scholars' Edition*, ed. C. G. Luckhardt and M. Aue (Oxford: Blackwell).
Wright, C. 1993. 'On an argument on behalf of classical negation', *Mind* 102, 123–31.

Index

Abstractness/abstraction 3, 16, 52, 67, 70, 100, 111, 122, 130-2, 141-2, 146, 160, 162-3, 165, 179-80, 194-5, 201-3, 213-17, 220, 230, 238, 261, 287, 291-2, 300, 307
Acquaintance: *see* Knowledge
Alien 4, 21-2, 256, 260-3, 267-70, 273-6, 280, 282
Ambiguity 2, 31, 37, 53, 121, 124-6, 130, 132-3, 168-9, 179-80, 212
Analysis/Analytical 12, 18, 26-7, 45, 51, 67, 73, 111, 113 n.5, 116, 129, 144, 163 n.7, 196, 221, 229, 268, 272-3, 294, 300, 303-6
Analytic(ity) 1, 33, 45-9, 53, 55, 60, 64, 66-8, 71, 74, 76, 112, 123, 169, 186
Anscombe, E. 1, 4-11, 13, 22, 24, 85, 91-3, 105, 163 n.9
Anti-realism 2, 162, 164-72, 174-7, 181-2, 188-9, 191, 293, 295 n.19
A posteriori 12, 63, 71 n.21, 106-7
A priori 1-2, 12, 21, 33, 45, 48-51, 55, 60-79, 83-6, 91 n.8, 105-6, 109, 113, 201, 264-7
Arbitrariness 5-7, 10-11, 250 n.5, 253, 255
Argument: *see* Function
Arithmetic: *see* Mathematics
Aristotle 116, 131 n.21, 139, 149, 183, 300 n.23
Assertion/Assertibility 89, 99, 104 n.18, 107, 124, 170, 183, 205, 214-21, 229, 268, 296-7
Austin, J. L. 133
Axiom 11 n.6, 183-5, 197-8, 225-7, 233, 293 n.17
Ayer, A. J. 288-92

Belief 25, 36, 39, 76-7, 88-9, 134, 164, 167, 172, 220, 303-5
Berto, F. 296-7
Bloor, D. 6, 11 n.5, 24-5
Bound/Boundary: *see* Limit

Carnap, R. 112
Cartwright, N. 169-70
Category 4, 27, 83-4, 111, 122, 139, 156, 166, 174, 178-9, 201, 238-40, 276, 305-7
Causation 19-20, 45, 48, 76, 83, 87-8, 90, 98, 100, 103, 108, 220, 285, 303
Character 203-4

Chomsky, N. 131 n.21, 140-1, 157, 165, 168, 171 n.14, 175, 180
Collins, J. 140
Colour 6, 9, 14, 17, 70-1, 74, 91, 99, 101, 103-7, 166, 185-6, 288-92, 298-9, 301, 303-7
Complexity 16, 26-8, 128, 131 n.21, 177, 277
Compositional(ity) 113-14, 116, 119 n.13, 135, 157, 184, 186, 190, 215, 260, 266, 273, 277, 281
Concept(ual) 5-10, 18, 27, 45, 62 n.6, 63-8, 72-3, 75, 78, 84, 88-90, 93, 107-8, 112-13, 120-1, 123, 130, 135, 139, 141, 147, 155-7, 163, 165-6, 174, 179-80, 186, 199, 202, 206, 209-10, 231, 239-40, 243-6, 252, 256, 274-6, 281, 285-7, 289-93, 296, 301-7
Consequence: *see* Entailment
Consistency/Inconsistency 3, 140-1, 162-3, 186, 220, 224-7, 232-4, 298, 302
Content 41, 48, 58-68, 72-7, 87-90, 93-4, 109, 112 n.2, 121-6, 130, 139-42, 147, 150, 155-6, 171, 202-3, 233-4, 241-4, 246, 273
Context (principle) 27-8, 96, 117, 120, 127, 148-50, 171, 183 n.28, 207-8, 254, 294
Contingency 7, 22-4, 33, 45-8, 64-5, 71, 78, 84-6, 106, 177, 263
Contradiction 16, 21, 43, 47, 54, 64, 66, 70-1, 140, 209-10, 221 n.1, 233, 299-300, 302
'Copernican' Turn 24, 82-3, 103
Copredication 2, 120-35, 141
Correct(ness) 91, 164, 166-70, 172-6, 179, 181, 185 n.31, 190, 240-6, 248-56, 281
Count/Mass (noun) 138-42, 144-57
Cramér, H. 220, 227-30, 234

Davidson, D. 21, 25, 94, 115, 117, 183-6, 189 n.37, 249 n.4, 251, 274-5
Davies, M. 197-8
Deduction 13-14, 197-8, 208, 220-5, 231, 234, 240, 245, 248-9, 251, 253-4, 277
Definition 27, 50, 66, 86, 90, 98-100, 106-8, 120-1, 138-40, 143-4, 147, 149, 152, 156, 165, 199, 202-3, 211-12, 215, 223, 225, 231, 248, 289-92, 301, 307
Denotation: *see* Reference/Referent
Descartes, R. 36 n.12

Describe/Description 3, 12–13, 16–17, 20, 23–4, 42, 44, 48–9, 63, 65, 68, 71, 86, 92–7, 101–2, 107, 126, 129, 134, 143, 146, 149, 153–7, 169–70, 172, 174–5, 181, 202, 204, 208, 221 n.1, 225–7, 231, 233, 237, 247–50, 253, 256–8, 261–4, 268–71, 276, 281, 283, 299, 301, 303

Determinacy/Determination 1, 9–23, 31–3, 39, 44–51, 58, 64–7, 71, 73, 78, 86, 88–91, 94–6, 99–108, 114, 117, 122, 127, 132, 134, 151, 160–3, 173, 185–6, 198, 201, 213, 225, 231, 248–9, 264, 269, 271, 279–82, 286–7, 289, 291, 299, 301, 306

Devitt, M. 124–5, 127

Double-Negation Elimination 292–5

Dummett, M. 87 n.3, 95, 102, 111, 212, 293, 295 n.19

Empirical 6, 9–10, 22–5, 28, 31–2, 34–6, 39–40, 45, 48, 58–9, 62–8, 71, 73–5, 82, 84–6, 92, 103–4, 109, 123, 163 n.7, 164, 166, 172, 177, 184, 186, 191, 212–13, 234, 256, 264, 277, 283, 285, 306

Empiricism 163 n.9, 167–9, 263–8

Engelmann, P. 38–9, 53–4

Entailment 11, 46, 92, 143–4, 160, 167, 183, 186, 220, 222–4, 233–4, 250, 286 n.7, 299, 301–2

Epistemic/epistemology: *see* Knowledge

Essence 5–11, 13, 20, 50, 52, 55, 59, 92, 100, 103–6, 154, 163 n.9, 165, 219, 277, 283–4, 286, 294–5, 306–7

Ethics 59–62, 66 n.12, 77–8, 103, 109, 166, 167 n.12

'Eulb' 288–92

Evans, G. 203, 206 n.14, 209

Exclusion: *see* Incompatibility/Exclusion

Experience/Perception 8, 17, 32–3, 36, 39, 41, 49–50, 64, 67, 71, 74, 85, 111, 150, 158, 174–5, 186, 194, 220–1, 235, 239–43, 246, 258–9, 296, 303

Explanation 19–21, 28, 60, 73, 75–6, 86–90, 95–104, 108–9, 114–15, 169–71, 181, 183, 198–9, 207, 213, 216, 222–34, 243–4, 247, 249, 251, 257, 259, 265, 278, 286, 292, 301

Expressibility/inexpressibility 22–4, 39, 43, 54, 58, 61, 64–6, 73 n.25, 74, 76, 78, 85, 219, 221–35, 261, 283

Extension(ality) 32, 106, 113, 138 n.2, 139, 144, 147–51, 298

Externalism 89, 105, 126, 276

Fact 14, 48, 50–1, 58–62, 64–5, 67–8, 71, 74, 77–8, 101, 103, 112–14, 123–4, 139, 167–9, 183, 185–6, 219, 221–30, 232–4, 237–8, 242, 256–8, 275–6, 279–80, 290, 295, 299, 302–3

Falsity 20, 23, 25, 47, 63, 72, 78, 91 n.8, 100, 113–14, 116, 129, 134, 160, 162, 167, 169–72, 177, 182, 185, 187–9, 196, 199, 201, 216, 219, 225, 247–8, 250, 271, 281, 290, 302, 306

Fiction 116–19, 122, 129–32, 134–5, 141, 167, 170, 185, 227

Form(al) 11–19, 21–5, 28, 34–5, 58–60, 63–78, 84–5, 88, 90, 93, 95–6, 99–100, 103, 112, 114, 119 n.13, 120, 128–9, 142, 149–51, 153, 157, 186–90, 200, 208–9, 216–17, 220–1, 225–7, 237–44, 256–7, 261, 268, 292

Formalization/Formulation 3–4, 15, 59, 170, 174, 181, 195 n.4, 197, 204, 207–11, 214–21, 224–8, 232, 235, 256–7, 262, 279

Frege, G. 3, 18, 26–8, 112 n.2, 116–17, 138, 140, 143–4, 195, 199–200, 209–11, 213–14, 223, 266, 268, 286–7

Function(al) 16–18, 25–8, 90, 101, 108, 124, 142, 149, 151, 155–6, 171, 173, 176, 187–8, 190, 199–200–1, 209, 213, 228, 266–74, 276–7, 280, 282

Gaskin, R. 94, 96, 112, 116 n.6, 119 n.13, 127, 139, 143, 161–3, 190–1, 194–6, 198 n.10, 202–11, 219, 231, 262–73, 275–82

Geometry: *see* Mathematics

Given 239–43, 245 n.3, 246–8, 251, 253–9

Gödel, K. 220, 224–7, 233–4

Grammar 2, 5–13, 25–8, 92, 97, 99–107, 129, 139, 154–5, 163 n.9, 165, 168, 173, 180, 190, 268, 272–3

Hacker, P. 13, 71 n.20, 91, 99

Hale, B. 195, 199–201, 211–13

Human(ity) 4, 8–10, 21–5, 35–7, 41–2, 48–9, 54–5, 78, 92, 117, 162, 167, 171, 174, 177, 219–20, 235, 265, 283–5, 293, 295, 305

Hume, D. 45

Idealism 46, 48–9, 51–2, 54–5, 59–62, 82, 85–8, 92–3, 109, 111–12, 116–17, 135, 161–3, 191, 219, 237–9, 253–5, 257, 259, 262, 278–9, 283–4, 304–7
  Empirical 31–5, 39, 45, 83, 85
  Linguistic 1–4, 6–11, 13–19, 22–5, 31–3, 47, 58, 62, 82, 91–4, 96–7, 109, 111–12, 116, 139, 143, 152, 154, 157–8, 161–3, 190–1, 194, 202–11, 208, 210, 219, 222, 230–5, 257, 260, 262–6, 271, 277–80, 282, 283–8, 291–2, 304–7
  Partial 9–11

Idealism (*Continued*)
  Transcendental 1–2, 11, 20, 31–9, 43–5, 58–62, 64, 66, 71, 82–7, 91 n.8, 92, 109, 191
Incompatibility/Exclusion 4, 44, 59–65, 70, 77, 128, 148–52, 232, 276, 283–7, 292–307
Inconsistency: *see* Consistency/Inconsistency
Indeterminate/Indeterminacy: *see* Determinate/Determinacy
Ineffability: *see* Expressibility/inexpressibility
Inference 34, 68, 90–1, 111, 115, 123, 160 n. 2, 210–13, 222–8, 237–59, 299
Instrumental(ism) 2–3, 108, 160, 164–8, 170, 172–3, 178, 181–91
Integrity: *see* Whole
Intension 117 n.10, 60, 187, 195
Interpretation 15, 23, 31, 78, 94–6, 100, 103, 108–9, 113–17, 126–9, 135, 167 n. 12, 171, 190, 214, 251–2, 274, 293, 306 n.31
Intuitionism 293
Isomorphism 3, 58, 100, 237–40, 247, 253–4, 258–9

Judg(e)ment 6, 52, 58, 65–7, 72–9, 88, 90, 185, 239–46, 253–6, 303
Julius Caesar problem 195, 198–202, 211, 213, 216–17
Justification 3, 6, 11, 27, 47, 72–3, 83, 97–105, 220–4, 227, 240, 243–8, 254–9

Kannisto, H. 64
Kant, I. 1–2, 11, 20, 24, 45, 58–69, 72–9, 82–7, 92, 95, 111, 124–5
Kaplan, D. 203
Keefe, R. 249
King, J. 125–7
Knowledge 60–3, 66–7, 69–71, 73 n.25, 74, 76, 78, 82–8, 92–3, 105–7, 114, 116, 118–19, 123, 131–4, 162, 186, 197, 202–6, 219–30, 234–5, 238 n.1, 245 n.3, 248, 254–8, 278–9, 281, 286, 297
Kripke, S. 23, 105–6, 112, 163, 238 n.1

Law 12, 21, 47, 59, 66, 70, 73–8, 84, 131, 164, 168–72, 176, 222–4, 227, 295
Lear, J. 21–2, 84 n.1
Leslie, S.-J. 186
Lewis, D. 118
Limits/limitations 11, 20–2, 32–3, 37, 40–1, 43–5, 49, 51, 58–63, 65, 74, 77–9, 84–5, 92, 96, 98, 108–9, 149–50, 165, 198, 200, 219, 275
Linguistic Given: *see* Given
Linguistic idealism: *see* Idealism, linguistic
Linguistic instrumentalism: *see* Instrumentalism

Linguistic practice: *see* Use
Linguistic Turn 103
Linguistics 3, 143, 147, 157, 160–71, 173, 177, 180–2, 188–91, 206 n.14
Linnebo, Ø 201, 213–17
Logic(al) 11–13, 14, 17, 21, 25–8, 43–8, 50–3, 55, 58–61, 64–6, 68, 70–7, 84, 91 n.8, 100, 112 n.2, 119 n.13, 128–9, 144, 154, 164 n.10, 182 n.27, 184–7, 190, 212, 217, 220, 222–7, 254, 261, 264–5, 268, 276, 292–3, 296, 303–5

Mach, E. 41–2
Mass (noun): *see* Count/Mass (noun)
Mathematics 3, 17, 59, 65–70, 72, 75–7, 84, 104 n.18, 111, 117, 138, 164, 166, 167 n.12, 188–90, 219–35
McDowell, J. 239–47, 251–7
McGinn, M. 40, 46
Meaning 10, 13–15, 21–3, 32–3, 39, 42–5, 50, 52–4, 58–65, 67–8, 70–1, 73, 76–8, 84–91, 93, 95–6, 99–108, 111, 115–31, 143, 157, 160–4, 168, 171–3, 177, 182–9, 194–204, 207, 245 n.3, 248–53, 274–9, 285, 287–8, 290–5
Meinong, A. 118, 120, 161
Mereology 144–5, 147–51, 153
Metalanguage 96, 102–3, 113 n.5, 214
Metaphysics 3, 9–19, 23, 27–8, 33–55, 58–9, 64, 75, 82–6, 92, 103, 111–13, 116–17, 122–5, 133–57, 161–4, 185–91, 260–4, 267, 270–2, 278–80, 285, 287–90, 293 n.15, 296, 300, 303–5
Mind(edness)/mentality 6, 21, 36, 39, 41, 49–51, 55, 87–9, 96, 111, 116, 139–43, 154, 157, 167–8, 175–6, 179–81, 202–3, 276, 283, 303–4
Misrepresentation: *see* Representation/Misrepresentation
Modality 7, 11 n.6, 19, 109, 245 n.3, 293 n.17
Model 94–7, 100, 177, 220–1, 226–30, 241, 249–50, 254, 277
Montague, R. 183, 187–9
Moral(alilty): *see* Ethics
Moltmann, F. 145–6, 148–50, 152
Moore, A. 20–1, 40, 59–65, 72–4, 221–2 n.1
Morphology 173–7, 179, 181, 188–9, 204
'Myth of the Given': *see* Given

Name/nominal/noun (phrase) 15, 25–7, 63, 98, 116, 119, 120–32, 138, 140–57, 163, 184, 198–213, 231, 237, 248, 250–1, 272, 275, 279, 285, 287 n.9, 297

INDEX 313

Natural language 111–15, 117 n.11, 128–9, 139–40, 147, 149, 153–7, 165, 177, 196–7, 211, 233, 275, 297
Natural science: *see* Science
Necessity 5, 7, 9–11, 13, 15, 18–20, 23, 31, 33, 43, 45–9, 53, 55, 65–7, 69–72, 75, 78, 82, 84–6, 92–3, 105, 112, 177, 194–5, 202–3, 214, 223–4, 228, 242–3, 264–7, 279, 283, 286, 300, 302
Negation/Negative 4, 101, 225, 283–307
Neo-Fregean: *see* Frege
Nominal: *see* Name/Nominal
Nominalism 165, 209, 217
Nonsense 19, 31, 33, 37–8, 45, 47, 50–2, 54–6, 59–63, 65, 72, 89, 97, 108, 201
Normativity 23, 47, 66, 71 n.20, 89–91, 93–4, 101, 109, 115
Noumenon/Noumena(l) 66, 72, 83
Noun: *see* Name/Nominal/Noun (phrase)
Numbers/numerals 3, 17–18, 91, 103, 111, 116–17, 138, 145–8, 154–7, 180, 188, 195, 198–202, 206, 208–16, 220, 225–30, 233–4

Object(hood)/objectivity 2–3, 5, 7–8, 10–16, 18, 24–7, 59, 61, 63–4, 66–7, 70–4, 82–9, 92, 98–9, 101, 104, 106, 111, 116–20, 122, 125–31, 135, 138–44, 146–8, 151, 153–8, 160, 163, 166–9, 180, 191, 194–202, 207–9, 213–17, 221, 230–4, 260–1, 269, 275, 287–92, 297–9, 306
Object-language 96, 102, 196–8, 208
Oneness: *see* Unity
Ontology 2–3, 15, 24, 27, 50–1, 55, 92, 103, 111–12, 116–34, 139–43, 154–7, 160–3, 171–2, 177, 182–5, 188–90, 210, 230–3, 285, 287–90, 300, 306

Peacocke, C. 88, 90–1, 139, 143
Pears, D. 13
Perception: *see* Experience/Perception
Perspective 34–5, 39, 221 n.1
Phenomenon/Phenomen(ologic)al 12–13, 16–18, 24, 70, 76, 92, 107, 112–16, 129, 145, 155, 169–70, 176, 190, 255, 260, 277, 281, 301
Phonology 173–6, 179, 181, 188–9, 204
Physics/physical 6, 17, 25, 48, 51, 55, 69–70, 89, 113, 121, 124–8, 140–3, 165, 168–71, 173–4, 176, 179–80, 220, 235, 276, 286–7, 295–6, 306
Pictures/depicting 26 n.33, 47, 50–1, 53, 55, 58, 63, 71, 78–9, 99, 273, 281
Plato/Platonism 3, 117, 163 n.9, 165, 174, 179, 188, 297–8, 306

Plural(ity)/Singular(ity) 138–9, 142–58, 195–202, 207, 211–16, 261, 269, 280–1
Polysemy 120–1, 124–7, 130, 133, 141–2
Positive 287–96, 299, 301–4
Possibility 1, 7, 10–13, 32–3, 39, 41–5, 48–51, 53–5, 58, 61, 63–4, 67–75, 77–8, 82–6, 92–3, 95, 100, 141, 160, 163, 187–8, 203, 210, 217, 224, 227, 247–8, 257, 260–4, 267–73, 276, 280–2, 294–5, 300, 305
Practice: *see* Use
Pragmatic 93–4, 114, 183 n.28, 254, 281
Predicate: *see* Subject/Predicate
Price, H. 296
Principle: *see* Rule
Proof 223–7, 233–4
Property 27, 49, 64, 70–2, 88–9, 103–4, 106, 114–16, 120, 124–7, 134, 138–43, 150, 156–7, 160, 174, 176–7, 181, 197–8, 202, 207, 228–30, 233, 240–2, 260, 269, 286, 288, 294, 298, 301–2
Proposition 5, 12, 17, 25–8, 38, 40, 43–52, 54–5, 58–69, 71–9, 97–8, 101, 103–5, 129, 143, 160 n.3, 182 n.26, 184, 197, 202, 219–34, 287, 290–1, 293–4, 300, 302–3
Psychology 6, 11, 37, 49, 84, 87–91, 93–4, 100, 108–9, 111, 113 n.3, 116, 122–3, 162, 165, 174 n.17
Putnam, H. 94–6, 107

Quantification 112–13, 117–22, 132, 152, 154, 156, 184 n.29, 212–13, 215–17, 261, 269, 300
Quine, W. V. 116–18, 132, 139, 147, 194, 249 n.4

Ramsey 16 n.18, 26 n.33, 27–8, 53
Rational 17, 59, 93, 116, 188, 197, 200, 239, 245, 297
Realism 6, 13, 15–17, 24, 31, 46, 48–9, 51–2, 54, 82, 85–6, 96, 100, 104–5, 109, 163 n.9, 164–9, 171, 177, 179–80, 188–91, 232–3, 238, 249, 253–4, 277, 286–7, 292
Reference/Referent 2, 15, 25–8, 87–9, 94–6, 101–3, 111, 117, 119 n.13, 123–31, 138, 140–4, 148, 150–4, 157, 162 n.6, 184–5, 194–211, 213–15, 268–9, 272, 277–81, 285–6, 290, 298
Regress 26–7, 73–4, 221–3, 245
Relation 12, 15–16, 26–7, 46, 49, 51, 64, 66, 68, 74, 79, 87, 93, 95, 98, 109, 116, 118, 121, 132, 139, 144–7, 155, 160, 201, 213, 230, 239–41, 250–1, 256, 261, 264, 285, 301, 305
Relativize/Relativism 93, 111, 117, 150, 166

Representation/Misrepresentation 1–2, 12, 14, 16–18, 25, 32–9, 41, 43, 45, 49–52, 54–5, 71–2, 82–3, 86–7, 91, 93–4, 97, 99–103, 105–6, 109, 118, 175–6, 180–1, 189–90, 260–73, 276, 281–2

Rey, G. 176, 178, 180, 190

Rule 5–11, 24–5, 54, 66, 72–7, 92, 97–101, 104, 108–9, 123, 164–75, 177, 179–82, 187–90, 196–8, 214, 222–7, 237–8, 243–4, 248, 250–2, 257–8, 293–4, 299

Russell, B. 16, 27, 36 n.12, 49, 116, 163, 200 n.11, 202, 300–1, 303–5

Ryle, G. 224

Satisfaction 116–17, 123, 161, 163, 182–6, 196–8, 202, 208–10, 226

Schopenhauer, A. 33, 36 n.12, 38–40

Scepticism 19, 83, 95, 102–3, 129, 138–41, 182, 223, 257, 261

Science 2, 33, 35 n.11, 48, 54, 71–2, 75–9, 92, 105 n.19, 113, 116, 157, 164–71, 177, 194

Self/Subject 1, 31–45, 48–9, 58–9, 64 n.8, 72, 74, 78–9, 83–5, 88–9, 108–9, 221 n.1, 232, 239, 242

Semantics/semantic value 2–3, 26, 68, 88–91, 93–6, 105, 109, 111–35, 139–40, 144–50, 153–7, 160–3, 173, 176–7, 182–91, 197, 203, 248–54, 260, 264, 277, 280, 285–7

Sensation 41, 103

Sense: *see* Meaning

Sentence 14–19, 25–8, 53–5, 95–6, 113–17, 120–1, 128–35, 143, 150, 160 n.3, 165, 171, 173–4, 177–87, 195–202, 205, 211–14, 237, 244–52, 256–8, 261, 264, 266–82, 290–4, 298–300, 303

Set 23, 84, 116, 144–9, 153, 160, 174–6, 187–8, 220–34, 250 n.5, 268, 270, 273, 289, 302

Sider, T. 161–2

Sign: *see* Symbol

Singular(ity): *see* Plural(ity)/Singular(ity)

Solipsism 48

Spatio-temporal(ity) 2, 66–7, 69–72, 74, 84–5, 99–100, 140–3, 286, 305

Spinoza, B. de 286–7, 295, 301

State of affairs 17 n.19, 20, 51, 61–4, 70–1, 74, 99, 269–70, 287, 290, 292, 295, 299–302

Stenius, E. 58–60, 62, 67, 69, 76

Strawson, P. 83, 86

Structure/Structural 2, 4, 12–13, 16–23, 26, 28, 47, 65, 68–71, 75–6, 85, 96, 100–1, 112–17, 129, 133, 149, 155, 171–81, 186, 189, 197–8, 200, 219–20, 225–6, 231, 234–8, 252, 260–74, 277–8, 280–3

Subject of willing/experience/cognition/subjective: *see* Self/Subject

Subject matter: *see* Category

Subject/predicate 4, 12, 15–18, 25–8, 66, 72 n.24, 99, 116, 120–9, 133, 141–8, 151–2, 155–7, 164, 178, 197–8, 201–2, 207–9, 213, 238, 248, 251, 261, 266, 268–9, 272–3, 280–1

Substance 13–15

Sullivan, P. 19–20, 28, 40, 59–63, 65, 70, 74, 76–8

Supersensible: *see* Noumena(l)

Symbol 12–13, 15, 17, 43, 46, 49–52, 54, 68, 118, 132, 171, 191, 253, 277, 284–6, 296, 300

Syncategorematicity 27

Syntax/Syntactic 26–8, 95, 113–16, 128, 131–5, 139, 143, 145–6, 151, 155–7, 162, 171, 173–4, 176–81, 189–90, 200, 215, 238–40, 260, 286–7, 289–92, 295, 300

Synthetic(ity) 1–2, 45, 60–3, 65–73, 77, 79, 83–6, 109, 265

Tarski, A. 247–8, 250–3, 274

Tautology 43–5, 47, 53–4, 66, 68–9, 73, 77, 79

Theorem 67, 72, 183, 185, 195–8, 207–8, 220, 224–8, 233–4

Theory/theoretical 18, 46, 51–2, 59, 61–2, 69, 77–8, 87–91, 94–6, 100, 103, 113–17, 129, 131, 134–5, 140, 144–5, 149, 160–74, 176–7, 179, 181–91, 194–202, 207–8, 220–34, 243, 248–53, 260, 269, 273–4, 277–8, 281, 285, 290, 293

Thought/thinking 10–11, 13, 20–3, 31–6, 39–46, 48–54, 58–62, 64–7, 71 n.20, 72, 74, 76–9, 82–3, 88–9, 93, 107, 111, 160, 171, 182, 191, 219, 241, 276

Time: *see* Spatio-temporality

Thomasson, A. 122–3, 130, 142, 161

Transcendental(ism) 2, 10, 13–15, 23–5, 31–40, 43–5, 58–62, 67, 69–70, 72–3, 77–8, 82–5, 92, 163 n. 7, 191, 219, 263–7, 270–2, 277, 283, 285, 306

Translation 21, 99–100, 258, 274–5, 289–92

Truth 3, 20, 23, 25, 43, 47–8, 60, 62–3, 65–8, 71–3, 75, 77–9, 87–90, 92–6, 105, 109, 111–22, 129–35, 160–74, 176–7, 179, 181–90, 195–201, 206–9, 211–17, 219–30, 234, 237–8, 245, 247–52, 256–8, 264, 268–71, 279–82, 290, 301–3

Truth-conditions: *see* Truth

Truth-values: *see* Truth

Types 28

Understanding 3, 7, 15, 23, 26, 34, 38–42, 46, 48–9, 52, 59, 66–7, 73, 77–8, 84, 100, 108,

114 n.6, 115, 133, 135, 146, 187, 194, 201–6, 217–30, 232–5, 239, 250–1, 253–4, 258, 267, 277–9, 296
Unity 2, 26–8, 33–4, 50, 55, 73, 138–42, 145, 149–50, 152–8, 233–4
Use/Useful 8–11, 14–15, 23, 32, 43–7, 51–2, 54, 73, 90, 92–109, 115, 139, 148, 154, 164, 166, 168, 171, 176–7, 179, 191, 197, 206, 212, 219, 243–59, 263, 265, 277–8, 281, 294, 305
Utter/Utterance 54, 108, 114, 134, 160, 171–82, 186–90, 196, 205, 233, 276, 284, 286, 297

van Fraassen, B. 164, 166–7, 170, 172
Verification(ism) 21–2, 46–7, 276–7, 293

Whole 139, 144–5, 147, 149–58
Will 32–4, 36–7, 40, 45, 59, 73, 78
Williams, B. 22–3
Wittgenstein, L. 1–2, 4–9, 11–21, 24–6, 31–56, 58–79, 84–5, 91–3, 97–109, 190–1, 251, 283–4, 287 n.8, 293–5, 298–300, 303–4
—*Notebooks* 13, 33, 35–40, 48–50, 64, 68–9, 293 n.15, 304
—*Tractatus* 1–2, 13–20, 25 n. 30, 26, 31–44, 46, 48–56, 58–79, 84, 98–100, 287 n.8, 298–300
—*Philosophical Investigations* 4–8, 11, 14–17, 24, 64, 74 n.26, 98, 108–9, 251, 284, 293–4
—*Zettel* 5–7, 13, 91
Wright, C. 195–7, 199–201, 211–13